A HISTORY OF GKN

By the same author

ACCOUNTANCY AND THE BRITISH ECONOMY 1840–1980:
The Evolution of Ernst & Whinney

*A HISTORY OF GKN: Volume 1, Innovation and Enterprise, 1759–1918

INDUSTRIAL ARCHITECTURE IN BRITAIN, 1750–1939

THE MEMOIRS OF EDWIN WATERHOUSE (*editor*)

Also published by Macmillan

A HISTORY OF GKN

Volume 2
The Growth of a Business, 1918–45

Edgar Jones

Foreword by
David Lees

MACMILLAN

First published 1990

Published by
MACMILLAN ACADEMIC AND PROFESSIONAL LTD
Houndmills, Basingstoke, Hampshire RG21 2XS
and London
Companies and representatives
throughout the world

Typeset by Footnote Graphics, Warminster, Wilts

Printed and bound in Great Britain by
Butler & Tanner Ltd, Frome and London

British Library Cataloguing in Publication Data
Jones, Edgar, 1953–
A history of GKN.
Vol. 2, The growth of a business, 1918–1945
1. Great Britain. Engineering industries
I. Title
338.7'62'000941
ISBN 0–333–44578–3

Contents

List of Maps and Figures

List of Tables

List of Illustrations

List of Colour Plates

List of Abbreviations

AEI	Associated Electrical Industries
AI&S	Australian Iron & Steel Co.
BCL	Bristol Central Library
BHP	Broken Hill Proprietory
BHPL	BHP Coated Products Division Library, Port Kembla
BIDC	Bankers Industrial Development Co.
BJB	Bayliss, Jones & Bayliss
BRL	Birmingham Reference Library
BSC	British Steel Corporation
DBB	*Dictionary of Business Biography*
DSBB	*Dictionary of Scottish Business Biography*
EJM	Exors. of James Mills
EWS	English Wood Screw Co.
GKB	Guest Keen Baldwins Iron & Steel Co.
GKN	Guest Keen & Nettlefolds
GKW	Guest, Keen, Williams
GRO	Glamorgan Record Office, Cardiff
GWR	Great Western Railway
GwRO	Gwent Record Office, Cwmbran
HWI	Henry Williams India
JLA	John Lysaght (Australia) Proprietory
MBA	Midland Bank Archives
MTL	Merthyr Tydfil Central Library
PNB	Patent Nut & Bolt Co.
PRO	Public Record Office, Kew
TVR	Taff Vale Railway
UWW	United Wire Works (Birmingham)
WAC	Welsh Associated Collieries
WwW	*Who was Who*

Foreword

When GKN commissioned the writing of its history it was thought that two volumes would suffice to tell the story from 1759 through to the 1970s. The many facets of GKN's business, its growth and the resultant multitude of sources, however, were such that the second volume to be of comparable length to the first cannot go beyond 1945 and spans therefore only the interwar period and the years of the Second World War. The story from 1945 to more recent times will be for a later volume and will again be an account of adaptation leading to success.

From small beginnings in 1759 this great enterprise in its early development mirrored the Industrial Revolution, and by 1918 its basic elements were still coal and steel with the addition of fasteners. The interwar years saw expansion in this country and overseas by acquisition and investment and the beginning of the grouping of a large number of subsidiaries in a variety of steel and engineering companies.

A large-scale and influential company, GKN was very different in its structure, composition and product at the end of the Second World War from 1918. It had once again demonstrated its inherent power to adapt to changing economic circumstances and the market-place.

It is inevitable that those now engaged in the business will find the more recent history, and that which is still in the making, the most interesting. Certainly a description of the change that has taken place in the 1970s, and perhaps even more so in the 1980s, when put in a proper historical perspective will in due course make fascinating reading.

However, without the efforts and strivings of those individuals who developed the business from 1918 to 1945, the story of which is so comprehensively contained in this second volume, more recent history could not have occurred.

Our thanks go to Dr Edgar Jones for his careful and thorough research and his scholarly treatment of the subject-matter. I hope that the many friends and acquaintances of GKN will enjoy reading this further episode in the history of a great company.

DAVID LEES

Acknowledgements

The publication of this history represents the culmination of almost eight years work. It was originally planned to cover the period 1759 to the mid-1970s in two parts but the wealth of source material and complexity of the subject matter resulted in this second volume being brought to a conclusion at 1945, opening the possibility for a third volume to describe the post-war years to the near present. In its execution a work of history may be compared with scaling a Lakeland peak: a sustained effort, anxiety tinged with excitement over the difficult parts, boredom in the trudge but once on the summit, with a vista below, 'awed, delighted and amazed' at a task completed.

Part of the second volume of the GKN History was researched and written at a time when, for a variety of reasons, the future of the project could not be guaranteed. Now that matters have assumed a satisfying solidity, it is gratifying to be able to contemplate thanking those who have helped to bring this project to fruition.

First and foremost there are the members of the GKN History Committee. Mr John Howard has done more than any other individual to assist in the research and writing of the history. Thanks are due to him for giving up so much time in his retirement, and for his consistent support for the project. Lord Briggs, who has commented on the text in its various drafts, has provided encouragement and a professional insight. Messrs Stephen Lloyd, Anthony George, Geoffrey Hughes and Ralph Smallwood, each with specialist and extensive knowledge of the GKN group, have produced detailed corrections and suggestions; I am most grateful. In addition, I have relied on the help offered by Sir Anthony Bowlby, Sir Richard Brooke, Sir Douglas Bruce-Gardner, W.W. Fea, E.C. Lysaght and Sir Henry Williams. Without the benefit of their comments, this study would have contained many errors of fact and judgement.

Considerable assistance has been provided by those who no longer have a direct connection with GKN or who have never been employed by the group. They include Lord Hartwell, who commented extensively on the coal chapter, Dr Mark Pegg of British Coal, Mr John A. Owen of British Steel, Mr Roy Stewartson, and Mr Alan Cox of Allied Steel and

Wire, Elizabeth Rowbottom formerly of European Industrial Services, Mr J.B. McDowall and Mr Peter Rose of the BSC Orb Works, Newport, and the Headmaster and Mr R. Whicker of Canford School.

Much of the archival material for the chapter on John Lysaght (Australia) Pty was provided by Mr Alan Stein, formerly Librarian and Chief Information Officer of BHP Coated Products Division. He has also offered the most detailed annotations on the text and served as a constant source of encouragement. Further criticism was generously provided by Mr Vincent Wardell.

In the general execution of this project a number of retired GKN executives have provided material assistance and though their contributions relate to the post-1945 period, I should like to thank them formally for their time and effort. They have included Lord Brookes, life president and chairman of GKN between 1965 and 1974, the late Sir Barrie Heath, chairman from 1974 to 1979 and Sir Trevor Holdsworth, chairman between 1979 until 1987, who was also responsible for setting up the history project. Others to whom gratitude is owed comprise Mr Michael Chester, Mr J.A. Collier, Mr Ian Donald, Mr J.F. Insch, Mr T.H. Keen, the late Mr L. Maxwell-Holroyd, Mr L.R.P. Pugh, Mr R.E.J. Roberts, Mr T.C. Rochford, Mr F.C. Rowbottom, Mr J.C. Sankey, Mr W.E. Simons, Mr R.N.M. Ward and Mr Basil Woods.

For providing research material or advice I am grateful to the following institutions or companies: Birmingham Reference Library, BSC Scunthorpe Works, Bristol Central Library, Bristol Record Office, British Coal, the British Steel Corporation, Broken Hill Proprietory, Business History Unit, Cyfarthfa Castle Museum, European Industrial Services, Glamorgan Archive Service, Cardiff, Institution of Mechanical Engineers, Metal Society, Rheemco, Sela Fasteners and the Walsall Local History Centre.

Many current employees of GKN have helped and are so numerous to defy listing. I am, nevertheless, equally grateful to them. May I offer my apologies to those who have assisted but not been named.

The author also acknowledges the assistance provided by the publishers, Macmillan, and in particular to Mr T.M. Farmiloe and Mrs Sophie Lillington. Mrs Janette Carney, who typed the manuscript, is owed much thanks for her expertise, skill and sympathetic support. Many of the photographs were processed by A.J. Knowler and I am grateful to them.

A career change, long contemplated but now irrevocably taken, albeit with a backward glance, leaves me unable to write the final volume in this trilogy. Should a successor be appointed, may I take this opportunity to wish him good fortune with what proves to be an exciting story.

Many have contributed, but the final text is mine and I take full responsibility for it.

EDGAR JONES

Chronology of Events

1919 F.W. Cotterill of Darlaston and its subsidiary, John Garrington & Sons, acquired by GKN.

1919 T.S. Peacock appointed a director of GKN.

1920 GKN merged with John Lysaght and its subsidiary, Joseph Sankey & Sons; H. Seymour Berry appointed a joint deputy chairman of GKN and T.S. Peacock became a joint managing director.

1920 Meiros Collieries, and their subsidiary, South Rhondda Colliery Co., acquired by GKN.

1920 Bayliss, Jones & Bayliss of Wolverhampton taken over by GKN.

1920 Death in December of the Earl of Bessborough, succeeded as chairman of GKN by Edward Steer.

1921 In April the Newcastle Works (New South Wales) of Lysaght's Galvanised Iron Pty. came into production.

1921 Acquisition of Gwaun-cae-Gurwen Colliery Co.

1922 The Cyfarthfa Collieries re-opened in September, and the steelworks dismantled.

1923 Acquisition of Henry Cox Screw Co. and A. Stokes & Co. by GKN.

1923 Authorisation of £80,000 to be spent on new coke ovens and by-product plant at Dowlais steelworks.

1923 Consolidated Cambrian group and D. Davis & Sons taken over by GKN.

1924 Decision taken to close the Stour Valley Works formerly belonging to the PNB.

1925 Nettlefolds Proprietory screw works, at Sunshine, near Melbourne, came into production.

1925 The Cyfarthfa Collieries were sold by GKN.

1925 The puddling furnaces and rolling mills at London Works (formerly PNB) were dismantled.

1926 F.W. Cotterill put into voluntary liquidation and its assets incorporated within GKN.

1926 A programme of major capital expenditure authorised over three years for the Dowlais and Dowlais–Cardiff steelworks.

1926 Joseph Sankey & Sons acquired a minority shareholding in Harris & Sheldon, shopfitters.

1927 Formation of Gueret, Llewellyn & Merrett.

1927 April, H. Seymour Berry appointed chairman of GKN upon the resignation of Edward Steer.

1927 Recess Screws (1926) acquired.

1927 Thomas Haddon & Co. taken over.

1927 October, death of Edward Steer.

1928 May, H. Seymour Berry, Lord Buckland, killed in a riding accident, succeeded as chairman of GKN by Sir John Field Beale.

1928 W.R. Lysaght appointed chairman of John Lysaght.

1928 October, Howell R. Jones retired as general manager of Dowlais Works and Collieries, and was succeeded by William Simons.

1929 Sale of Gwaun-cae-Gurwen Colliery Co. to Amalgamated Anthracite.

1930 Formation of the British (Guest, Keen, Baldwins) Iron & Steel Co. to include the heavy steel interests of GKN and Baldwins.

1930 Incorporation of Welsh Associated Collieries, GKN's coal holdings.

1930 June, Frederick Mountford (Birmingham) acquired.

1930 Exors. of James Mills of Bredbury, Stockport, taken over.

1930 Aug. Stenman AB of Eskilstuna, Sweden, acquired by GKN.

1930 October, election of J.H. Jolly and T.Z. Lloyd to GKN board.

1930 The reconstruction of Normanby Park Steelworks, Scunthorpe, for £400,00 authorised.

1930 Cessation of iron and steelmaking at Dowlais.

1931 December, Nettlefolds resigned from the International Woodscrew Union.

1933 July, T.S. Peacock appointed deputy chairman in succession to F.W. Keen; C.H. Keen and K.S. Peacock elected to the GKN board.

1933 Scheme to reconstruct the Dowlais–Cardiff steelworks, East Moors, approved by Bankers Industrial Development Co.

1933 Transfer of rolling operations from Rogerstone to Cardiff approved in principle.

1934 English Wood Screw Co. of Croydon taken over.

1934 A majority interest in Henry Williams India (1931) acquired by GKN.

1934 J.H. Jolly appointed a joint managing director of GKN.

1934 Death of George H. Sankey, managing director of Joseph Sankey & Sons.

1935 Sale of Welsh Associated Collieries to Powell Duffryn Associated Collieries.

1935 Cardiff rod mill opened.

1935 English Wood Screw Co. wound up.

1935 Uddeholms, Swedish woodscrew makers, acquired.

1935 December, death of Sir John Field Beale, succeeded as chairman by S.R. Beale.

1936 January, Dowlais–Cardiff steelworks returned to production, after reconstruction costing £3 million.

1936 K.S. Peacock appointed a joint managing director.

1940 December, death of Sir David Llewellyn, succeeded as chairman of John Lysaght by S.R. Beale.

1941 July, T.S. Peacock retired as a joint managing director but retained his deputy chairmanship.

1942 Uskside Engineering Co. of Newport acquired by John Lysaght.

1942 Somerset Wire Co. taken over by GKN.

1943 April, J.H. Jolly appointed deputy chairman.

1944 January, Sankey Electrical Stampings at Worli, Bombay, began production.

1944 Twisteel Reinforcement became a wholly-owned subsidiary of GKN.

1945   April, death of W.R. Lysaght.

1945   Nettlefold & Sons, woodscrew factors, acquired by GKN.

1945   GKW bolt factory under construction at Bhandup, near
Bombay.

Introduction

Time present and time past
Are both perhaps present in time future
And time future contained in time past.
T. S. Eliot, 'Burnt Norton' (1935)[1]

The interwar period, sandwiched between two world wars and divided in half by a deep and prolonged slump, was a particularly testing time for British business. The bursting of the post-war boom saw the beginning of a contraction in the traditional industries (coal, steel, shipbuilding and textiles) which was to dominate the economic climate for a decade, and raise the problem of persistent mass unemployment.[2] The nation was faced not only with stronger foreign competition but also with a more unsettled and sluggish international market. The depression made matters worse: steel output was halved between 1929 and 1931; shipbuilding, by 1930, reduced to half its output of the immediate post-war years, almost came to a complete standstill in 1932, while coal production fell by one-fifth in the three years from 1929. Although an upswing followed in 1933, world trade had merely recovered to the level of 1929 by the outbreak of the Second World War.[3]

Within this picture of economic vicissitude, GKN, a major manufacturing group, constituted an important test case, a litmus paper for British industry. The first question, which perhaps might be asked, is why should the first one hundred and fifty-nine years of GKN's history and the subsequent twenty six both demand studies of roughly equal length? First, this is not a fair comparison as this second volume includes the stories of both John Lysaght and Joseph Sankey before their takeover by GKN in 1920; they, together with Cotterills, Garringtons, Bayliss, Jones & Bayliss and Exors of James Mills (all acquired in the interwar period), had their origins in the nineteenth century. However, this point alone is not sufficient to justify such a striking imbalance in the number of words needed to discuss two periods of history. Another explanation relates to the survival of archival evidence. Much more could have been written on the company in the eighteenth and early nineteenth centuries had more information been available. Although there remain significant gaps (not least the output records of Nettlefolds and the profit figures for certain subsidiaries), the source material generated in the twenties and thirties was of such variety and quantity to make the historian's problem one of selection rather than discovery.

In 1918, when the war in Europe came to a halt and the engine peacetime commerce started to turn, GKN did not find itself in perfect mechanical order. Although the screw-making business of Nettlefolds remained very profitable, the other principal elements in the group were either in need of capital investment or faced declining markets: the London Works of the former Patent Nut & Bolt Co. required widescale modernisation;[4] the Dowlais steelworks suffered from comparatively old plant and machinery together with serious locational problems, while its more recent companion, Dowlais-Cardiff, sited beside Roath Dock, had been designed for the manufacture of plate, and demand by the shipbuilding industry was shortly to collapse; many of the group's colleries had seen their most productive days, and with falling prices, a number were soon to close. In addition, GKN had not succeeded in attracting talented new blood to its senior ranks. The main board in 1918 comprised five members under the chairmanship of the Earl of Bessborough, the group's first non-executive leader; his fellow directors comprised F.W. Keen, Edward Steer, E. Windsor Richards and Sir John Field Beale. Richards, aged eighty-seven, retired in that year to be succeeded by H. Probyn, the company secretary.[5] Although Beale was later to serve as chairman, he was by profession a solicitor and occupied a non-executive seat. Only Keen and Steer possessed detailed knowledge of the business and had gained personal experience of manufacturing.

During 1914–15 Dudley Docker (1862–1944), the acquisitive and determined head of the Metropolitan Carriage, Wagon & Finance Co., had proposed that his group merge with GKN.[6] The scheme collapsed because of Arthur Keen's death and the nervousness of his son and successor. Clearly, Docker had judged that as matters stood within GKN, some form of amalgamation would be propitious. Perhaps encouraged by the deepening post-war depression, in February 1920 the GKN board decided not to resist proposals for a merger with John Lysaght, the steel making, rolling and galvanising group, when they were presented by the latter's chairman, H. Seymour Berry. Because GKN was the larger of the two groups, it qualified as the holding company, and Lysaghts became the subsidiary.

The union between GKN and John Lysaght was the most significant event in the history of the company during the interwar period. The merger had a number of important implications. First, it introduced a number of able and highly motivated senior managers to the GKN board, principal among these being H. Seymour Berry (later Lord Buckland),[7] Sir David Llewellyn[8] and W.R. Lysaght.[9] Although Berry did not immediately succeed Bessborough in 1920 as chairman (the post falling to Edward Steer), he was appointed joint deputy chairman and assumed a position of considerable influence. Born in Merthyr Tydfil and a former assistant to D.A. Thomas, Viscount Rhondda, his business experience had been gained in the South Wales coalfield. Accordingly, his friends and associates were either colliery owners, mining

1 The principal players in this history: H. Seymour Berry, Lord Buckland, chairman of GKN, entertaining a group of directors at Buckland Estate, Bwlch, shortly before his death. From left to right, back row, —, Sir William Ewert Berry [Lord Camrose], Lt. Col. C.H.C. Guest, James Gomer Berry [Lord Kemsley], Lord Glanely, Sir David Llewellyn; middle row, —, T.S. Peacock, —, —, Lady Glanely, Lady Beale, F.W. Keen, Sir John Field Beale; front row, Mrs Dease, —, —, Lady Buckland, Lord Buckland, Lady Llewellyn; seated on the ground, the three Miss Berrys.

engineers or coal merchants. Basing his strategy on the success achieved by the industry in the late Victorian and Edwardian periods, he encouraged GKN to invest heavily in the region's collieries. With these acquisitions, the membership of the GKN board altered appreciably: Sir Leonard W. Llewelyn, T.J. Callaghan, John Paton, E.A. Mitchell-Innes and latterly Edmund L. Hann and Sir Stephenson H. Kent owed their appointment to this strategy. In addition, Berry's younger brothers, William Ewert, later Lord Camrose, and James Gomer, Lord Kemsley, were also elected to directorships.[10] Thus, the Lysaght merger had an indirect though profound influence on the composition of GKN's senior management in the mid-1920s and 1930s.

The union between the two groups also broadened their manufacturing capabilities: Lysaghts and their major subsidiary, Joseph Sankey & Sons, had a number of specialisms not offered by GKN. Although loss making in the early 1920s, when it experienced closure and short-time working, the Normanby Park steelworks, opened by Lysaghts at Scunthorpe in 1912, served as a valued source of billets for the company's Orb Rolling Mills, Newport. The latter, as suppliers of sheet steel to the automotive and electrical industries, proved to be a most profitable enterprise. In the nineteenth century the bulk of the mills' output, after galvanising at St Vincents Works, Bristol, was exported to Australia where it was extensively employed in the construction of houses, shops and warehouses. This market was progressively lost to Orb and St Vincents Works during the interwar years as indigenous production was able to supply a growing proportion of the nation's demands from the Newcastle Works of John Lysaght (Australia) Pty. in New South Wales. Deprived of this trade, St Vincent's Works, fell into difficulties and escaped threats of closure by continuing to produce agricultural hollow-ware and prefabricated farm buildings. The Construction Department, nearby at Netham, was badly affected by the depression but flourished during the 1930s and won government contracts for re-armament and repairs caused by the war itself.

The indirect acquisition of Joseph Sankey & Sons broadened GKN's industrial base, extending it still further into two of the economy's most important areas. The company's Bankfield Works had established a reputation as the leading supplier of electrical stampings and laminations, while the Hadley Castle Works at Wellington sold wheels, chassis frames and body pressings to the largest of the car makers. The impressive record of profits earned by Sankey's throughout the interwar years underlined the importance of being associated with the truly dynamic areas of the economy.

The strategic turn of direction in favour of coal, after the appointment of Berry and Llewellyn, resulted in the following major acquisitions: Gwaun-cae-Gurwen Colliery Co. (1921), Meiros Colliery Co. and the South Rhondda Colliery Co. (1920), D. Davies & Sons (1923), and the Consolidated Cambrian group (1923), which alone employed 14,000 men.[11] A host of reasons (including the return to the Gold Standard from 1925, the age of the collieries and their inherent geological problems, labour disputes, and cheap imports) conspired to undermine the commercial success of this policy. The death of Lord Buckland in 1927 removed its protagonist from the board and from then GKN gradually withdrew from the South Wales coal industry. In an attempt to discover whether collieries might fare better if grouped together under a single autonomous board, Welsh Associated Collieries was formed in 1930 as a wholly-owned subsidiary of GKN. Battling through particularly unfavourable market conditions, its profit record remained unimpressive and in March 1935 WAC was sold to its principal competitor Powell Duffryn, and GKN's historic involvement with coal, dating back to the earliest days of the Dowlais Iron Co., was finally severed.

The decision by GKN to set up Welsh Associated Collieries corresponded with the partial divestment of their heavy-steel interests, another activity with a poor commercial record in the twenties. On 1 January 1930, Baldwins and GKN established a joint company, Guest Keen Baldwins, to run their four steelworks: Dowlais, Dowlais–Cardiff, Port Talbot and Margam. Almost the first act of GKB was to blow out

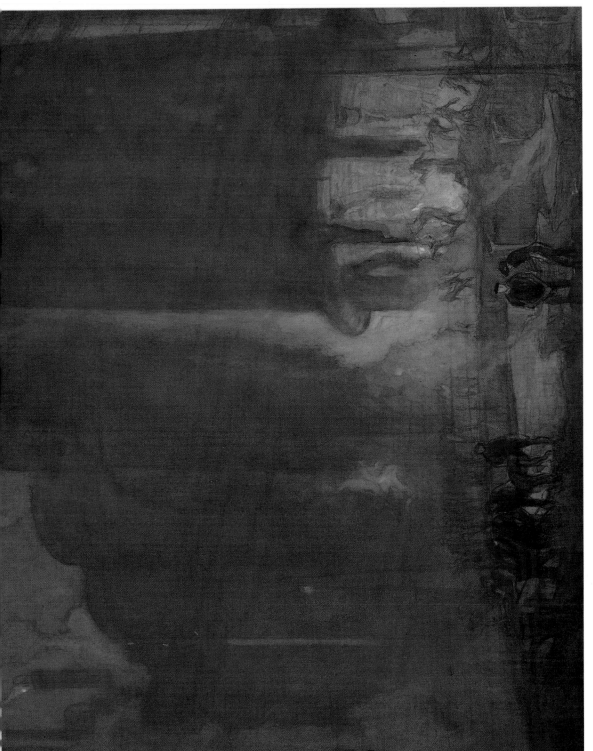

1 'The Blast Furnaces at Dowlais' by Sir Frank Brangwyn (1867–1956). A watercolour of the blast furnaces at Dowlais during the 1920s. Brangwyn, who was born in Bruges, studied under William Morris before going to sea, returning to practise as an artist (*Cyfarthfa Castle Museum & Art Gallery, Merthyr Tydfil, Mid Glamorgan*).

the furnaces and Bessemer converters at Dowlais, though it maintained a flicker of its former glory as the foundries and engineering shops at Ifor Works continued to employ several hundred men. Faced with a depression in the shipbuilding industry, the Dowlais–Cardiff steelworks at East Moors had found it impossible to earn consistent profits during the twenties. The only solution was to close the works in the autumn of 1933 and embark on a reconstruction which would enable it to produce billets, colliery arches, pit props and light sections. The £3 million required was raised with assistance from the Bankers Industrial Development Co. and in conjunction with Baldwins. Once the rebuilding at East Moors was completed in January 1936, the works remained under the control of GKB.

Having partially divested themselves both of their coal and heavy-steel interests in South Wales, from 1930 GKN could concentrate a greater proportion of its managerial talent and resources in the various engineering subsidiaries it owned in the Midlands. Principal among these were Bayliss, Jones & Bayliss (whose Victoria Works, near Wolverhampton, produced castings, nuts, bolts and spikes, together with gates and fencing in great variety), F.W. Cotterill (whose Darlaston works made nuts, bolts, rivets, washers and studs) and the Albert Works of John Garrington & Sons, also at Darlaston, which produced drop forgings for the aircraft, automobile, agricultural, tube engineering and electrical trades.

However, of crucial importance throughout the interwar years were the profits earned by Nettlefolds, the leading European maker of woodscrews. Neither the Guest nor the Keen elements were able to maintain the commercial good fortune they had enjoyed in the nineteenth century and the group became increasingly reliant on the surpluses generated by the Heath Street screw mills. In 1929 and 1930, for example, when GKN's traditional activities steel and coal suffered, Nettlefolds produced profits of £387,412 and £364,975 respectively.[12] By taking over both well-established and embryonic woodscrew makers in the UK, notably Henry Cox Screw Co. and A. Stokes & Co. (both 1923), Thomas Haddon & Co. (1927), Frederick Mountford (1930), the English Wood Screw Co. (1934), Thomas P. Hawkins & Sons (1938), and George Goodman (1938), they were able to retain their monopoly of the British market. However, to a greater extent than before they felt the impact of foreign competition. In part this reflected the International Woodscrew Union's difficulties in regulating conduct between its national members and the aggressive policies pursued by Swedish manufacturers in the face of falling prices. In 1930 this resulted in GKN acquiring Sweden's largest producer, Aug. Stenman of Eskilstuna, and in 1935 they took over a second Swedish company, Uddeholms. Having successfully defended its territory from importers, in the late 1930s and throughout the war years, GKN embarked on a major programme of capital spending to up-date and renew the plant and machinery at Heath Street.

The shift in emphasis away from coal and steel towards engineering in the Midlands was reflected in appointments to the main board after 1930. In August of that year, for example, T.Z. Lloyd, general manager of Heath Street since 1906, was elected to a directorship of GKN. In July 1933 T.S. Peacock, former general manager of Cotterills, the nut and bolt manufacturers of Darlaston, rose to be both deputy chairman and managing director, while his son, K.S. Peacock, responsible for sales and marketing at Nettlefolds, was appointed to the board; aged thirty-one, he was the youngest director in the history of GKN. K.S. Peacock was promoted to joint managing director in January 1936, and thereby became one of the principal decision-makers in the group.[13] His father retired as joint managing director in 1941, but retained his post as deputy chairman until his death five years later. The balance of power, therefore, had swung away from coal and steel in South Wales, in favour of light engineering in the Black Country. The appointment of Allan Macbeth to the GKN board in July 1937, emphasised this shift. As managing director of Exors. of James Mills, the Bredbury manufacturers of railway fixtures and fittings, he had invited GKN to acquire the business in 1930.

Of crucial importance in the management of GKN from the mid-1930s onwards was James Hornby Jolly.[14] A chartered accountant from Lancashire, he had joined the group as company secretary in 1918, and was elected to the board in 1930, and four years later, at the comparatively young age of forty-seven, he became joint managing director. Jolly held this post until October 1947, when he succeeded Sir Samuel Beale as chairman,[15] having been appointed a joint deputy in April 1943. Never allowing himself to become immersed in the intricacies of technology, he took a financial and administrative overview of the group. His cumulative knowledge of the various constituent companies and accountancy expertise, provided Jolly with a central role in strategic policy-making.

The interwar period produced a greater interest in the establishment of overseas subsidiaries than ever before.[16] The union with John Lysaght fortuitously introduced GKN to manufacturing in Australia. Towards the end of the Great War the former had been planning the construction of rolling mills and galvanising plant at Newcastle, NSW, and in 1920 at the time of the merger much of the construction was complete, so that when the works came into operation in April 1921, GKN had become the new owners. Committed to the success of this embryonic enterprise and encouraged by the Federal Government, Lysaghts were able to attract capital investment for the progressive enlargement of the Newcastle Works. Having temporarily operated the Port Kembla works of the former Australian Iron & Steel Co. from 1936, they then constructed their own rolling mills and galvanising plant there. Called the Springhill Works, these opened in January 1939. In addition, John Lysaght (Australia) Pty. had signed an agreement with the American Rolling Mills Co. to set up sheet rolling mills near the Port

Kembla Works. Completed in February 1939, Commonwealth Rolling Mills Pty. (the CRM Works) formed the third major manufacturing unit operated by Lysaghts in Australia.

By comparison, the acquisition in 1930 of Aug. Stenman AB, the Swedish manufacturer of fasteners and hinges, was part of a considered strategy devised by Nettlefolds to maintain the integrity of its UK market from ruinously cheap imports. The takeover of Henry Williams (1931) was at the invitation of its chairman, Owen R. Williams. The company, which had experienced a short-term financial crisis, found itself competing with exports of railway bolts and spikes from the former Cotterill mills at Darlaston. GKN, which sold a variety of products to the sub-continent through its agents, Macbeth Bros. & Co., was anxious to establish a manufacturing base and network of wholesale outlets. The purchase was based, therefore, on complementary interests and a desire to broaden the group's trading options. With capital provided by GKN, the works at Howrah continued to grow and in 1944, following encouragement from the Indian government, it was decided to transfer the bolt mill to a new purpose-built factory at Bhandup, Bombay. There, shortly afterwards, Guest Keen Williams were joined by Sankey Electrical Stampings, the Indian subsidiary of Joseph Sankey & Sons, set up in 1943–44 with encouragement from their customer Crompton Parkinson, whose works at Shalimar they leased until the transfer to Bhandup in 1946.

One of the problems faced by GKN in these difficult years was related to their organisation. As Figure 1 demonstrates, the number of subsidiaries belonging to GKN, both at home and abroad, rose significantly during the period. The fact that this diagram does not include the many colliery companies purchased by GKN and its associated companies (Guest Keen Baldwins, Welsh Associated Collieries and the Orconera Iron Ore Co.), adds to the complexity of the group's structure. To overcome the administrative problems this growth had produced, several committees were formed to operate between the main board and individual manufacturing enterprises. These included the Colliery, Nettlefolds (later 'Birmingham'), South Wales and Steel Committees. In addition, the Investment Registration Committee met in order to monitor the performance of GKN's holdings on the stock market and to offer suggestions as to how the company's profits might most advantageously be placed in the financial markets. In British business, the 1930s saw considerable efforts made to improve reporting techniques in accountancy and witnessed the presentation of the first set of consolidated accounts by the Dunlop Rubber Co. for 1933.[17] No such innovation occurred at GKN, nor until the 1940s did the group take any steps to provide further information on matters such as depreciation policies or how their investments had been valued, despite the fact that the latter constituted a major balance sheet item.[18] In this, GKN were the rule rather than the exception, though it was perhaps surprising given the accountancy qualification held by Jolly.

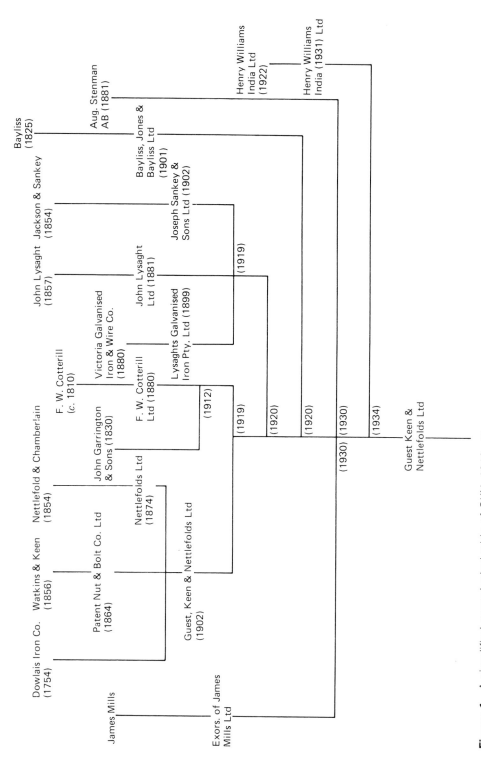

Figure 1 A simplified genealogical table of GKN, 1918–45

The group's reporting procedures improved dramatically after the passing of the 1948 Companies Act when GKN moved into the vanguard of companies adopting accounting reforms.[19]

What follows, therefore, is an assessment of GKN's performance judged against the adverse economic backcloth of the interwar period. How did the group perform in terms of output, profits and the return on company investments? Which elements earned the greatest income, and was the company successful in channelling investment into the most dynamic of its subsidiaries? Were talented young managers given opportunities to develop their abilities and win promotion? Equally important is the need to elucidate the beliefs and strategies of main board members. On what basis did they acquire certain companies, how did they regard the workforce, what were their attitudes to organisational problems and reporting procedures, and what, indeed, was their general philosophy of business? To have answered some or part of these questions, will be to add a little to the sum of business history.

References

1. T.S. Eliot, *The Complete Poems and Plays*, London (1969), p. 171.
2. John Stevenson, *British Society 1914–45*, Harmondsworth (1984), p. 107.
3. Ibid., p. 108.
4. Interview J. Cockcroft with J.H. Jolly, 12 May 1972.
5. *DBB*, Vol. 4, London (1985), J.K. Almond, 'Edward Windsor Richards', p. 900.
6. R.P.T. Davenport-Hines, *Dudley Docker, The Life and Times of a Trade Warrior*, Cambridge (1984), pp. 46–7.
7. *DBB*, Vol. 1, London (1984), Graeme Holmes, 'H.S. Berry', pp. 299–301.
8. *DBB*, Vol. 3, London (1985), Graeme Holmes, 'D.R. Llewellyn', pp. 822–26.
9. Ibid., Edgar Jones, 'W.R. Lysaght', pp. 897–904.
10. *DBB*, Vol. 1, London (1984), Christine Shaw, 'W.E. Berry and J.G. Berry', pp. 301–9.
11. *An Outline History of GKN*, Birmingham [c. 1926], pp. 60–61.
12. BRL, 298/16 GKN, Nettlefolds Department, Annual Accounts General, 1921–34.
13. *DBB*, Vol. 4, London (1985), Edgar Jones, 'Sir K.S. Peacock', pp. 570–3.
14. *DBB*, Vol. 3, London (1985), Edgar Jones, 'J.H. Jolly', pp. 523–26.
15. *Dictionary of Scottish Business Biography 1860–1960, Vol. 1, The Staple Industries*, Aberdeen (1986), Charles W. Munn, 'Sir Samuel Beale', pp. 156–58.
16. Geoffrey Jones (Editor), *British Multinationals: Origins, Management and Performance*, Aldershot (1986), Edgar Jones, 'Steel and Engineering Overseas: GKN's multinational growth, 1918–1965', pp. 164–83.
17. J.R. Edwards, *A History of Financial Accounting*, London (1989), pp. 127–8.
18. J.R. Edwards, *Company Legislation and Changing Patterns of Disclosure in British Company Accounts 1900–1940*, London (1981), pp. 27, 30.
19. R.H. Parker, *Understanding Company Financial Statements*, Harmondsworth (1972), pp. 21, 48, Appendix D, p. 34.

Part 1

Steel and Coal in South Wales, 1919–39

1 GKN and the Post-War Boom, Merger and Acquisitions, 1919–23

In November 1918 when war came to an end, Guest, Keen & Nettle-folds (GKN) stood as one of Britain's largest manufacturing companies. Comprising three steelworks, a substantial collection of fastener factories in the Midlands and a group of collieries in South Wales, it had followed paths of both vertical and horizontal integration. According to a ranking prepared for 1919 based upon the estimated market value of capital, GKN came sixteenth (£8.2 million), and within the metal industry only Vickers (fourth, £19.5 million), United Steel (tenth, £13.2 million) and Armstrong, Whitworth (eleventh, £12.2 million) were higher.[1] It remained in essence a trading company (Guest, Keen & Nettlefolds), with a small number of manufacturing subsidiaries (such as the British Screw Co.), and its operational base was limited to England and Wales. The only overseas venture in which GKN had an interest was a one-third holding in the Orconera Iron Ore Co. of Bilbao, which leased a major group of hematite mines at Obregon, Santander.[2]

As regards the management of GKN, Edward Ponsonby (1851–1920), the eighth Earl of Bessborough, had succeeded to the chairmanship on the death of Arthur T. Keen in July 1918.[3] An Irish aristocrat who had been called to the Bar in 1879, he served as secretary to the Speaker of the House of Commons from 1884 to 1895. His other directorships, including the London, Brighton & South Coast Railway, provided him with general business experience but he remained unschooled in the practicalities of GKN's operations and qualified, therefore, as the group's first non-executive leader. Francis Watkins Keen (1863/4–1933), younger brother of Arthur T., had been appointed deputy chairman and joint managing director in the same year.[4] The other members of the main board comprised the joint managing director, Edward Steer (1851–1927), E. Windsor Richards (1831–1921), H. Probyn (d. 1926),[5] Sir John Field Beale (1874–1935), and Lt. Col. C.H.C. Guest (1874–1957), while J.H. Jolly (1887–1972) served as company secretary from August 1918. Steer, whose father had married into the Nettlefold family, was responsible for the operation of the Castle steelworks and rolling mills at Rogerstone.[6] Sir John Field Beale, senior partner of the London firm of Beale & Co., solicitors, whose Birmingham office had established a long professional relationship with GKN,[7] had been elected in 1916–17 as a replacement for Sir Joseph Weston-Stevens.[8] E. Windsor Richards, who would have been eighty-seven in 1918, retired from GKN later in that year, not having attended any board meetings since the end of 1916.[9] H. Probyn, formerly company secretary of both the Patent Nut & Bolt Co., and GKN, suffered from ailing health so that his elevation to director in July 1918 had the advantage of allowing Jolly, a talented and ambitious chartered accountant, to take over his post and duties.[10] Lt. Col. C.H.C. Guest, the second son of Lord Wimborne and currently the Liberal MP for Pembroke Boroughs,[11] held a non-executive directorship from his appointment early in 1918.[12] The able but autocratic Arthur Keen had not seen the need to advance many talented or technically expert directors, his death in 1915 creating a considerable managerial gap. Hence, the GKN board which welcomed the news of the end of the Great War was both small and aged: Bessborough, the chairman, Beale and Guest while Probyn was shortly to resign in 1921[13] (though he remained a member of the Birmingham Committee), leaving just F.W. Keen and Steer with operational experience.

Beneath the main board were four specialised committees ('Nettlefolds', 'Colliery', 'Works' and 'Finance', the last, in the main, concerned with managing the group's investment portfolio), to which on the succession of the Earl of Bessborough, was added a fifth, the Executive Committee. Composed of the senior managers of the largest works – Howell R. Jones (Dowlais), T.Z. Lloyd (Smethwick), A.K. Reese (Cardiff), J.H. Whitehouse (Cwmbran) and John Williams (Rogerstone) – it was designed to buttress the decision-making of the directors with practical advice.[14] In time both Jones and Lloyd would be promoted to the main board but for the moment their expertise and technical understanding were sought at one remove.

Whilst the GKN board had established a subsidiary committee system, it was still acknowledged that their membership required reinforcement. Accordingly in January 1919 John Paton (1864/5–1943),[15] chairman and managing director of Partridge, Jones & Paton, owners of six collieries in South Wales and a steelworks at Newport, was appointed (see p. 74). He probably owed his election to a friendship with Edward Steer (who was a director of Partridge, Jones & Paton), both men living in the region, the former in Pontypool and the latter at Malpas. Although an able businessman, Paton, because of his existing responsibilities, could never be other than a non-executive director. A transfusion of new blood was to be provided for the board but it was to come from an unexpected direction.

MERGER WITH JOHN LYSAGHT

John Lysaght, was a galvanising and sheet steel business which had grown from a small plant in Bristol to embrace a steelworks at

Normanby Park, Scunthorpe, and extensive rolling mills in Newport (see Chapter 2). Founded by John Lysaght (1832–95)[16] in 1857, it had remained in essence a family-run company even after resort to limited liability in 1880. Gerald S. Lysaght (1869–1951),[17] who had held the chairmanship since 1905,[18] became increasingly concerned that a post-war depression would be ruinous for many industrial concerns. By chance H.G. Hill, a director of Lysaght responsible for the management of the St Vincent's Works in Bristol, was returning home by train, having attended a Ministry of Munitions Committee.[19] He was joined in his compartment by William Trimmer (1872/3–1926), then managing director of Uskside Engineering.[20] Having heard of the pessimism felt at Lysaghts, Trimmer passed on this news to his long-standing friend, Henry Seymour Berry (see p. 77), who was at this time a director of some sixty South Wales collieries. Discussing a possible acquisition with his closest business associate, [Sir] D.R. Llewellyn (see p. 79), they enlisted the help of their former employer's daughter, Viscountess Rhondda. With her financial support, Berry and Llewellyn acquired Lysaghts for £5 million in 1919, a considerable coup given the modernity of its rolling mills and strength of its export market to Australia. Berry, Llewellyn and Viscountess Rhondda all joined the Lysaght board, the former as its chairman.[21] The precise catalogue of events remains a mystery because of the loss or destruction of the crucial Lysaght Minute Book covering the period 1917 to 1921.[22] It appears, nevertheless, that the takeover was not contested and that Gerald Lysaght was content to retire from the family business. For his part in the acquisition, Trimmer was rewarded with a seat on the board. Other appointments included H. Seymour Berry's two younger brothers, William Evert Berry and James Gomer Berry,[23] Sir Leonard W. Llewelyn and M.H. Llewellyn, while S.A. Putnam, an old business colleague of Berry's (p. 83), became company secretary. Three Lysaghts remained on the board, Sidney Royse ('S.R.'), William Royse ('W.R.') and Daniel Conner ('D.C.').[24]

Having taken over Lysaghts, Berry swiftly turned his attention to another established family-run industrial concern which had temporarily run low on managerial drive, Joseph Sankey & Sons. Founded during the 1850s as a firm of hollow-ware manufacturers in Bilston by Joseph Sankey (1827–86),[25] the business had grown rapidly during the late nineteenth and early twentieth centuries diversifying into the field of electrical laminations, and pressings for the automotive trade at their Hadley Castle Works near Wellington, Shropshire (see Chapter 7). The death of their able chairman, John William Sankey, in 1913[26] and the fact that his son and designated successor, Sidney (1889–1915), had been killed at the battle of Loos, resulted in a substantial section of the shareholding falling into the hands of female members of the family, who felt less confident about running the business. In addition, although the company was profitable (a surplus of £39,103 had been earned in the year 1917–18),[27] they had made insufficient allowance during the war for their liability under Excess Profits Duty. For the year ended 31 March 1918 an assessment amounting to £80,000 had been received but only £50,000 had been placed in a revenue fund for this contingency.[28] The Lysaghts, who were long-standing friends (because the former had owned two rolling mills, the Swan Garden and Osier Bed, nearby in Wolverhampton), provided the Sankeys with an example of how to escape from this predicament. Accordingly when George H. Sankey (1865–1934), as chairman, returned from a meeting with the Lysaght directors in Newport to announce that H. Seymour Berry had offered £27.10s. for each Sankey share, it was agreed that the proposal be accepted.[29] On 3 December 1919 Berry became the new chairman of Sankeys, while D.R. Llewellyn and Sir Leonard W. Llewelyn also joined the board. With the resignation of Harry T. Sankey, only Frederick Ernest (d. 1931) and George Herbert Sankey remained to represent the family.[30] Thus, within a period of less than six months Berry and his partner, D.R. Llewellyn, had gained control of two potentially profitable and inter-related businesses which could be added to their widespread holding in the South Wales coal industry.

Having been born, educated and spent his early working life in Merthyr (p. 77), it was not surprising that among Berry's ambitions had been a desire to be associated with Guest, Keen & Nettlefolds. The company had dominated the town being the principal employer, whilst its managers and owners had exerted a considerable influence on local affairs.[31] GKN had built up a reputation as one of the leading industrial concerns in South Wales; it had a distinguished history, a prestigious name and was profitable. No sooner had they consolidated their hold over John Lysaght and its subsidiary, Joseph Sankey, then Berry and Llewellyn planned a takeover of GKN.

The Earl of Bessborough successfully defended GKN against the threatened acquisition at a specially-arranged meeting held at the Queen's Hotel, Birmingham, on 20 February 1920 but was unable or unwilling to resist the notion that the two companies should amalgamate. Accordingly, it was agreed that the two companies should merge, Lysaght and Sankeys becoming subsidiaries of GKN.[32] The differences in size and profitability between the two groups had not been great, so that it had been a finely judged decision as to which became the master. Critical in saving GKN was probably the decision in 1919 to disclose the existence of an internal reserve fund (then standing at £900,729), which had been accumulated during the Great War, the result of an overly generous provision for retrospective Excess Profits Duty.

The merger, effective from January 1920, remained a question of ownership rather than a matter of fundamental managerial change. Although the membership of the respective boards was revised, all the companies concerned continued to operate under their existing names and no new organisational structure was introduced. From the Lysaght team, H. Seymour Berry, D.R. Llewellyn, W.R. Lysaght, William E.

Berry and H.G. Hill were elected to the GKN board.[33] Only Edward Steer, then deputy chairman and managing director of GKN, joined the Lysaght board.[34] Berry remained chairman of Lysaghts and became joint deputy chairman of GKN.[35] Although he then became the really dynamic force within GKN's highest echelon, he did not possess sufficient personal authority to assume the reins of power when the Earl of Bessborough died suddenly in December 1920 while attending a company dinner for directors and Birmingham officials.[36] Edward Steer, who had become a director of Nettlefolds in 1882 and joined the GKN board on its formation in 1902, had the weight of tradition and accumulated experience behind him to become chairman on 15 December 1920.[37]

ACQUISITIONS IN ENGINEERING

The two years following the end of the Great War witnessed a booming economy as the brake on pent-up demand was released and industry returned to its customary peace-time activities. However, the disruption caused by the hostilities and the return of servicemen to their civilian occupations cancelled out any gains that GKN may have made in a context of rising GNP. The company's profits fell from £446,645 in 1918 to £417,141 in 1919 (Table 1.1).[38] With the exception of Nettlefolds, the engineering factories within the group had been neglected. As J.H. Jolly observed, Arthur Keen had preferred to invest capital in gilt-

Table 1.1   GKN profits, 1918–30

		£	£ Adjusted
To 30 June	1918	446,645	571,706
	1919	417,141	567,312
	1920	860,510*	1,359,606
	1921	810,102	1,158,446
9 months to 31 March	1922	567,220	657,975
12 months to 31 March	1923	844,919	946,309
	1924	874,743	970,965
	1925	937,613	1,050,127
	1926	948,298	1,033,645
	1927	909,279	963,836
	1928	966,244	1,014,456
	1929	956,071	994,314
	1930	968,698	968,698

*Including John Lysaght Ltd
Note: Figures adjusted by the Bank of England's index of consumer prices, 1930 = 100.

Source: *GKN Annual Report and Accounts*, 1918–30.

edged stock rather than machinery at London Works and his son, Arthur T. Keen, being of an indecisive disposition, had done little to correct the imbalance.[39] Accordingly, Frank Keen, having been given responsibility as deputy chairman for GKN's nut and bolt plant, realised that the quickest way to recover their position in the fastener market was to acquire a major competitor, F.W. Cotterill Ltd of Darlaston (see Chapter 6). In August 1919 the annual accounts of Cotterills, together with those of their subsidiary, John Garrington & Sons Ltd., drop forgers of Darlaston, were scrutinised[40] and shortly afterwards both businesses were acquired by GKN. Tom Swift Peacock (d. 1946), who had joined F.W. Cotterill as their company secretary, becoming the managing director in 1900, was appointed to the GKN board after the takeover.[41] An able man who was both feared and respected by the workforce, Peacock was promoted to joint managing director of GKN in 1920[42] after the merger with John Lysaght.

Still under the influence of the post-war boom, GKN made a second important acquisition in the Midland's engineering trade. In 1920 they purchased the Wolverhampton business of Bayliss, Jones & Bayliss, manufacturers of nuts, bolts, spikes and castings, with a specialism in gates and fencing.[43] This further strengthened the group's hold over the fastener market and provided additional outlets for the pig iron and steel produced by its South Wales steelworks.

PROFITS AND PERFORMANCE: 1918–23

It is difficult to assess to what extent GKN benefited from the immediate post-war boom (Table 1.1) as the group's profit figures for 1920 were dramatically increased by the incorporation of the Lysaght accounts. The impact of the severe slump of 1921–22 did, however, reveal itself in the published profit figures. In general, the British economy subsequently produced a weak and uneven recovery which reached a high point in 1929.[44] This trend, too, may be discerned in GKN's performance as profits climbed gently to a peak in 1928 when they levelled off before crashing in the depression of 1931–34.

During the period January 1919 to April 1920 the board minutes regularly recorded the contribution of various parts of the group to its overall profits. Four areas were categorised: the Dowlais and Cardiff steelworks, together with their collieries (the Guest element), London and Stour Valley Works with Cwmbran (the former Patent Nut & Bolt Co.), Nettlefolds, and income from investments and bank interest. This short series of figures clearly revealed that the Nettlefold screw works was subject to the least variation. It consistently recorded high profits and was able to sustain the group's steelworks and collieries when their viability fluctuated dramatically in response to market forces. Both the former Guest and PNB elements fell into loss periodically, though the former with its collieries and modern plant in Cardiff was able to earn

Table 1.2 The profitability of GKN by constituent parts 1918–20

Period	Dowlais, Cardiff & Collieries (£)	London, Stour Valley and Cwmbran (£)	Nettlefolds (£)	Investments & Bank Interest (£)
5 months to 30 November 1918	76,349	40,484	200,313	57,075
5 months to 5 June 1919	42,803	34,058	342,468	126,500
5 months to 30 November 1919	(187,866)	2,712	165,146	68,593
8 months to 29 February 1920	135,854	(21,969)	339,443	—
10 months to 30 April 1920	471,996	33,259	472,001	—

Note: Figures in brackets indicate a loss.

Source: GKN Minute Book, Vol. 3, March 1916–September 1922, it. 3226, 3310, 3433, 3479, 3518.

substantial surpluses when conditions proved favourable. After the merger with John Lysaght calculations on this sectoral basis were no longer recorded.

SUMMARY

The five years following the end of the Great War witnessed a quiet revolution within GKN, producing changes as far-reaching as had occurred in 1900–2 when the group had been formed. The merger with John Lysaght and its subsidiary, Joseph Sankey, brought not only a range of new and related steel products, it introduced two formidable managers, H. Seymour Berry and D.R. Llewellyn. They were, in effect, to run GKN for the next five years and the strategy which they were to devise influenced the company for a further decade.

Because the London and Stour Valley Works had fallen into a state of neglect, GKN decided to strengthen their position in the fastener market by the takeover of two established nut and bolt companies. F.W. Cotterill (with its subsidiary, John Garrington & Sons) and Bayliss, Jones & Bayliss. These three businesses were to prove profitable acquisitions for over fifty years and became key elements in its engineering activities. Thus, within a dramatically short period of time the scale and variety of GKN's operations had been greatly extended and the composition of its senior executive team radically altered.

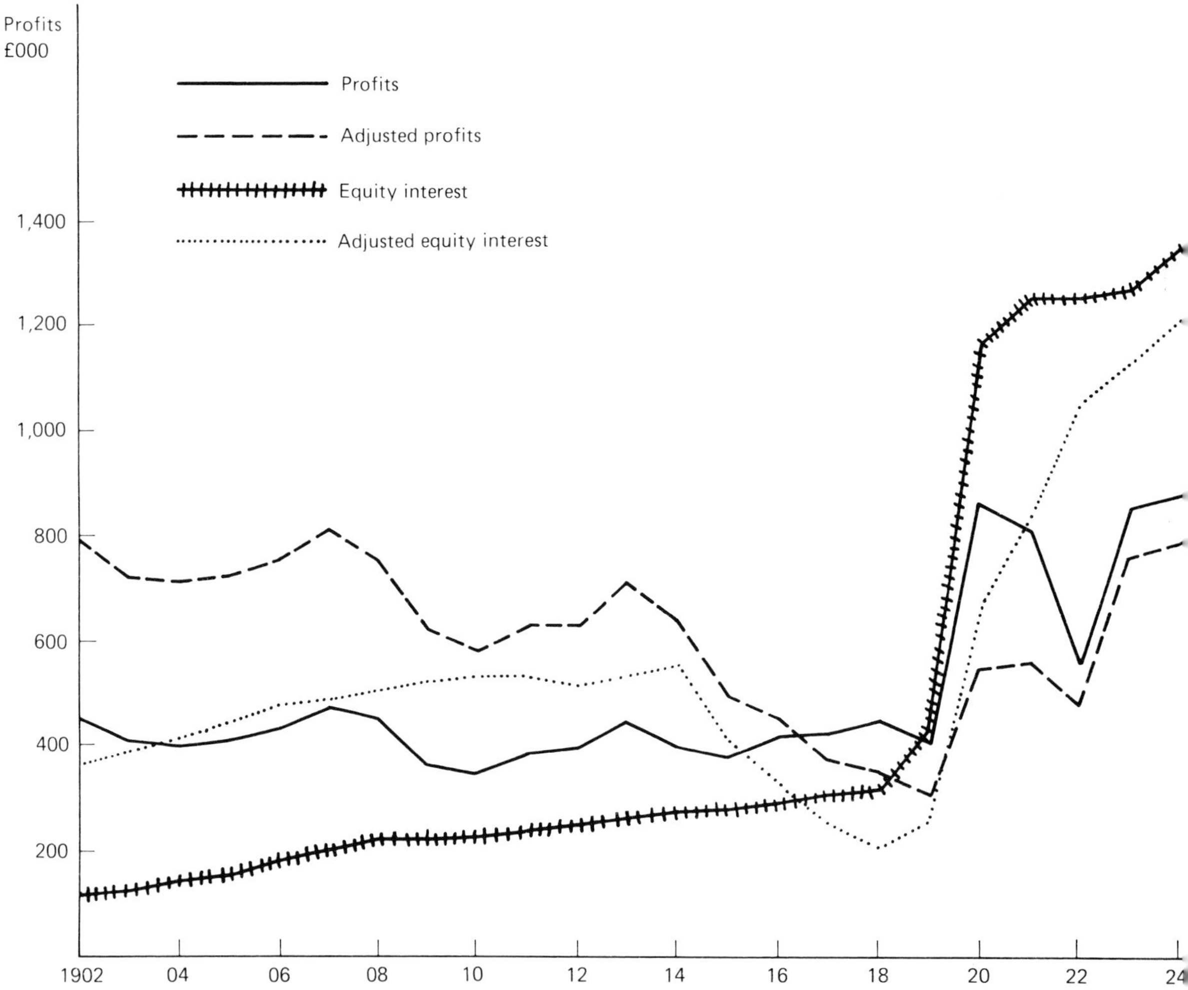

Figure 2 GKN profits and equity interest, 1902–47

References

1. Leslie Hannah, *The Rise of the Corporate Economy*, London (1983), p. 189.
2. G.G. Jones (Editor), *British Multinationals: Origins, Management and Performance*, Aldershot (1986), Edgar Jones 'Steel and Engineering Overseas: Guest, Keen & Nettlefolds' Multinational Growth 1918–1965', pp. 165–6.
3. GKN Minute Book, Vol. 3, March 1916–September 1922, 4 July 1918, it. 3102; 22 August 1918, it. 3142.
4. *The Engineer*, Vol. CLV, 21 April 1933, Obituary, p. 391; Jones, *GKN, Vol. One*, op. cit., p. 188.
5. GKN Minute Book, Vol. 7, September 1926–April 1928, 9 September 1926, it. 4989.

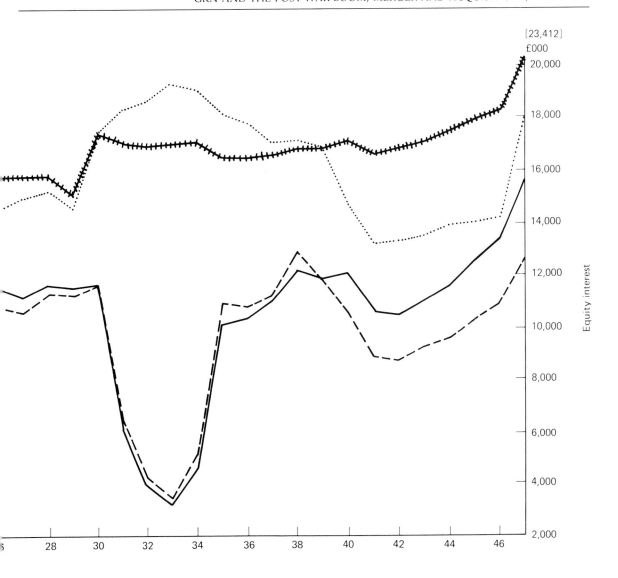

6. For further details of Edward Steer, see Jones, *GKN, Vol. One*, op. cit., pp. 222–24.
7. Ibid., p. 391.
8. GKN, Annual Report and Accounts (1916) and (1917).
9. GKN Minute Book, Vol. 3, 1917–18, passim.
10. Ibid., 22 August 1918, it. 3142; *DBB*, Vol. 3 (1985), Edgar Jones, 'J.H. Jolly', pp. 523–26.
11. Stenton and Lees, *WWMP*, Vol. 3, 1919–45, Brighton (1979).
12. GKN, Annual Report and Accounts (1918).
13. GKN Minute Book, Vol. 3.
14. Ibid., 3 October 1918, it. 3161.
15. *Colliery Guardian*, Vol. CLXVI, No. 4287, 26 February 1943, Obituary, p. 260.

16. *DBB*, Vol. 3 (1985), Colin Baber and Trevor Boyns, 'John Lysaght', pp. 895–99.
17. Ibid., Edgar Jones, 'W.R. Lysaght', p. 902.
18. *The Lysaght Century, 1857–1957*, Bristol (1957), p. 61.
19. Interview E. Jones with E.C. Lysaght, December 1983.
20. *Colliery Guardian*, Vol. CXXXII, No. 3430, 24 September 1926, Obituary, p. 680.
21. *The Lysaght Century*, op. cit., p. 29; J.C. Carr and W. Taplin, *History of the British Steel Industry*, Oxford (1962), p. 386.
22. This would have been Vol. 3 in the series and is the only gap.
23. *DBB*, Vol. 1 (1984), Christine Shaw, 'William Ewert Berry and James Gomer Berry', pp. 301–9.
24. J. Lysaght Minute Book, Vol. 4, August 1921–March 1926, 19 August 1921, p. 1.
25. *DBB*, Vol. 5 (1986), Edgar Jones, 'Joseph Sankey', p. 63.
26. Ibid., Edgar Jones, 'John William Sankey', pp. 60–2.
27. Joseph Sankey & Sons, Minute Book, Vol. 3, 1917–1921, 4 July 1919, p. 113.
28. Ibid., 30 January 1919, p. 92.
29. Ibid., 19 November 1919, p. 130.
30. Ibid.
31. See Jones, *GKN, Vol. One*, op. cit., pp. 87–90, 120–25.
32. GKN Minute Book, Vol. 3, op. cit., 20 February 1920, it. 3457.
33. Ibid., 20 February 1920, it. 3458.
34. J. Lysaght Minute Book, Vol. 4, op. cit., 19 August 1921, p. 1.
35. GKN Minute Book, Vol. 3, op. cit., it. 3459; *GKN Annual Report and Accounts*, No. 20, (1920).
36. GKN Minute Book, Vol. 3, op. cit., 4 December 1920, it. 3623.
37. Ibid., 15 December 1920, it. 3626.
38. *GKN Report and Accounts* (1918–1919).
39. Interview J. Cockcroft with J.H. Jolly, 25 July 1972, p. 2.
40. GKN Minute Book, Vol. 3, op. cit., 28 August 1919, it. 3367.
41. *DBB*, Vol. 3 (1985), Edgar Jones, 'Sir Kenneth Swift Peacock', p. 570.
42. *GKN Annual Report and Accounts*, No. 20, (1920).
43. *An Outline History of GKN*, Birmingham [*c.* 1926], pp. 57–8.
44. B.W.E. Alford, *Depression and Recovery? British Economic Growth, 1918–1938*, London (1979), p. 15.

2 *John Lysaght Ltd*

PART 1, 1857–1918

Corrugated and galvanised sheet iron was the product upon which the commercial success of John Lysaght Ltd rested. Black sheets were rolled to specific gauges and lengths at their various rolling mills either in Wolverhampton or later at Newport and then shipped to the St Vincent's Works in Bristol where they were dipped in baths of molten zinc and tin, a coating designed to prevent the metal rusting.[1] From there corrugated iron was exported to those Imperial territories, such as India, where hot, dry climates rendered this a practical and cheap building material, Australia becoming Lysaght's chief market. The principle of enhancing the rigidity of sheet iron by grooving or corrugating had been long known, though technical problems had prevented the introduction of mass-production methods until the late 1820s when the adoption of fluted rolls enabled red-hot sheets of wrought iron to be shaped quickly and efficiently.[2] The first patent to be concerned with the process, and using the then novel term 'corrugation', was granted to Henry R. Palmer, a London civil engineer, in 1829.[3] In that year Richard Walker, a carpenter and builder, purchased Palmer's patent and began to manufacture corrugated iron at his factory in Grange Road, Bermondsey.[4] In 1844, John Spencer, an agent for Thomas Edington & Sons of the Phoenix Iron Works, Glasgow, was granted a patent for producing corrugated iron, using either a hot or cold sheet passed between grooved rolls, thereby refining the method devised by Palmer. However, untreated black iron was vulnerable to corrosion. Galvanising (by immersing the object in a bath of molten zinc) provided a protective coat and by the 1840s one British maker, Morewood & Rogers of Steel Yard Wharf, Upper Thames Street, London, had resorted to this expedient for corrugated sheet exported to America,[5] and in the following decade large quantities of galvanised iron were being sold abroad.[6] Although not one of the firms responsible for pioneering these developments, John Lysaght Ltd, founded in 1857, and therefore a second generation manufacturer of the product, was by 1875 the largest of its kind in Britain,[7] and ultimately became the first and only manufacturer in Australia.

JOHN LYSAGHT: FOUNDATIONS OF THE BUSINESS

John Lysaght (1832–1895), an Irishman, was born in Hazelwood, Mallow, the youngest son of William Lysaght a small landowner.[8] He spent his early years in the locality but was sent in his late teens to Birmingham where he was employed at Morewood & Rogers' Patent Galvanised Ironworks, 11 Broad Street.[9] Lysaght then moved to Bristol where his family had both business and kinship connections. Crucial in his business success, however, was a friendship formed with Robert Clarke who inherited, on the death of his father, a small factory which galvanised buckets and ship's ironwork, at Temple Backs, close to Temple Meads Station.[10] Yet, the youthful Clarke exhibited neither the interest nor the commercial aptitude to succeed his father and being comfortably provided for, made a gift of the works to John Lysaght in 1857. However, the business which Lysaght took over employed only six men and a boy, and the wage bill for its first week's work, ending on 4 July 1857, amounted to £6 11s 3d.[11]

Continuing emigration to South Africa and Australia resulted in a rapidly rising demand for corrugated iron sheets to build the prefabricated homes, shops and workplaces of the new and fast-growing pioneer settlements. During the gold rush years in Australia, for example, the price of galvanised iron reached £30–£40 per ton.[12] This encouraged Lysaght to diversify. By 1860 the works were galvanising corrugated iron sheet,[13] which was then stamped with the distinctive 'Orb' trademark, selected in the first year of business.[14] Success in this market soon resulted in the need for larger premises, and in 1869 Lysaght acquired the St Vincent's Works, a four-acre site formerly occupied by the mechanical engineers, Acraman, Morgan & Co., who in 1837 had made most of the machinery for Brunel's *Great Western*, the first steamship to cross the Atlantic on a regular schedule. Entered from Silverthorne Lane, this was a prime industrial location bounded to the south by the feeder canal to the River Avon and to the north by the Great Western main line with connections to the Midland Railway.[15] There a large galvanising shop, 150 ft × 120 ft and 70 ft high was constructed, supported internally by four massive Bath stone pillars.[16] Inside these lead pipes were inserted to channel rainwater from the glazed roof to the drains. The use of timber for its framework, rather than iron or steel, and the concealment of the pipes within masonry columns was to guard against the corrosive effect of the acid in the atmosphere produced by the pickling of the sheets before they were galvanised. The factory appears to have been designed by Thomas Royse Lysaght, a Bristol architect and elder brother of John Lysaght.[17] In the early 1850s the former moved his architectural practice to the St Vincent's Works, possibly because Lysaghts had become involved in the manufacture of ironwork and in 1876 set up a Constructional Engineering Department which would have benefited from the presence of a friendly professional.

2   St. Vincent's Works, Bristol — a view of the office building. It was designed in 1891 by Richard Milverton Drake, a local architect. No expense had been spared in the construction, the entrance hall and staircase being finished in intricate Doulton tiling (*Author*).

John Lysaght purchased his supplies of corrugated black sheet from a variety of Midlands' rollers during the 1870s, these being carried along the Severn Canal to the company's wharf.[18] Upon unloading, the sheets were placed on small trucks and transported around the works over narrowgauge tracks. To attack surface oxide the iron was pickled in sulphuric acid, and then placed in one of ten galvanising pots filled with molten zinc, called 'spelter'. For the more expensive grades a small quantity of tin was added as it was believed to improve the adherence of the coating. The galvanised iron was washed in water to cool the metal and dried in a machine, patented by Mr. Lysaght, which resulted in a 'great saving of labour'.[19] The finished product was boxed for despatch either by ship or railway.

The workforce at Bristol increased rapidly: from twenty-nine men and boys in 1864[20] to 400 in 1883 when over 1,000 tons of galvanised iron were turned out.[21] Ultimately, numbers at St Vincents and nearby Netham rose to almost 1,000 by 1900.[22]

Since John Lysaght was manufacturing the material used for walls and roofs in prefabricated buildings, it was natural that he should consider extending his operations to include the structural ironwork which held these edifices together. Accordingly, in 1876 he acquired thirteen acres of land nearby at Netham, also served by the canal feeder,[23] where he set up a Constructional Engineering (originally called 'Structural Ironwork') Department. This specialised in the design of roof structures and its commissions included: Swansea Market, the Round House at Woolwich Arsenal, Llanelli Market, the concert pavilion on Aberystwyth Pier, the car sheds for the Bristol Tramway & Carriage Co., machine shops for Vickers, Son & Maxim at Barrow and sheds for the Avonside Engine Co., Portsmouth Dockyard and Llanelli Steel Co.[24] Their expertise was such that in 1887 they won the competition to provide the steel frame to the Manchester Royal Jubilee Exhibition Hall.[25] In addition, the Department manufactured ironwork for footbridges, platform coverings and viaducts,[26] in particular for the Great Western and London & South Western Railways.[27]

Having expanded the range of his products to include hollow-ware manufacture (buckets, tubs, coal scuttles and so forth), galvanised iron sheet, structural ironwork and the production of wire-netting (intro-duced c. 1875), it was natural that he should consider a measure of vertical integration to safeguard his extended activities. Reliant upon Midland rollers of sheet over extended lines of communications, John Lysaght decided to acquire his own rolling mills, and in 1878 purchased the Swan Garden Iron Works at Wolverhampton from G.B. Thorneycroft & Co., rollers of rails, plates, a little sheet and merchant iron. He wrote of the transaction in his 'Private Letter Book' for 12 January.

> I will purchase the whole works as they stand, exclusive of finished or half-finished iron and pig iron, for the sum of £23,000 ... Possibly to others on the spot the works are worth more, but to me they are not, because I should have to alter the entire plant in the course of a couple of years or so to bring the works into a form consistent with the improvements in the rolling of sheets.[28]

Because of the prolonged trade recession the Swan Garden Works had, in fact, been closed temporarily and at Bristol John Lysaght recorded that he too had been 'only jogging on, trying to avoid as much loss as possible merely to keep the works going and my business together'.[29] His shrewd decision to buy, at the bottom of the market, revealed a measure of courage and optimism. The Wolverhampton plant was converted for the rolling of sheet, eventually seven mills being installed, with an annual capacity of 25,000 tons. By 1883 almost 700 men were employed there.[30] Initially the mills were 'singles' (one set of rolls to each shaft) giving them an output of 30 tons a week but in time, and particularly after the substitution of steel for wrought iron in the mid-1890s, the figure rose well over 50 tons, and reached 100 tons by the 1930s. The black sheets were then loaded into narrowboats in Wolverhampton (the Swan Garden Works abutting on to the Wyrley & Essington Canal) and transported via the Severn Canal directly to the St Vincent's wharf to be galvanised and corrugated.

So great was the demand for corrugated iron by the Empire that in October 1885 John Lysaght felt it necessary to increase his sheet-rolling capacity still further and purchased the Osier Bed Iron Works, Horsley Fields.[31] Also situated in Wolverhampton it had an annual output of 15,000 tons, which in October 1888 was increased considerably by the decision to lay down a further six mills at a cost of £23,000.[32]

By 1880, having developed the St Vincent's site, acquired Netham and Swan Garden with rapidly expanding order books, John Lysaght's business had outgrown the organisational limits of the family partnership. Accordingly, in the summer of 1881, the firm was floated as a private limited liability company with a capital of £162,000 in the form of 3,240 shares.[33] Of these 3,223 were allotted to John Lysaght who became the chairman, while the three other directors, Albert Petter, John Bramwell Hollom and Richard Dodd, were each allocated one share.[34] The remaining shareholding was divided accordingly: St John George Lysaght (ten), George W.W. Webb, manager, (one), Charles Julius Ryland, the auditor, (one), John Latham Press (one) and Robert Donaldson (one). Sydney Royse Lysaght became the company secretary, a post he retained until November 1884, when he was succeeded by Edward Davey.[35] In April 1888, an issue of 3,000 additional preference shares of £50 (paying a dividend of 5 per cent) raised the capitalisation of the business from £162,007 to £312,007.[36] Of these, 2,000 were purchased by John Lysaght himself, consolidating his position of absolute authority over the shareholding.[37] This situation persisted until 1902, when to help finance the construction of a steelworks, John Lysaght became a public limited liability company (see p. 24).

PROFITS AND PERFORMANCE: THE 1880s, 1890s AND 1900s

The export of galvanised sheet lay at the root of John Lysaght's business success, and of all sales overseas those to Australia were of paramount importance. In 1903 about 81 per cent of the sheet produced by Wolverhampton and Bristol was exported, and of this about 80 per cent went to Australia.[38] The correspondence of John Lysaght during the years 1885–86 suggested that this trade was of vital importance in keeping the business solvent. A depression in the UK had forced prices for galvanised iron from £15 10s per ton in August 1884 to £13 7s 6d by July 1886 and in doing so drove some English makers into bankruptcy. Throughout 1886 Lysaght complained that he received hardly any orders from British customers.[39] The Australian economy, by contrast, remained buoyant, and by the time that a collapse in the land boom speculation and tight money markets brought a recession in 1891, this situation at home had recovered. However, the Australian market had become sufficiently important that it resulted in stoppages and a reduction in the number of staff and workers.[40] Equally, a slight improvement, beginning in 1893, encouraged the Lysaght board to believe that their business's fortunes would improve during 1894,[41] though in reality the recovery was more gradual than they had predicted due to formidable competition and the catastrophic effects of the depression.[42]

Given the overwhelming importance of sheet exports, the board deliberated long and hard over changes in price as these could have a disproportionate effect on sales. In July 1888, for example, when the cost of both black sheets and spelter had risen, they refused to pass on the increments to the consumer and maintained the price of £15 per ton f.o.b. London.[43] The decision later in the year to acquire the Osier Bed Works at a cost of £23,000 can be seen in the context of obtaining greater control over their inputs so that they could regulate the final price of galvanised sheet even more effectively.[44] This interpretation was confirmed by the Directors' Report for 1891 in which John Lysaght recorded that heavy losses had been recorded at the Swan Garden, Osier Bed and Spelter Works during 1890 but despite this the St Vincent's Galvanising and Trading Department had achieved a 'very fair profit'.[45] In other words, during recessions deficits were tolerated at subsidiary manufacturing plants so long as sales of galvanised sheet showed a surplus overall. In good years such as 1891 the Wolverhampton rolling mills earned a profit of £17,000 in contrast to the £15,000 loss accumulated in 1890, while the Spelter Works at Bristol were £1,300 in the black rather than £3,500 in the red for the corresponding periods.

When the depression affecting the 'Australian colonies' of 1891 deepened in the following year, shipments of galvanised iron from Bristol fell by over a third and prices tumbled. As a result, a considerable gap had opened up between the estimated income the company could expect from orders received and the actual sums being paid when the goods were delivered. To accommodate the discrepancy, and, in effect, to subsidise the reductions a 'consignment adjustment fund' of £25,000 was created in 1892.[46] Toward the end of the year, as the slump reached its low point, the need for the fund almost disappeared, 'goods abroad having sold at or near the invoiced prices'.[47] The impact of these

Table 2.1 Reported pre-tax profits of John Lysaght, 1885–1918

	£	Adjusted		£	Adjusted
to 31 Mar. 1885	67,887	94,287	1904	129,016	184,308
1886	50,849	73,694	1905	99,451	138,126
1887	75,626	111,215	1906	128,302	166,626
1888	120,425	172,036	1907	169,677	212,096
1889	123,377	171,357	1908	221,056	302,816
1890	92,823	128,921	1909	306,650	414,392
1891	122,401	170,001	1910	374,006	479,495
1892	109,978	161,732	1911	447,880	559,850
1893	101,773	149,968	1912	414,777	487,973
1894	92,925	147,500	1913	478,143	562,251
1895	111,777	180,285	1914	507,441	596,989
1896	117,959	193,375	1915	633,005	586,116
1897	95,370	153,822	1916	—	—
1898	103,871	162,298	1917	—	—
1899	144,142	211,973	1918	—	—
1900	151,184	201,579			
to 31 Dec. 1901	121,731	173,901			
1902	135,306	196,096			
1903	121,759	176,462			

Note: Figures adjusted by the Sauerbeck-*Statist* price index, 1867–77 = 100.

Source: John Lysaght, Old Company Minute Book,
June 1881–March 1897, Vol. I;
Minute Book, March 1897–November 1901, Vol. II;
John Lysaght New Company Minute Book,
November 1901–December 1909, Vol. I;
Minute Book, January 1910–March 1917, Vol. II.

economic trends revealed itself in the profits of John Lysaght (Table 2.1) as the steady rise from 1885 onwards was halted in 1892 and the high figure of £122,401 for the year ending 31 March 1891 was not surpassed until 1899, though in real terms a peak had in fact been achieved in 1888, overtaken in 1895.

The profit figures adjusted for the effects of price movements have proved to be a better guide to the fortunes of John Lysaght for the jump evident in 1895 accurately reflects the company's own analysis of its performance. From 1891 until mid-1895 supply outstripped demand but by the end of the year they observed

a condition of activity to the iron market which had been unexampled since 1889. We had to face the pleasant difficulty of not being able to produce as large a quantity of iron as we could sell, having cries from all our agents in all parts of the world for more supplies, and even to purchase black sheets from outside makers to keep pace with the requirements of the home market.[48]

The second half of the decade saw ever climbing outputs and a trend of rising profits.[49] Nevertheless, the strategy which had brought John Lysaght to this powerful market position remained unchanged:

> the lines laid down and pursued by our honoured chief, the late head of the firm [John Lysaght] – 'A policy of cautious progress and well-considered extension'. We have avoided all doubtful business and taken no steps without deliberation, but we have not been content to stand still, and the forward steps we have taken have all been justified by results.[50]

Profits fell slightly in 1897 and recovered to a degree in 1898, the result of severe competition which, in turn, depressed prices,[51] despite high levels of output.[52] Greatly increased demand in 1899 produced a 'brilliant total', the bulk of profit being made from the manufacture of black and galvanised sheets.[53]

A breakdown of the figures for 1903 revealed that after the deduction of £18,982 for depreciation, 20.1 per cent of the company's profits had been earned by the Constructional Engineering Department at Netham, 3.0 per cent by the Spelter Works at Bristol and 76.9 per cent on sales of galvanised iron, which comprised the rolling of black sheets at Newport and Wolverhampton and manufacture of wire netting and hollow-ware at Bristol.[54] Considering the last category, the company found it difficult to apportion profits between black-sheet rolling and galvanising operations. The assumed surplus shown in the books at Newport was £79,370 (56.6 per cent of the total), leaving £28,671 for Bristol (or 20.3 per cent). However, by this calculation the latter was thought to be bearing all the charges of the former and since the sale of the finished sheets was the result of a joint enterprise, they re-worked the figures on the basis that the apportionment of profit should be proportionate to the selling price of black and galvanised sheet at the port of sale. This gave a surplus of £38,061 (27.1 per cent) to Newport and Wolverhampton and £69,980 (50 per cent) to Bristol. Yet these results appear equally unsatisfactory since the profit gained on the rolling of those black sheets which were subsequently galvanised was, in effect, transferred to Bristol. A more complex equation, taking into account the costs of the respective manufacturing operations, was needed to produce an accurate reckoning of the contribution of the various plants to John Lysaght's overall commercial success.

With the exception of 1905, the company's profits climbed steadily throughout the Edwardian period, increasing dramatically from 1909 when they passed £300,000 for the first time. The loss of a minute book has prevented the calculation of a full series to their takeover in 1920.

CHANGES IN MANAGEMENT

The founder and the first chairman of the limited liability company, John Lysaght remained the prime mover in the business until the early 1890s when poor health forced him to take a less active role.[55] Undoubtedly a strong personality, like Arthur Keen, he did not believe greatly in the delegation of power, arguing that committees were largely a waste of time. He preferred the directness of the spoken or written word: 'I have always been averse of meetings because I cannot recollect any meeting that has been productive of the smallest good'.[56]

In common with other enlightened entrepreneurs of the period, John Lysaght took a paternalistic interest in the welfare of his employees. By the 1880s the St Vincent's Works could boast a canteen with separate accommodation for men and women, a large hall and recreation centre, a well-stocked library and a sick and medical club. In 1879 he had negotiated with the rector of the local parish, Revd. John Gladstone (whose daughter was to marry W.R. Lysaght in 1890), for the purchase and conversion of an unused church as a social centre. In a letter he described his motives:

> I do not feel entitled to claim anything except that in giving, or assisting to give, an impetus towards the development of a movement by which the working man may learn to find some rational amusement, enjoyment and comfort outside the public house, I am taking a step in the right direction. I am happy to say that so far the men are taking advantage of the room, etc., and show every intention to profit by it.[57]

In addition, he offered employment to prisoners released from Bristol's Horfield Jail, an act of altruism and generosity of spirit.

Although he could not be prevailed upon to stand for the Town Council, John Lysaght became a magistrate in Bristol and was appointed its High Sheriff in 1882.[58] A Conservative supporter, in 1883 he gave the local party a block of buildings in Baldwin Street, Bristol, to serve as their headquarters.[59] He owned houses in Gloucestershire, Suffolk (the 5,000 acre Hengrave Hall estate), and a marine villa at Teignmouth, where, as a member of the Royal Yacht Club, he pursued his favourite pastime of sailing. As a result of his successful business career, John Lysaght amassed a considerable fortune and when he died on 1 October 1895, suffering from a tumour of the neck,[60] left £424,214 gross.[61] Sir William Henry Wills, M.P. for Bristol, remarked at the time that though he and John Lysaght had occasionally disagreed, he retained 'a great regard for him as an honourable and upright man of business'.[62]

John Lysaght had three sons and three daughters by his marriage to Emily (d. 1882), daughter of Sidney Moss, and the eldest, St John George Lysaght (d. 1893) was the only other member of the family to be

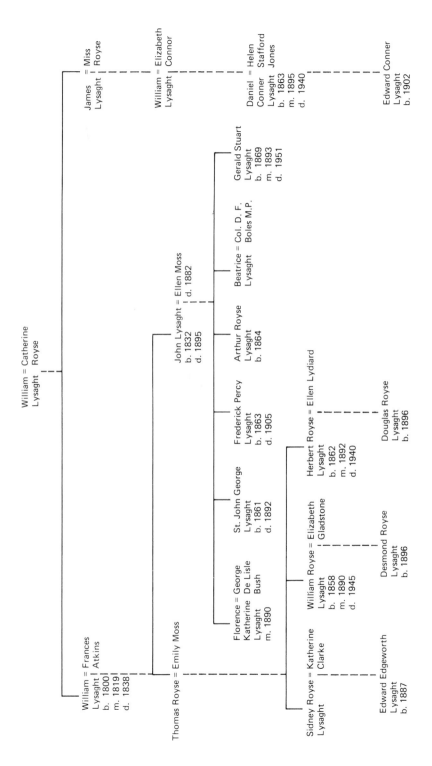

Figure 3   A simplified family tree of the Lysaghts

included within the shareholding when the private limited liability company was floated in the summer of 1881.[63] Although St John Lysaght became a director in March 1889,[64] it appears that his suddenly failing health caused him to resign on 6 March 1893 to be replaced on the board by his brother, Frederick Percy Lysaght (1863–1905).[65] The youngest of the three brothers, Gerald S. Lysaght (1869–1951) also joined the family business and was appointed a director in October 1895 immediately after the death of his father.[66] George De Lisle Bush, who had married John Lysaght's eldest daughter, became a member of the board in October 1893.[67] Earlier in the year J.B. Hollom had retired and was replaced as a director by Dennis F. Boles.[68]

However, the second-generation managerial impetus was provided not by the children or in-laws of John Lysaght but by those of his elder brother Thomas R. Lysaght, the Bristol architect. His sons entered the business in three distinct areas and each achieved a considerable degree of success. The eldest, Sydney Royse Lysaght (1856–1941) began work at St Vincent's and upon the flotation in 1881 became the company secretary, a post which he resigned in November 1884.[69] More interested in writing poems and novels, he did not entirely renounce his interest in the business and in February 1886 was appointed a director.[70] Although adopting something of a non-executive standpoint, he took responsibility for monitoring the company's performance, particularly with regard to exports, undertaking a number of trips to Australia, South Africa and Canada.[71] An intelligent man with a keen eye for society's mores, and occupying a slightly detached position, S.R. Lysaght was able to offer a dispassionate overview of the business's various activities. He, for example, was the protagonist in favour of transferring the galvanising plant from St Vincent's to the Orb Rolling Mills at Newport (see p. 49). Having no particular axe to grind, and impressed by the economies that such a move would produce, his persistent advocacy of this strategy, supported by costings, was not immediately successful and it was some years before the scheme obtained the board's approval.

In March 1891 William Royse Lysaght (1858–1945), younger brother of 'S.R.' was elected to the board.[72] Educated privately, in the autumn of 1874 he had entered the Gospel Oak Co.'s works at Tipton, Staffordshire, to learn the business of producing sheet iron.[73] Doubtless he had been encouraged to do this by John Lysaght so that when the latter purchased his own rolling mills at least one member of the family would have already acquired the relevant technical expertise. Accordingly, when in 1878 the Swan Garden Works became part of the Lysaght group, John Lysaght wrote to the nineteen-year old 'W.R.' to suggest he might be interested in 'a good opening . . . and the chance of a more permanent position if you should wish to avail yourself of it'.[74] Under the management of W.R. Lysaght a number of innovations took place: double and treble mills were put down and the diameter of rolls increased by 24 inches. Overhead cranes were installed, but weekly output remained at about 45 tons per mill until the substitution of steel for wrought iron in the mid-1890s corresponded with additional gains in productivity. The rolling mills at the Osier Bed Iron Works also fell under W.R. Lysaght's control.

The third brother, Herbert Royse Lysaght (1862–1940) appeared to have eschewed all involvement with the family firm when having emigrated to Australia to join Lysaght Bros. & Co., wire netting importers and makers,[75] he left them to enter the Commercial Bank of Sydney. He worked there for seventeen years, for much of this time as a branch manager,[76] before in the summer of 1899 agreeing to take charge of Lysaght's selling agency in Sydney and when the company commenced manufacture in 1921 at Newcastle, New South Wales, as the chief executive of the Australian subsidiary.[77]

When John Lysaght died in October 1895 the chairmanship passed to his son, Frederick P. Lysaght, and S.R. Lysaght became the managing director.[78] When the former died in September 1905 he was succeeded not by his deputy but his younger brother Gerald S. Lysaght,[79] who in the event possibly proved to be the poorer choice (see p. 5). In November 1901 on resort to limited liability, Lt. Col. D.F. Boles (elected MP for West Somerset in August 1911)[80] and Herbert George Hill were both elected to the board. The latter had originally replaced C.J. Ryland as the company's auditor in 1885[81] and having served in that capacity for fifteen years accepted the post of chief accountant in October 1898.[82] As a result, Ernest Cooper (1848–1926), the eminent Victorian chartered accountant and senior partner of Cooper Brothers,[83] was appointed auditor,[84] and a remuneration of £105 was agreed for the 1899 accounts.[85]

In 1911 Edward Davey was promoted to be both company secretary and director, having held the former post for sixteen years. He remained in these offices until his death in September 1915,[86] when Edward P.M. Davey became secretary and Daniel Conner Lysaght (1869–1940), a cousin of 'W.R.', 'S.R.' and 'H.R.', filled the vacancy on the main board.[87]

From the transfer of the business to the St Vincent's site, Silverthorne Lane, in 1869, this became the company's headquarters. Managers from Wolverhampton and later Newport or Scunthorpe reported to Bristol, where the board meetings were held. In 1891, it was decided that larger and more prestigious offices were needed.[88] Accordingly, the Bristol architect R. Milverton Drake was commissioned to design an elaborate two-storey building, entered through a battlemented gateway.[89] Completed by 1893, its baronial facade was matched in richness by the Doulton tiled interior. The grandiose style and lavish expenditure on materials was doubtless seen to match the company's importance within Bristol's industry. Following the flotation of 1901 the offices were extended at a cost of £2,000.[90]

ST VINCENT'S WORKS AND NETHAM, BRISTOL

The principal manufacturing process at the St Vincent's Works was the galvanising of sheet steel, and as the demand for this product grew so additional galvanising pots had to be installed. By 1895 its capacity had risen to 1,000 tons a week,[91] but in 1901 it was recognised that the Silverthorne Lane site could no longer alone cope with the rising volume of orders.[92] In that year an expenditure of £6,725 was authorised to install galvanising pots at Netham[93] to deal with those products destined for the UK market, while St Vincent's handled the export trade. The volume of business handled by the two Bristol works increased in a steady and continuous fashion (Table 2.2) to reach a peak in 1913 when 143,000 tons of galvanised sheet were manufactured in a single year[94] – a record which was never to be surpassed in Britain.

A substantial proportion of the wire netting manufactured at St Vincent's was exported to the colonies.[95] The department was particularly successful in 1894 when 5.25 million yards, then a record, were produced, a response in part to a booming Australian market.[96] Output rose to 6 million yards in 1895[97] and 8 million in the following year.[98] In 1897, when output records were again broken chiefly due to an order for 800 miles from Lysaght Bros. & Co. of Australia, a profit of £6,504 (10.7 per cent) was made on a turnover of £60,614, in comparison with £5,500 (12.6 per cent) on £43,500 in 1896.[99] Output fell in 1898 to 6.9 million yards from 8.94 million in 1897, surpluses being £4,530 (9.9 per cent) and £6,100 (10.0 per cent) respectively.[100] However, reliant upon a buoyant export trade, the department suffered considerably in 1900 when orders fell to 4.8 million yards. Amongst the causes were the disruption caused by the Boer War and fearsome competition from German manufacturers.[101]

The Structural Ironwork Department at Netham was subject to severe fluctuations in its profitability. In 1895 the surplus recorded was only one-quarter of that achieved in 1893 and the worst figure since 1891.[102] In part, this resulted from an unprecedented scarcity of work during the first six months of 1895, while a subsequent influx of orders produced congestion and the need for costly overtime payments. The perennial problem of obtaining raw-material supplies quickly also persisted. The need for continuous and regular levels of orders and inputs was illustrated by the following calculation: during the first six months of 1895 wages per ton of iron produced amounted to £7, but fell in the second half of the year to £5, the average cost being £1 per ton greater than in 1894 when output was both higher and more stable.[103]

Given the high levels of capital locked up in the department in plant and stocks but also the difficulty in carrying through contracts, the board believed that the department ought to be able to earn profits equivalent to 10 per cent of its turnover. For most of the 1890s it failed to meet this budget, but suddenly produced remarkable figures in

Table 2.2   Total output of galvanised sheet from St Vincent's Works, Bristol, 1869–1941

	Tons		Tons		Tons
1869	2,600	1894	30,155	1920	93,740
1870	2,302	1895	38,788	1921	45,268
1871	3,796	1896	49,124	1922	116,068
1872	3,566	1897	52,095	1923	107,017
1873	4,036	1898	48,453	1924	111,574
1874	5,786	1899	47,705	1925	108,673
1875	6,898	1900	59,191	1926	96,509
1876	5,802	1901	56,110	1927	107,551
1877	7,735	1902	68,000	1928	86,383
1878	8,604	1903	77,801	1929	92,523
1879	7,748	1904	78,691	1930	49,641
1880	8,858	1905	87,096	1931	30,932
1881	12,550	1906	86,783	1932	23,306
1882	11,902	1907	88,607	1933	29,541
1883	12,929	1908	72,206	1934	40,125
1884	17,184	1909	105,635	1935	51,861
1885	22,881	1910	113,643	1936	50,730
1886	19,287	1911	134,392	1937	36,758
1887	25,118	1912	134,149	1938	32,600
1888	29,595	1913	142,756	1939	92,477
1889	25,547	1914	120,118	1940	26,872
1890	26,039	1915	66,641	1941	13,655
1891	34,582	1916	33,706		
1892	26,228	1917	12,603		
1893	32,171	1918	9,569		
		1919	57,981		

Note: The output of galvanised sheet from Orb Works, Newport was included in these figures.

Source: 'The Story of John Lysaght, Limited, England' (typescript 4 February 1946).

1898.[104] On orders totalling 200 tons less than in 1897 the surplus tripled, the result of increased demand, higher prices and their success in securing a £200,000 contract to supply the Admiralty with structural ironwork at Gibraltar harbour.[105] The upturn was sustained during 1899 when record profits were recorded.[106]

THE ORB ROLLING MILLS, NEWPORT

In their report for 1895 the directors suggested that

> by our organization and the established excellence of our brands, our distributing agencies and our sound financial position we

3 Orb Rolling Mills, Newport, from the railway embankment crossing Corporation Road. The transporter bridge and the River Usk is just visible in the distance (*Rheemco*).

have been able to make a profit, but we have done this in the teeth of certain disadvantages. . . Our works are badly placed for manufacture, our steel has to be taken to Wolverhampton from the North of England or from South Wales, and our black sheets from Wolverhampton to Bristol. Firms manufacturing in the North of England and South Wales escape these charges, and it is probable that if better placed we could save a sum annually which would in itself be . . . very large.[107]

In March 1895, having suffered what they termed 'irregularity of quality' for the past eighteen months,[108] it was decided to seek a site near the Barry Docks, in South Wales, for the laying down of rolling mills.[109] With their rolling capacity divided between two middle-aged plants in Wolverhampton and linked to their galvanising works by 120 miles of canal or railway, the company's transport network had become over extended. In February 1896 after negotiations over the Barry site had been suspended, it was resolved to continue looking for land possessing a 'deep water frontage and connected with two or three main railway systems of the United Kingdom'.[110] Accordingly, Mr T. Forster Brown, a consultant mining engineer based in Cardiff, was asked to prepare a report on a further site at Barry and two plots at Newport. However, the presentation of his findings in June 1896[111] had been forestalled by W.R. Lysaght's own investigations of the two Newport possibilities. The one closest to the sea proving unsuitable, the Pill Farm site, originally discovered by W.R. Lysaght, on the east side of the River Usk opposite the Newport Docks, had been selected. The company's solicitor, Mr. Press, was instructed to negotiate with Colonel Lockwood, owner of the land, to obtain a 99-year lease for

4 The office staff of Orb Works photographed in front of the former house on Pill Farm in 1903. (*BSC Orb Works*).

about 70 acres at an annual rental not to exceed £15 per acre.[112] In January 1897, having obtained an agreement over the site, the board sanctioned the expenditure of £15,000 on plant and machinery.[113] In October they decided to name the new mills after their well-known trademark, the 'Orb Iron Works',[114] and in January 1898 announced that they intended to start sheet rolling in March with three mills.[115] Impressed by the success of the project, the directors sanctioned the expenditure of a further £25,000 in 1898 to increase the number of mills.[116]

Once in production, it soon became clear that the most efficient way to transport black sheets from Newport to Bristol was by coasting vessel down the River Usk across the Bristol Channel to the Avon. Accordingly in January 1899 it was agreed that £3,450 be spent on building a wharf at the Orb Works.[117]

From the outset, in March 1898, Daniel Conner Lysaght had been placed in charge at Newport. Arriving from Wolverhampton with three men, he recruited Welsh labour to bring the first three mills into operation.[118] They were worked in eight-hour shifts by nine teams of men who had been induced to emigrate from the remote village of Ynysmeudwy in the Tawe Valley, a few miles to the north of Neath. In

5 No. 25 Mill team at Orb Works in 1903 (*BSC Orb Works*).

addition, groups of workers transferred from Wolverhampton as the number of mills at Newport increased. In 1901, when Orb Works had outgrown its Swan Garden progenitor, W.R. Lysaght himself left the Midlands to take command with D.C. Lysaght as his deputy.[119] It no longer made commercial sense to keep the comparatively small Osier Bed Mills in operation, six of its mills having been transferred to Newport;[120] the works were offered for sale in May 1905,[121] though a purchaser was not found until July 1911, when Mr A.H. Marks of Birmingham agreed to pay £3,000.[122] In 1902–3 the seven remaining rolling mills at Swan Garden Works were removed at a cost of £20,000[123] and the buildings converted for use as a foundry to supply Newport (and later the Normanby Park steelworks) with chilled cast-iron rolls.[124]

The Orb rolling mills grew rapidly from their opening, fuelled by ever-increasing demand from overseas and the Empire. By 1899 their weekly capacity had reached 700 tons and by the end of 1900 was approaching 1,000 tons.[125] In 1903 when the transfer from Wolverhampton was complete, 29 mills had been installed at Newport with a weekly capacity of 2,150 tons.[126] A further five mills were authorised in August 1909 at a cost of £30,000[127] and in the following summer

6 Looking down the length of Orb works; it was one of the longest industrial buildings in Britain. Note the heavy steel plates which formed the floor (*BSC Orb Works*).

7 The flywheel of No. 10 engine, with mills and re-heating furnaces beyond, in 1921 (*BSC Orb Works*).

another four were ordered (estimated at £25–30,000) to be in operation by February 1911,[128] which brought the total to 42 with a weekly capacity of 3,500 tons and an annual output, allowing for stoppages, of 165,000 tons.[129]. When 3,750 tons were rolled during one week in November 1911 this was acknowledged as a record for the Orb Works.[130] The output for 1912 totalled 169,000 tons, of which 120,000 tons were sent to Bristol chiefly for galvanising.[131]

THE NORMANBY PARK STEELWORKS, SCUNTHORPE

With the completion and rapid growth of the Orb rolling mills and ever-rising demand for galvanised and black sheet, it was natural that the directors of John Lysaght should consider a further measure of vertical integration and plan the construction of an integrated steelworks. They were reliant on various steel makers and on occasion purchased bars from America[132] or Germany,[133] but these external suppliers could not always be relied upon to satisfy their requests in times of heavy consumption. However, the laying down of blast furnaces, open hearth furnaces and rolling mills to produce the sheet bar required by Newport would prove to be the most capital intensive project undertaken by John Lysaght. To help with the finance of the scheme and to rid the business of its indebtedness to the trustees of

John Lysaght's will,[134] in December 1900 it was decided to float the company on the Stock Exchange to permit 'a very large cash payment being made to the trustees and at the same time give the new company about £150,000 additional working capital'.[135] After further consideration, the board agreed that the new business would be capitalised as follows:

Debentures @ 4% or 4½%   £500,000
Preference Shares @ 5%   £100,000
Ordinary Shares   £400,000
Management Shares   £1,000[136]

All the debentures and two-thirds of the preference shares were to be issued to the public. Of the £500,000 to be raised from the former, £100,000 was to be retained by the new company whilst the remaining £400,000, together with £400,000 raised from the sale of ordinary shares and outstanding £100,000 in preference shares, be paid to the old, private company as its purchase price.

The task of finding a suitable site for a steelworks fell to W.R. Lysaght who toured the country looking for a location with access to ample supplies of iron ore and coal, efficient transport links with Newport and space for expansion. John Henry Darby (1856–19), the pioneering steelmaker of the Brymbo Works, near Wrexham who had erected the first basic open hearth furnace at Brymbo in 1884–85,[137] was called upon as a consultant. He, together with W.R. Lysaght and H.G. Hill, discussed the relative merits of building a steelworks either at Frodingham, near Scunthorpe, or at Newport.[138] The former had the advantage of being situated beside the extensive Lincolnshire iron-ore fields, while any works at Newport would have to rely on imports or coastal shipments. However, in the spring of 1905 the company changed direction, favouring a scheme by which they would purchase the ironworks and iron-ore mines belonging to the new Westbury Iron Co. Ltd., Wiltshire, rather than construct their own works on a green-field site. The offer price was £120,000, though W.R. Lysaght thought them worth only £80–90,000.[139] In May 1905 a provisional agreement was signed with them, pending a report by J.H. Darby.[140] A month later, having made several trial borings into the ironstone, he 'expressed himself absolutely satisfied with the quantity of the ironstone ... no better or more suitable supply of ore could be found in Great Britain, Germany or America'.[141] When ratification of the proposed sale appeared as almost a formality, a further series of borings were undertaken and proved to be 'very unsatisfactory'. In addition, the New Westbury Iron Co. failed to obtain mining rights over those lands contiguous to the smelting works in order to bring the ore field up to 550 acres.[142] Consequently, Lysaghts requested the return of their £1,000 deposit and abandoned any thoughts of acquiring the company.[143]

W.R. Lysaght and H.G. Hill again turned their attention to North Lincolnshire.[144] By October 1905 ninety samples of ore taken from Sir Berkeley Sheffield's estate, Normanby Park, were subject to tests,[145] and in November Darby was able to report on the satisfactory nature of the mineral from which, he estimated, with a doubtful over-accuracy, sheet bars could be made and delivered to Newport at a cost of £3 11s 7d per ton.[146] His conclusions provided the signal for serious negotiations with Sir Berkeley Sheffield over royalty payments to begin.[147] In December 1905 Darby provisionally agreed terms for a seventy-five year lease over 891 acres,[148] and in April 1906 the royalty on the extraction of ore was reduced from the original figure of 1s per ton to 9d.[149] F.W. Cooper, of the North Eastern Steel Co. later to be appointed general manager,[150] who had been asked to comment on the feasibility of the scheme, affirmed Darby's conclusions and added that he was satisfied 'that steel bars could be produced and delivered at Newport at a cost of £3 17s 6d per ton after providing for depreciation and interest on the capital of £350,000, which he considered sufficient for the output of 2,000 tons per week'.[151] J.H. Darby was appointed as consulting engineer at a fee of £3,500 a year with a bonus of £8,000 to be paid if the entire cost of the project remained beneath the estimate of £350,000.[152]

This was an ambitious scheme not only in the sense that it involved considerable capital expenditure, but also because it represented a comparatively early excursion into the field of basic steelmaking. At this time most works adhered to acid technology and with the gradual exhaustion of British reserves of hematite, were increasingly reliant on imported ores. The introduction of basic steelmaking techniques which could consume ores containing high levels of phosphorus opened up the North Lincolnshire fields which were rich in phosphorus but low in iron content (20–30 per cent).[153] However, because the ore lay close to the surface beneath an overburden of clays and shales, it could be easily worked by open-cast methods, rendering their extraction on a large scale relatively inexpensive,[154] which, in turn, compensated for the poor mineral content. J.H. Darby, who had undertaken much pioneering research into basic steelmaking, was an obvious choice to design the works.

Construction began in 1910, contracts having been let to Lamberton & Co. of Glasgow for the rolling mills (£33,133), Pearson & Knowles for the blast furnaces (£25,000) and the Nuremberg Co. for the gas engines (£23,000),[155] while the Yorkshire Semet-Solvay Co. won the order to supply the coke ovens, by-product plant and coal washery for £155,400.[156] In April 1911 when the steelworks committee recommended that the planned third blast furnace be erected so as to bring the output up to 2,000 tons of sheet bars per week, it was discovered that costs had escalated. The total cost had risen to about £543,000, compared with J.H. Darby's original estimate of £350,000.[157] Accordingly, S.R. Lysaght was empowered to write to Darby asking him to resign.[158] In order to finance the over-spending, Lysaghts arranged for the issue of 300,000 £1 preference shares at 6 per cent,[159] and the flotation, in June 1912, was greatly over subscribed.[160]

On 8 July 1912, Nos. 1 and 2 blast furnaces at Normanby Park were blown in and the open hearth steel furnaces came on stream two weeks later.[161] The steelworks, when completed, consisted of three blast furnaces, each with eleven-foot hearths, a battery of 152 coke ovens, four 45-ton hearth Siemens furnaces, a 400-ton mixer, twelve 28-ton soaking pits (to handle two-ton ingots) and rolling mills, with an annual output of 100,000 tons of sheet bar.[162] Although by no means as large as some of the established steelworks in Britain or the latest designs in America or Germany, Normanby Park was a modern and integrated plant. W.R. Lysaght and J.H. Darby had been careful to select the latest technology when assembling the various components. In the autumn of 1908, for example, they had visited a number of German works, including the Dusseldorf plant of the German Steel Works Union, to study their methods of producing sheet bar.[163]

As regards transport to Newport, a light railway had been laid from the Great Central's line between Grimsby and Doncaster at Scunthorpe to run due north through the steelworks to a dock on the River Trent at Whitton.[164] Steamers would then ship the steel around the coast to the Orb Works tidal jetty on the River Usk.

OVERSEAS SALES TO THE EMPIRE

So long as exports of corrugated sheet and holloware to the colonies remained within manageable limits, John Lysaght was able to deal through agents, paying a commission on sales. Yet the volume of business conducted with Australia alone rose to such levels that it became essential to establish their own sales outlet, and in 1879, with a head office in Melbourne, they set up the Victoria Galvanised Iron & Wire Co.,[165] which from 1899 was re-named as Lysaght's Galvanised Iron Pty. Ltd.

In 1884 the decision was taken to begin manufacturing, albeit on a limited scale, in Australia and the company laid down plant for the production of wire netting in Sydney.[166] Because there were as yet no makers of sheet steel in the sub-continent, it would have been almost impossible to have established a hollow-ware or galvanising business despite the existence of import tariffs of 18 per cent in New South Wales and 25 per cent in Victoria on the finished product. However, transport costs for netting wire were comparatively low, and the value-added in the process of weaving was comparatively high. The machines recently patented by John Lysaght were sufficiently advanced to compensate for the higher wage costs existing in Australia, while the low capital costs of the steam-powered equipment obviated the need for substantial investment at a time when demand was nascent.[167] In deciding whether to set up their own factory in Sydney or Melbourne local politics were a consideration: although the protective duty on imports of wire netting was lower in New South Wales than in the state of Victoria, the administration in the former could be relied upon to maintain this level for some years. Further, Sydney was better placed geographically to serve the potentially large markets of western NSW and Queensland.

The manufacture of wire netting flourished and in August 1886 a special meeting of the John Lysaght board was called to discuss the future of their Australian enterprises. The overseas managers wished to buy out both the Sydney factory and the Melbourne sales agency under the style, Lysaght Brothers & Co.[168] However, this scheme did not meet with John Lysaght's approval and in the event the new company (with a capital of £15,000)[169] was formed virtually as his possession; he held all but nine of the £10 shares.[170] Despite this financial reconstruction, Lysaght Brothers remained undercapitalised.

Almost immediately after the formation of Lysaght Bros. John Lysaght began to dispose of his shares, these being acquired by the Sydney directors, interstate agents of the company and managers. By 1895 Arthur R. Lysaght, as nephew of John, had acquired a controlling interest. The agency agreement by which Lysaght Bros. acted for its Bristol parent had ended in 1890 and relations between the two had deteriorated. In August 1895 when 'in consequence of the present financial position of Lysaght Bros & Co., and the indebtedness to them of Mr Arthur Lysaght', it was proposed that John Lysaght acquire a controlling interest in the Australian company by purchasing

from Mr. A.R. Lysaght £5,000 worth of shares at par, giving him the option within three years of redeeming all or any of the shares at par, the purchase money of such shares being applied . . . to the reduction of his indebtedness to Lysaght Bros & Co.[171]

The proposal was never effected, and in 1902 Arthur R. Lysaght owned 1,500 of the 1,507 shares. However, Lysaght Bros. acted again as the UK company's agents in New South Wales and Victoria (but not the other states in Australia). Yet in June 1899 after the visit of S.R. Lysaght to the colony, it was decided to terminate this arrangement from 31 December of that year.[172] Management of the Sydney branch then passed to the newly recruited H.R. Lysaght (p. 335) and a new firm, Lysaght's Galvanised Iron Pty, was established in Melbourne;[173] Thomas Davey of Melbourne was appointed the managing director.[174] The decision proved to be a sensible one for a comparison of sales between 1897–99 when Lysaght Bros were acting for the company and 1900–2 when they had direct control themselves, revealed an increase of 33 per cent.[175]

Within Australia the major distribution points were Melbourne and Sydney. During the month of July 1889, for example, they received 600 and 700 tons of galvanised sheet, of lesser importance were Brisbane (300 tons), Adelaide (100), Tasmania (50), and Swan River (50), while New Zealand accounted for 150 tons.[176] Having visited Australia early in 1894, S.R. Lysaght reported that competition was severe throughout the continent but was particularly fierce in Melbourne.[177] As a result, it was decided to offer merchants a bonus, on a scale from 1s 6d per ton for a buyer of 300 cases to 3s 6d per ton on 750 cases, who exclusively stocked Lysaght's 'Orb' brand of galvanised sheet.[178] This scheme applied only to Victoria where trade rivalry was at a peak, while in Sydney a system of prices graduated according to quantity had already been introduced. The overseas tour undertaken by S.R. Lysaght also included Canada, South Africa and New Zealand and he concluded that in the manufacture of galvanised and corrugated iron, Lysaghts were 'far and away in front of every other firm, but the extent of our operations, the system of management and the soundness of our financial position, places us in the very first rank of the industrial houses of the world'.[179]

The company also made a concerted effort to export to other overseas territories, but without the success they had achieved in Australia. In 1894, for example, 2,030 tons were shipped to South Africa (an increase of 30 per cent of the 1893 total of 1,550 tons), but stiff competition there had reduced prices to such a level that 'the business had been done at little or no profit'.[180] The same was true of South America (principally Argentina) and Canada where falling sales had produced a loss.[181] A recovery in their trade with South Africa was blighted in 1899 on the outbreak of the Boer War and the 'political troubles' which preceded it.[182] A gradual improvement in sales to South America, rising by twenty per cent during 1897,[183] encouraged the opening of a galvanising and sheet rolling plant at Buenos Aires. In Canada during the 1890s and 1900s, the company accounted for about 50 per cent of the total sales of galvanised sheet, though in South Africa (around 15 per cent) and South America (around 15 per cent), the proportion was much lower.[184] A tacit agreement existed between Lysaghts and John Summers not to compete in each other's markets, the latter having secured a powerful position in India where the cheaper grades of sheet were consumed.

By the 1890s, John Lysaght had established itself as the principal importer of galvanised sheet into Australia. In 1895, for example, 67 per cent of the sheet purchased in Melbourne had been manufactured by the company, while the corresponding figure for the state of Queensland was 84 per cent. They were responsible for supplying 58 per cent of all the galvanised sheet imported by Australia in 1895. This represented an impressive performance given that in 1880, the year they opened their Melbourne office, the figure was only 17 per cent (Table 2.3).[185]

No manufacture of sheet took place in Australia. The company

Table 2.3 Exports of galvanised sheet by Lysaghts to Australia, (1880–1905)

	Percentage of all* (tons)	Percentage in NSW (tons)	Percentage in Queensland (tons)
1880	17		
1885	30		
1890	41		
1891	—		
1892	—		
1893	—		
1894	46	50	64
1895	58	51	84
1896	54.5		
1897	66		
1898	64		
1899	57		
1900	58		
1901			
1902	64		
1903	62		
1904	—		
1905	—		

Note: Including New Zealand.

Source: John Lysaght Old Company Minute Book, Vol. I (1881–97); ibid, Vol. II (1897–01); John Lysaght Minute Book, Vol. I (1901–09).

limited itself to establishing a network of sales and distribution offices, each with their own warehouse and corrugating plant (it was more economical to transport flat galvanised sheet, which occupied less space, and then put them through a corrugating machine once they had arrived at their designated depot).[186] Given the volume of trade from Bristol to Australia (70,000 cases were shipped during 1901),[187] savings in freight charges would have been considerable.

Table 2.4   John Lysaght sales of galvanised sheet to Australia 1900–18 (tons)

	Melbourne	Adelaide	Fremantle	Sydney*	Brisbane
1900	7,736	2,545	5,764	2,419	1,955
1901	9,193	2,879	6,128	5,421	2,684
1902	7,942	2,658	6,366	8,578	5,799
1903	8,277	3,592	6,311	10,827	4,904
1904	9,971	3,522	6,540	11,967	5,215
1905	11,145	3,823	5,692	12,554	5,758
1906	12,717	5,179	5,640	13,531	6,612
1907	12,742	5,471	4,542	15,696	7,265
1908	12,866	6,225	4,029	20,235	7,778
1909	14,897	7,045	4,228	21,399	10,382
1910	18,237	9,342	5,323	24,321	11,316
1911	19,556	10,417	6,868	27,698	13,824
1912	18,979	9,885	6,183	33,472	14,847
1913	18,595	10,174	7,416	31,978	14,871
1914	18,081	8,812	6,371	28,608	15,415
1915	12,583	4,846	3,630	22,086	11,003
1916	7,820	2,914	1,973	12,949	5,933
1917	4,044	1,561	1,281	6,559	3,332
1918	698	394	295	34	50

Note: *Including Newcastle and Suva.
Note the totals from 1900 to 1911 are estimates and those from 1912 to 1918 are actual figures.

Source: 'Day Book Totals' (typescript, n.d.).

How the mounting pressure applied by the Australian government through the imposition of tariffs[188] and the construction of a steelworks by the Broken Hill Pty Ltd. in New South Wales,[189] encouraged Lysaghts to set up their own sheet rolling and galvanising plant at Newcastle in 1919–21 forms the subject of Chapter 10.

THE GREAT WAR

Once the manufacturing capabilities of the company had fallen under the Ministry of Munition's control, they were diverted to producing the material of war.[190] Handicapped by the voluntary enlistment of many of their workers (by September 1914 1,400 men from Bristol, Newport and Normanby Park had joined the forces),[191] the number of mills in operation at the Orb Works fell to 30 (of 44) by the spring of 1915.[192] They produced trench plates, sheet steel for helmets and after 1916 sheet brass for cartridges.[193] The great demand for steel encouraged Lysaghts to spend £260,000 on an additional blast furnace (with a capacity of 1,000 tons a week) and two open hearth furnaces (of 160 and 80 tons capacity) at Normanby Park, £118,000 being contributed by the Ministry of Munitions.[194] By 1918 the annual ingot make at Scunthorpe had risen to 137,000 tons.[195] In December 1915 the company granted W.R. Lysaght permission to move to London where he worked as Spelter Adviser to the Ministry of Munitions, being concerned with the allocation of steel output and the fixing of prices for raw materials.[196] For his service he was awarded a CBE in 1918.

The one plant within the Lysaght group to suffer grievously was the St Vincent's galvanising works. Reliant for its volume of orders upon exports, its business almost disappeared overnight. Shipping having been diverted to supply the Allies with basic items of consumption and the inputs of a mechanised war, and the Orb rolling mills diverted to other uses, output from Bristol fell from 143,000 tons in 1913 to a mere 9,500 tons in 1918.[197] Overseas sales declined to an even greater extent, collapsing from 127,000 tons in 1913 to 5,000 tons in 1918. The Structural Ironwork Department at Netham did not suffer to the same extent as it was employed on Admiralty and War Office contracts for the construction of air stations and ordnance depots both at home and abroad.[198] In addition, it benefited from the general expansion which was taking place in the steel industry and erected sheds or roofs for several works, including Normanby Park.

SUMMARY

The sixty-one years from the foundation of John Lysaght in 1857 to the end of the Great War had witnessed a spectacular story of business success. The reinvestment of rapidly growing profits, together with the flotation of the family firm successively as a private and a public limited liability company, had enabled its managers to integrate vertically first into sheet rolling and then into the manufacture of iron and steel. The company, which entered the interwar years, possessed an integrated, medium-sized steelworks with adjacent ore fields and the second largest sheet-rolling works in Britain (after the Corby Works of John Summers), together with galvanising plant at St Vincent's and a thriving Structural Ironwork Department at Netham, Bristol.

If the business had a weakness it did not concern the structure of its manufacturing operations, nor indeed the specific components within this chain; neither was it related to the calibre of its managers but concerned the nature of its commercial dealings, and the reliance Lysaghts placed upon high levels of exports to Australia. Several Australian states were not content that its economy, which possessed the necessary coal and iron ore, should remain hostage of overseas producers of steel.[199] The Great War, by cutting them off from vitally needed imports, had demonstrated the need to establish indigenous industries. Henceforth, they would place increasing pressure on John Lysaght to lay down manufacturing plant in Australia and this, in turn, would have major implications for both their galvanising works at Bristol and rolling mills in Newport.

In a sense, the company had become a victim of its own good fortune. Because of its very success in capturing and developing the Australian sheet steel market, which had then become the keystone of its business, Lysaghts were vulnerable to any changes in this region and product. Just as the hostilities had revealed to the Australians how reliant they were upon British industry, so too it showed them how much the fortunes of individual companies had come to rest on their goodwill and co-operation. However, the two industries which in the 1920s were to generate a major source of demand for the Orb Mills had both been supplied in lesser quantities before the Great War. The seeds for necessary diversification had already been sown and were soon to flourish.

PART 2, 1919–45

POST-WAR RECOVERY

The immediate post-war boom and the restoration of trade with Australia resulted in high levels of demand for sheet steel.[200] Those men who had been employed by John Lysaght before the hostilities and who had enlisted in the forces were entitled to return to their original job upon demobilisation and, the board stated, 'in order to create a vacancy – if none existed – the unmarried man in that position with the shortest term of service is to be displaced'.[201] The return of ex-servicemen created a few initial difficulties. At the Orb Works, for example, outputs fell below pre-war standards largely because the men had both to re-acquire skills and build up physical strength to cope with the particular demands of rolling.[202] Nevertheless, soaring demand and mounting prices for steel resulted in sound profits and high wage levels.

At Orb Works men were paid according to how much they produced, the rate being determined by a sliding scale governed by the Sheet Trade Board (of which W.R. Lysaght was chairman) which fluctuated in relation to the final price of steel sheet. Over the three months from January 1920, some 800 'turns' (or shifts) were lost at the Orb Works as a result of absenteeism, mostly on Fridays and Saturdays.[203] D.C. Lysaght suggested to the Whitley Committee (a monthly meeting between senior managers and the men's representatives) that high rates encouraged the younger men to be satisfied with three or four turns a week. The position improved during the summer of 1920, and by the late autumn, when the short-lived boom had collapsed, the problem solved itself as prices tumbled. In November, the Whitley Committee at Orb Works reported that galvanising trade prices for sheet steel had fallen to £10 per ton and that almost every manufacturer was working short time.[204]

Matters deteriorated in 1921 as Britain entered one of the worst depressions of its industrial history. As D.C. Lysaght observed,

> orders were being accepted at cost and even below cost to provide work for the men ... Men were being discharged from our Scunthorpe Works, as owing to the high costs obtaining here, foreign bars could be imported into this country £5 to £6 per ton cheaper than we could manufacture them.[205]

As the slump deepened, stocks of galvanised sheet mounted. In February, the St Vincent's Works in Bristol had to be closed for the first time in its forty-year life.[206] The congested state of the warehouse at Orb Works also necessitated the shutting down of the rolling mills. To keep the men in employment, Lysaghts were

> prepared to continue rolling even at a loss, but the sheets could not be sold, as no orders were coming in. Whilst in pre-war times the orders for galvanized sheets received by the trade averaged nearly 20,000 tons per week, the total ... received by the trade last month was 1,800 tons, of which quantity nearly half was executed by our Bristol Works.[207]

In March they reported that the total number of orders received by the British galvanising trade during the previous month amounted to 1,336 tons as against an average pre-war week of 18,000 tons.[208] If demand for galvanised sheet was at an all time low, and the Newport rolling mills had been reduced to a standstill, then there was little rationale in keeping the Scunthorpe steelworks in operation. The furnaces were blown out and in June 1921 the low level of continental steel prices resulted in the directors confidently predicting that the Normanby Park open-hearth furnaces (see Table 2.5) would not be re-lit until the following year.[209]

The loss or destruction of the John Lysaght Ltd Minute Book Volume 3, which covered the period 1917–21, has made it difficult to uncover the events surrounding the company's take-over by GKN and obfuscated the decisions which took place during these tough post-war years.[210] The reported profits (Table 2.4) did not reflect the severity of the

Table 2.5 Annual ingot production at Normanby Park Steelworks, 1913–45

	Tons		Tons
1913	101,701	1930	167,929
1914	107,569	1931	122,935
1915	116,304	1932	161,838
1916	112,101	1933	228,948
1917	120,131	1934	247,388
1918	130,879	1935	282,770
1919	123,478	1936	308,427
1920	152,461	1937	339,697
1921	19,300	1938	259,102
1922	98,641	1939	311,245
1923	168,100	1940	265,535
1924	173,698	1941	254,088
1925	169,548	1942	255,489
1926	68,204	1943	247,675
1927	200,987	1944	241,443
1928	199,555	1945	232,930
1929	204,598		

Source: 'The Story of John Lysaght, Limited, England' (typescript, 4 February 1946).

depression as the figures for 1920 (£499,090) and 1921 (£495,329) compared favourably with those for 1913 (£478,143) and 1914 (£507,441). Yet, if the effects of war-induced inflation are discounted, then the picture appeared more worrying: £316,280 and £346,142 respectively for 1920 and 1921 as against £757,754 and £809,316 for 1913 and 1914.[211] However, companies were not then in the habit of indexing annual results and decisions would have been taken on the basis of the published figures.

By August 1921 the nadir of the depression had passed,[212] and the rolling mills and galvanising works, but not the steel plant, were back in operation. Piece rates had fallen considerably and the price of coal had been reduced, both of which increased the competitive position of Lysaghts enabling them to recover parts of their formidable pre-war export trade. During the month of September 1921, output at Newport rose to 11,448 tons, two-thirds of the corresponding pre-war figure, 'the increase being mainly due to the larger Bristol demand for the Australian market'.[213] In January 1922 it was reported that overseas sales of galvanised sheet had doubled over the past three months.[214] Throughout the year demand built up, though not to an extent to lift prices, and in December 1922 orders had reached a point where they were sufficient to keep the Orb Mills in operation for two to three months ahead.[215]

ORB WORKS, NEWPORT

Once the post-war depression had been cleared, Lysaghts' profitability during the interwar period relied on the efficiency of their rolling operations. The steel plant remained closed until the spring of 1922, and only moved into commercial success in the mid-1930s when the developing electrical and automobile industries widened the market for steel sheet of particular qualities (pp. 46). The Bristol galvanising works found it increasingly difficult to compete for exports and was gradually run down (pp. 49). As a result, it fell to the Orb rolling mills to generate the profits the company needed.

During the 1920s, a high proportion of the steel sheet rolled at Newport was destined for constructional purposes, whether corrugated, galvanised or untreated as 'black sheet'. The techniques and plant had scarcely altered in their basics since the latter part of the eighteenth century. Until the interwar period the Orb Works had been one of the largest sheet plants in the world. Yet its huge output had been achieved not by the introduction of sophisticated units of production, but by the duplication of relatively simple and uncomplicated machinery. By 1923, for example, there were 48 2-high hot mills with an annual capacity of around 200,000 tons. The bottom roll alone was driven by steam power and the gap between the rolls was controlled by manually operated screws,[216] so that the work of feeding the sheets backwards and forwards into the mill was performed by hand labour. Each mill had a team of eight men (a roller, who received 21.5 per cent of the tonnage rate), finisher (16.5), shearer (17.5), heaver-over (11.5), marker-holder-up (10.5), charger (8.5) and a scrap lad (5.5 per cent).[217] Promotion up a ladder of increasingly skilled tasks was rigidly governed by length of service. The extremely arduous nature of the jobs (the heaver-over, for example, handled 95 tons of sheet in each shift) demanded considerable physical strength and in times of hot weather encouraged the consumption of several gallons of beer per man during each eight-hour stint[218] in order to keep salt levels high. During periods of exceptionally high temperatures, the workrate fell and output was considerably reduced.[219]

Steel bars, in pairs, were fed into the mill having been pre-heated in a coal-fired furnace (which involved the shovelling of 1.75 tons of coal each turn). The flattened metal was then folded over repeatedly into a 'pack' as it was passed to and fro in the mill and became thinner. Great skill was required to maintain the correct temperature (in order to keep the steel malleable but not too hot lest the doubled pack adhere to itself) and to preserve an even thickness throughout. The packs, which required to be re-heated, at regular intervals, were manhandled by tongs, an act that required considerable dexterity. Mechanisation, even as late as 1945, was limited to reversing on the mill and the installation of a few conveyors to move the sheets short distances.[220]

High levels of output and consistent quality relied on teamwork and

Table 2.6   The reported profits of John Lysaght, (1919–45)

	£	Adjusted* £
to 31 December 1919	595,286	437,710
1920	499,090	316,280
1921	495,329	346,142
1922	580,845	500,728
1923	616,332	552,269
1924	545,505	492,778
1925	—	—
1926	—	—
1927	507,580	477,948
1928	674,652	—
1929	483,404	648,704
1930	—	483,404
1931	—	—
1932	199,892	—
1933	409,230	226,122
1934	441,718	458,264
1935	397,746	487,010
1936	548,370	428,144
1937	315,270	563,587
1938	445,682	319,422
1939	401,136	445,682
1940	345,859	344,619
1941	351,205	274,056
1942	388,565	277,194
1943	364,511	307,896
1944	358,168	286,791
1945		278,947

Note: *Figures adjusted by Bank of England's Index of Consumer Prices, 1930 = 100.

Source: John Lysaght Ltd Minute Book Vol. 4 (1921–26), Vol. 5 (1927–31); Vol. 6 (1931–35); Vol. 7 (1935–40).

strenuous labour. If hot weather sometimes encouraged absenteeism in periods of high wage rates and one or two members of the team took an unscheduled holiday, then the remainder were unable to work. Nevertheless, the overall profitability of the rolling mills resulted in comparatively well paid employment, the leader of a mill team being able, on occasion, to earn £10 a week (the equivalent of £400 today). Although minor injuries and burns were relatively common (in February 1927, for instance, 748 cuts, 74 burns, 73 bruises and 51 sprains were sustained resulting in the payment of £257 in compensation),[221] the work was not as dangerous nor unpleasant as being in a coal mine, and was, in general, much better paid. In addition, some workers were provided with subsidised housing. In November 1923 the Ministry of Health sanctioned a scheme to build 100 homes for Lysaght employees. The company contributed £150 towards the cost of each structure, while the Corporation of Newport loaned the balance at 5 per cent over two years.[222]

Although Lysaght were not permitted to offer rates other than those specified by the Sheet Trade Board, the fact that they rolled a substantial proportion of special quality sheet resulted in the men receiving regular payments over the standard rate. They took a concerted interest in their employees' welfare. When W.R. Lysaght decided to close the Orb Works in advance of a vote on the General Strike, the company granted a loan of over £50,000 to its workers to keep their families provided with necessities.[223] In December 1928 a large sports pavilion and recreation hall, unveiled as the 'W.R. Lysaght Institute', was completed, having cost an estimated £25,000.[224] Apart from being a humanitarian way of treating employees, this was also a sensible policy. Since the works did not rely upon technically advanced machinery, its commercial success was founded upon a highly skilled labour force (numbering around 3,500 during the inter-war period).[225] Given the importance of teamwork, it was in Lysaghts' interest to maintain a stable and contented workforce; strikes, absenteeism and difficulties in recruitment could have crippled a business which was based upon consistent output and a high quality product. In this respect, the company were remarkably far-sighted in establishing a 'Whitley Committee' for the Orb Works in November 1917.[226] With a constitution designed 'to afford regular opportunities for discussion between the management and the operatives on matters of mutual interest',[227] it met monthly and comprised delegates from the ten lodges, the works representative, the three senior mill managers and selected Lysaght directors; printed minutes were circulated to all members. The excellent labour relations which existed at Newport and the absence of strikes in the period to 1945 must, to a great part, have been a product of the regular and open discussions which took place in this forum.

How, then, did the Orb Works fare during the interwar period? Of considerable significance was the winning of large orders for sheet from Japan throughout 1923.[228] The product was destined for housing[229] and the trade, which had been facilitated by low prices, continued throughout 1924,[230] but in the following year an import duty of £2 per ton, together with the depressed level of the yen, conspired to stop the flow of sheet orders from Japan.[231] An attempt was made in July 1925 to revive the market when Lysaghts quoted at 'cost price or less'[232] and by September the situation was described as 'hopeful', as a few orders arrived.[233] Although the Japanese intermittently purchased black sheets,[234] the volume of orders attained in 1923–24 was not repeated.

A substantial proportion of the sheet produced at the Orb Works in the 1920s was sent to Bristol for galvanising and export, the bulk of which was sold to Australia. In 1923, for instance, of the 170,000 tons produced at Newport, 65,000 tons were sold directly as black sheets, while the balance, 105,000 tons, were sent to Bristol for galvanising.[235] However, with the completion of rolling mills and galvanising pots at Newcastle, New South Wales, in April 1921 (see Chapter Ten) Lysaghts principal export market was effectively set to die in the medium-term. As overseas production rose, the company could no longer expect to sell large quantities of galvanised and black sheet to Australia. In 1924, for example, when output at Newport achieved a new record of 187,775 tons, the growing Newcastle plant achieved a total of 15,564 tons.[236] Whilst scope for increasing the former was comparatively limited, it was planned to duplicate capacity in Australia so that output rose to 36,000 tons in 1930 and 58,000 tons in 1932.[237]

If the Orb Works were to maintain its levels of production, new customers had to be discovered. Of great importance for the future were contacts forged with the automotive trade. In 1924, six of the 48 mills were turning out sheet used in the production of car bodies, and their principal customers at that time included Humber, Vauxhall Motor Co., Standard Motor Co., Arrol-Johnston, Midland Light Bodies and Harper, Sons & Bean.[238] Because the technical initiative in the rolling of sheet steel for the automotive industry had been captured by America where mass-production methods were considerably advanced, D.C. Lysaght and W.E.C. Hudden were sent to the USA to inspect the latest techniques.[239] On their return, D.C. Lysaght warned of the dangers of competition from America, adding that the Morris Motor Co. had decided to build their cars with all-steel bodies. Unless Lysaghts could attain a high standard of output, Morris 'would put down a body pressing works and obtain their sheets from America'.[240] In the event, Orb Works became a major supplier of Morris and they, together with Ford at Trafford Park, became the company's major customers.

The other area of new business was the rolling of sheet steel for the electrical trade – principally in the manufacture of transformers and laminations. This activity served as a valuable buffer against the impact of general recession in the late 1920s. In January 1928 when output was at 60 per cent of capacity and demand from the automobile trade was described as being 'very poor', orders for electrical sheets increased.[241] In April, Lysaghts were involved in negotiations with British Thomson–Houston & Co. and Metropolitan Vickers Electrical Co. for exclusive contracts which, if successful, would secure them 80 per cent of the British market in electrical sheets.[242]

Although it had access to orders from two new industrial sectors – automobile and electricity – the Orb Works felt the impact of the depression which centred upon 1929. Towards the end of the year the motor trade showed signs of revival and those mills rolling sheet for car bodies were reported as being 'busier than for some considerable time'.[243] Nevertheless, during December the works remained operating at 70 per cent of capacity.[244] In mid-1931, inspired by the abandonment of the Gold Standard (which, in effect, reduced the value of the pound), a short-lived recovery followed,[245] lifted further by a temporary revival in the automobile sheet business.[246] Yet in the spring of 1933 orders from the electrical and motor trades were still below average, though the former showed some signs of improvement.[247] A sustained recovery occurred in September when output rose to 10,183 tons, noted as being the largest monthly total for some years.[248] By October 1935 the automobile sheet department was working to maximum capacity,[249] while in the autumn of the following year demand for electrical and motor sheets was so heavy that difficulties were encountered in supplying customers.[250] Output for January 1937 reached 14,117 tons, with orders secured for four months ahead.[251]

Whilst the 1920s and early 1930s had not witnessed a revolution in rolling mill technology, a limited programme of mechanisation had been effected – designed in the main to eliminate the most arduous handling tasks. In the meantime, a dramatic innovation had been pioneered in America by the Columbia Steel Co., which had succeeded in mass-producing sheet steel in two stages: wide hot strip rolling followed by 'cold-reduction'.[252] Rather than pass the steel backwards and forwards through the same rolls, altering the gap each time and doubling up the sheet as it became thinner, the Americans set up a series of mill stands arranged in tandem, one after another in a straight line, into which hot slabs were fed, being rolled down to plate thickness. The strip was then coiled, cleaned and cooled before being rolled cold in a separate set of stands to the required gauge.[253] In November 1935 E.C. Lysaght and J.B.R. Brooke (the son of W.J. Brooke) visited the United States to study the latest techniques.[254] Modifying the process which they had witnessed to suit the manufacturing capacity of Orb Works, they recommended the installation of an 80in., 3-stand Tandem cold-reduction mill, which operated from 1936 with consistent success on sheet for the motor industry until the late 1940s when, following the formation of the Steel Company of Wales, it was broken up and employed in finishing at the Abbey Works at Margam.[255]

By the spring of 1938 there were signs that the boom had ended. Output for February had fallen to 8,680 tons at Newport and trade was reported as being 'very slack'.[256] No improvement followed during the summer and S.R. Lysaght observed in September that the 'demand for galvanised iron both for home and export continued to decrease'.[257] Exports of galvanised iron and black sheets for the first seven months of 1938 were only half the quantity for the same period in 1937. Rearmament came to the rescue of the Orb Works, as it did to the steel industry as a whole. The need to construct thousands of air-raid shelters brought a considerable volume of orders. By the time that the first delivery was made on 22 February 1939, 1,500 tons of sheet were being rolled each week for shelters,[258] this contributing to a new record output of 19,330 tons in March.[259] In May, an order for a further 38,000 tons of sheet was received.[260]

ST VINCENT'S WORKS, BRISTOL

From July 1915, when the Australian government requested Lysaghts to begin manufacturing in their country, the future of the St Vincent's Works as a galvanising plant was doomed. It lay at the end of a chain of production which began in Scunthorpe, advanced to Newport, and then arrived in Bristol to pass on, for the most part, overseas. Once the Orb Works had become established there remained little commercial sense in shipping large quantities of sheet across the Bristol Channel down the Avon to Silverthorne Lane for finishing and despatch. The dis-economies present in this exercise could be accommodated so long as trade was buoyant and expanding, but as soon as markets contracted and prices fell, the need to improve efficiencies would fall upon the weakest link in the chain. The St Vincent's Works closed briefly during the 1921 slump (p. 41), and by June 1922 there were 15 galvanising pots in operation, with a monthly capacity of 7,962 tons.[261] Although output climbed to 102,215 tons for the year,[262] the low levels to which prices for galvanised sheet had fallen, resulted in the St Vincent's Works struggling to make a profit. In December 1922 a scheme to transfer galvanising to Newport was costed at £150,000 but was not

10   The manufacture of wire netting by Lysaghts at their Netham Works. This is possibly a post-1945 photograph (*Rheemco*).

implemented.[263] Among the arguments that the Lysaght directors might have considered, was the hardship to a loyal Bristol workforce that such a closure would have caused. In addition, St Vincent's was the company's headquarters and a loss of prestige would have followed if a major part of its manufacturing activity had disappeared.

The General Strike forced the St Vincent's Works to close for a second time and when operations re-started only eight pots were at work, output being about 70 per cent of the pre-dispute level.[264] S.R. Lysaght raised the issue of closing the Bristol galvanising operations and transferring them to Newport; figures showing the possible saving were discussed but not recorded in the minutes.[265] At the next meeting he proposed that plans be finalised 'for the immediate provision of a galvanising plant of three pots, with a capacity for gradual development'.[266] The board took the view that the scheme was not urgent, though agreed to the preparations of costings. The gradual decline in the fortunes of the St Vincent's Works was revealed in figures produced in January 1927: the total output of galvanised sheets had reached a peak in 1913 of 122,835 tons, falling to 94,483 tons in 1925 and 83,960 tons in 1926.[267] Again in October 1927 S.R. Lysaght raised the issue arguing 'that a substantial saving in production costs would be effected'.[268] Berry, as chairman, prevaricated and asked for further reports, believing perhaps that galvanising in the UK was set in terminal decline.

As the additional rolling mills and galvanising plant at Newcastle came on stream, so output at St Vincent's continued to dwindle – in the eight months to the end of August 1928, 45,165 tons were produced.[269] This had 'resulted in increased costs at Bristol and steps were being taken to obtain new business in other markets'.[270] Total output in 1928 (71,516 tons) was considerably down on 1927 (96,704 tons).[271] In September 1929 when production at St Vincent's had fallen to around 1,500 tons a week (with a potential capacity of 2,500 tons), the notion of transferring galvanising to Newport was again discussed.[272] It was estimated that the cost of setting up galvanising pots with the latest improvements, such as crane handling to reduce manual labour, would be £120,000. Substantial savings could be made as fewer works would be required and possibly only one-third of the office staff employed in Bristol would be needed.[273] However, nothing happened.

Commercial conditions worsened during the 1929 depression, making it impossible for the works to compete successfully. In March 1930, for example, when the market price for galvanised sheet was £11 17s 6d per ton, Lysaghts' price for the cheapest brand was £13 2s 6d.[274] With declining economies of scale, the cost of production at Bristol had risen above that of their smaller rivals. The question of ending galvanising was considered yet again, but the board refrained from taking action.[275] In November 1930, figures demonstrated that when the extensions to the Newcastle Works were completed, 75 per cent of the company's galvanised sheet would be made abroad, leaving only 25 per cent in Bristol.[276] At the December board meeting S.R. Lysaght argued again in

11 Galvanised steel products made by Lysaghts (*Rheemco*).

favour of a transfer, adding that the St Vincent's Works had been in operation for only six days in October producing a mere 1,300 tons.[277]

In order to try to save jobs at Bristol, a plan was prepared to modernise the galvanising plant there. Yet as S.R. Lysaght pointed out it would result in savings of 1s 7d per ton, while the move to Newport would reduce costs by 14s per ton.[278] In March 1931, when a mere four pots were in operation and the company's export requirements for the year were estimated at 19,000 tons (the works having an annual capacity of 120,000 tons),[279] the board could no longer defend the St Vincent's Works and authorised the *Bristol Evening Times* to announce the phased end of galvanising.[280] In the event, the works turned out 20,428 tons of galvanised sheet in 1931 (at a time when Lysaghts' overseas plant produced 41,313 tons)[281]

Galvanising began at Newport in March 1932 with a single pot, a second following in April.[282] Output at Orb Works climbed steadily from 1,292 tons in May to 2,182 tons in June.[283] Although Newport soon overtook Bristol as the principal galvanising plant (in October 1937, for example, Orb produced 1,913 tons to St Vincent's 1,066 tons),[284] the decision to close the latter was postponed until April 1940 when it was decided to transfer the last sheet galvanising section.[285]

While the galvanising works at Bristol experienced a torrid time during the interwar period, the Constructional Department, its neigh-

JOHN LYSAGHT'S BRISTOL WORKS LIMITED.
Redcliffe BRAND AGRICULTURAL SPECIALITIES & ORB BRAND WIRE NETTING

12 A post-war trade exhibition of Lysaghts galvanised agricultural ware (*Rheemco*).

bour at Netham, had better fortune. Extensions, estimated at between £40–50,000, were authorised in June 1922.[286] The works appears to have been largely successful during the 1920s until the slump. In 1927, for example, when output rose to 7,523 tons, nearly equal to the record figure for 1913, prospects were considered 'favourable', though competition remained 'extremely keen'.[287] The drift into depression revealed itself in the total for 1928, 7,289 tons,[288] while that for 1931 (4,984 tons) was the lowest since 1923.[289] Recovery followed in the mid-1930s, as the company established links with the major building contractors in Bristol and the West of England.[290] Among their principal structures were the swing bridge over the Avon at Ashton Gate, the steelwork for the Portishead power-station and the Great Western goods station at Temple Meads. In July 1939 in anticipation of the damage that would be caused by enemy aircraft, Lysaghts' Construction Department, along with Dorman Long & Co. and the Cleveland Bridge Co., were authorised by the Ministry of Transport to undertake repairs to bridges throughout the 'Southern Area' (Cornwall to Berkshire including Wales and Monmouth).[291]

NORMANBY PARK STEELWORKS, SCUNTHORPE

Prompted to expand during the hostilities by the Ministry of Munitions desperate for supplies of shell steel and further encouraged by the post-war boom, Lysaghts completed a fifth blast furnace (with a 13ft hearth) in 1920. It could not have been worse timed. In February of the following year, as Continental steel prices tumbled, business dried up and the steelworks was closed. During October, in response to a request from the Orb workforce who were dissatisfied with the Continental billets that they were forced to use, the board replied that it was impractical to re-open Scunthorpe, which normally supplied their steel. The directors noted that they were prepared to run the steelworks at a loss of £1 per ton, if necessary, to keep the men in employment, but after discussions with the manager, W.J. Brooke, even this target proved impossible. Two blast furnaces (one for the production of foundry iron and the other for basic iron)[292] were blown in during November 1921,[293] a third following in March 1922.[294] Shortly afterwards plans were effected to bring the open hearth furnaces back into operation.[295] In June 1922 a total of 14,958 tons of pig iron were produced, together with 9,500 tons of tin bars and 1,422 tons of billets.[296]

Although Normanby Park came back into operation, it worked only briefly to full capacity during the 1920s.[297] Orb Works continued to purchase a proportion of their billets from the Continent as they were considerably cheaper than the home product.[298] This was a rare example of a downstream company being allowed to tender beyond the group and was permitted to do so in order that it remain profitable in competitive economic circumstances. During the depression of 1929–30, when prices fell to such levels as to make the steelworks no longer viable, a major reorganisation was the only choice if it were to continue in being. Being medium-sized and some twenty-years old, Normanby Park could not realistically hope to compete with the largest Continental or British steelworks in the mass-market. Its favoured option was to concentrate on the manufacture of specialised steels. Accordingly, in

13 The visit of the GKN board to Normanby Park Steelworks, Scunthorpe, on 20 September 1923. Seated in the middle was H. Seymour Berry with W.R. Lysaght to his left and Edward Steer to his right. Third from the left, standing, was Sir John Field Beale, a future chairman of the group.

October 1930 a scheme of reconstruction costing over £400,000 was embarked upon.[299] The programme included a new battery of coke ovens, fired by blast furnace gas; the re-building of two of the open-hearth furnaces to increase their capacity to 120 tons; the erection of an iron-ore screening and crushing plant; and equipment for the utilisation of all coke-oven and blast-furnace gases.[300] To have undertaken such a capital-intensive scheme at almost the nadir of the depression took considerable nerve and revealed commercial acumen.

The wisdom of this initiative was soon demonstrated. In 1932 when many British steelworks were producing less than half their 1929 capacity, Normanby Park had achieved 80 per cent.[301] Nevertheless, to obtain these levels of production, orders had been accepted with the smallest margin of profit,[302] and had been made possible by the improvements, which had reduced costs to a new record low of 44s 4d per ton in March 1932.[303] Efficiency had reached such levels by March 1933 that the Orb Works could purchase their entire supply of billets from Scunthorpe (the first time since 1918 that they had been able to do so), and the steel plant was almost at full capacity.[304] The key to this success story was the installation of the coke ovens which not only reduced the cost of coke to 8s 0d per ton, but also provided sufficient gas to fire the steel plant and maintain steam for general requirements.[305]

Being employed at full capacity, a further £45–55,000 was authorised to be spent in January 1934 at Normanby Park for the construction of a second 400-ton mixer and the enlargement of No. 2 blast furnace.[306] Given that shortages of coke in the UK led to violent fluctuations in price, it was agreed in April 1936 that a further twenty-three coke ovens be constructed at a cost of £151,103.[307] During that month record outputs were obtained in both the steel plant and at the rolling mills,[308] while the total make for 1937 reached 33,000 tons.

Because Lysaghts had decided to concentrate on producing certain special steels, in 1937 they were unable to meet the precise specifications demanded by shell steel but were able to meet the less rigorous requirements of bomb steel.[309] This additional demand proved particularly well timed, as in March 1938 orders for sheet bars decreased considerably and specifications for electrical steels fell to their lowest for two years.[310] By May the situation had worsened and very large stocks of American and Continental semi-finished material were held by most re-rollers.[311] Mill production at Scunthorpe had fallen from 5,300 tons per week in 1937 to around 4,000 tons the spring of 1938 and declined to 3,200 tons by May.[312] Overheads rose accordingly, making it difficult to compete or make a reasonable profit. In June one of the blast furnaces was blown out and Lysaghts temporarily closed the mills and the melting shop.[313] With no improvement in their trading position anticipated,[314] re-armament proved to be a mixed blessing for the steelworks. A new sintering plant had come into operation in the spring of 1939 and this had the desirable effect of saving 8s 0d on every ton of pig iron made.[315] The production of billets for ARP shelters had

14   An aerial view of Normanby Park Steelworks taken in July 1935 (*Aerofilms*).

helped to raise output considerably, but the major increase in demand came in December 1939 when the Steel Controller notified Lysaghts that Normanby Park would shortly be expected to manufacture shell steel.[316] By January 1940 they were producing this at the rate of 400 tons per week in the expectation that demand would rise to 1,000 tons.[317]

OVERSEAS VENTURES: FRANCE AND IRELAND

Early in 1930, E.C. Lysaght travelled to France to meet the representatives of Citroen who had heard of Lysaghts' growing reputation as rollers of sheet for automobiles. Their suggestion was either that

Lysaghts manufacture sheets in conjunction with their company or jointly with an established French rolling firm. For Lysaghts the attraction of the scheme was that it provided an entrée to a large market for high-grade black sheets in which labour costs were lower than in Britain.[318] Accordingly they decided to look for a four-mill plant in the region of Le Havre, a port, or Rouen (on the Seine), either of which could be supplied with billets from Britain and would be within reasonable distance of the Parisian automotive works.[319] In October 1930 a company, Société Française Lysaght, was set up to provide the necessary administrative and legal framework for any enterprise.[320] A survey of existing manufacturers produced the Beautor Works, at Beaucort on the River Aisne ninety miles north of Paris.[321] Cooper Bros., the chartered accountants, submitted a financial report on the company in May 1931 and as a result, it was suggested that Lysaghts purchase 25,000 ordinary shares (each valued at 650 francs) in the company, in order to obtain a controlling interest. The Beautor management, which had little knowledge of rolling high quality sheet, would gain expertise from their British partners, while Lysaghts would gain a solid footing in a protected French market.

Although the Lysaght directors were in general enthusiastic about the scheme, the GKN representative on their board, Sir John Field Beale, was opposed to the plan because he believed that the steel trade on the Continent was unlikely to improve and possibly be subject to further recession. As a result, Lord Camrose moved that the report assembled by Cooper Bros. should be left with Beale who would then present the case at the GKN board meeting the following day. At these discussions it was observed that,

> the Lysaght Management Committee were strongly in favour of making the purchase, which would involve an outlay of £130,000 ... The Board's [GKN's] inclination was not strongly in favour of proceeding with the matter because of the general uncertainty of trade and the probable further setback in French economic conditions. In view, however, of the strong recommendation of the Lysaght management, it was decided that discussions with French interests should proceed...[322]

In August 1931, W.R. Lysaght recorded that the visit of three representatives from Newport to Beaucort to study technical matters had proved satisfactory. Nevertheless, a further report prepared by Cooper Bros. revealed that the company had failed to make a profit for at least four years. The discovery of this commercial failure caused the Lysaght board to abandon the proposed takeover, though the Orb Works did not lose its connection with Citroen and supplied them with sheet from Newport.[323]

Five years later, in 1936, Lysaghts considered setting up a works in Ireland as this was a market dominated by Continental producers.[324] A site at Queenstown, near Cork, had been found on which a galvanising plant could be erected, and supplied by sea with black sheets from the Orb Works. The land was offered at £10,000 and the entire cost of the project was estimated at £60–70,000.[325] However, this scheme foundered over negotiations with the Irish Department of Commerce and Industry. In meetings at Dublin, S.R. Lysaght had asked the government to introduce a duty on Continental black sheet imported to Ireland for galvanising to protect British makers.[326] This request had been refused. The scheme was put into a state of abeyance until April 1937 when the Department of Industry informed Lysaghts that a Mr Frame was contemplating rolling black sheets in Ireland. In the event of such an enterprise proceeding, the government had promised to provide protection and to introduce a duty on imported black sheet. If sheet from Newport were subject to a levy, then the final galvanised product turned out from Queenstown would always be more expensive than that manufactured indigenously by Mr Frame. Lysaghts proceeded with the purchase of the land at Rushbrooke for £14,000 but also informed the Irish Government that unless they could guarantee the free entry of English black sheet for a period of at least ten years, the project would have to be abandoned.[327] In the event the guarantee was not forthcoming and the site was sold.[328]

MANAGERS AND MANAGEMENT

After the merger between John Lysaght and GKN the boards of the respective companies were re-arranged to bring a measure of integration. Nevertheless, the directors of Lysaghts remained in essence those of the pre-merger organisation. H. Seymour Berry and D.R. Llewellyn, for example, retained their respective positions of chairman and deputy chairman, while Sir William E. Berry, J.G. Berry, H.G. Hill, Sir Leonard W. Llewelyn, M.H. Llewellyn, the Viscountess Rhondda, S.R. Lysaght, W.R. Lysaght, D.C. Lysaght, G.H. Sankey and W. Trimmer also continued to serve as directors.[329] In order that senior members of GKN could be actively involved in decision making, both Edward Steer and Sir John Field Beale were appointed to the board. As regards the practical management of the various plants, responsibility fell upon W.R. Lysaght, who based himself at Chepstow almost equidistant from Newport and Bristol, and D.C. Lysaght (1869–1940) who ran the Orb Rolling Mills. The former's career has already been described (p. 23), while the latter, a younger cousin of W.R., had been born and educated in County Cork.[330] Emigrating to England to improve his career prospects, D.C. Lysaght first joined the army but the death of his father precluded this career and he entered the St Vincent's Works to learn about the galvanising business. When John Lysaght died in 1895, and additional executive authority passed to W.R. Lysaght, D.C. was transferred to the Swan Garden Works to assist the latter in running the

15 W.R. Lysaght (1858–1945). He joined the family business in 1878, worked at the Swan Garden Mills, was responsible for selecting the Orb and Normanby Park sites, and served as chairman of Lysaghts from 1928 to 1939 (*E.C. Lysaght*).

rolling mills. Having acquired a considerable expertise in sheet rolling, it was not surprising that he was asked to move to Newport in March 1898 to begin operations there. From the initial three mills and workforce of three skilled men, D.C. Lysaght built up the Orb Works to comprise 42 hot mills and a staff of 3,000 by 1913.[331]

The composition of the board altered gradually throughout the 1920s. The death of H.G. Hill on 22 August 1925 created one vacancy,[332] while William Trimmer, whose 'non-executive' responsibilities included the joint managing directorship of the St Vincent's Works, died in September 1926.[333] No replacements were made, however, until July 1927 when the retirement of Edward Steer from both the chairmanship of GKN and the Lysaght board prompted the appointment of T.S. Peacock to the latter.[334] A joint managing director of GKN with special responsibilities for their Darlaston bolt and nut factories, Peacock was there to see that GKN interests were represented and to obtain first-hand knowledge of Lysaght thinking.[335]

When Lord Buckland was killed in a riding accident,[336] W.R. Lysaght's claim to be his successor was both natural and compelling.[337]

The latter, having served fifty years with the company, possessed an intimate knowledge of the business, had been a long-serving member of the wages boards for the Midlands and the South Wales Sheet Trade and sat on the Council of the Iron and Steel Institute.[338] Perhaps the one negative feature of this promotion was W.R. Lysaght's age, for he celebrated his seventieth birthday in July 1928[339] and continued in office until retirement in December 1939. However, as in the case of H. Seymour Berry, his was a non-executive role, a co-ordinator and voice of experience rather than a manager responsible for detailed, daily decisions. These, in the case of the Orb Works fell to D.C. Lysaght. Indeed, the success of the Newport operations resulted partly from the complementary relationship which existed between the two.[340] D.C. Lysaght, akin to a chief of staff, intuitively perceived the issues at stake in technical problems and labour relations, and possessed an Irish love of debate, while W.R. was sparing in the use of words and deliberate in thought. Paradoxically, it was D.C. Lysaght who was the firmest in negotiations and W.R., whose apparently tough and authoritarian manner, in fact concealed a conciliatory heart.[341]

In April 1930 S.R. Lysaght, a 'consulting director', was elevated to the post of joint managing director.[342] Having been described by H. Seymour Berry as a capable 'business ambassador . . . to the foreign and colonial markets',[343] he had developed a considerable understanding of commerce with Australia, Canada, South America and South Africa. Being the director who presented the company's trade statistics to the board, S.R. Lysaght spoke with a slightly detached authority on the business's performance and played a crucial role in encouraging the transfer of galvanising from Bristol to Newport. Not being associated

16 The three Lysaght brothers: left to right, H.R., W.R. and S.R. (*BHP Steel*).

with any particular manufacturing plant, he judged issues on a financial basis and attached considerable importance to costings.

In October 1933 W.J. Brooke (1875–1952), who had been general
manager of Normanby Park Steelworks since 1920, was elevated to the
board.[344] Brooke had originally worked for a firm of analytical chemists
in Birmingham, after which he became successively steel plant manager
of the Frodingham Iron and Steel Co. and general manager of the
Shelton Iron and Steel Co. at Stoke on Trent. In 1918 he returned to
Scunthorpe as chief executive of the Redbourne Works, moving two
years later to Lysaghts.[345] In July 1933, S.R. Lysaght remarked, following a visit to Scunthorpe, that he had much appreciated

> the manner in which Mr Brooke was filling his post as manager . . .
> He referred particularly to Mr Brooke's standing in the locality. Mr
> Brooke took a prominent part in social activities and was obviously
> regarded as a kind of local leader.[346]

The appointment of Brooke was an important one, as the number of
directors with direct managerial responsibilities in the business on the
Lysaght board had fallen to two, D.C. Lysaght and W.R. Lysaght, the
latter taking an increasingly non-executive role. This partly reflected
late nineteenth-century attitudes whereby managers were not generally
made members of the board unless they were particularly senior or had
a family connection, directorships being reserved for prominent public
figures. In January 1935, for example, the Lysaght board included the
Viscountess Rhondda, who took the opportunity provided by board
meetings to edit *Time and Tide*, William Berry, Lord Camrose, and Sir J.
Gomer Berry (both newspaper owners), together with Sir David
Llewellyn and M.H. Llewellyn (both colliery company owners), while
G.H. Sankey (whose death in December 1934 resulted in the appointment of Harold B. Sankey),[347] Sir John Field Beale and T.S. Peacock
were representing the interests of other companies. This imbalance had
arisen, in part, because of the take-over of Lysaghts in 1919 by H.
Seymour Berry in conjunction with D.R. Llewellyn and the Viscountess
Rhondda. All three had joined the board along with several of Berry's
nominees.

The appointment of Desmond Royse Lysaght (1903–70) and Edward
Conner Lysaght (b. 1902) to the board in March 1935[348] indicated that
the Lysaght–GKN forces were re-establishing their authority over the
Berry grouping. Both D.R. and E.C. Lysaght held managerial posts at
the Orb Works, the former being the only child of W.R. and the latter
the son of D.C. At the time of their promotion, Sir David Llewellyn
observed that the board would be 'strengthened by this inclusion of
younger men'.[349] Educated at Cheltenham College and intending to
pursue a military career, E.C. Lysaght had passed the entrance
examinations to Woolwich but then decided to join the family business
arriving straight from school in 1921.[350] Viscountess Rhondda resigned

from her directorship in 1936, being paid £2,000 in compensation for the loss of her office,[351] and in June of that year both Lord Camrose and Gomer Berry, now Lord Kemsley, retired from the board because of pressure from other commitments.[352] With the exception of Sir David Llewellyn who remained as deputy chairman, all the figures of the Berry era had departed.

In May 1939 J.H. Jolly, a joint managing director of GKN from August 1934, was appointed to the Lysaght board.[353] But the major event of the year was the resignation of W.R. Lysaght as chairman in December. Aged eighty-one and with sixty-four years with the company, he decided to opt for retirement.[354] In recognition of his achievements (in particular the transfer of rolling operations from Wolverhampton to Newport and the founding of the Scunthorpe steelworks), W.R. Lysaght was elected life president of the company.[355] He was succeeded by his second-in-command, Sir David Llewellyn, and S.R. Beale took the deputy chairmanship.[356]

The unexpected death of D.C. Lysaght in May 1940, following a heart attack at the works, led to his son, E.C. Lysaght, and D.R. Lysaght both being appointed joint managing directors.[357] Between them they ran the Newport and Bristol ends of the business, with W.J. Brooke being in executive control of the Scunthorpe steelworks. When Sir David Llewellyn died in December 1940, the chairmanship passed to S.R. Beale, a post he retained until his retirement in 1947.[358]

When GKN acquired its controlling interests in John Lysaght Ltd, the directors of the latter were assured that they would retain their own 'entity' and 'the relations existing between the operatives and management would not be affected at all'.[359] In essence this remained the case throughout the interwar period. Although the GKN board remained the final arbiter on questions of heavy capital expenditure (as the instance of the French take-over illustrated, p. 54), the Lysaght executives were granted considerable latitude to make strategic decisions. The company continued to trade under its original name, from the same head office, with no change to its manufacturing chain.

In so far as the merger exercised an influence on Lysaghts, it was largely administrative. In 1924 after a visit to Australia by T.S. Peacock, GKN executives were favourably impressed by the network of sales offices established by Lysaghts there and suggested that they ought to be integrated with the more limited agencies belonging to the former.[360] Later in the year, Lysaghts were asked to bear a greater proportion of the overheads incurred by GKN.[361] They agreed to contribute £5,000 per annum on the understanding that the Smethwick head office would deal with share transfers, dividend payments and other administraive matters.

In the absence of centralised banking within the GKN, Lysaghts were asked on occasion to loan capital to other members of the group. In March 1934, for example, they agreed to lend Exors. of James Mills £40,000 at 3½ per cent a year,[362] and in 1935 Welsh Associated

17 The Lysaght Institute, Newport. Completed in 1928 at a cost of £25,000, it comprised a sports pavilion and recreation hall (*Author*).

Collieries borrowed £30,000 from them at the same rate of interest.[363]

Occasionally, being a member of a vertically integrated group could present problems. When Sankeys began pressing sheet for motor bodies for S.S. Cars in 1937, Lysaghts observed that this was an injudicious step as

> it might prejudice the relations of J. Lysaght Ltd. with such large customers as the Pressed Steel Co. and Fisher & Ludlow. Both of these firms had already referred to the fact that they would not view Sankey's competition with equanimity.[364]

As a result, Sankeys limited their activities in this trade.

THE SECOND WORLD WAR

Because of its strategic importance in what was to prove a war whose character was determined by industry, from 11 September 1939 the British iron and steel trade fell under the control of the government. As in the Great War, employees volunteered for military service before this became prohibited by a system of 'reserved occupations'. The company agreed to pay the wives of married men 10s a week and the parents of single men 5s a week.[365] At first, the Orb Works was constrained not by orders but by a dearth of steel. Once the heavy initial orders for Anderson shelters and nissen huts had been completed,[366] Sheet from

Newport was despatched to manufacture helmets, ammunition boxes, jerricans and the thicker grades were used in the production of land mines.[367] In addition, the Orb Works laid down a sizeable foundry for cartridge brass which was then rolled for the manufacture of 20mm cannon shells.[368] Of great importance for the aircraft industry was the production of duralumin, an aluminium alloy, one-third the weight of steel, used in the construction of airframes. After one refusal by the Ministry of Aircraft Production in 1939, E.C. Lysaght succeeded in persuading the authorities that the company could perform this highly specialised work on the 3-high mill at Newport.[369] From 1941 until January 1945, when the Light Alloy Department was closed,[370] considerable quantities of duralumin were rolled at Orb Works. In the production of brass cartridges and duralumin around 600 women were employed.

The Construction Department at Netham was chiefly engaged on the assembly of tanks,[371] modifying American designs for use by the British Army,[372] and was one of the companies entrusted with completion of the top-secret amphibian tanks needed for the Normandy invasion. They also manufactured anti-submarine netting, pre-fabricated ship superstructures, anti-aircraft guns and shells, while the engineering shop produced radar equipment. St Vincent's Works concentrated on making the components which formed the ubiquitous Bailey Bridge, and was also involved with the preparations for the laying of 'Pluto' (the pipeline under the Channel which supplied the invading armies with petrol from England) and with the 30ft by 9ft buoyancy tanks for the Mulberry harbours.[373]

SUMMARY

On 5 November 1945, six months after the war in Europe had ended, E.C. Lysaght, addressing the Whitley Committee in Newport, stressed the importance 'of getting ahead with our overseas trade, if the country were not to suffer the loss of our export markets'.[374] Because of the enlistment of men in the forces and the diversion of operations for munitions and the machinery of war, Lysaghts could not respond to all the orders they had received.[375] The company had every reason to be wary of the post-war economy. The boom, which had followed the armistice in 1918, had proved short-lived and had ushered in a period of tough competition. Would it be the same for the decade after 1945? In addition, Lysaghts had seen the recovery of the mid-1930s subside and orders at the Normanby Park steelworks and Orb rolling mills had fallen off, rearmament having saved both from the effects of yet another recession. In one respect Lysaghts were better prepared to face the future in 1945 than they had been in 1918, the galvanising operations at Bristol, which had been costly and unproductive throughout the 1920s, had finally been closed and the plant transferred to

Newport. In the event, demand outstripped supply in the post-war period and the steel industry was granted the luxury of being able to allocate its goods, rather than having to compete for customers, and Lysaghts entered a particularly profitable phase of their history. Judged by past experience, however, E.C. Lysaght had every reason to exhort the Orb workforce to greater levels of efficiency and new records of output.

References

1. BCL, *Work in Bristol, A Series of Sketches of the Chief Manufactories in the City, Reprinted from the Bristol Times and Mirror*, Bristol (1883), St Vincent's Galvanising Works, pp. 3–7.
2. Gilbert Herbert, *Pioneers of Prefabrication, The British Contribution in the Nineteenth Century*, Johns Hopkins, Baltimore (1978) p. 34.
3. Ibid., No. 5786, 1829.
4. H.W. Dickinson, *Transactions of the Newcomen Society*, Vol. 24 (1943–44), 'A Story of Galvanised and Corrugated Metal', p. 27.
5. Herbert, *Pioneers of Prefabrication*, op. cit., p. 47.
6. Ibid., p. 57.
7. BCL, *Bristol and Its Environs*, British Association, London (1875), P. 209.
8. *Bristol Times & Mirror*, 2 October 1895, Obituary *DBB*, Vol. 3 (1985), Colin Baber and Trevor Boyns, 'John Lysaght', p. 895.
9. Information provided by Mr. Alan Stein, formerly Chief Library and Information Officer, BHP Steel International.
10. *The Lysaght Century 1857–1957*, Bristol (1957), p. 7.
11. *Lysaght Century*, op. cit., p. 9.
12. Dickinson, 'Galvanised and Corrugated Metal', op. cit., p. 32.
13. *Mathews's Annual Directory for Bristol* (1864), J. Lysaght, Temple Back, p. 330.
14. *Lysaght Century*, op. cit., p. 11.
15. BCL, *Work in Bristol*, op. cit., p. 4.
16. Ibid., p. 5; R.A. Buchanan and Neil Cossons, *The Industrial Archaeology of the Bristol Region*, Newton Abbot (1969), p. 61.
17. Edgar Jones, *Industrial Architecture in Britain 1759–1939*, London (1985), pp. 129–31; Andor Gomme *et al.*, *Bristol, An Architectural History*, London (1979), p. 438.
18. BCL, *Work in Bristol*, op. cit., p. 5.
19. Ibid., p. 5.
20. *Lysaght Century*, op. cit., p. 12.
21. BCL, *Work in Bristol*, op. cit., p. 8.
22. *DBB*, Vol. 3 (1985), 'John Lysaght', op. cit.
23. *Lysaght Century*, op. cit., p. 13; *Bristol Survey (Part Two) 1960 Histories of Famous Firms*, 'John Lysaght Ltd', p. 24.
24. *John Lysaght Ltd., Bristol, Constructional Engineering Department* [*c.* 1900], pp. 2, 44, 48, 49, 50, 55, 27–8, 30–1, 37, 52–4.
25. *Royal Jubilee Exhibition, Manchester 1887, Official Catalogue*, p. 19.
26. John Lysaght Old Company Minute Book, Vol. I, op. cit., 19 May 1892.
27. Ibid., 21 July 1893; 21 May 1896;
28. John Lysaght 'Private Letter Book', 12 January 1878, quoted from *Lysaght Century*, op. cit., p. 50.

29. 'Private Letter Book', op. cit., 15 May 1877; *Lysaght Century*, op. cit., p. 14.
30. BCL, *Work in Bristol*, op. cit., pp. 5, 8.
31. Lysaght Old Company Minute Book, June 1881–March 1897, Vol. I, 9 October 1885; *Trades Directory of Wolverhampton*, London (1862–63), p. 27; Kenneth Warren, *The British Iron & Steel Sheet Industry since 1840*, London (1970), p. 37.
32. Ibid., 4 October 1888.
33. Lysaght Old Company Minute Book, Vol., I, 30 June 1881; Charlotte Erickson, *British Industrialists, Steel and Hosiery 1850–1950*, Cambridge (1959), p. 210.
34. Lysaght Old Company Minute Book, Vol. I, 15 December 1881.
35. Ibid., 12 November 1884.
36. Ibid., 14 March 1887; 16 April 1888.
37. Ibid., 14 May 1888.
38. John Lysaght Minute Book, Vol. I, op. cit., Directors' Report for 1903, 3 May 1904, p. 113.
39. Information provided by Mr Alan Stein, 21 January 1987.
40. Lysaght Old Company Minute Book, Directors' Report for 1891, 7 March 1892.
41. Ibid., Directors' report for 1893, 5 March 1894.
42. Ibid., Directors' Report for 1894, 29 March 1895.
43. Ibid., 16 July 1888.
44. Ibid., 4 October 1888.
45. Ibid., 7 March 1892.
46. Ibid., Directors' Report for 1892, 16 March 1893.
47. Ibid.
48. Ibid., 23 June 1896.
49. Ibid., Directors' Report for 1896, 31 March 1897.
50. Ibid.
51. Ibid., 31 March 1896.
52. Lysaght Old Company Minute Book, Vol. II, Directors' Report for 1897, 6 April 1898.
53. Ibid., Directors' Report for 1899, 31 May 1900.
54. Lysaght Minute Book, Vol. I, op. cit., Directors' Report for 1903, 3 May 1904, p. 113.
55. Lysaght Old Company Minute Book, Vol. I, op. cit., 16 November 1888; *Bristol Times & Mirror*, Obituary, 2 October 1895.
56. Quoted from *Lysaght Century*, op. cit., p. 50.
57. Quoted from *Lysaght Century*, op. cit., p. 48.
58. *The Western Daily Press*, Vol. 75, No. 11,644, 2 October 1895, Obituary, p. 5.
59. *Bristol Times & Mirror*, Obituary 2 October 1895; *Bristol Mercury*, Obituary, 2 October 1895.
60. *Midland Evening News*, Obituary, 2 October 1895.
61. *DBB* Vol. 3 (1985), Baber and Boyns, op. cit., p. 898.
62. *Western Daily Press*, Obituary, op. cit., p. 5.
63. Lysaght Old Company Minute Book, Vol. I, op. cit., 15 December 1881.
64. Ibid., 11 March 1889.
65. Ibid., 6 March 1893.
66. Ibid., 15 October 1895.
67. Ibid., 30 October 1893.
68. Ibid., 6 March 1893.

69. Ibid., 12 November 1884.
70. Lysaght Old Company Minute Book, Vol. I, op. cit., 24 February 1886.
71. Ibid., 24 October 1893.
72. Ibid., 16 March 1891.
73. *DBB*, Vol. 5 (1985), Edgar Jones 'W.R. Lysaght', pp. 899–904.
74. Quoted from *Lysaght Century*, op. cit., p. 50.
75. G.G. Jones (ed.), *British Multinationals*, op. cit., Edgar Jones, 'Steel and Engineering Overseas: GKN's Multinational Growth, 1918–1965', pp. 172–3.
76. Lysaght Old Company Minute Book, Vol. II, op. cit., 20 June 1899.
77. Edgar Jones, 'GKN Multinational Growth', op. cit., p. 167.
78. Lysaght Old Company Minute Book, Vol. II, op. cit., 15 October 1895.
79. John Lysaght, New Company Minute Book, Vol. I, op. cit., 26 September 1905, p. 174.
80. *John Lysaght Ltd., Prospectus, 28 November 1901*; John Lysaght Minute Book, Vol. II, 22 August 1911, p. 71.
81. Lysaght Old Company Minute Book, Vol. I, op. cit., 13 February 1885.
82. Lysaght Old Company Minute Book, Vol. II, op. cit., 27 October 1898.
83. *DBB*, Vol. 1 (1984), Edgar Jones 'Ernest Cooper', pp. 778–80.
84. Lysaght Old Company Minute Book, Vol. II, op. cit., 20 June 1899.
85. Ibid., 21 August 1900.
86. Lysaght Minute Book, Vol. II, op. cit., 22 September 1915, p. 267.
87. Ibid., p. 268.
88. *The Lysaght Century*, op. cit., pp. 22–3.
89. St. Vincent's Works, plans and office elevations, signed by R. Milverton Drake, December 1891.
90. Lysaght Company Minute Book, Vol. I, op. cit., 11 December 1901, p. 11; 21 January 1902. p. 17.
91. Lysaght Old Company Minute Book, Vol. I, op. cit., Directors' Report for 1895, 22 April 1896.
92. Lysaght Old Company Minute Book, Vol. II, op. cit., Directors' Report for 1900, 23 May 1901.
93. Ibid., 23 April 1901.
94. *The Lysaght Century*, op. cit., p. 26.
95. Lysaght Old Company Minute Book, Vol. I, op. cit., 6 March 1893.
96. Ibid., 1 June 1894.
97. Ibid., 22 April 1896.
98. Ibid., Lysaght Old Company Minute Book, Vol. II, op. cit., Directors' Report for 1896, 31 March 1897.
99. Lysaght Old Company Minute Book, Vol. II, op. cit., Directors' Report for 1897, 6 April 1898.
100. Ibid., Directors' Report for 1898, 20 June 1899.
101. Ibid., Directors' Report for 1900, 23 May 1901.
102. Lysaght Old Company Minute Book, Vol. I, op. cit., 22 April 1896.
103. Ibid.
104. Lysaght Old Company Minute Book, Vol. II, op. cit., Directors' Report for 1898, 20 June 1899.
105. Ibid., 8 November, 18 November 1898.
106. Ibid., Directors' Report for 1899, 31 May 1900.
107. Lysaght Old Company Minute Book, Vol. I, op. cit., Directors' Report for 1895, 22 April 1896.
108. Lysaght Old Company Minute Book, Vol. I, op. cit., 29 March 1895.

109. Ibid., 19 November 1895.
110. Ibid.
111. Ibid., 23 June 1896.
112. Ibid.
113. Ibid., 13 January 1897.
114. Lysaght Old Company Minute Book, Vol. II, op. cit., 21 October 1897.
115. Ibid., 26 January 1898.
116. Ibid.
117. Ibid., 17 January 1899.
118. *The Lysaght Century*, op. cit., p. 18.
119. Ibid., p. 18.
120. Lysaght Old Company Minute Book, Vol. II, op. cit., Directors' Report for 1897, 6 April 1898.
121. Lysaght Minute Book, Vol. I, op. cit., 16 May 1905, p. 158.
122. Lysaght Minute Book, Vol. II, op. cit., 18 July 1811, p. 68.
123. Lysaght Minute Book, Vol. I, op. cit., 15 July 1902, p. 46.
124. *Lysaght Century*, op. cit., p. 18.
125. Lysaght Minute Book Old Company, Vol. II, op. cit., Directors' Report for 1899, 31 May 1900.
126. Lysaght Minute Book, Vol. I, op. cit., Directors' Report for 1903, 3 May 1904, p. 113.
127. Ibid., 17 August 1909, p. 335.
128. Lysaght Minute Book, Vol. II, January 1910–March 1917, 23 May 1910, p. 19.
129. Ibid., 17 January 1911, p. 44.
130. Ibid., 21 November 1911, p. 80.
131. Ibid., 21 January 1913, p. 141.
132. Lysaght Old Company Minute Book, Vol. II, op. cit., Directors' Report for 1900, 23 May 1901.
133. Lysaght Minute Book, Vol. I., op. cit., 5 May 1903, p. 122.
134. Lysaght Old Company Minute Book, Vol. II, op. cit., 5 November 1901.
135. Ibid., 5 December 1900.
136. Ibid., 13 December 1900.
137. 'The Story of Brymbo' (typescript), pp. 12, 14–15, 19; Carr and Taplin, *British Steel Industry*, op. cit., pp. 103, 269.
138. Lysaght Minute Book, Vol. I, op. cit., 22 November 1904, p. 132.
139. Ibid., 24 January 1905, p. 135.
140. Ibid., 16 May 1905, p. 158.
141. Ibid., 2 June 1905, p. 162.
142. Ibid., p. 163.
143. Ibid., 20 June 1905, p. 167.
144. Ibid., 18 July 1905, pp. 169–70.
145. Ibid., 17 October 1905, p. 176.
146. Ibid., 21 November 1905, p. 178.
147. Ibid., p. 179.
148. Ibid., 18 December 1905, pp. 181–2.
149. Ibid., 24 April 1906, p. 196.
150. Lysaght Minute Book, Vol. II, op. cit., 16 November 1910, p. 37.
151. Lysaght Minute Book, Vol. I, op. cit., 17 July 1906, p. 209.
152. Ibid., 14 May 1907, pp. 247, 253.
153. Carr and Taplin, *British Steel Industry*, op. cit., p. 290.

154. G.R. Walshaw and C.A.J. Behrendt, *The History of Appleby-Frodingham*, Scunthorpe (1950), pp. 5, 7–10.
155. Lysaght Minute Book, Vol. I, 21 December 1909, pp. 345–6.
156. Lysaght Minute Book, Vol. II, 16 August 1910, p. 29.
157. Ibid., 12 April 1911, p. 55.
158. Ibid.
159. Ibid., 6 June 1912, p. 113;
160. *Bristol Times & Mirror*, 'Lysaghts' Preference Issue', 5 June 1912.
161. Lysaght Minute Book, Vol. II, 16 July 1912, p. 122.
162. *The Lysaght Century*, op. cit., p. 24; *Lysaght's Scunthorpe Works* [1964], p. 3.
163. Lysaght Minute Book, Vol. I, op. cit., 20 October 1908, pp. 304–5.
164. Ibid., 17 August 1909, pp. 335–6.
165. *Lysaght Venture*, Sydney (1955), p. 2; Jones, 'Steel and Engineering Overseas', op. cit., pp. 165, 166.
166. *Australian Economic History Review*, Vol. X, March 1970, C.B. Schedvin, 'Rabbits and Industrial Development: Lysaght Brothers & Co. Pty. Ltd, 1884–1929', p. 27.
167. Ibid., p. 28.
168. Lysaght Minute Book, Old Company, Vol. I, op. cit., 28 August 1886.
169. Schedvin, 'Rabbits and Industrial Development', op. cit., p. 29.
170. Lysaght Minute Book, Old Company, Vol. I, op. cit., 16 September 1886.
171. Lysaght Minute Book, Old Company, Vol. I, op. cit., 30 August 1895.
172. Ibid., 20 June 1899.
173. Ibid., 7 July 1899.
174. Lysaghts' Galvanised Proprietory Ltd with Thomas Davy, 7 September 1900.
175. Lysaght Minute Book, Vol. I, op. cit., 16 June 1903, p. 79.
176. Lysaght Minute Book, Old Company, Vol. I, op. cit., 25 June 1889.
177. Ibid., 1 June 1894.
178. Ibid.
179. Ibid.
180. Ibid., 29 March 1895.
181. Ibid.
182. Lysaght Old Company Minute Book, Vol. II, op. cit., 6 April 1898; 20 June 1899.
183. Ibid., 20 June 1899.
184. Ibid., 23 May 1901.
185. Lysaght Old Company Minute Book, Vol. I, op. cit., 22 April 1896.
186. Lysaght Old Company Minute Book, Vol. II, op. cit., 23 May 1901.
187. Lysaght Minute Book, Vol. I, op. cit., 15 July 1902, p. 45.
188. Ibid., 20 August 1907, pp. 256–7.
189. Lysaght Minute Book, Vol. II, 2 November 1911, p. 81.
190. *Lysaght Century*, op. cit., p. 25.
191. Lysaght Minute Book, Vol. II, 22 September 1914, p. 224.
192. Ibid., 20 April 1915, pp. 243–44.
193. Ibid., 16 December 1915, p. 281.
194. Ibid., 18 April 1916, p. 295.
195. *Lysaght Century*, op. cit., p. 26.
196. Lysaght Minute Book, Vol. II, 16 December 1915, p. 279; Carr and Taplin, *British Steel Industry*, op. cit., p. 305.
197. *Lysaght Century*, op. cit., p. 26.
198. Ibid.

199. 'Some Facts in connection with the establishment of the Galvanised Industry in Australia' (typescript, n.d.).
200. *Lysaght Century*, op. cit., p. 29.
201. BSC Orb Works, 'Whitley Committee Minute Book, No. 1, November 1917 to November 1918', 11 February 1918, p. 14.
202. Whitley Committee Book, No. 2, January 1919 to April 1927, 3 November 1919, p. 24.
203. Ibid., 12 April 1920, p. 37.
204. Ibid., 1 November 1920, p. 54.
205. Ibid., 10 January 1921, p. 58.
206. Ibid., 14 February 1921, p. 59.
207. Ibid.
208. Ibid., 7 March 1921, p. 63.
209. Ibid., 13 June 1921, p. 66.
210. The missing Vol. III would have covered the period 1917 to July 1921.
211. Figures adjusted by the Bank of England's index of consumer prices, 1930 = 100.
212. Ibid., 11 August 1921, p. 69.
213. Lysaght Minute Book, Vol. 4, op. cit., 26 October 1921, p. 18.
214. Ibid., 2 January 1922, p. 83.
215. Ibid., 4 December 1922, p. 112.
216. Lecture delivered to the Newport & District Metallurgical Society, Newport, on 6 October 1987 by E.C. Lysaght.
217. *Sheet Trade Board, Extracts from Minutes 1920–1935*, No. 515, 'Pack Mill, Newport', p. 180.
218. Ibid., p. 181.
219. Whitley Committee Book, Vol. 2, op. cit., 7 May 1923, p. 123.
220. Orb Works, 'Film of the Rolling Operations', (*c.* 1946).
221. Whitley Committee Book, Vol. 2, op. cit., 7 March 1927, p. 225.
222. Ibid., 5 November 1923, p. 140.
223. *Lysaght Century*, op. cit.
224. Lysaght Minute Book, Vol. 5, op. cit., 24 July 1928, p. 153.
225. *Lysaght Century*, op. cit., p. 29.
226. Whitley Committee Book, Vol. 1, 14 November 1917, p. 1.
227. Orb Works Whitley Committee, Constitution, March 1955.
228. Whitley Committee Book, Vol. 2, op. cit., 5 February 1923, p. 117; 2 July 1923, p. 127.
229. Interview by E. Jones with E.C. Lysaght, December 1983.
230. Whitley Committee Book, Vol. 2, op. cit., pp. 7 January 1924, p. 146; 7 April 1924, p. 150.
231. Ibid., 2 February 1925, p. 172.
232. Ibid., 6 July 1925, p. 183.
233. Ibid., 7 September 1925, p. 187.
234. Ibid., 4 April 1927, p. 227.
235. Lysaght Minute Book, Vol. 4, op. cit., 19 December 1923, p. 182.
236. Lysaght Minute Book, Vol. 4, op. cit., 27 January 1925, p. 258.
237. *Lysaght Venture* Sydney (1955), p. 7.
238. Whitley Committee Book, Vol. 2, 12 May 1924, p. 153; *John Lysaght Ltd., Sheet Steel for Motor Bodies* [n.d.]
239. Ibid., 8 March 1926, p. 200.
240. Ibid., 14 June 1926, p. 209.

241. Lysaght Minute Book, Vol. 5, 18 January 1928, p. 125.
242. Ibid., 20 April 1928, p. 136.
243. Ibid., 21 November 1929, p. 242.
244. Ibid., 17 December 1929, p. 247.
245. Lysaght Minute Book, Vol. 6, June 1931–November 1935, 7 January 1932, p. 56.
246. Ibid., 3 June 1931, p. 1.
247. Ibid., 6 April 1933, p. 164.
248. Ibid., 2 November 1933, p. 207.
249. Ibid., 3 October 1935, p. 350.
250. Lysaght Minute Book, Vol. 7, op. cit., 3 September 1936, p. 60.
251. Ibid., 4 March 1937, p. 100.
252. *Lysaght Century*, op. cit., p. 32.
253. W.K.V. Gale, *The British Iron and Steel Industry, A Technical History*, Newton Abbot (1967), pp. 149–50; Carr and Taplin, *British Steel Industry*, op. cit., p. 407.
254. Lysaght Minute Book, Vol. 7, December 1935–July 1940, 5 December 1935, p. 4.
255. *Lysaght Century*, op. cit., p. 42.
256. Ibid., 7 April 1938, p. 182.
257. Ibid., 1 September 1938, p. 210.
258. Ibid., 2 March 1939, p. 247.
259. Ibid., 4 May 1939, p. 261.
260. Ibid., 6 April 1939, p. 253; 4 May 1939, p. 262.
261. Lysaght Minute Book, Vol. 4, op. cit., 26 July 1922, p. 79.
262. Ibid., 24 January 1923, p. 121.
263. Ibid., 20 December 1922, p. 115.
264. Lysaght Minute Book, Vol. 5, April 1926–May 1931, 21 June 1926, p. 15.
265. Ibid., 20 October 1926, p. 34.
266. Ibid., 18 November 1926, pp. 39–40.
267. Ibid., 19 January 1927, p. 50.
268. Ibid., 20 October 1927, p. 102.
269. Ibid., 19 September 1928, p. 161.
270. Ibid.
271. Ibid., 16 January 1929, p. 183.
272. Ibid., 18 September 1929, p. 226.
273. Ibid., p. 227.
274. Ibid., 18 March 1930, p. 269.
275. Ibid.
276. Ibid., 5 November 1930, p. 310.
277. Ibid., 3 December 1930, p. 318.
278. Ibid., 7 January 1931, p. 326.
279. Ibid., 4 March 1931, p. 341.
280. Ibid., p. 343; *Bristol Evening Times*, 5 March 1931, 'Section of Lysaghts Works to leave Bristol'.
281. Lysaght Minute Book, Vol. 6, June 1931–November 1935, 4 February 1932, pp. 65–6.
282. Ibid., 7 April 1932, p. 81.
283. Ibid., 3 August 1932, p. 104.
284. Lysaght Minute Book, Vol. 7, op. cit., 2 December 1937, p. 157.
285. Ibid., 4 April 1940, p. 329.

286. Lysaght Minute Book, Vol, 4, op. cit., 23 June 1922, p. 70.
287. Lysaght Minute Book, Vol. 5, op. cit., 20 October 1927, p. 121.
288. Ibid., 18 December 1928, p. 184.
289. Lysaght Minute Book, Vol. 6, op. cit., 4 February 1932, p. 66.
290. Interview, E.C. Lysaght, December 1983.
291. Lysaght Minute Book, Vol. 7, 6 July 1939, p. 277.
292. Whitley Committee Book, Vol. 2, op. cit., 3 October 1921, p. 74.
293. Lysaght Minute Book, Vol. 4, op. cit., 29 September 1921, p. 15; 23 November 1921, p. 25.
294. Ibid., 25 April 1922, p. 53.
295. Ibid.
296. Ibid., 26 July 1922, p. 78.
297. *Hull and Lincolnshire Times*, 28 July 1923, 'Interesting Gathering at Normanby Park Works', output in 1920 averaged 2,600 tons per week and rose to 3,500 tons in 1923.
298. Lysaghts Minute Book, Vol. 5, op. cit., 6 August 1930, p. 293.
299. Ibid., 1 October 1930, p. 301.
300. *Lysaght Century*, op. cit., p. 35.
301. Ibid.
302. Lysaght Minute Book, Vol. 6, op. cit., 7 January 1932, p. 55.
303. Ibid., 7 April 1932, p. 88.
304. Ibid., 4 May 1933, p. 170.
305. Ibid.
306. Ibid., 4 January 1934, pp. 224–5.
307. Lysaght Minute Book, Vol. 7, op. cit., 2 April 1936, p. 29.
308. Ibid., 4 June 1936, pp. 44–5.
309. Ibid., 4 November 1937, pp. 149–50.
310. Ibid., 3 March 1938, p. 174.
311. Ibid., 5 May 1938, pp. 188–9.
312. Ibid., 2 June 1938, p. 194.
313. Ibid., 7 July 1938, p. 201.
314. Ibid., 1 September 1938, p. 208.
315. Ibid., 6 April 1939, pp. 252–3.
316. Ibid., 7 December 1939, p. 299.
317. Ibid., 8 January 1940, p. 311.
318. Lysaght Minute Book, Vol. 5, 20 February 1930, p. 261.
319. Ibid., 4 June 1930, p. 285.
320. Ibid., 1 October 1930, p. 303.
321. Lysaght Minute Book, Vol, 6, op. cit., 3 June 1931, pp. 1–2.
322. GKN Minute Book, Vol. 9, op. cit., 4 June 1931, it. 5929.
323. Lysaght Minute Book, Vol. 6, op. cit., 5 August 1931, pp. 21–2.
324. Lysaght Minute Book, Vol. 7, op. cit., 6 February 1936, pp. 16–17.
325. Ibid., p. 17.
326. Ibid., 4 June 1936, p. 47.
327. Ibid., 8 April 1937, p. 102.
328. Ibid., 3 June 1937, p. 125.
329. Lysaght Minute Book, Vol. 4, op. cit., 19 August 1921, p. 1; 29 September 1921, p. 9; 24 January 1923, p. 119; *The Ironmonger*, 13 September 1919, p. 75.
330. Interview with E.C. Lysaght, December 1983.
331. *DBB*, Vol. 3 (1985), Jones, 'W.R. Lysaght', op. cit., p. 900.
332. Lysaght Minute Book, Vol. 4, 25 September 1925, p. 303.

333. Lysaght Minute Book, Vol. 5, 22 September 1926, p. 25.
334. Ibid., 22 July 1927, p. 92.
335. *DBB*, Vol. 4 (1985), Jones, 'K.S. Peacock', op. cit., p. 570.
336. Lysaght Minute Book, Vol. 5, 26 June 1928, p. 146.
337. Ibid., p. 147.
338. *DBB*, Vol. 3 (1985), Jones, 'W.R. Lysaght', op. cit., p. 902.
339. Lysaght Minute Book, Vol. 5, op. cit., 24 July 1928, p. 152.
340. *Lysaght Century*, op. cit., p. 56.
341. Interview with E.C. Lysaght, September 1987.
342. Ibid., 16 April 1930, p. 280.
343. Lysaght Minute Book, Vol. 4, op. cit., 25 May 1922, p. 59.
344. Lysaght Minute Book, Vol. 6, 5 October 1933, pp. 197–8.
345. Information from Sir Richard Brooke, July 1988; *Lysaght Century*, op. cit., p. 59.
346. Lysaght Minute Book, Vol. 6, op. cit., 5 July 1933, p. 177.
347. Ibid., 3 January 1935, pp. 303–4.
348. Ibid., 7 March 1935, pp. 315–16.
349. Ibid.
350. Interview, E. Jones with E.C. Lysaght, December 1983.
351. Lysaght Minute Book, Vol. 7, 7 May 1936, p. 37.
352. Ibid., 4 June 1936, p. 50.
353. Ibid., 4 May 1939, pp. 260–1.
354. Ibid., p. 310.
355. Ibid., 4 January 1940, pp. 308–9.
356. Ibid., p. 309.
357. Ibid., 6 June 1940, pp. 339–40.
358. *Lysaght Century*, op. cit., p. 61.
359. Whitley Committee Book, Vol. 2, 2 February 1920, p. 32.
360. Lysaght Minute Book, Vol. 4, op. cit., 24 April 1924, p. 208.
361. Ibid., 22 July 1924, p. 229.
362. Lysaght Minute Book, Vol. 6, op. cit., 1 March 1934, p. 243.
363. Ibid., 7 March 1935, p. 319.
364. Lysaght Minute Book, Vol. 7, op. cit., 2 September 1937, p. 140.
365. Lysaght Minute Book, Vol. 7, op. cit., 4 January 1940, p. 311.
366. Whitley Committee Book, Vol. III, 7 July 1941, item 1853.
367. Ibid., 4 March 1940, item 1775.
368. Lysaght Minute Book, Vol. 7, op. cit., 4 July 1940, p. 352.
369. Interview with E.C. Lysaght, September 1987.
370. Whitley Committee Book, Vol. III, 2 November 1942, item, 1908; 1 January 1945, item 2007.
371. Lysaght Minute Book, Vol. 7, op. cit., 4 July 1940, p. 353.
372. *Lysaght Century*, op. cit., pp. 37, 39.
373. Ibid., pp. 36–7.
374. Whitley Committee Book, Vol. III, 5 November 1945, item 2042.
375. Ibid.

3 Coal: Rise and Fall, 1919–35

> Everything being now relative, there is no longer
> absolute dependence to be placed on God, Free
> Trade, Marriage, Consols, Coal or Caste.
> John Galsworthy, *A Modern Comedy* (1929)[1]

In 1925, when the extensive colliery interests belonging to GKN had achieved an annual output of over 6 million tons and employed 36,000 men,[2] coal was perceived as being the most important holding within the group, more significant than steel or fasteners. In South Wales only the Powell Duffryn Steam Coal Co. was larger, and in 1938 after the two had merged they were responsible for one-third of the productive capacity of the region. The directors with responsibility for the colliery subsidiaries held sway on the board and chief among them, Henry Seymour Berry, Lord Buckland, was elected chairman in 1927. Supported by his deputy and close friend, Sir David Llewellyn, a possessor of technical expertise and extensive local knowledge, he had been able to alter the shape of GKN's senior management team so that by the late 1920s it had become dominated by executives recruited from the South Wales coal industry. Among those introduced by Berry were T.J. Callaghan, E.A. Mitchell-Innes and Sir Leonard Llewelyn. The growth in output achieved from the 1880s to 1914 by the South Wales coalfield[3] was not sustained in the interwar period when annual totals were consistently lower in response to declining and increasingly competitive markets, which prompted pit closures and high unemployment and, in turn, a greater level of industrial unrest. In response to poor profits and over-capacity, GKN's many colliery subsidiaries were brought together in 1930 to form a single, merged company, Welsh Associated Collieries (WAC). Although not conceived with such a motive at the time, this consolidation prepared the ground for disposal in 1935 when WAC was sold to Powell Duffryn. This, in effect, brought the involvement of GKN in coal mining to an end, an activity which had its roots in the Dowlais Iron Co.'s decision in 1861 to enter wholeheartedly the 'sale coal trade'.[4] The intensification of this policy in the early nineteen-twenties proved to have been a costly mistake, though it was a course of action which had been carefully planned and had obtained a considerable measure of support, not only from within the group but in financial circles as well.

THE POST-WAR BOOM: BERRY AND LLEWELLYN

Although not on the scale of the Powell Duffryn Coal Co., the number of pits owned by GKN at the end of the Great War was nevertheless substantial and it was among the principal colliery companies of South Wales. In addition to the Dowlais Collieries (which included the Nantwen, Bedlinog, Cwmbargoed and Fochriw pits), they had acquired the Cyfarthfa Collieries, had sunk a deep pit at Abercynon (employing 2,835, with an output of ½ million tons per annum) and owned several mines at Cwmbran inherited from the Patent Nut & Bolt Co.[5] By 1924 this group of collieries employed 9,600 workers underground and a further 1,880 above ground with an annual output of 1.6 million tons of coal.[6] In 1918 membership of the Colliery Committee, which took responsibility for the daily operation of the group's pits, was composed of Edward Steer (chairman), Lt. Col. C.H.C. Guest, F.W. Keen and H. Probyn with J.H. Jolly as secretary. Because the coal trade had hitherto been considered a subsidiary activity, none of these directors had any direct working interest in the industry so that technical expertise and practical information had to be supplied by Howell R. Jones,[7] the general manager of the Dowlais Works and Collieries, and H.W. Martin, chief colliery manager there.[8] The only director on the main board with experience of the coal trade was John Paton (1864/5–1943), who had been appointed in January 1919.[9] Nevertheless, as chairman of Partridge, Jones & Paton Ltd., owners of six pits and a steelworks at Newport,[10] his involvement was rather that of a consultant, being elected, along with Howell R. Jones, as GKN's representative on the board of the Meiros Colliery Co. in March 1920.[11] In view of his non-executive position, Paton did not become a member of the Colliery Committee until September 1925,[12] and resigned as a director of GKN in August 1930 because of growing commitments to his own undertakings.[13] An opportunity existed, therefore, for an ambitious director whose power-base lay in the South Wales coal industry to establish a position of authority on the GKN board.

The accounts which survive for 1919 do not show adequately the scale of the profits earned by GKN's coal companies. Over the ten months to 30 April 1919 Dowlais and Cardiff Works together with the collieries made a profit of £42,803, a negligible figure in comparison with the screw works which achieved a surplus of £342,468.[14] Matters improved appreciably during the post-war boom and during the eight months to 29 February 1920 Dowlais Works and the collieries recorded a profit of £171,248, though Nettlefolds, including Rogerstone Works, made £339,443.[15] The buoyancy of their exports extended the boom experienced by the coal trade until the end of 1920 even though it had broken for the economy as a whole in April.[16] Consequently, the contribution made by the Dowlais Works and collieries rose and in the ten months to 30 April 1920 they earned £435,630 of the total manufacturing surplus of £910,738.[17]

18 The Dowlais–Cardiff Colliery, Abercynon, seen from the north-west (*c.* 1935). Opened in 1894, two pits were eventually sunk to a depth of 740 yards. It was established to provide the Cardiff steelworks with supplies of coking coal (*Welsh Industrial and Maritime Museum*).

Concerned to improve the supply of coking and steam coal to their steelworks at Dowlais, Cardiff and Rogerstone, the Colliery Committee offered to purchase the Meiros Collieries, and its subsidiary, the South Rhondda Colliery Co. (1898) Ltd., in August 1919. The price was considered too high,[18] and GKN's takeover was delayed until March 1920.[19] By this time, however, a fundamental change had occurred in the disposition of the main board, one which was to have major implications for the group's interest in coal. For on 20 February 1920 a merger had been concluded between GKN and John Lysaght (p. 5), resulting in H. Seymour Berry and D.R. Llewellyn being elected as directors and the former as deputy chairman.[20]

19 Nantwen Colliery, Bedlinog (*c.* 1910) (*Welsh Industrial and Maritime Museum*).

20 A tour of inspection to Dowlais. Left to right: Howell R. Jones, possibly Edward Steer, H. Seymour Berry, Sir David Llewellyn, Lt. Col. C.H.C. Guest, —, — (John A. Owen).

Both men had been brought up in South Wales, were of middle-class origins and became intimately involved in the coal industry. Henry Seymour Berry (1877–1928), later Lord Buckland and chairman of GKN from 1927 until his death, was born at Merthyr Tydfil, the eldest son of Alderman John Mathias Berry, J.P., (1847–1917), an estate agent.[21] Born in Haverfordwest, the latter then lived at Camrose in Pembrokeshire working as a station master for the Great Western.[22] The move to Merthyr in 1874 followed marriage to Mary Ann Rowe of Pembroke Dock and a transfer to the Taff Vale Railway.[23] J.M. Berry subsequently worked as a travelling salesman, principally in tea, but in 1894 established himself as an auctioneer and estate agent. A strict nonconformist, Berry contributed towards the cost of building the Congregationalist Chapel in Market Square. His enthusiasm was for politics and he served as first secretary of the Merthyr Liberal Party and in 1911 was elected the town's mayor. D.A. Thomas (1856–1918), later

Viscount Rhondda, commented that he had little trouble with electioneering as these matters could be safely entrusted to his capable agent, J.M. Berry. A respected member of Merthyr's middle class, he built up a profitable estate agency practice and on his death in 1917 left £23,842.

The eldest of J.M. Berry's three sons, H. Seymour Berry was educated at St. David's Primary School (paying 2d. a week) and at Abermorlais Higher Grade School, the first in South Wales to provide free teaching to those passing an examination. Eventually he trained and qualified as a school teacher at Abermorlais but in 1898 was sued for hitting a child.[24] Although the case was dismissed the magistrate advised Berry to abandon teaching and he joined his father's estate agency business in Victoria Street, Merthyr. When J.M. Berry retired in 1909, Seymour ran the firm.[25] Prepared to take risks, yet with determination and attention to detail, he pursued the career of estate agent with considerable success. He gambled on property on his own account as well as on his father's firm but was also prepared to offer a small margin on a large deal.[26] It was, perhaps, in this period that H. Seymour Berry learnt the rudiments of business, and was later able to re-apply his skills to the buying and selling of companies rather than houses.

By 1915 H. Seymour Berry felt that he could exercise his talents no further in the estate agency firm and sought a new challenge. In December 1914 he had acquired his first directorship in a colliery, the Britannic Merthyr Coal Co. and decided that this was an industry in which he might be able to make his name. Berry approached his father's lifelong friend, D.A. Thomas, to ask whether he might work in his mighty organisation, the Cambrian Trust. Unimpressed, the latter replied on 20 June 1915:

> My dear Berry,
> Reverting to your suggestion of yesterday, I do not see at the moment how I can utilise your service in any official capacity. You will probably find that a trip to the United States at the present time would prove of much interest, and to a young businessman like yourself with your future before you, of great educational value.[27]

Not perturbed by this rebuff, Berry arranged to visit Thomas, and offered to work without a salary until his value was established. Thomas granted him a trial, suggesting that Berry attempt to close a deal which the former had himself failed to conclude. Succeeding in the enterprise, H. Seymour Berry found himself appointed as a close financial aide.[28]

D.A. Thomas, although more interested in politics than business, had become one of the leading figures in the South Wales coal industry. The son of a Merthyr grocer, who spent his latter years running two deep mines, the Cambrian Collieries at Clydach Vale, he took a second-class degree in mathematics from Gonville and Caius College, Cambridge. His ambition to pursue a political career in London was frustrated by the death of his father in 1879, and he returned to join the family business and to study mining. From 1907 and the acquisition of the Glamorgan Coal Co., Thomas pursued a policy of growth through take over, purchasing pits adjacent to the Cambrian collieries. These retained their separate names and identities but fell under the overall control of the Cambrian Trust, a holding company, which by 1910 embraced 6,868 acres centred on the Rhondda with an output of 3 million tons.

In order that he could pursue his career in Parliament (he served as Liberal MP for Merthyr from 1888 until 1910) and manage such a large organisation, Thomas delegated to young men of ability. He once advised 'it is not only a question of finding the right man, the great thing is to know how to use him when you have got him'.[29] Berry was fortunate in the timing of his approach to Thomas for as the latter's daughter, Margaret, later Viscountess Rhondda, recounted, her father had

> for some time been on the look out for younger men of enterprise and energy. 'You must always have a good man to swing a deal on', he would say – during the last two or three years of his life he used Mr Berry as his right-hand man on many occasions.[30]

Thomas himself desired 'the prize of success, of recognition. He loved praise almost as a child does; it was very sweet to him'.[31] He was also highly ambitious with a contempt for those who were not. Extremely shy as a young man, Thomas remained taciturn and intimidating with those whom he did not like.[32] Berry, however, met with his approval and respect, becoming a trusted adviser.

The real turning point for Berry came in 1916 when Thomas joined Lloyd George's War Cabinet and subsequently became Minister of Food Control. He could no longer run his colliery group himself and Berry together with Thomas's daughter, Margaret, took increasing control.[33] During this period the Consolidated Cambrian group (the name having changed in 1913) expanded rapidly. In 1916, for example, six undertakings were added to the Thomas empire, including the Elder Collieries in Maesteg, D. Davis & Sons' pits in Ferndale, North's Navigation Collieries, the Gwaun-cae-Gurwen Co. and the International Coal Co. The combine, which employed 6,000 miners, had an annual output of over 8 million tons or about one-seventh of the South Wales coalfield. By 1919 Berry held sixty-six directorships, mainly in colliery companies, many of them the result of acquisitions effected in 1918–19 in conjunction with D.R. Llewellyn. However, they also included the chairmanship of the publishers of the *Merthyr Express*, Tarian Printing & Publishing Co. of Aberdare and the deputy chairmanship of the Cambrian News Co., Aberystwyth, and Messrs Gee & Co. of Denbigh. Within a period of less than ten years he had risen from being a successful estate agent in Merthyr to one of the most powerful industrialists in Wales. He was fortunate, indeed, that D.A. Thomas, a noted administrator, was called out of political retirement to visit America in 1915 and in the following year was appointed president of the Local Government Board.

Whilst Berry owed his rise to financial organisational and negotiating skills, David Richard Llewellyn (1879–1940) followed a different path to eminence in the South Wales coal trade. The eldest son of Alderman Rees Llewellyn (1857–1919),[34] manager of the Bwllfa Colliery, Cwmdare, he was educated at Aberdare Higher Grade School and Llandovery College. Llewellyn, known as 'D.R.', began his career in the coal industry as a mining surveyor, like his father. Having served his articles with R. Vaughan Price at the Maris Collieries, near Neath, in 1900 he took a two-year course in mining at University College, Cardiff, qualifying as a mining engineer. In 1903, whilst in America to study mechanical mining, his obvious abilities brought him two offers of employment, one as a mining engineer and the other as chief engineer for the State of British Columbia. However, his prospective wife, Magdalene, the daughter of the Rev. H. Harries of the Libanus Baptist Church, Treherbert, did not wish to emigrate to the United States. In 1905, on returning to Wales, he acquired the Windber Colliery and developed this small drift mine with the aid of electrically driven coal cutters, believed to have been the first introduced to South Wales.[35] He was said to have been a pioneer in the working of seams considered too thin or unworkable to be developed commercially.

In 1916, having proved both his technical skills and business acumen, Llewellyn was offered the chairmanship of the Gwaun-cae-Gurwen Co.'s extensive anthracite mines, a company recently acquired by D.A. Thomas. Until this time Llewellyn and Berry's paths had never crossed, and their first meeting, one of chance, occurred in a railway carriage whilst travelling on the Great Western from Porthcawl to Cardiff.[36] From this beginning developed a close friendship and complementary business association. Both were around forty and from similar backgrounds; Berry provided the commercial acumen and contacts, while Llewellyn understood the mining industry in all its technical aspects. Talented and ambitious, they made a formidable partnership.

Their most spectacular acquisition took place in September 1919, when in conjunction with D.A. Thomas's daughter, Margaret Mackworth,[37] they obtained a controlling interest in John Lysaght Ltd. (p. 5) at a cost of £4.5 to £5 million. This gave them a secure entrée into the steel industry and subsequently led to their involvement with GKN following the amalgamation of the two companies in January 1920.

Berry and Llewellyn followed their Lysaght coup in October 1919 by taking over Graicola Merthyr Co. of Swansea for £2 million.[38] With an output of 600,000 tons of anthracite, it was the largest manufacturer of patent fuel in South Wales at over one million tons per annum. Early in 1920 they purchased two more collieries through existing holdings: North's Navigation bought Celtic Collieries and the Imperial Navigation Coal Co. absorbed the Cynon Colliery Co., Berry becoming chairman of both acquisitions.[39] In May 1920 Llewellyn, Berry and H.H. Merrett took over the Crown Patent Fuel Co. for £2 million which gave them 80 per cent of the briquette output of the UK.[40] The Aberpergwm Mineral Estate (2 million tons) was purchased for around £4 million in July 1920 by Llewellyn, Berry and associates. A tract twenty miles by two, it contained estimated coal reserves of 1,200 million tons and they planned to increase its existing daily output of 1,000 tons by ten times. Similarly, Berry and Llewellyn purchased the Idle Rock Colliery at Glyn Neath in June 1921 with a view to re-opening its workings and thereby offer employment to around 500 men.[41]

Of the two, perhaps Llewellyn received the best press in South Wales. One obituary described him as

> a masterful, determined personality, with a sense of humour ... He had, too, a charm of manner which endeared him to all who knew him ... Naturally quick-tempered, his passion was not long lasting.[42]

His son, Sir Harry Llewellyn, the Olympic showjumper, recounted an incident which occurred when his father was teaching him to drive. He had impetuously waved his fist at another motorist whereupon Sir David Llewellyn quickly told him to pull up and explained that this was 'for that other chap to come back and beat the hell out of you for being so rude'.[43] His son also recalled a sense of responsibility towards the coal trade. This led him to delay the closure of a pit which would cause heavy unemployment, which, in turn, forced Llewellyn to lean on the banks to maintain colliery companies that had little prospect of profitability.[44] Unfortunately there were so many of these in the interwar period that no amount of prevarication could solve the inherent problems of the South Wales economy. Nevertheless, he remained faithful to his dictum 'coal stood by my family and I will stand by coal'.[45]

Herbert H. Merrett (1866–1957), chief commercial advisor to Llewellyn and with whom he founded a coal marketing company, Llewellyn, Merrett & Price, in 1918–19, decribed his old friend 'D.R.' as

> a pioneer and a producer, with a faith in the coal industry which could never be broken down – a heritage from his father ... He might have been a greater personality than the late Lord Rhondda had he not found it necessary to devote so much attention to other interests. 'D.R.' was at his best in defence of his principles, and I have sat beside him many times when he faced organised attack by disgruntled people who, by reason of his sincerity and fearlessness, soon became his greatest admirers.[46]

By contrast, it is more difficult to gather an appreciation of the personality of H. Seymour Berry. Contemporary descriptions were both rare and brief, while his unexpected death, aged fifty, produced few detailed obituaries. However, a typescript, 'The Berry Brothers' written by a grandson of Lord Buckland, Robert Smyly, quoted several of his speeches which revealed something of his philosophy. The first, delivered at the Merthyr Drill Hall in 1922, was in support of the Conservative candidate, Sir Richard Mathias. Against a barrage of hostile interruptions he spoke:

> I say to the Labour Party in Merthyr in all seriousness that I have endeavoured to be, in my position, as big a friend to labour as any man amongst you. (Cheers) . . . Two years ago I was elected a director of Guest Keen & Nettlefolds. I was a Merthyr boy . . . I was educated in the town, and not sent out of the town at great expense for my education. I had myself as a boy very definite views in this upon the responsibility of the great employers of capital in this district . . . My opinion was that the great employers in this district had not done their duty. When I got inside I resolved to find out what the real state of things was . . . I found that the position of the old collieries at Dowlais was appalling, and that coal was being produced at a price that could not possibly compete with other collieries in South Wales.
>
> It was felt that the older collieries had had their day and must sooner or later cease, but fortunately we had on the board a man of imagination and genius [D.R. Llewellyn] who understands mining thoroughly and who recommended, contrary to the wishes of the rest of the directors, that the upper measures should be explored and that we should see if it were possible to get the measures worked . . That has been tried.
>
> A little over twelve months ago the Dowlais Works had been idle for many months . . . No man had greater worry than I did . . . I felt it was our duty, even if we lost heavily . . . I succeeded (and I think that I am entitled to the credit for it) to my joy in starting the Dowlais Works . . . When half of the iron and steel works in the country were idle, and at enormous loss month by month for the last twelve months.[47]

As Berry himself noted in a further speech, delivered two days later, he was the first GKN director to address a meeting in Merthyr, which in view of the stormy circumstances was an act of some courage. As regards his personal qualities, he was undoubtedly a man of ability. With a facility for mental arithmetic and a passion for detail, Berry could intuitively decipher a balance sheet.[48] More impetuous than his younger brothers, he considered risk taking an essential ingredient of success.

H. Seymour Berry revelled in pitting his wits against a business rival and gloried in a successful deal. For example, in 1928 when Sir Alfred Mond refused to pay an additional £10,000 for the Gwaun-cae-Gurwen Co., Berry suggested that they spin a coin to settle the matter. He won the call. A gifted salesman, he could sway a slower mind, a fact, together with his success, which contributed to a degree of unpopularity.

An unashamed entrepreneur, Berry coined the motto: the labourer is worthy of his hire, but so is capital. He genuinely believed in the virtues of capitalism and pursued its principles with enthusiasm and determination, even if these would involve conflict with established interests and the trade unions. An interventionist state could only ruin people's initiative and drive, he believed. A generous patron of hospitals, Berry once observed that 'people are spoonfed to such an extent that one wondered if there were any spirit of fatherhood left' and hoped that 'the day would never come when the state would interfere with the running of the hospitals'.[49] He was not, however, cold-hearted. A vital person, restless when alone and animated in company, he became a philanthropist. Amongst his larger gifts were £25,000 to establish a technical institute in Merthyr,[50] £20,000 towards the building of a new hospital at Ponsarn,[51] £8,000 for a swimming pool,[52] £7,000 towards the new science wing at University College, Cardiff,[53] and in addition he donated many smaller sums to local charities and bodies such as the Merthyr Town Football Club, Dowlais Male Voice Choir, Brecon County Infirmary, and the National Museum of Wales in Cardiff. On 6 July 1923 H. Seymour Berry became the third Freeman of Merthyr,[54] Lord Merthyr and Viscount Rhondda being the other two. When he received his peerage in July 1926, as Lord Buckland of Bwlch, the title was listed as being for 'public, political and philanthropic services'.

From October 1922, Berry lived at the Buckland Estate at Bwlch in Breconshire. Comprising 2,600 acres, it included five miles of trout and salmon fishing on the Usk and some of the finest shooting in South Wales. The large house, built in 1895, featured a 70ft hall. As a result of his involvement in the coal industry, Berry had become very wealthy and on his death left unsettled property to the value of £1,116,447. His will, drafted in September 1920, established a trust which was to grant relief to the poor of Merthyr. It was to be funded by the grant of ordinary or second preference shares in GKN to the value of £50,000. Other GKN shares were allocated for the provision of prizes at local schools and for the Market Square Congregational Chapel.[55]

On 23 May 1928, while riding with his groom, Weaver, Berry was killed. He had a habit of taking an early morning ride before settling down to the business of the day. The two were galloping through a field across which ran a line of telegraph poles. Chatting to Weaver, he did not notice that the horse was heading dangerously close to a pole. The mare swerved at the last moment sending Berry headlong; his skull was fractured and death instantaneous.[56]

How, then, did people regard Berry? Doubtless there were groups of miners and steelworkers, particularly those who had been thrown into unemployment by closures or rationalisation, for whom his name would not have been held in high esteem. However, there were others whose jobs he had sought to preserve. Lord Hartwell, his nephew, recalled that at his funeral the streets were lined three deep.[57] Berry appears to have been unpopular among the Cardiff merchants who are said, according to anecdote, either to have drunk champagne or sung the Nunc Dimittis on hearing the news of his death.[58] Their grievance undoubtedly had its roots in D.A. Thomas' decision to diversify into sales and marketing, thereby making the coal exchange redundant. Berry had administered this strategy for Thomas and reapplied it when at GKN. In addition, it is possible that both by virtue of their large holdings were able to force favourable rates from the merchants, which would have added to any resentment.

Paying tribute to Berry shortly after his death, T.P. O'Connor, father of the House of Commons, observed that 'he loved a great joke as hugely as a great stroke of business. He never took himself with any pretentious seriousness'.[59] How can Berry be summarised? The son of an austere, hard-working, Non-conformist estate agent, he was a risk taker, quick-thinking, a man who took pleasure from striking a bargain or entertaining friends. Not afraid to disturb established interests, if this would result in economies or improved profits, Berry upset the Cardiff merchants, some doubtless jealous of his rapid success.

As well as never forgetting his roots in Merthyr, Berry remained tenaciously loyal to those who had helped him in his rise to power and rewarded them with directorships in his various holdings. When he discovered that the tax affairs at Lysaghts required considerable clarification he approached S.A. Putnam, an income tax inspector at Merthyr, in whom he had great confidence.[60] Putnam was persuaded to leave the Civil Service to become company secretary and ultimately a director of John Lysaght. Similarly, William Trimmer (1872/73–1926),[61] managing director of the Uskside Engineering Co. and who had informed Berry of the lack of confidence held by Gerald Lysaght in the family business, was rewarded with directorships in Lysaghts (becoming managing director of the St Vincent's Works) and Joseph Sankey & Sons.

To increase the representation of the coal industry on the GKN board and to include its sales and marketing activities, T.J. Callaghan (1859/60–1935) was elected a director in December 1920.[62] Born in Cardiff and educated at Ratcliffe College, Leicester, in 1874 he had entered the coal exporting firm of Louis Gueret. Succeeding the founder as head of the business, he became a director of Consolidated Cambrian and was chairman of its subsidiary, the Naval Colliery Co. (1897) Ltd. During the Great War, Callaghan served as vice-chairman of the Central Executive for the Supply of Coal to France and Italy and in 1918–19 was President of the Cardiff Chamber of Commerce.[63] Callaghan remained a director of GKN until his death, having also been appointed to the board of WAC.

COLLIERY ACQUISITIONS

The strategic policy adopted by GKN toward the coal industry, under the auspices of Berry and Llewellyn, was essentially that devised by the former's mentor and master, D.A. Thomas. Until the Edwardian period when Thomas began his combination movement, the South Wales coal trade had been characterised by myriad producers of varying sizes surrounded by a considerable number of sales and marketing companies. He preferred to view the entire coalfield as a single gigantic interest with common economic needs, and argued that the existing structure was fair neither to capital nor labour.[64] Taking advantage of falling values from the mid-1890s, he campaigned for a co-operative organisation which could regulate both production and prices. Steam coal, claimed Thomas, had an inelastic demand so that small variations in either supply or demand had equally disproportionate effects on prices. When these fell individual owners boosted output in an attempt to reduce unit costs and in doing so inadvertently exacerbated a saturated market. However, Sir William Lewis, later Lord Merthyr (1837–1914),[65] chairman of the Monmouthshire and South Wales Coal Owners Association and the architect of the sliding scale agreement with the miners, had little sympathy for any scheme that might control output and ensured in 1896 that although owners representing 79.3 per cent of output agreed to the adoption of Thomas's plan, it was in the event rejected.

Having failed to persuade the South Wales coal industry as a whole to accept a degree of co-operation, Thomas then set out to implement his theories in a more limited business context. In 1906 the board of Cambrian Collieries, under his auspices, initiated a policy of purchasing neighbouring pits, beginning with the acquisition of the Glamorgan Coal Co.[66] Other pits soon followed including those of the Naval Colliery Co. Defying commercial convention, Thomas decided to sell and ship his own coal. In 1907 he took over L. Gueret Ltd., a sales agency, in order to develop a network in France and Italy, while the formation of Amaval, Sutherland & Co. extended it to South America. In the previous year he had set up Lysberg Ltd. to break the monopoly held by Cardiff merchants over the import of pit props from south-west France, and claimed to have saved a million pounds during its first twelve months of operation. A holding company, the Cambrian Trust, had been set up to consolidate the new vertically integrated organisation. In 1916 when the Consolidated Cambrian Trust bought the Ferndale Collieries, Thomas defined his motives as being,

> the standardisation so to speak of policy, management and administration ... The effect of a combination of this kind will be to eliminate the speculative middle-man but not to interfere with the bona fide merchant, to whose enterprise in the development of foreign markets for the distribution of the Welsh product colliery owners owe so much.[67]

This strategy of obtaining control over groups of neighbouring collieries (which, given the geological conditions of the region, determined the type of coal extracted) and then integrating vertically into sales and marketing was studied by Berry while working for Thomas during the Great War. Once he and Llewellyn had joined the board of GKN they set about extending this grand plan to the group's colliery holdings and those in which they had a personal interest.

With Edward Steer assuming an increasingly non-executive role as chairman of GKN, and H. Seymour Berry growing in authority, the group turned its attention towards the South Wales coal industry. In October 1921 it was agreed that GKN should purchase the Gwaun-cae-Gurwen Colliery Co. from the Disposal and Liquidation Commission,[68] and the acquisition was completed during the following year. Situated near Swansea with two pits, the company was one of the largest anthracite mines in Wales with 1,500 employees and an annual capacity of 300,000 tons.[69] Whilst GKN owned pits producing coking, steam, gas, household and bituminous coals, this takeover represented their entry into the anthracite market and indicated that their coal holdings were no longer merely considered as a profitable sideline nor as a means of supplying their various manufacturing enterprises.

Ironically, in 1921, the year that GKN turned its attention to coal and took a strategic change of direction, a note of warning had been sounded by Thomas Evans, a director and commercial manager of the Ocean Coal Co., in a local publication headed 'The Achievements of the South Wales Coalfield':

> While the outlook is clouded, there is no cause for apprehending a calamity which would involve the entire commercial structure of the coalfield. There are unfortunately many signs and portents which gave rise to anxiety, but it is easy to over-colour the position, and give false emphasis to the shadows in the picture.[70]

Doubtless both Berry and Llewellyn would have concurred with this interpretation, though events were to prove the predictions of Evans to be optimistic.

The two most important acquisitions in GKN's strategy for coal were effected in 1923. On 13 November a special meeting of the board was called with the sole purpose of considering proposals for obtaining control of D. Davis & Sons Ltd and Consolidated Cambrian Ltd by purchase of their ordinary shares,[71] both formerly major parts of the Thomas' empire with a combined value of around £2.5 million. The latter then comprised five colliery companies: Cambrian Collieries, Glamorgan Coal Co., Britannic Merthyr Co., Naval Collieries and Duffryn Aberdare Colliery Co. In addition, it held a half interest in the Blaenclydach Colliery Co. and the Cambrian Wagon Co. D. Davis & Sons, which operated nine pits at Ferndale in the Rhondda Fach, had an output of about 1½ million tons per annum, while the Consolidated

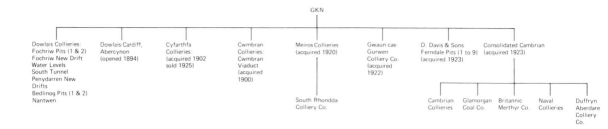

Figure 4   The principal coal holdings of GKN, c. 1925

Cambrian produced 2¼ million tons.[72] In both cases the takeover was to be effected by an exchange, one ordinary share in GKN for an ordinary share in D. Davis, and two ordinary shares in GKN for one ordinary share in Consolidated Cambrian. By 12 December 1923 owners of 86 per cent of the former's share capital and 91 per cent of the latter's had agreed to the conversion, and the acquisition went ahead.[73] As a result, the total output of GKN's collieries was raised to 6½ million tons per annum, which represented nearly a ninth of the South Wales coalfield's capacity.[74]

Why, then, did Edward Steer and his fellow directors of GKN agree to take over these two colliery companies? Aside from the question of why the group became more deeply involved in the coal industry, personalities lay at the root of the acquisition of these particular businesses. Sir David Llewellyn was chairman of D. Davis & Sons and H. Seymour Berry sat on the board.[75] The latter had succeeded to the chairmanship of the constituent companies in Consolidated Cambrian group and Sir David Llewellyn was in effect his deputy.[76] In effect, therefore, the senior management of two companies were requesting their share-holders to agree to an acquisition by another company in which they occupied an almost equally powerful position. It was not so much a takeover as a rationalisation of two men's personal authority.

Added to these personal and specific reasons for merger, the macro economic situation encouraged managers to believe that the future was propitious for investment. Two astute American commentators on the British coal mining industry characterised the years 1922 to 1924 as the 'era of New Hope'.[77] It was an apt description since the period corresponded with a marked revival in the export demand for coal. However, the factors responsible for this upturn were not likely to prove of a lasting nature: the 1922 miners' strike in America of sixteen weeks duration whose beneficial effect on prices and output was recorded by GKN's Colliery Committee;[78] and the military occupation of the Ruhr throughout 1923 which drastically curtailed German output. The latter's effect on prices, and the anticipated fall which would result from a restoration of normal activities, encouraged GKN in April to sell coal forward for the remainder of the year.[79] As a result of international events, UK output rose from 163.25 million tons in 1921 to 249.61 in 1922 and 276.0 in 1923, coal exports being 24.7, 64.2 and

79.5 million tons respectively.[80] South Wales was particularly reliant on overseas sales, exporting 53 per cent (29,875,916 tons) of its total output in 1913 as compared with 25 per cent by the UK as a whole, and 42 per cent (20,229,802 tons) and 15 per cent respectively in 1919.[81] Exports from the region totalled 15.47 million tons (33 per cent) in 1920 and 21.45 million tons (48 per cent) in 1925. In response to rising prices during August 1922, for example, GKN decided to re-open the Cyfarthfa Collieries which had been closed in June because of 'falling demand, the poor working conditions and the heavy loss sustained'.[82] Taking a short-term view of events in the early 1920s, it is possible to see why the directors of GKN could be persuaded by Berry and Llewellyn to increase the group's holding in coal.

On a more fundamental level it is not difficult to comprehend why so much business faith should have been vested in collieries. 'Our civilisation', observed George Orwell in 1937,

> *is* founded on coal ... The machines that keep us alive, and the machines that make the machines that make the machines, are all directly or indirectly dependent upon coal. In the metabolism of the Western world the coal-miner is second in importance only to the man who ploughs the soil. He is a sort of grimy caryatid upon whose shoulders nearly everything that is *not* grimy is supported.[83]

In the 1920s coal was the primary fuel for nearly all energy used, including most forms of transport other than a few railways and a growing proportion of shipping.[84] Like bread or potatoes, coal was an article of universal consumption in Britain and the industrialised economies. Used in houses, factories, power stations and by steam locomotives, liners and cargo vessels, how could its extraction and sale be anything but a profitable enterprise? Against the background of the lush decades of the 1870s, 1880s and 1890s when many of the pits of South Wales had been sunk, it seemed that they had only to overcome labour and organisation problems to turn their collieries into veritable gold mines.

South Wales, as a region, was particularly suited to the creation of combines. It possessed a virtual monopoly within the UK of dry steam coal (which was purchased in large quantities by the Royal Navy because when burnt it did not give off a tell-tale smoke plume on the horizon; coal of this quality was also sold at the upper end of the market to domestic consumers as a naturally smokeless fuel). Further, the topography of the district, focusing human activity within a number of self-contained valleys added to the degree of concentration. Dependence on the export trade enhanced the links between the many colliery companies and the various selling agencies, which in times of adversity also provided a motive for common action. The existence of steelworks in the valleys and on the coastal strip beside the ports provided yet a further element in any combination designed to secure economies of scale through vertical integration.[85]

The acquisition of the Cambrian combine and D. Davis & Sons was followed in January 1924 by the election of two new directors to the GKN board, Edward Alfred Mitchell-Innes K.C. (1863–1932), and Sir Leonard Wilkinson Llewelyn (1874–1924).[86] The former owed his appointment to his chairmanship of the Consolidated Cambrian and its subsidiary, the Glamorgan Coal Co.[87] Sir Leonard Llewelyn, who died aged fifty of heart trouble in June 1924,[88] had extensive experience of the South Wales coal trade and had been a former general manager of the Cambrian combine. The son of Llewellyn Llewelyn, a general manager of Powell Duffryn, he was educated at Monmouth Grammar School, Cheltenham and Heidelberg, serving an engineering apprenticeship in various South Wales pits.[89] Aged twenty-four Llewelyn became manager of the Clydach Vale Pit, part of the Cambrian Colliery Co. and after several other posts became general manager of the Cambrian group when it was being extended by D.A. Thomas. Like Sir David Llewellyn he was able, ambitious and hard-working. 'Genial in his relations with the miners', the *Colliery Guardian* recorded that

> he was fearless during strikes, and capable of real heroism in colliery disasters. At the time of the Clydach Vale explosion in 1915, he fought night and day the fire which raged in the pit and for his bravery, he was the recipient of the first silver medal awarded by the Royal Humane Society for saving life in mines ... His work in the Senghenydd disaster, when he led rescue parties into the danger zone was also memorable.[90]

The loss of Sir Leonard Llewelyn clearly detracted from the expertise and experience that GKN could draw upon regarding the coal industry, though as events were to work out it is unlikely that his premature death was of overwhelming consequence.

Soon after the acquisition of D. Davis & Sons and the Cambrian combine, affairs in the South Wales coal industry took a turn for the worse. Throughout 1924 the depression in the UK economy deepened. With the resumption of coal production in the Ruhr and reparations deliveries in the aftermath of the Dawes Agreement of August, the British coal industry with a cost structure consistent with pre-war levels of prosperity, was exposed for the first time to the realities of the long-term market.[91] The situation worsened in 1925 when the UK coal industry operated with an average loss of 10.25d per ton, in comparison with a profit of 1s 2d per ton in 1924 and 2s 2.25d per ton in 1923. From September 1924 to March 1925 more than half the collieries in Britain ran at a deficit, a proportion which had risen to 67 per cent by the end of May 1925. The level of unemployment in the industry climbed from 2.1 per cent in March 1924 to 25 per cent by June 1925.[92] Reliant as it was upon exports, South Wales suffered more acutely than most coal-producing districts in the UK.

The deteriorating situation encouraged GKN to rationalise its production and wind up its less profitable and loss-making pits. This was a process which had begun as early as January 1923 when Sir David Llewellyn had reviewed the 'serious losses' incurred at the Dowlais Collieries. Bedlinog had the worst record and was to be closed as soon as possible.[93] In part, the age of these pits lay at the root of their commercial failure. An inspection of the Cwmbran Colliery revealed that 'it was clear that the working conditions there were difficult owing to the long haulage, and particularly to the very difficult formation of the roofs'.[94] It was agreed that these old seams be abandoned and new ones opened in undeveloped measures. Soon afterwards GKN resolved not to renew the leases on the Cyfarthfa Collieries, and the Viaduct Colliery near Cwmbran was offered for sale.[95]

In view of the 'considerable losses' which were accruing at the Dowlais Collieries, the closure of the Bedlinog, Fochriw and South Tunnel pits (opened for the most part in the 1880s)[96] was considered.[97] To maintain production and reduce the level of redundancies a series of new drift mines were opened as quickly as possible in the Dowlais area 'so that at a later suitable date when output had increased from the new drifts, the old collieries of the company could be closed down'.[98] In October 1923 it was decided that work at South Tunnel pit would cease and the men employed would be transferred to Bedlinog to form a double shift.[99] By now the board recognised that demand for coal would not continue to grow as in the period preceding the Great War and that the problem facing GKN, and other coal producers, was not how to satisfy a rapidly expanding market but how to rationalise output and introduce efficiencies. The Dowlais New Drifts did not meet expectations and in February 1924 it was reported that 'only one seam had proved economical to work'.[100] The company also announced that Fochriw and South Tunnel pits were to close in April.[101] In June, as the situation worsened, the decision was taken to end working at Bedlinog. 'The serious unemployment which would be caused by the closing down of the pits was considered at length', by the GKN board and they 'agreed that if some suitable scheme could be evolved for the workmen themselves to operate the colliery for the remainder of its years of life, such a plan would receive every consideration'.[102] In the event, no such plan materialised and the two pits at Bedlinog had closed by October 1923.[103] Thus, the Dowlais Collieries, once a source of great wealth to GKN, had been effectively wound up.

Declining orders and falling prices prompted GKN to shut down the Cyfarthfa Collieries temporarily in October 1924. Because they had an estimated ten years working life and the numbers of unemployed were already large in the Merthyr district it was felt, in the opinion of H. Seymour Berry, 'that the effect of stopping permanently at the present time would . . . react very unfavourably on the company'.[104] In

November, when the new workings at Cwmbran had failed to generate the profits anticipated, it was decided to stop this pit, though in view of the adverse publicity generated over the Dowlais Collieries the date of closure, at some point in 1925, was to be deferred.[105] The opinion of the Colliery Committee, advanced at the end of 1924, that 'prices and conditions in the coal trade were about as low as they were ever likely to reach'[106] proved to be optimistic as matters continued to deteriorate throughout the following year.

In an attempt to raise the overall profitability of the group's holding in coal, in February 1925 it was decided to transfer managerial responsibility for the few remaining units (the Nantwen Colliery and the new drifts) of the Dowlais Collieries to the neighbouring steelworks.[107] In April it was reported the drifts were nearing a remunerative level and that the loss on this group of workings for 1925–26 would probably not exceed £20,000.[108] The Colliery Committee, anxious to dispose of the Cyfarthfa Collieries (mature pits with a low level of mechanisation), gave notice to staff that their services could be terminated by 31 July 1925.[109] In the event the mines were sold to W.M. Llewellyn (d. 1943),[110] Sir David Llewellyn's younger brother, the purchase price to be satisfied by the allotment of 15,000 £1 shares in the new private company to be called Llewellyn (Cyfarthfa) Ltd.[111] When, in November 1926, Hills Plymouth Co. went into liquidation and its collieries threatened with closure, W.M. Llewellyn and H. Seymour Berry agreed to purchase them. As the latter pointed out in an interview with the press, his motive was not, as in previous acquisitions, a commercial one, but concern for the people of Merthyr, given the unemployment that would have resulted. The new company, styled Llewellyn (Plymouth) Ltd, was run by W.M. Llewellyn.

Since wages accounted for around 70 per cent of total costs,[112] employers adhered consistently to the belief that the most effective way of improving productivity was either to cut piece rates or to increase the length of the working day. In December 1924 Sir David Llewellyn offered his support to the lobbying by South Wales coal owners for the re-establishment of the eight-hour day and Parliament's removal of the seven-hour maximum.[113] The Samuel Commission, which investigated the coal industry in 1925 and reported in March 1926, elucidated a gloomy analysis of the immediate market situation and its future prospects.[114] This prognosis encouraged the Colliery Committee in their view that the South Wales coalfield could only be saved if the men accepted 'longer hours or reduced wages' but recognised the difficulties entailed in accomplishing this object.[115] Sir David Llewellyn concluded that their only realistic course of action was to 'obtain deals on an individual pit basis, and to reduce costs. Pits would be closed from time to time to secure the necessary reforms'.[116]

With surplus capacity and low prices, matters remained bleak throughout 1925. Even more modern and well planned mines were affected: after touring D. Davis & Sons, Sir David Llewellyn and Howell

R. Jones recommended that Pits 2 and 4 and a district in one other pit be closed. This action would reduce the company's output from 1.4 million to 1 million tons and, they hoped, would trim costs, though the 'close proximity of the pits ... and the working of seams above one another' created considerable problems of rationalisation.[117] In view of the continuing depression in the coal market it was decided in November 1925 that new seams proven at the South Rhondda Colliery Co. would not be exploited and plans for sinking a new shaft and installing equipment were postponed.[118]

The fortunes of the coal industry in Britain improved only marginally during the autumn and winter of 1925–26. In the December quarter of 1925, for example, 90 per cent of the tonnage in South Wales was raised at a loss.[119] By April 1926 the average price of coal for export had fallen by two shillings per ton since the previous summer, a situation exacerbated by the return to the Gold Standard in April 1925. The consequent over-valuation of sterling did not help the industry's international competitiveness[120] but the claim that this was directly responsible for the 1925–26 crisis ignores the fact that the colliery companies' financial difficulties pre-dated this new fiscal policy and were directly linked to the re-opening of German coalfields with their superior production techniques (p. 100), following the Franco-Belgian withdrawal from the Ruhr in April 1924.

Pressure to accept reduced wages persisted throughout April 1926 and on 1 May when the owners' demand for district agreements and lower rates of pay was refused, the miners were locked out. Three days later a national stoppage was called and it lasted until May 12. Although the General Strike was comparatively short-lived, the miners refused to return to work until compelled to do so by suffering, having held on for a further six months. In the meantime the government, under Stanley Baldwin, had suspended the maximum seven-hour day in coal mines for a period of five years.[121] However, the depression which persisted in the coal industry throughout the remainder of the 1920s simply served to demonstrate that its troubles were deep-seated such that longer hours and lower wages were not in themselves sufficient to restore the profitability of the pre-war years.

Conditions in the British coal industry deteriorated after 1926, and particularly so in South Wales, for several reasons. Prime among them was the success of the large and efficient mines in Germany and Poland.[122] Output per manshift of saleable coal grew at a greater rate there than in the UK (Table 3.2) and as a result the Poles were able to undercut markets.[123] The introduction of import restrictions in France and Spain in the summer of 1927,[124] both countries to which South Wales collieries sold extensively, and the continuation of coal reparations by Germany to Belgium, France and Italy served to reduce the demand for GKN's coal further (see Table 3.1).

Having increased the working day and cut wages as far as was acceptable, the coal owners were forced to consider other strategies to

Table 3.1 UK coal production, 1919–38

Year	Total output (million tons)	Exports (million tons)
1919	229.8	35.2
1920	229.5	24.9
1921	163.3	24.7
1922	249.6	64.2
1923	276.0	79.5
1924	267.1	61.7
1925	243.2	50.8
1926	126.2	20.6
1927	251.2	51.2
1928	237.5	50.1
1929	257.9	60.3
1930	243.9	54.9
1931	219.5	42.7
1932	208.7	38.9
1933	207.1	39.1
1934	220.7	39.7
1935	222.3	38.7
1936	228.5	34.5
1937	240.4	40.3
1938	227.0	35.8

Source: Supple, *History of the British Coal Industry, Vol. 4*, op. cit., pp. 174–5, 273.

Table 3.2 Output per manshift of saleable coal, 1913, 1925–36 (Statute Tons)

Year	UK	Germany (Ruhr)	Poland
1913	1.016	0.930	1,125
1925	0.901	0.931	0.923
1926	0.923	1.096	1.102
1927	1.031	1.114	1.172
1928	1.065	1.172	1.247
1929	1.085	1.251	1.244
1930	1.081	1.332	1.233
1931	1.081	1.464	1.348
1932	1.124	1.599	1.388
1933	1.147	1.649	1.564
1934	1.168	1.651	1.677
1935	1.177	1.665	1.746
1936	1.168	1.683	1.810

Source: Coal Mining, [Reid] Report of the Technical Advisory Committee, Cmd. 6610, London HMSO (1945), p. 141.

improve performance. Being so reliant on exports, the South Wales colliery companies were among the first to discuss schemes of combination and co-operation. At the suggestion of Berry and Llewellyn, GKN forged closer links with the selling agencies. The group decided to use its 50.1 per cent holding in L. Gueret & Co. to take over another sales and marketing business, Llewellyn, Merrett & Price.[125] The amalgamation was completed in January 1927 and the new company called Gueret, Llewellyn & Merrett.[126] As foreign demand for Welsh coal continued to be described as 'poor', the various colliery companies met to organise an 'arrangement to avoid the drastic cutting of prices which had taken place recently. Most of the larger companies which had stood aloof from such a proposal were now willing to consider it'.[127] However, negotiations were not immediately fruitful and in September 1927 GKN's directors were still urging the adoption of a co-operative scheme to avoid unnecessary competition, this being 'absolutely essential in order to prevent a serious loss occurring in the coalfield in South Wales'.[128]

The serious nature of international competition was revealed in the autumn of 1927 when the sales agents wrote to T.J. Callaghan, chairman of Gueret, Llewellyn & Merrett, to point out

> the difficulty in keeping the collieries working when competitors were selling under the price of 20 shillings per ton f.o.b. ports. [As a result the GKN] board considered that in order to avoid serious losses to the collieries of the group arising from irregular working, the sales agents should be authorised to exercise their judgement so that they [can] . . . take orders below 20 shillings per ton f.o.b. if that means collieries could be kept working approaching full time.[129]

Nevertheless, it was not until January 1928, when it had become clear that the only alternative was the closure of several collieries, that Sir David Llewellyn could report that plans to introduce a co-operative selling system for South Wales were well advanced.[130] By May serious efforts were being made to get the scheme working effectively.[131] The events of 1928 dealt the final blow to the most ardent optimists. With overall losses as high as 11d per ton and unemployment reaching 23 per cent of the insured workforce, this was the worst year for the coal trade since 1920, discounting 1921 and 1926 when there were labour disputes. During 1928 other districts followed the example of South Wales and set up regulatory bodies to control prices.[132]

The policy of rationalisation and concentration within the many colliery subsidiaries owned by GKN was pursued during the tough three years from 1926. The process of acquisition and incorporation had not resulted in any major changes to individual colliery companies which continued to operate under their original names with a largely unchanged management, maintaining existing work practices and

Table 3.3   Output of coal in South Wales and Monmouthshire, 1913–39

Year	Output (tons)	South Wales as % of UK	Output per man year (tons)
1913	56,830,317	—	—
1914	53,879,752	—	—
1915	50,452,600	—	—
1916	52,080,765	—	—
1917	48,507,965	—	—
1918	46,716,552	20.51	213.46
1919	47,552,306	20.68	184.79
1920	46,248,967	20.15	170.34
1921	30,572,003	18.73	131.65
1922	50,325,094	20.16	207.09
1923	54,251,587	19.66	214.51
1924	51,085,135	19.12	204.04
1925	44,629,522	18.35	204.67
1926	20,272,572	16.05	93.00
1927	46,256,363	18.41	238.12
1928	43,311,966	18.24	257.10
1929	48,149,613	18.67	269.70
1930	45,107,912	18.50	260.75
1931	37,084,852	16.90	234.31
1932	34,874,302	16.71	239.18
1933	34,354,884	16.59	240.22
1934	35,173,317	15.94	251.35
1935	35,025,110	15.76	265.63
1936	33,886,179	14.83	268.06
1937	37,773,013	15.71	277.56
1938	35,901,100	15.55	259.28
1939	—	15.24	269.32

Source: Colliery Year Book and Coal Trades Directory (1924), p. 629; (1939), p. 561; Ministry of Fuel and Power, South Wales Coalfield, Regional Survey Report, London HMSO (1946), p. 53.

customers. Early in 1927 it was decided to concentrate the office staffs of these discrete organisations, which resulted in further redundancies and 'substantial economy'.[133] Berry had been responsible for devising the scheme and carrying through the alterations 'which although vitally necessary were unpleasant in execution'.[134]

Ageing and unprofitable pits in the group continued to be closed. In May 1927 Sir David Llewellyn recommended that if, for example, the Cwmbran Colliery could not be sold soon, working there should cease as it had proved impossible to bring costs below 2 shillings per ton over the current selling price.[135] When matters failed to improve in November it was decided to terminate the leases before the expiry, paying £10,000 in compensation for loss of royalties and rent, so that the pit could be closed,[136] and the colliery shut at the end of the month after its horses had been sold.[137] Another problem company was Duffryn Aberdare; a producer of steam coals, whose market had collapsed, the colliery operated at a loss.[138] Not surprisingly the offer to sell the business went unanswered, so the Colliery Committee recommended that GKN, in effect, settle the debts of Duffryn Aberdare (in the order of £40–£50,000) and that the company be transferred to a new merged organisation comprising Llewellyn (Cyfarthfa) Ltd and Hills Plymouth Ltd.[139]

The major problems within the GKN colliery holdings concerned the Consolidated Cambrian group of companies, of which Duffryn Aberdare was one. The level of overdrafts had caused their bankers, the National Provincial, to express concern in July 1926. As a result a block of debentures in Naval Collieries (to the value of £75,000) had been deposited with the bank as further security and various cost-saving measures had been introduced but, because of the depth of the depression in the coal trade, these had failed to have any impact on the group's debts by October 1927.[140] To keep the Consolidated Cambrian in operation, Berry was empowered to meet Sir Alfred Lewis of the National Provincial Bank with a view to raising £100,000 to support the enterprise. It was agreed in November that GKN and the National Provincial would each advance £50,000, the latter at bank rate.[141]

Yet with no improvement in the Consolidated Cambrian's performance and the death of Berry in May 1928, the chairman of GKN to whom the colliery group had held a particular interest, it was decided to consider selling this collection of pits. An unspecified 'South Wales colliery company', which turned out to be Powell Duffryn, expressed an interest in acquisition. Although GKN encouraged the deal, hoping that it would also lead to links with their marketing company (Gueret, Llewellyn & Merrett),[142] and Edmund L. Hann of Powell Duffryn began an inspection of the various pits,[143] the worsening financial predicament of the Cambrian group appears to have interrupted any scheme of amalgamation. For in October 1928 the GKN board was warned that writs could soon be served on constituent companies for the non-payment of royalties and other debts.[144] The pits of the Naval Colliery Co. had been closed temporarily and a similar course of action was considered for the Glamorgan Coal Co. Nevertheless, having completed their survey, Powell Duffryn indicated that they wished to continue with the negotiations.[145] At this point the GKN board became wary. They had been warned by Sir David Llewellyn that owing to the depressed state of the coal trade, Powell Duffryn were not as financially sound as might be thought. W.M. Llewellyn, who had accompanied the Powell Duffryn officials on their tour, advised the board that,

> conditions underground [in the Cambrian group of collieries] were probably the best that could be found in South Wales, and that, from a mining point of view, practically the only unsatisfactory feature was the short life (approximately ten years) of the Glamorgan pits. In his opinion it would be a mistake to allow the Powell

Duffryn Co. to acquire the collieries at the relatively small price which they would be likely to offer. Mr. Howell Jones reported on his inspection of the surface plant, which he considered generally satisfactory, and capable of dealing with 30/40% more tonnage than at present.[146]

Given that the pits appeared to be capable of improvement only by radical and expensive methods, and in view of the substantial debts that the colliery group had amassed, GKN concluded that they 'would not be justified in providing further monies which would probably be immediately utilised in the discharge of pressing creditors'. In addition, large sums would be required for working capital over an indefinite period so long as the depression in the South Wales coal trade endured.[147] Consequently, it was decided to liquidate the individual companies forming the Cambrian group. To this end Sir Gilbert Garnsey (1883–1932), the eminent accountant and partner in Price, Waterhouse & Co., was approached to advise on the winding up. In December 1928 when the voluntary liquidation had been effected, Garnsey was appointed receiver of the Glamorgan and Britannic Merthyr Collieries and jointly with Sir Harry Peat as receivers of the Cambrian and Naval Collieries.[148]

Whether the entire scheme of putting the Cambrian group into voluntary liquidation was simply a ruse to rid the collieries of their burdensome debts, and to provide managers with an opportunity to make troublesome miners redundant can never be properly established. The fact that GKN re-acquired the four colliery companies (Cambrian, Naval, Glamorgan and Britannia) in August 1929, when the price from the receiver had fallen to £745,000,[149] suggests that there was at least a measure of calculation in the entire episode.

The other major disposal from the GKN coal holdings was the anthracite mines of the Gwaun-cae-Gurwen Co. In May 1928 a provisional agreement was concluded between Sir Alfred Mond (1868–1930) and Frederick Szarvasy (1875–1948), the company 'doctor' and financier, of the Amalgamated Anthracite Collieries by which they would take over the properties of the Vale of Neath Co. and Gwaun-cae-Gurwen.[150] In August 1928 GKN confirmed that the business would be sold,[151] though its purchase by the recently formed Amalgamated Anthracite Collieries (capitalised at £5 million, with an annual output of 2 million tons and employed 8,000 men) was not announced until January 1929.[152] This, too, was an example of consolidation to achieve economies and marketing leverage.

WELSH ASSOCIATED COLLIERIES AND SALE TO POWELL DUFFRYN

The beginning of 1929 witnessed a slight improvement in the coal trade as an increasing volume of exports pushed prices upwards.[153] This, in turn, encouraged companies to break agreements on minimum prices in order to obtain extra orders and from the autumn of 1929,[154] when production quotas were introduced, to exceed their assigned totals.[155] In view of weakening cartel arrangements, perhaps, and as a residue from the discussions over the purchase of the Consolidated Cambrian group, a scheme to merge GKN's coal interests with those of Powell Duffryn together with the personal interests of Sir David Llewellyn and W.M. Llewellyn was discussed in the summer of 1929. Yet on receipt of a report from Sir William McLintock (1873–1947) on the accounts of GKN's and Powell Duffryn's respective selling organisations thoughts of a grand amalgamation were shelved.[156] The plan, had it come to fruition, would have created the largest colliery company in Britain and one that would have dominated the South Wales coalfield.

The notion of consolidation, however, was not abandoned by GKN. For the main board meeting which rejected the merger, approved a scheme to unite the interests of Gueret, Llewellyn & Merrett, Abercynon, D. Davis & Sons, the four collieries purchased from the receiver of the Cambrian group, and certain companies controlled by Sir David and W.M. Llewellyn.[157] Later in the month the constituents of the new company (to be called Guest, Keen, Gueret & Llewellyn) were defined more closely: Abercynon colliery, the four Cambrian properties, D. Davis & Sons and 180,000 shares in Llewellyn (Nixon), together with GKN's shareholding in Gueret, Llewellyn & Merrett and Llewellyn (Cyfarthfa). In addition, Sir David Llewellyn and W.M. Llewellyn agreed that those companies in which they held a substantial interest (Duffryn Rhondda (1929) Colliery Co., Bwllfa & Cwmaman Collieries, Troedyrhiw Coal Co., Llewellyn (Plymouth), D.R. Llewellyn & Sons, Aberdare Graig Coal Co. and Cynon Colliery Co.) were to be included in the merger.[158] It was also agreed that should the Duffryn Aberdare Steam Coal Co. come on to the market it should be acquired and incorporated within the combine. GKN had sold this colliery to Llewellyn (Cyfarthfa) only two years before (p. 90). The company was, in fact, purchased from the receiver in December for £51,250.[159] In November 1929 it was decided that the name of the new combine bore too much of a resemblance to Gueret, Llewellyn & Merrett and the new style 'Associated Welsh Collieries' was chosen,[160] although in December when Sir David Llewellyn was appointed chairman this too was altered to Welsh Associated Collieries (WAC).[161] W.M. Llewellyn and H.H. Merrett were the managing directors, while Sir John Field Beale, T.J. Callaghan and J.H. Jolly also sat on the board.[162]

Registered on 23 January 1930, WAC had a nominal capital of £8.5 million, GKN being the majority shareholder. It was said to control about one-quarter of the steam coal output of South Wales. Comprising some 60 pits, levels and drifts, the group produced around 10 million tons per annum and employed a workforce of over 32,000 men.

The decision to bring GKN's coal holdings together in a single subsidiary company was not designed solely to improve the management of those collieries. It was in part a move to divide the least profitable activities of the group from its core activities. For at the same time the British (Guest, Keen, Baldwins) Iron & Steel Co. was established to separate their loss-making, heavy steel interests (the steelworks at Dowlais and Cardiff, together with their attendant collieries in the Dowlais area) from the company's other steel activities.[163]

Welsh Associated Collieries did not have an auspicious beginning,[164] as April 1930 was judged to be 'one of the worst months experienced by the South Wales coal trade'.[165] In fact, both total UK production and exports of coal fell every year from 1930 to 1934 when a marginal improvement followed (Table 3.3). Unified control, however, did permit the directors of WAC to co-ordinate the stopping of certain pits and advancing of others 'to an extent that would not have been possible if the collieries had been working as separate units'.[166] By May 1932 Sir David Llewellyn observed that most of the economies which could be achieved through merger had now been secured; they included: a rationalisation of underground workings in those areas of adjacent pits, the introduction of coal-cutters and conveyors, electrification of collieries, the linking up to power-stations, enabling two out of three to be closed at weekends and the centralisation of coal washeries.

As a result, the profits generated by WAC (unspectacular in relation to the capital invested and scale of business) were reckoned to be better than those of other companies operating in the South Wales coalfield.[167] Because WAC felt obliged to appropriate most of the surpluses it earned for depreciation, no dividend on ordinary and preference shares was paid until 1934. In essence, the difficult five years to 1935 when WAC was sold, were made marginally profitable by the existence of price-fixing and quota schemes. Under the South Wales marketing plan WAC was permitted to extract 9 million tons of coal per annum and was guaranteed a minimum price for the various types of coal mined.[168] In June 1932 WAC purchased the Maerdy group of collieries and Lockets Merthyr Co. for a total of £15,000.[169] Although this was described as 'an important addition' it may be that the acquisition was seen as a way of raising the group's quota and eliminating competition rather than as an important output in its own right.

Declining exports encouraged an even greater degree of co-operation within the South Wales coal trade. In October 1932 it was announced that the six largest producers of steam coal, representing 76 per cent of output, had formed a body, Associated Welsh Mines, to regulate marketing and sales.[170] GKN believed that if those organisational links proved successful they might serve as the prelude to a formal merger. Despite this action, however, the profits earned by WAC in the last third of 1932 were 'seriously curtailed' and the collieries worked at below their agreed quota.[171] In February 1933 WAC reported that costs of production had been considerably reduced but no improvement in the level of demand had arisen,[172] and by April their pessimism was complete as prospects for the summer months were described as 'not promising'.[173] At this point WAC threatened to leave the selling organisation, Associated Welsh Mines, because two members had failed to honour the terms of the agreements[174] – a continuing weakness of such bodies since the federations formed by the iron-masters in the eighteenth century. They agreed to withdraw their resignation in July providing that penalties to a maximum of 1s 6d per ton be re-imposed on transgressors and compensation of up to 6d per ton be paid to those abiding by the rules.[175]

In June 1933 because of severe contractions in both domestic and international markets WAC had reduced its output to 70,000 tons per week, a figure well below their quota of 118,000 tons.[176] In August the Colliery Committee reported that 'it was becoming difficult to keep the collieries working at a sufficient tonnage to avoid losses'.[177] T.J. Callaghan acknowledged in November that 'conditions had been poor for some months' but believed that 'there would be, from now on, a gradual improvement'.[178] In fact, the exporting districts, of which South Wales was a prime example, did not share in the general trade revival of the mid-1930s.[179]

In 1930, on its formation, WAC had been loaned £745,000 by GKN at 7 per cent.[180] Because of the unprofitable nature of the South Wales coalfield, the company had been unable to repay any of the principal and in 1934 requested, in view of current money rates and the size of the loan, that the interest be reduced to 5 per cent. On condition that WAC re-organise their financial structure by making a fresh issue of debenture stock to the public, GKN agreed to accept 5 per cent as from 30 June 1932.[181] In August WAC announced the issue of debenture stock, to the value of £1.5 million which, if successful, would allow them to repay GKN at a stroke.[182] Whether this had been conceived primarily as a means of making WAC more attractive to any purchaser is not clear but on 7 December 1934 'after long negotiations a scheme of amalgamation with Powell Duffryn had been agreed'.[183] In effect, GKN's direct involvement with coal was now, after 176 years, at an end.

A new enterprise, Powell Duffryn Associated Collieries, was to be formed to take over the entire assets and liabilities of both companies. Powell Duffryn would acquire 50 per cent of the ordinary share capital of WAC at 10 shillings per share[184] to be paid for by an exchange of Powell Duffryn ordinary stock to the value of £1,181,509 and £87,995 in cash. As a result, the Powell Duffryn element was entitled to two-thirds share of any distribution from the merged company up to £450,000, the remainder going to the former WAC shareholders. J.H. Jolly had represented GKN during 'the long and arduous negotiations',[185] and he, Sir David Llewellyn, H.H. Merrett, W.M. Llewellyn and Sir John Field Beale were elected to the board of the merged company.[186] The amalgamation, formally ratified on 31 March 1935,[187] resulted in GKN's withdrawal from the coal industry except as a consumer and minority shareholder in the Powell Duffryn group.[188] The latter was now the largest coal-producing company in the UK[189] With an output of 12.5 million tons per annum.[190] Its chairman, Edmund L. Hann (1881–1968), descended from a family of mining engineers and colliery owners, as the chief executive of the Powell Duffryn Steam Coal Co., had obtained extensive working experience in the South Wales coalfield,[191] and was the obvious candidate to lead the new merged organisation.

How, then, was it that Powell Duffryn could take over such a large group as WAC? First, Powell Duffryn was the bigger and more profitable company, and one which had pursued a different strategy for growth. In contrast to the coal holding of GKN, a collection of pits purchased from existing owners, some of which had fallen into receivership, Powell Duffryn was a generic mining company. It had a rolling policy of sinking new pits, and through a commitment to technical innovation had some of the best equipped collieries in South Wales. Average profits of almost £340,000 between 1921 and 1925 enabled it to finance new mines and these, in turn, generated surpluses every year but 1928. The colliery companies acquired by GKN or which amalgamated to form WAC were often encumbered by debts, which had prevented either group from sinking any, but a very few, new workings.

REASONS FOR FAILURE: TECHNICAL INNOVATION AND LABOUR RELATIONS

As previous sections have demonstrated, the excursion into coal by GKN could not have been worse timed. The market conditions operating in the 1920s were some of the most depressed that the industry had experienced. However, two further factors played a significant part in the failure of GKN's strategy for coal: an inability to keep pace with technical innovation, and troubled labour relations.

Table 3.2 reveals that as a whole, the UK's productivity fell far short of that achieved in Poland and Germany, while Table 3.3 shows how South Wales declined in relation to Britain as a whole. At the root of these two trends were the techniques by which coal was extracted and the geomorphology of the coalfield. Harry Llewellyn, whilst in the employment of the Amalgamated Anthracite Group, visited Germany and at Essen was

> impressed with the Matthias Stinnes pits with their railway-tunnel-like drivages underground and the efficient manner in which they used their coal cutters, brought the coal to the surface and classified it. In this respect they were probably, on average, technically ten years ahead of British mining methods.[192]

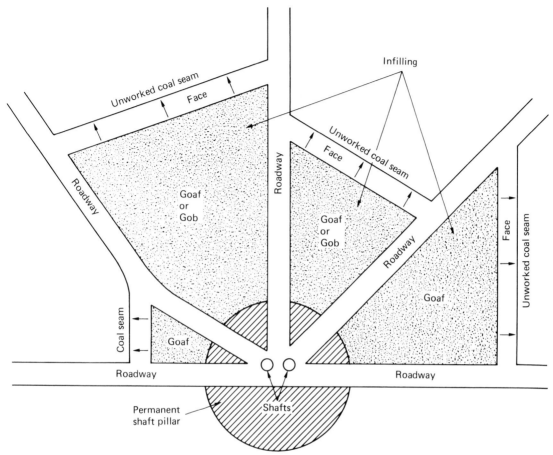

Figure 5 Coal mining by longwall advancing method (*British Coal*).

Llewellyn's description refers to the adoption of 'horizon mining', as distinct from the traditional method of driving roadways to the face through the coal seams themselves. In the latest German pits roads were driven towards one constant horizon at each level, regardless of the strata, before mining operations began. The result was an efficient and well-planned transport system established at the outset, though it required a heavy initial capital expenditure while the enterprise remained unproductive.[193] Pits in South Wales, whether sunk in the late nineteenth century or in the interwar period operated for the most part on the 'longwall advancing' system. This method was relatively swiftly and cheaply applied and provided quick profits, at the expense of continually rising transport costs. In essence, a face was established near the shaft and driven into unknown territory. The roadways cut from each end of face and ran at right angles between it and the shaft. As the coal seams followed irregular and varying gradients the roadways often went up and down and around sharp bends making it difficult or impractical to install mechanical conveyors.

These problems were exacerbated in South Wales by the particularly difficult geological conditions which existed in the region. Although the basin shape of the coalfield made the theoretical extent of known reserves easy to calculate, in practise the great variations in the thickness of seams and the extensive faulting which occurred across the strata made it difficult to estimate the quantity of coal that could be extracted from any given face. Sharp variations in quality compounded the problem. An engineer would be loathe, therefore, to commit his company to heavy capital expenditure in conveyors and cutting equipment only to find that the rich reserves he had expected were proved unworkable by a fault or suddenly narrowing seam.

It was also claimed that the South Wales region suffered from a more than usually powerful 'squeeze', that is, forces of compression acting upon the excavated site. Because the area was worked under the longwall advancing system it was necessary to fill or support the entire space (or 'gob') left by removing the coal. In other districts of Britain where the pressures were less severe, engineers needed to stow only those areas immediately beside the roadways. Because the longwall face was always advancing, dramatic changes in physical conditions could be encountered without warning and this, in turn, could hold up production or cause the abandonment of a particular seam.[194] These factors compounded operating costs in South Wales and generated heavier maintenance charges required to keep the roadways in safe and passable condition.[195] In such geological circumstances locomotive-hauled trains to take coal from the face and take the miners to and from their work, installed at the outset under the horizon system, were almost a practical impossibility for South Wales. As George Orwell observed, 'men commonly travelled three miles to the face from the pit bottom in Britain so that they had already expended considerable physical labour before they began to cut coal'.[196] Orwell was in fact writing of his experiences in Lancashire where mines were generally larger than in South Wales. The smaller nature of pits resulted in Welsh miners rarely having to spend three hours walking to and from the face. However, the more extensive the colliery, the more likely it was that mechanical transport facilities would be introduced. Travelling from shaft was laborious and would have reduced the amount of energy available to the hewer to cut coal.

Until 1938 the British system whereby a landowner also held mineral rights to his property militated against the sinking of large mines. Even when a single owner possessed large estates, he sometimes pursued a deliberate policy of granting leases for comparatively small areas with the intention of increasing his royalty receipts by having several undertakings work the coal simultaneously.[197] South Wales, in particular, was typified by such a system of operation where clusters of small and medium-sized pits extracted coal in close proximity to one another.

Patterns of consumer demand also served to slow the pace at which the industry mechanised in South Wales. The house-coal market was characterised by a demand for large coal which could be handled more easily and would not slip through grates. Mechanised cutting reduced the proportion of large-sized coal and therefore lowered the value of any given quantity. As a result, when attempting to improve efficiency and reduce physical labour, the industry in South Wales tended to adopt pneumatic picks, rather than coal-cutting machines. The former enabled miners to keep the proportion of large coal high but did not raise productivity to the extent desired. Conveyors with their related transfer points and bunkers were considered a source of further breakage. Collieries supplying the domestic market also needed to maintain extensive and labour-intensive surface facilities to sort and clean the coal (screens and washeries), which both added to costs.

Faced with this pattern of ownership and operation, Berry and Llewellyn were severely constricted in the extent to which they could modernise the GKN collieries. Attempts were made to introduce new machinery (in June 1925, for example, a Jeffrey crusher was installed at Nantwen Pit to reduce the size of large coals since demand for them had fallen),[198] however the age and character of WAC's pits prevented wholesale mechanisation. A survey of the South Wales coalfield revealed that the proportion of machine-cut coal there was considerably below the average for Britain (Tables 3.4 and 3.5) and after 1930 fell further behind.[199]

In addition, Berry and Llewellyn inherited a tradition of poor labour relations. Mutual suspicion, often breaking into hostility in the form of strikes or lock-outs, was a feature of the interwar coal industry in Britain. In March 1919, for example, the Dowlais Collieries came out on strike,[200] and when national wage cuts were implemented in the spring of 1921 a three-month stoppage resulted.[201] Industrial disputes were common in the Cambrian Collieries,[202] including a lengthy strike during 1925.[203] The stoppage during 1926 was the most bitter dispute

Table 3.4   The use of coal cutting machines in South Wales, 1930–36

Year	Number of machines	Quantity of coal cut (tons)	Percentage of total output
1930	460	4,328,714	10
1931	484	—	12
1932	437	—	12
1933	454	4,404,169	13
1934	472	—	15
1935	476	—	18
1936	482	7,151,019	21

Source: Ministry of Fuel and Power, South Wales Coalfield Regional Survey Report, London HMSO (1946), p. 64.

Table 3.5   Coal conveyed by machinery in South Wales, 1930–36

Year	Number of conveyors	Number of loaders	Tons conveyed	Percentage of total output
1930	973	5	7,804,660	17
1931	932	16	—	20
1932	975	10	—	20
1933	937	9	7,284,241	21
1934	966	19	—	26
1935	1,052	18	—	32
1936	1,063	19	12,263,303	36

Source: Ministry of Fuel and Power, South Wales Coalfield Regional Survey Report, London HMSO (1946), p. 65.

and although the men returned to employment compelled by hardship, this did not prevent further confrontations. In the winter of 1931–32 the miners in several WAC pits ceased working; Sir David Llewellyn estimated that this strike had cost GKN in the order of £40,000.[204]

It is not difficult to understand why poor industrial relations persisted in the South Wales coal industry. In a period of contracting demand and depression, owners were continually attempting to reduce costs, and given their inability or reluctance to mechanise ageing and medium-sized pits, this limited their options to reducing wages or increasing the length of the working day. Sir David Llewellyn resolutely canvassed for a return to the eight-hour day[205] as the best way of raising the profitability of ailing pits. The miners were implacably opposed to the increase and reluctantly agreed to work the extra hour only after their defeat in 1926.[206] Given the arduous and unhealthy nature of mining and the fact that the working day began when the men reached the coal face (possibly having spent an hour travelling along tortuous roadways from the shaft),[207] it is easy to appreciate why the issue aroused so much resentment.

Perhaps because of the severe cost restraints under which they operated and because collieries in general remained small or medium sized, the South Wales industry had a poor record for the provision of social and welfare facilities for their employees, compared with such enlightened companies as Bolsover or Wigan.[208] Industrial relations would not have been improved by the absence of pithead baths and other welfare buildings.[200]

Sir David Llewellyn, one of the moderate coal owners and one who regularly visited pits to get to know his workforce personally, believed that suspicion and hatred had reached such levels in South Wales that permanent good relations were an impossible goal.[210] He had become resigned to cyclical variations: prosperous spells when piece rates could be raised, moderate periods and then bad times when cuts and stoppages would predominate. The experience of GKN during the 1920s and 1930s did not prove him wrong.

SUMMARY

The decade following the Great War had witnessed a re-ordering in the ranking of GKN's various activities, with coal for the first time being placed at or near the top of the list. Steel-making and engineering in the Midlands often had to take second and third places to the extraction of coal. This strategic re-emphasis occurred principally because the two most dynamic and forceful personalities on the board, H. Seymour Berry and Sir David Llewellyn, had risen to prominence as industrialists by virtue of their careers in the South Wales coalfield. In addition, they believed that the policies introduced so effectively by D.A. Thomas before the Great War could be developed with equal profit afterwards. Accordingly, they assembled an even mightier empire than his, later called Welsh Associated Collieries, comprising pits throughout the region vertically integrated with selling agencies on the one side and steelworks on the other. That their grand plan ultimately failed had much to do with the inherent nature of the industry in South Wales. Old pits, or mines not sufficiently large or well-planned to accommodate the latest machinery and a tradition of poor labour relations conspired in a period of unprecedented economic difficulty to scupper their scheme. After the sudden death of Berry in May 1928, Sir David Llewellyn's enthusiasm declined. As the intractable nature of the problems facing WAC became readily apparent and the composition of the GKN board altered to accommodate representatives of its steelworks and engineering factories, so support for a strategy based upon coal dwindled, and in 1935 the group formally renounced its interest in the industry.

Nevertheless the legacy of coal lived on. To safeguard its minority shareholding, GKN continued to appoint representatives on the Powell Duffryn board (Lt. Col. C.H.C. Guest, J.H. Jolly, Sir David Llewellyn and H.H. Merrett in 1939),[211] and, in turn, elected members of the coal industry to its own ranks. For example, Edmund L. Hann, chairman of Powell Duffryn, became a director of GKN in 1935 and remained on the board until the spring of 1952.[212] In the mould of Sir David Llewellyn or Sir Leonard Llewelyn, Hann had been born into a mining environment, trained and qualified in South Wales and risen rapidly up the ranks of management. In July 1937 Sir Stephenson H. Kent (1873–1954) became a director of GKN.[213] As chairman of the Powell Duffryn subsidiary, Stephenson Clarke, coal factors, distributors of wagon and shipowners, he was a figure of wide influence in the sale and marketing of coal.[214] His vice-chairman, John Scott Hindley (1883–1963), later Lord Hyndley, joined the GKN board for the duration of the Second World War and was, along with Hann, Sir Evan Williams (1871–1959)[215] and Sir Stephenson Kent, one of the senior executives responsible for strategic decision-making in Powell Duffryn.[216] Hindley's particular expertise lay in the sale of coal though he subsequently became the first chairman of the Coal Board. With the retirement of Edmund L. Hann in 1952, GKN's involvement with the industry finally came to an end, an association which may be traced back to the foundation of the Dowlais Iron Co.'s furnace at Merthyr in 1759 when coal was extracted for conversion into coke and later to fuel the ironwork's steam engines.

References

1. John Galsworthy, *A Modern Comedy* (1929), Preface p. xiii.
2. *An Outline History* [c. 1925], op. cit., pp. 60–1.
3. Roy Church, *The History of the British Coal Industry, Vol. 3, 1830–1913; Victorian Pre-Eminence*, Oxford (1986), p. 3.
4. GRO, D/DG, Letter, W. Menelaus to G.T. Clark, 7 November 1861.
5. Jones, *GKN, Vol. One*, op. cit., pp. 341–51.
6. *The Colliery Year Book and Coal Trades Directory* (1924), pp. 129, 201.
7. 'GKN Colliery Committee Minute Book, Vol. IV, January 1918 to May 1920', 4 June 1918, it. 1824.
8. Elizabeth Phillips, *A History of the Pioneers of the Welsh Coalfield*, Cardiff (1925), p. 184.
9. GKN Minute Book, Vol. 3, op. cit., 2 January 1919, it. 3223.
10. *Colliery Year Book* (1924), op. cit., pp. 334, 745; R. Lyttleton's 'Newspaper Cuttings', obituary, February 1943, p. 106; *Colliery Guardian*, Vol. 166, No. 4287, 26 February 1943, obituary.
11. GKN Minute Book, Vol. 3, op. cit., 4 March 1920, it. 3472.
12. GKN Minute Book, Vol. 4, op. cit., 28 September 1925, it. 4818.
13. GKN Minute Book, Vol. 8, op. cit., 7 August 1930, it. 5762.
14. GKN Minute Book, Vol. 3, op. cit., 5 June 1919, it. 3310.
15. Ibid., 1 April 1920, it. 3479.
16. M.W. Kirby, *The British Coalmining Industry 1870–1946*, London (1977), p. 53.
17. GKN Minute Book, Vol. 3, op. cit., 3 June 1920, it. 3518.
18. Ibid., 7 August 1919, it. 3349.
19. Ibid., 4 March 1920, it. 3472.
20. Ibid., 20 February 1920, it. 3458, 3459.
21. For accounts of H.S. Berry's life see: *DBB*, Vol. 1 (1984), Graeme M. Holmes, 'H.S. Berry', pp. 299–301; *Colliery Guardian*, Vol. CXXVI, No. 3283, 30 November 1923, 'Men of Note, No. 17, H.S. Berry', p. 1321; *Colliery Guardian*, Vol. CXXXVI, No. 3517, 25 May 1928, obituary, p. 2052.
22. Information supplied by Lord Hartwell, 1987.
23. Robert Smyly, 'The Berry Brothers' (typescript, June 1982), p. 43.
24. Interview Lord Birkenhead with Hon. Richard Lyttleton, 1976; text supplied by Lord Hartwell.
25. Ibid., p. 1.
26. Information provided by Lord Hartwell.
27. Quoted from Smyly 'Berry Brothers', op. cit., p. 2.
28. Ibid., p. 2.

29. Ibid., pp. 56–7.
30. Margaret H. Mackworth, *D.A. Thomas, Viscount Rhondda*, London (1921), p. 295.
31. Ibid., p. 183.
32. *DBB*, Vol. 5 (1986), M.J. Daunton, 'D.A. Thomas', p. 474.
33. Margaret H. Mackworth, The Viscountess Rhondda, *This was My World*, London (1933), pp. 217, 220, 223–4.
34. *DBB*, Vol. 3 (1985), Graeme Holmes, 'Sir David Richard Llewellyn', pp. 822–26.
35. *Colliery Guardian*, Vol. CLXI, No. 4173, 20 December 1940, Obituary, p. 579.
36. R. Lyttleton's 'Newspaper Cuttings', December 1940, 'Funeral of Sir D.R. Llewellyn', p. 99.
37. The Viscountess Rhondda [Margaret H. Mackworth], *This was My World*, London (1933), pp. 217–24.
38. Smyly, 'Berry Brothers', op. cit., p. 4.
39. Ibid.
40. Ibid., p. 5.
41. Ibid., p. 6.
42. R. Lyttleton's 'Newspaper Cuttings', op. cit., p. 99.
43. Harry Llewellyn, *Passports to Life, Journeys into Many Worlds*, London (1980), p. 14.
44. Ibid., p. 15.
45. Ibid.
46. R. Lyttleton's 'Newspaper Cuttings', ' "D.R." As a Colleague saw Him', *Western Mail*, January 1941, p. 102.
47. Smyly, 'Berry Brothers', op. cit., pp. 7–9.
48. Information provided by Lord Hartwell.
49. Smyly, 'Berry Brothers', op. cit., p. 23.
50. *Colliery Guardian*, Vol. CXXXV, 25 May 1928, op. cit., p. 2052.
51. Smyly, 'Berry Brothers', op. cit., p. 17.
52. Ibid., p. 18.
53. Ibid., p. 20.
54. *Colliery Guardian*, Vol. CXXVI, No. 3282, 30 November 1923, 'Men of Note in the British Coal Industry, No. 17, Mr H.S. Berry', p. 1321.
55. Smyly, 'Berry Brothers', op. cit., p. 25.
56. Ibid., p. 24.
57. Letter Lord Hartwell to E. Jones, 16 December 1987.
58. Letter Lord Hartwell to E. Jones, 10 August 1988.
59. Quoted from Smyly, 'Berry Brothers', op. cit., p. 24.
60. Interview of W.E. Simons by J. Cockcroft, 18 September 1973, p. 11.
61. *Colliery Guardian*, Vol. CXXXII, No. 3430, 24 September 1926, Obituary, p. 680.
62. GKN Minute Book, Vol. 3, op. cit., 4 December 1920, it. 3624.
63. *Colliery Guardian*, Vol. CL, No. 3878, 26 April 1935, Obituary, p. 785. *Colliery Guardian*, Vol. CXXX, No. 3379, 2 October 1925, 'Men of Note, No. 65, T.J. Callaghan', p. 797.
64. *DBB*, Vol. 4, Daunton, 'Thomas', op. cit., p. 475.
65. *DBB*, Vol. 3 (1985), L.J. Williams, 'William Thomas Lewis', pp. 773–8.
66. D.J. Williams, *Capitalist Combinations in the Coal Industry*, Labour Publishing Co., London (1924), p. 96.
67. Quoted from Mackworth, *D.A. Thomas*, op. cit., p. 142.

68. GKN Minute Book, Vol. 3, 6 October 1921, it. 3849; 1 December 1921, it. 3889.
69. *Colliery Year Book* (1924), op. cit., p. 203.
70. A.P. Barnett and D. Willson-Lloyd, *The South Wales Coalfield*, Cardiff [*c*. 1921], p. 21.
71. GKN Minute Book, Vol. 4, October 1922–December 1923, 13 November 1923, it. 4402.
72. Ibid.
73. Ibid., 12 December 1923, it. 4405, 4406.
74. *Colliery Guardian*, Vol. CXXVII, No. 3288, 4 January 1924, p. 25.
75. *Colliery Yar Book* (1924), op. cit., p. 140.
76. Ibid., pp. 729, 742.
77. I. Lubin and H. Everett, *The British Coal Dilemma*, New York (1927), p. 52.
78. GKN Minute Book, Vol. 3, op. cit., 6 April 1922, it. 3983.
79. Ibid., 5 April 1923, it. 4256.
80. Quoted from Barry Supple, *The History of the British Coal Industry, Volume 4, 1913–1946, The Political Economy of Decline*, Oxford (1987), pp. 174–75.
81. *Proceedings of the South Wales Institute of Engineers*, Vol. XXXVI (1920), Hugh Bramwell, 'The Economics of the South Wales Coal-Field', pp. 322–3.
82. GKN Minute Book, Vol. 3, op. cit., 29 June 1922, it. 4047; 7 September 1922, it. 4098.
83. George Orwell, *The Road to Wigan Pier*, London (1937), Harmondsworth (1962), p. 19.
84. William Ashworth with Mark Pegg, *The History of the British Coal Industry, Vol. 5, 1946–1982, The Nationalised Industry*, Oxford (1986), p. 38.
85. D.J. Williams, *Capitalist Combination in the Coal Industry*, London (1924), pp. 98–9.
86. GKN Minute Book, Vol. 5, op. cit., 3 January 1924, it. 4426.
87. *Colliery Year Book* (1924), op. cit., pp. 186–7; *Who was Who*, Vol. III, p. 949; Barnett and Willson-Lloyd, *South Wales Coalfield*, op. cit., p. 99.
88. GKN Minute Book, Vol. 5, op. cit., 27 June 1924, it. 4539.
89. *Colliery Guardian*, Vol. CXXVII, No. 3312, 20 June 1924, Obituary, p. 1584; *Who was Who*, Vol. II, p. 636. *Colliery Guardian*, Vol. CXXXVII, No. 3309, 30 May 1924, 'Men of Note, No. 30, Sir Leonard Llewelyn', p. 1341.
90. *Colliery Guardian*, Vol. CXXVII, No. 3312, op. cit., p. 1584.
91. Kirby, *British Coalmining*, op. cit., p. 68.
92. Ibid.
93. GKN Minute Book, Vol. 4, op. cit., October 1922–December 1923, 2 January 1923, it. 4125.
94. Ibid., it. 4126.
95. Ibid., 4 January 1923, it. 4172, 4182.
96. Jones, *GKN Vol. One*, op. cit., pp. 314–16.
97. GKN Minute Book, Vol. 4, op. cit., 1 February 1923, it. 4205.
98. Ibid., 7 June 1923, it. 4294.
99. Ibid., 10 October 1923, it. 4373.
100. GKN Minute Book, Vol. 5, December 1923–February 1925, 7 February 1924, it. 4493.
101. Ibid., their closure was confirmed, 1 May 1924, it. 1511.
102. Ibid., 27 June 1924, it. 4732.
103. Ibid., 2 October 1924, it. 4585.
104. Ibid., 2 October 1924, it. 4585.
105. Ibid., 6 November 1924, it. 4606.

106. Ibid.
107. GKN Minute Book, Vol. 6, op. cit., 4 February 1925, it. 4670.
108. Ibid., 2 April 1925, it. 4710.
109. Ibid., 8 May 1925, it. 4728.
110. R. Lyttleton's 'Newspaper Cuttings', Obituary, W.M. Llewellyn, September 1943, p. 115.
111. Ibid., 26 June 1925, it. 4764, 6 August 1925, it. 4779.
112. The Ministry of Fuel and Power, *Coal Mining, Report of the [Reid] Technical Advisory Committee Cmd. 6610*, London HMSO (1945), p. 6.
113. GKN Minute Book, Vol. 5, op. cit., 4 December 1924, it. 4627.
114. *Report of the Royal Commission on the Coal Industry* (1925), Vol. 1, Cmd. 2600 (1926), pp. 3–14.
115. GKN Minute Book, Vol. 6, op. cit., 8 April 1926, it. 4915.
116. Ibid.
117. Ibid., 5 November 1925, it. 4837.
118. Ibid., it. 4844.
119. Kirby, *British Coalmining*, op. cit., p. 77.
120. In October 1931 Sir David R. Llewellyn reported that departure from the Gold Standard had resulted in more enquiries for South Wales coal, GKN Minute Book, Vol. 9, op. cit., 1 October 1931, it. 5998.
121. E.D. Lewis, *The Rhondda Valleys, A Study in Industrial Development 1800 to the Present Day*, London (1959), pp. 251–53.
122. *The Reid Report*, op. cit., p. 7.
123. Kirby, *British Coalmining*, op. cit., p. 108.
124. GKN Minute Book, Vol. 7, op. cit., 2 June 1927, it. 5149.
125. Ibid., 2 December 1926, it. 5044.
126. Ibid., 13 January 1927, it. 5059.
127. Ibid., 3 February 1927, it. 5063.
128. Ibid., 8 September 1927, it. 5196.
129. Ibid., 7 October 1927, it. 5207.
130. Ibid., 5 January 1928, it. 5252.
131. GKN Minute Book, Vol. 8, op. cit., 3 May 1928, it. 5313.
132. Kirby, *British Coalmining*, op. cit., p. 116.
133. GKN Minute Book, Vol. 7, op. cit., 7 April 1927, it. 5117.
134. Ibid.
135. Ibid., 4 May 1927, it. 5135.
136. Ibid., 3 November 1927, it. 522.
137. Ibid., 1 December 1927, it. 5235.
138. Ibid., 2 June 1927, it. 5169.
139. GKN Minute Book, Vol. 8, op. cit., 3 May 1928, it. 5039.
140. GKN Minute Book, Vol. 7, op. cit., 7 October 1927, it. 5210.
141. Ibid., 3 November 1927, it. 5219; 5 January 1927, it. 5245.
142. GKN Minute Book, Vol. 8, op. cit., 2 August 1928, it. 5363.
143. Ibid., 4 October 1928, it. 5378.
144. Ibid.
145. Ibid., 1 November 1928, it. 5401.
146. Ibid.
147. Ibid.
148. Ibid., 6 December 1928, it. 5416.
149. Ibid., 1 August 1929, it. 5573.
150. *Colliery Guardian*, Vol. CXXVI, 25 May 1928.

151. GKN Minute Book, Vol. 8, 2 August 1928, it. 5361.
152. Ibid., 3 January 1928, it. 5432.
153. Ibid., 4 April 1929, it. 5484.
154. Ibid., 7 November 1929, it. 5613.
155. Kirby, *British Coalmining*, op. cit., p. 116.
156. GKN Minute Book, Vol. 8, op. cit., 1 August 1929, it. 5572.
157. Ibid., it. 5574.
158. Ibid., 23 August 1929, it. 5580.
159. Ibid., 5 December 1929, it. 5650.
160. Ibid., 7 November 1929, it. 5588, 5601.
161. Ibid., 5 December 1929, it. 5621.
162. *Colliery Year Book* (1933), pp. 359–60.
163. GKN Minute Book, Vol. 8, op. cit., 6 February 1930, it. 5667.
164. R. Lyttleton's 'Newspaper Cuttings' (p. 45): *Western Mail & South Wales News*, 31 January 1931, p. 11.
165. Ibid., 1 May 1930, it. 5739.
166. Ibid.
167. Ibid., 2 October 1930, it. 5794; December 1931, it. 6037.
168. Ibid., 8 January 1931, it. 5859.
169. Ibid., 2 June 1932, it. 6138.
170. Ibid., 4 August 1932, it. 6163; 6 October 1932, it. 6180.
171. Ibid., 3 November 1932, it. 6204.
172. Ibid., 2 February 1933, it. 6261.
173. Ibid., 6 April 1933, it. 6304.
174. Ibid.
175. Ibid., 6 July 1933, it. 6347.
176. Ibid.
177. Ibid., 3 August 1933, it. 6367.
178. Ibid., 2 November 1933, it. 6405.
179. Kirby, *British Coalmining*, op. cit., p. 145.
180. GKN Minute Book, Vol. 9, op. cit., 1 February 1934, it. 6456.
181. Ibid., 1 March 1934, it. 6474.
182. Ibid., 22 August 1934, it. 6553.
183. GKN Minute Book, Vol. 10, December 1934–June 1938, 3 January 1935, it. 6636.
184. Ibid.
185. Ibid.
186. Ibid., 6 June 1935, it. 6717; R. Lyttleton's, 'Newspaper Cuttings', 'Gigantic Welsh Combine', p. 42.
187. Ibid., 7 November 1935, it. 6767.
188. *Colliery Year Book* (1939), p. 337.
189. Lewis, *The Rhondda Valleys*, op. cit., p. 254.
190. *Colliery Year Book* (1939), p. 271.
191. *Colliery Guardian*, Vol. CXXX, No. 3371, 7 August 1925, 'Men of Note, No. 61, E.L. Hann', p. 289.
192. Harry Llewellyn, *Passports to Life*, op. cit., p. 74.
193. Ashworth and Pegg, *British Coal Industry, Vol. 5*, op. cit., pp. 70–71.
194. Ibid., pp. 72–3.
195. *Proceedings of the South Wales Institute of Engineers*, Vol. XXXVI (1920), Hugh Bramwell, 'The Economics of the South Wales Coalfield', pp. 325–27.
196. Orwell, *Road to Wigan Pier*, op. cit., pp. 22–3.

197. *Reid Report*, op. cit., p. 30.
198. GKN Minute Book, Vol. 6, op. cit., 26 June 1925, it. 4765.
199. Ministry of Fuel and Power, *South Wales Coalfield*, op. cit., p. 67.
200. GKN Minute Book, Vol. 3, op. cit., 6 March 1919, it. 3267.
201. E.D. Lewis, *The Rhondda Valleys, A Study in Industrial Development 1800 to the Present Day*, London (1959), p. 250.
202. GKN Minute Book, Vol. 5, op. cit., 1 May 1924, it. 4505; 27 June 1924, it. 4541; 15 January 1925, it. 4649.
203. Ibid., 11 September 1925, it. 4802.
204. Ibid., Vol. 8, 5 February 1931, it. 5885.
205. GKN Minute Book, Vol. 5, op. cit., 4 December 1924, it. 4627; 8 April 1926, it. 4915.
206. Ibid., 4 November 1926, it. 5031, 'a good number of men at the Meiros Colliery were back on the eight hour day'.
207. Orwell, *Road to Wigan Pier*, op. cit., p. 34.
208. Supple, *History of the British Coal Industry, Vol. 4*, op. cit., pp. 474–78.
209. For an illustration of this problem see The Arts Council, *Coal, British Mining in Art 1680–1980*, London (1982), pp. 80–81.
210. *DBB*, Holmes, 'D.R. Llewellyn', op. cit., p. 825.
211. *The Colliery Year Book* (1939), p. 270.
212. *Colliery Guardian*, Vol. CXXX, No. 3371, 7 August 1925, 'Men of Note, No. 61, Edmund L. Hann', p. 289; *Who was Who*, Vol. VI, p. 486; *GKN Annual Report and Accounts* (1951), p. 5.
213. GKN Minute Book, Vol. 10, op. cit., 1 July 1937, it. 7009.
214. *Who was Who*, Vol. V, p. 612.
215. *DBB*, Vol. 5 (1986), M.W. Kirby, 'Sir Evan Williams', pp. 823–4.
216. *DBB*, Vol. 3 (1985), Jenny Davenport, 'John Scott Hindley', pp. 256–7.

4 *Steel and GKN, 1919–39*

We tore the iron from the mountain's hold,
By blasting fires we smithied it to steel;
Out of the shapeless stone we learned to mould
The sweeping bow, the rectilinear keel.
                    John Masefield (1878–1967), 'The Ship'

Ironmaking, and later the manufacture of steel, was the one continuous thread running through the history of GKN from the foundation of the company's antecedent at Dowlais in 1759. Steel had an aura, a fascination and a magic about it; steelworks were exciting, noisy and lively with a touch of danger, where basic materials were roasted to high temperatures and fashioned while red hot into objects of enormous strength and resistance. The men who worked there had to be physically tough, their skills, experience and the ever present threat of hazard contributing to an industrial camaraderie. The senior managers and directors of steelworks, by virtue of the numbers they employed and the vast nature of the plant and machinery which they controlled often became powerful figures whose voices carried authority in boardroom meetings. However, in 1919 steel could be purchased relatively cheaply and within a year was to be found in abundance. Moreover, the costs of either setting up a steelworks or of updating an existing enterprise were enormous. For example, no other part of the GKN group, whether its fastener factories, pressing and stamping shops or collieries, absorbed so much capital investment during the interwar period. Yet steel remained at the very core of this vertically integrated company. To have sold GKN's steelworks would have deprived its pits of valuable customers and left its sheet rolling mills and various engineering works without a major source of supply. Steel was a necessary, glamorous and costly aspect of the group's operations during the interwar period.

INTO ADVERSITY: DOWLAIS AND DOWLAIS–CARDIFF, EAST MOORS, 1919–29

On the cessation of war, the principal steelmaking plants of GKN were at Dowlais and Cardiff. The former, once the largest ironworks in the world, had tended to live off past achievements rather than future promise during the Edwardian period while its companion built beside the Roath Docks at East Moors had then been one of the most modern works in the country. In 1919 Dowlais still concentrated on the production of rails, and Cardiff made plate, mainly for ships, but also turned out billets. In addition, GKN owned and sometimes operated the Cyfarthfa Works whose blast furnaces and rolling mills had been called out of retirement in 1916 by the insatiable demand for shell steel. Despite the promise offered by the post-war boom, GKN closed this subsidiary of Dowlais as soon as the Ministry of Munitions relinquished their period of control. With the blowing out of the two blast furnaces and stopping of the rolling mills, the Cyfarthfa Works shut for ever.[1] Although the group was in general optimistic about their commercial fortunes, the plant and machinery at Cyfarthfa was sufficiently old and functioned on such a limited scale as to make it uneconomic. GKN had resisted attempts by the Ministry of Munitions to have the works re-opened and conceded only from a sense of patriotism combined with the offer of financial incentives.[2]

The release of the wartime brake placed on the European economies and removal of state controls resulted in a feverish boom in 1919–20. In the expansive spirit which swept through the steel industry in December 1919, GKN authorised the expenditure of £39,475 on the relining of No. 3 blast furnace at East Moors.[3] This also represented an attempt to redress an imbalance which had arisen during the war between the UK's capacity to make pig iron and steel respectively.[4] The former required greater capital expenditure and needed to be produced in far larger quantities. In response to this market situation John Lysaght erected a third blast furnace with a 13ft hearth at Normanby Park Steelworks in 1920. However, for the five months ended 30 November 1919 Dowlais, Cardiff and their collieries suffered a substantial loss of £187,866.[5] The figures produced for the eight months to 29 February 1920 revealed that the coal mines above were not responsible for this failure as the steelworks at Cardiff individually recorded a deficit of £35,394, while Dowlais and the collieries had moved into a profit of £171,248.[6] The strength of the economic recovery was such that for the ten months to the end of April 1920, Cardiff returned to profitability, achieving a surplus of £36,366.[7] The confidence that GKN placed in its steelworks received tangible expression in June when the expenditure of £20,000 was authorised for the construction of new offices for the Cardiff works.[8]

The short-lived boom of 1919–20 collapsed into the severe slump of 1921–22.[9] The staple industries suffered especially hard during this unexpected depression. As Table 4.1 shows, the price of steel plate and rails collapsed. Production fell back drastically both at Dowlais and Cardiff where large numbers of workers were laid off until orders recovered. The coal strike of April–June 1921 resulted in the cancellation of many profitable contracts which, if renewed, were concluded at less favourable prices.[10] In October 1922 it was decided not to restart the plate mill at East Moors because of insufficient demand from shipbuilders.[11] At Dowlais the mills were similarly under-employed and

2 'Dowlais Works at Night' (1929) by C.W. Mansel Lewis (1872–1930). A panoramic view of the steelworks shortly before its closure which reveals its scale and awesome aspect (*Cyfarthfa Castle Museum & Art Gallery, Merthyr Tydfil, Mid Glamorgan*).

Howell R. Jones, the general manager, agreed to accept low prices to keep as many men in work as possible;[12] in January 1923 they were tendering at £7 7s 6d per ton for rails,[13] which stood in stark contrast to the average figure of £15 per ton for the late nineteenth century.[14]

Because Continental steel prices had fallen faster than those in the UK, British consumers were tempted to purchase imports as Table 4.2 reveals. Rates of unemployment in the iron and steel industry were far higher than in other branches of manufacturing or in commerce and services; in January 1922 35.7 per cent of those working in the steel industry had been made redundant, compared with 16.2 per cent for UK industry, trade and services, while in July 1922 the figures were 27.6 and 12.3 per cent respectively.[15] Nevertheless GKN was able to pay a dividend of 7.5 per cent for the year ended March 1922. Edward Steer, the chairman, described the situation as 'fair' and attributed the group's comparatively reasonable performance to the variety of business undertaken and the possibilities for mutual aid amongst its branches.[16]

The slump which centred on 1921–22 was followed by a weak and

Table 4.1   UK prices of steel products, 1919–22 (per ton)

Date	Soft billets net price			Ship's plates 3/8in. & over Scotland			Heavy rails England		
	£	s	d	£	s	d	£	s	d
1919									
May	14	10	0	7	10	0	15	0	0
July	13	17	6	18	5	0	16	0	0
Oct.	15	0	0	18	15	0	16	10	0
1920									
Jan.	17	0	0	21	10	0	17	10	0
April	24	10	0	24	10	0	21	0	0
July	26	0	0	27	0	0	23	0	0
Oct.	21	10	0	27	0	0	25	0	0
1921									
Jan.	16	0	0	25	10	0	25	0	0
April	13	10	0	19	0	0	18	0	0
July	10	10	0	15	0	0	15	0	0
Oct.	7	10	0	14	0	0	12	10	0
1922									
Jan.	7	5	0	10	10	0	9	10	0
April	7	2	6	10	10	0	9	10	0
July	7	7	6	10	0	0	9	10	0
Oct.	7	1	3	8	17	6	8	15	0

Source: J.C. Carr and W. Taplin, *History of the British Steel Industry*, Oxford (1962), p. 361.

Table 4.2   UK output of iron and steel and total imports (000 tons), 1922–39

	Pig iron and ferro-alloys	Open-hearth acid	Steel basic	Total imports of iron and steel
1922	4,902	1,709	3,626	881
1923	7,441	2,568	5,284	1,322
1924	7,307	2,411	5,125	2,429
1925	6,262	2,016	4,750	2,720
1926	2,458	1,055	2,265	3,738
1927	7,293	2,571	5,929	4,406
1928	6,610	2,219	5,669	2,897
1929	7,589	2,451	6,488	2,822
1930	6,192	1,805	5,099	2,912
1931	3,773	1,182	3,785	2,845
1932	3,574	1,123	3,912	1,594
1933	4,136	1,552	5,140	971
1934	5,969	1,751	6,678	1,366
1935	6,242	1,858	7,361	1,152
1936	7,721	2,159	8,772	1,483
1937	8,493	2,276	9,673	2,033
1938	6,761	1,721	7,743	1,341
1939	7,980	2,157	9,705	Not available

Source: J.C. Carr and W. Taplin, *History of the British Steel Industry*, Oxford (1962), pp. 366, 370, 429, 430, 484, 488.

uneven upswing which reached its high point in 1929, though in certain important respects (the export sector in particular), the UK's economic performance remained below the pre-war level.[17] In January 1923 the Cardiff plate mill restarted on receipt of 24,000 tons of orders.[18]

In attempt at limited diversification it was also agreed, at a cost of £10,000, that one of the open-hearth furnaces should be converted to basic steelmaking,[19] which would allow the works to purchase cheap ores from both Britain and the Continent. However, so long as the company retained its 50 per cent holding in the Orconera Iron Ore Co. which supplied them with hematite from Northern Spain, they were obliged to persist with some form of acid steelmaking. Yet as new steelworks were constructed with basic facilities and as deposits of ores high in phosphorus were far greater than those with lower levels of impurities, it was clear that in both technical and supply terms the future of acid steelmaking was doomed. In April 1923 the GKN board decided to convert seven of their eight open-hearth furnaces and the Talbot furnace at Cardiff[20] to basic operation.[21] Dowlais would continue to make acid steel in its Bessemer converters and open-hearth furnaces as this would enable the company to consume its quota of

21 An aerial view of Dowlais steelworks in the late 1920s. The Ifor Works stands in the middle distance to the right (*Welsh Industrial and Maritime Museum*).

Orconera ores and continue to supply the fastener factories which preferred acid billets for their cutting qualities. To try to ensure sufficiently high levels of orders, it was agreed that Dowlais should have first refusal on all tenders submitted from both the Rogerstone rolling mills (which fed the Nettlefolds' screw mills) and other steel-consuming factories within the GKN combine.[22]

Nevertheless, the age and piecemeal fashion in which the Dowlais Works had developed concerned GKN. It relied almost exclusively on steam power in an era when the latest mills were driven by electric motors. Accordingly, in 1921 it was decided, to convert the entire works to electricity. A power station was constructed in the Ifor Works to supply the steelworks and, by an overhead transmission line, the Dowlais collieries which were also undergoing a process of limited modernisation.[23] The coke ovens formed a weak link in the chain of production, so that it was decided in April 1923 to renew them at an estimated cost of £75–£80,000.[24] When completed the 65 Otto regenerative by-product ovens, laid down in two batteries of 30 and 35, had an

22 The bottom end of the Dowlais rail bank, November 1926. The structural steelwork on the trucks in the foreground is from John Lysaght's Netham Works (*Glamorgan Archive Service*).

output of 4,000 tons a week.[25] To supply these and maintain output at a time when the works' Victorian collieries were being closed, a series of drift mines were opened (p. 89). A new steel sleeper plant (able to manufacture pressed sleepers up to eleven feet in length) had also been laid down and came into operation in May.[26]

By the spring of 1923 the slight recovery in trade was thought sufficient to have justified the re-opening of the works, particularly in view of the large expense that would have been incurred in leaving them idle.[27] This policy prevailed throughout the rest of the year when following both low prices and the falling off in orders, the board considered the idea of closure in August[28] and again in September when it

23 The rail bank at Dowlais with its overhead cranes, October 1927 (*Glamorgan Archive Service*).

was observed 'that the cost of running Dowlais Works was more than would be the loss on standing charges if the works were idle'.[29] The merger with John Lysaght also came to the workers' aid as the Orb rolling mills at Newport agreed in August 1923 to purchase 1,000 tons of sheet bar a week from Dowlais.[30] Nevertheless, in April 1924 greatly reduced orders again brought the issue of closure before the board.[31] John Paton argued that 'the cost of manufacture [at Dowlais] should be brought down considerably so that the loss on working at current prices should prove not very material'.[32] Given the age of much of the plant, it may have been thought impractical to try to effect economies, so the directors decided to investigate whether any further business could be found within the GKN combine and from railway companies before deciding to suspend operations at Dowlais. In the following month these proposals, having been agreed by the company's steel committee, were ratified by the board: 'no works should place orders with other firms in this country without first affording Dowlais the opportunity of taking the order, provided that Dowlais can make the billets of the quality desired'.[33]

In such a period of adversity, it was natural, as in previous eras, that manufacturers became increasingly interested in trade associations designed to limit competition.[34] By January 1924 the Rail and Steel Plate Associations had been revived and were in operation. In essence, the

24 Steel sleepers manufactured at Dowlais (*c.* 1923). These were sold to hot countries where termites would consume the timber variety (*Glamorgan Archive Service*).

idea was to get every British manufacturer of these products to agree to fix their prices, and work to quotas based on the relative capacities of their plant. The difficulty occurred in enforcing these rules as any steel-works that was prepared to offer a discount could obtain potentially substantial orders so long as its competitors adhered to the negotiated higher figure. Indeed, dissensions among members of the Rail Makers Association during the early months of 1925 made it likely that the body would break up.[35]

In such circumstances of sluggish activity new orders were greeted with enthusiasm. In June 1924 William Simons, general manager of Dowlais–Cardiff, announced that his steelworks had obtained con-tracts to supply the Admiralty with plates for new battleships.[36]

In a climate of adverse market trends, Dowlais was hampered further by ageing plant and machinery. Railway companies ordered rails of increasing length and whilst the Goat Mill could roll them, the rail bank where they were stored and inspected could not accommodate the new 60ft lengths.[37] If the works were to survive, the rail bank needed to be rebuilt. In December 1924 £10,000 was allocated to extend the plant,[38] but in April 1925 when the estimate had risen to £15,000, the scheme was cancelled in an effort to reduce expenditure.[39] In the event, the modifications were effected later in the year increasing the weekly capacity of the bank to 250 tons.[40] A further £10,000 was spent during 1926 to increase its efficiency and to enable greater lengths of rail to be handled.[41]

Nevertheless, despite the electrification of the Goat Mill, construction

25   The coke ovens and by-product plant at Ifor Works, Dowlais, in 1928 (*John A. Owen*).

26 The finishing mill, part of the Goat Mill, originally laid down in 1859 but extensively re-built, and in operation for the production of rails (c. 1920–23) (*John A. Owen*).

of new coke ovens and by-product plant and improvements to the rail bank, the extreme competition engendered by depressed world markets kept Dowlais in difficulties throughout 1925.[42] The order book for the works recovered considerably during 1926 and by March contracts totalling 67,200 tons had been received;[43] but, while the quantity of work was satisfactory, prices still remained below pre-war levels.[44] In April 1926 when the general condition of both Cardiff and Dowlais was reviewed by the board, it was decided to spend £15,000 at the latter on a turbo blower.[45] However, since there was already sufficient blast for the two existing furnaces, the new plant could generate greater efficiencies only if a third blast furnace were brought into operation. In view of the precarious demand for rails, the board decided against such an expansive policy. These uncertain market forces also encouraged the reconstitution of the International Rail Association during the autumn of 1926.[46]

In September 1927 recovery was sufficient for Howell R. Jones to be able to report that the Dowlais trading account had passed from loss into profit over the last few months, this in part being the result of new plant coming into production.[47] In November, so that the turbo blower might work at full capacity, a third blast furnace was blown in, even though the works was operating at two-thirds of its potential output.[48] This optimistic tactic soon proved ill-founded and when a number of specifications failed to match the orders, the furnace had to be damped down,[49] thereby nullifying the effectiveness of the new blower. The trading position of the Dowlais Works was described in January 1928 as being 'unsatisfactory' despite contracts for 10,000 tons of rails being placed by the GWR and 6,000 tons of steel sleepers by the Ugandan railways.[50]

By July 1928 the situation at Dowlais had become desperate. For the first time in fifty years the steelworks had been unable to secure any orders from a single UK railway company.[51] Once the world's greatest manufacturer of rails, it could no longer compete successfully with other British manufacturers. With the exception of the new power house and coke ovens, the plant and machinery was generally outdated or in a few cases run down, while the gradual evolution of the works over one hundred and seventy years had resulted in the layout being not of the most efficient design.[52] With an ominous foreboding, William Simons noted that South Wales steelworks were rejecting the traditional acid technology in favour of basic methods. Dowlais, unlike Cardiff which had switched almost all of its furnaces to basic, retained a rigid adherence to hematite practice.

Psychologically, the fate of Dowlais as a steelworks was finally sealed, it appears, by the poor standard of the rails supplied to the Egyptian government. There were serious complaints concerning their quality and the Crown Agents intervened to settle the matter.[53] The problems which arose with this contract were used as the excuse to close the works, though, in reality, its demise was the product of insufficient capital investment. In view of the mediocre record of output and performance recorded by Dowlais throughout the 1920s, the GKN board appear to have been reluctant to introduce able executives to the works, and able managers who had received their training there subsequently attained senior positions at East Moors and Port Talbot. In 1926, on completion of 50 years services, Howell R. Jones asked to be relieved of some of his responsibilities as general manager of the steelworks and its attendant collieries. Because of his experience (albeit in coal rather than steel), he was persuaded to remain in office despite being sixty-six years old.[54] The trouble which arose over an order as important as the Egyptian rail contract emphasised to GKN that the management at Dowlais needed to be revitalised if the works were to continue in existence. Howell R. Jones took the retirement which was overdue, and William Simons was appointed general manager in his place for a period of twelve months.[55] The latter was the son of David Simons (1842–92) a gentleman puddler at Dowlais, who then trained in Bessemer steel-making, and was employed at various South Wales steelworks including Blaenavon.[56] Having served an apprenticeship with Miller & Co. of Coatbridge, Scotland, William Simons qualified as a member of the Institution of Mechanical Engineers and obtained posts at a number of works including Dowlais, Cyfarthfa and Workington. In 1902 he joined the Shelton Steelworks rising to become the managing director and in 1922, on the retirement of A.K. Reese, was appointed general manager of Dowlais–Cardiff at East Moors.[57]

In September 1928 T. Tottenham, the Egyptian government's chief inspecting engineer, visited Dowlais to discover whether their latest

3 'Caeharris Post Office, Dowlais' (1935) by Cedric Morris (1889–1981). This oil painting depicts the disused blast furnaces and the tips behind (*Cyfarthfa Castle Museum & Art Gallery, Merthyr Tydfil, Mid Glamorgan*).

rails were acceptable as suitable replacements for those rejected earlier. He judged the quality unsatisfactory and the state exercised their right to obtain new orders from other works.[58] Although constantly updated, the mill in which they had been produced had been laid down in 1859 and, given the additional transport costs, may have found it difficult to compete with those more modern plants sited on the coast. One of their principal rivals would have been Margam Steelworks, belonging to Baldwins and built near Port Talbot. Planned during the Great War, it came into operation in 1922, specialising in the output of slab, bars and heavy rails.[59] The subsequent news that all rails recently supplied by Dowlais to Egypt were to be lifted and scrapped was not the kind of publicity designed to inspire confidence in customers.[60]

At this point other members in the GKN group rallied to the aid of Dowlais. The Orb Works at Newport placed an order for sheet bar with them, while contracts for billets from the Rogerstone and other Midland rolling mills were thought sufficient to keep the steelworks employed.[61] Dowlais still had 5,000 tons of rails to roll under the existing Egyptian contract and it was decided to make a second attempt to satisfy their conditions, the company applying to be placed on the Crown Agent's list again.[62] To this end, in February 1929, GKN authorised the expenditure of £8,000 on the Goat Mill bank to improve the handling of bars and billets.[63] Paradoxically the position of the works continued to improve during the early part of 1929. In March the Dowlais order book had filled appreciably and it was calculated that if this trend held till the end of the year a profit would be returned.[64] With this optimism in mind, new boilers were purchased at a cost of £5,000 to increase steam power. Although Bayliss, Jones & Bayliss complained in March about the quality of billets supplied to them by Dowlais for rolling into rod for rail screws and bolts, the prospects for the steel trade in South Wales, with the exception of plate, were viewed as being 'better than for some time'.[65]

In 1929, the last full year of its operation, the Dowlais Steelworks comprised four blast furnaces ('A' and 'B' which each produced 2,300 tons a week), No. 11 (hand-charged with a capacity of 1,700 tons) and No. 3 (old and used occasionally but able to turn out 1,200 tons a week when required),[66] and two 20-ton Bessemer converters. Rolling was performed by the Goat Mill and the 20". Big Mill which produced colliery arches. Responding to the slight upturn and in view of the latter's age (it had been put down in 1830),[67] plans were laid to install a new mill to roll light rails and colliery arches.[68]

In October 1929 William Simons prepared a report on the viability of both Dowlais and Cardiff. He came to the conclusion that the economic future of both works was questionable. The former was in doubt because of a low and fluctuating level of orders and the need to adopt basic technology in view of the increasing scarcity of low phosphorus coke required by the acid process.[69] This pessimistic outlook combined with falling demand resulted in plans for a mill to roll colliery arches

27 The idle blast furnaces in silhouette at Dowlais (*c.* 1936) (*Welsh Industrial and Maritime Museum*).

being deferred.[70] Early in 1930 the situation worsened. Although sufficient orders were being received, prices had tumbled, while the cost of raw materials, including coal, had advanced.[71] With the formation of Guest Keen Baldwins on 1 January 1930 (p. 129), the Dowlais Works passed from the direct control of GKN and its future became increasingly consequent upon the fortunes of steel in South Wales rather than the specific needs of a vertically integrated industrial group. Although Lt. Colonel Guest and I.L.F. Elliot, as GKN's representatives, had been able to negotiate terms with the Egyptian government such that the £74,000 owed to the works would be paid in exchange for an extension from six to twelve years as the guarantee period on their rails,[72] the new owners scarcely paused before announcing that 'conditions in the iron and steel trade continued to be extremely depressed and it was likely that Dowlais Works, on the termination of the present run [of orders], would be closed down permanently'.[73]

On 4 October 1930, after 171 years of continuous operation, the Dowlais Works ceased to be a manufacturing entity. The blast furnaces were blown out, the two 20-ton Bessemer converters de-commissioned and the 30in Goat Mill shut down. Such plant and machinery that was considered of any value was transported either to Cardiff or Port Talbot.[74] The 21″ Big Mill continued in operation until 1936, when the foundries, coke ovens and engineering shops of the Ifor Works alone remained, employing several hundred men.[75] On the closure of the steelworks around 3,000 became redundant and in 1935, at the time the Royal Commission investigated unemployment in Merthyr, 12,460 or 63.7 per cent of the insurable population were recorded as being out of work.[76] In November 1936, when King Edward VIII visited the dismantled plant to see for himself the extent of the deprivation, he was

4 'The Tips, Dowlais' (1935) by Cedric Morris (1889–1981). The bleak and depressed nature of Merthyr in the 1930s is conveyed in this contemporary picture (*Cyfarthfa Castle Museum & Art Gallery, Merthyr Tydfil, Mid Glamorgan*).

28 The destruction of the blast furnaces at Dowlais (c. 1937) (*Welsh Industrial and Maritime Museum*).

reported as saying: 'these works brought all these people here. Something ought to be done to find them employment'.[77] In response to a general revival in the steel trade which, in turn, raised the price of coke, Dowlais coke ovens were re-opened in 1936, but provided jobs for a mere 200.[78] The major part of the site remained derelict, like the memorial to Ozymandias,[79] until after the Second World War when fresh opportunities came to Dowlais. The need for ingot moulds generated by a worldwide demand for steel encouraged investment in the Ifor Works[80] and in November 1958 a new foundry was opened.[81]

To return to the mid 1920s and the fate of Dowlais–Cardiff, the slump in orders for plate resulted in the works rolling steel for manufacture of pipes. During 1924 they supplied Cardiff Corporation with around 5,000 tons of plates for this purpose. In order to increase their market share, GKN proposed a joint enterprise with Thomas Piggott & Co., pipe manufacturers of Birmingham. The plan was to construct a plant in East Moors beside the steelworks at an estimated cost of £40,000, of which 60 per cent would be found by GKN and 40 per cent by Piggotts.[82] In the event, GKN subscribed two-thirds of its preference capital and Thomas Piggott & Co. one third, while the ordinary shares were divided equally between them.[83] W. Simons became the managing director of Guest, Keen & Piggotts and W.R. Lysaght also joined the board. Plates supplied by Dowlais–Cardiff were cold rolled to form pipes of up to 48″ diameter which were then welded along the seam and hand finished. Having come on stream in the autumn of 1925,[84]

29 The demolition of the hot blast stoves at Dowlais (*c.* 1937) (*John A. Owen*).

30 From the top of the old coal storage bunker, a view of the Ifor Works in 1945 when used by the Admiralty as a storage depot. To the right stands the derelict by-product plant (*John A. Owen*).

the works continued to operate until 1930 when its closure was forced by the depression and the introduction of cheaper manufacturing methods from America.[85]

So severe was the competition affecting the heavy steel trade in 1925 that when the plate mill at Cardiff had to close for repairs in October, it was uncertain whether it would re-start.[86] In view of the continuing losses at Dowlais–Cardiff, a special meeting of the GKN board was called for 16 April 1926 to consider the future of the steelworks.[87] In presenting his report, William Simons emphasised that wholesale capital expenditure had now become a necessity. The Steel Committee of GKN, under the chairmanship of W.R. Lysaght, had already discussed the matter and concluded that the steelworks should be permitted to continue to produce plate but that commercial viability could be achieved only if the plant were improved and a measure of

31 An aerial view of Dowlais–Cardiff, East Moors, September 1929 (*Aerofilms*).

diversification introduced. It was agreed that over the period 1926–29 £117,000 would be spent at Cardiff on new plant, including mechanical hoist equipment for No. 2 and No. 4 furnaces (£30,000), gas cleaning plant for two blast-furnaces (£35,000), extensions to the pig-bed crane gantry (£2,000), four hot-blast stoves (£20,000), and ore bunkers for the blast furnaces (£30,000). In addition, a further £79,750 was authorised for the steel-making plant: a mechanical furnace charging machine, the rebuilding of the smelting furnace and completion of the casting-shop gantry (£47,250), a new gas-fired slab heating furnace (£25,000) and the electrification of the auxiliary engines for the slab and plate mill (£7,500). It was estimated that these innovations would save Dowlais–Cardiff £51,500 in operating costs per annum, a figure which would re-coup the initial expenditure (£196,750) within four years.

In tune with national trends (Table 4.2), the second half of 1926 and 1927 witnessed a slight recovery in the fortunes of GKN's steelworks. In September 1926, for example, Dowlais–Cardiff reported that orders for plate had risen to 32,000 tons guaranteeing them work until June of the following year.[88] Recovery in the spring of 1927 encouraged an acceleration in the construction of the new hot blast stoves, the problem being that Cardiff could not produce sufficient pig iron to keep its open-hearth furnaces in operation and was compelled, as a result, to purchase from other ironworks.[89] In April, William Simons reported that the newly lit blast furnace had achieved a record output for the UK over a five-week period, and that apart from the price of coke, costs were satisfactory.[90]

Given the cost advantages of Continental steelworks (labour was cheaper and governments tended to be more supportive), the Steel Committee considered purchasing the Isbergne Steelworks at Calais.[91] Although price differentials suggested short and medium-term advantages in such a strategy, the main board concluded that it was 'probably better, in the long run, to continue to buy the GKN group requirements rather than supply them from a Continental works'.[92] After a tour of inspection the notion was finally discarded.[93]

The recovery of 1926–27 proved short-lived for Cardiff. By November a scarcity of plate orders resulted in the steelworks lying idle for two weeks,[94] and a weak recovery could stimulate only part-time working.[95] In February 1928 orders remained below the 2,000 tons per week needed to ensure profitable operation.[96] The situation worsened. During June only two weeks were worked and there seemed little prospect of earning a surplus.[97] By August 1928 only one blast furnace was in operation and the steel plant operated at 50 per cent capacity.[98] Unlike the rail market which brightened in 1929, that for plate continued to be depressed,[99] though a slight improvement was noted during the summer when plans were laid for a second blast furnace to be blown in during September.

With sluggish markets and gloomy prognosis, an offer to purchase the Cardiff steelworks was entertained in July 1929. An American, called Brassert, was interested in introducing a new process for making wrought iron to Britain and needed an operational works for his technical adventure.[100] However, negotiations floundered because the GKN board, willing to part with their East Moors plant because of the 'seemingly permanent loss of certain ship plate orders', thought it unlikely that Brassert would agree to buy Dowlais as well, and they were not prepared to sell Cardiff without its ageing subsidiary.

The Dowlais–Cardiff steelworks struggled to obtain orders for plate throughout 1929.[101] In view of these evident difficulties, Sir Charles Wright (1876–1950),[102] chairman of Baldwins, rival steelmakers based at Port Talbot, approached Sir John Field Beale on 20 December to suggest that the two companies merge their heavy steel interests. The amalgamation, by removing the competition which existed between them, would provide an opportunity for rationalisation and modernisation, while the combined resources of the two companies would increase the scope for capital investment. Within three days, GKN provisionally agreed to the scheme.[103] On 2 January 1930, the board ratified the plan to form a new company with an ordinary share capital of £3,855,000, of which £2,100,000 was to be subscribed by GKN and £1,575,000 by Baldwins. Sir John Field Beale was to serve as the chairman, Sir Charles Wright as deputy chairman and managing director, while a further eight directors were to be elected equally from the two-parent companies. In February it was agreed that the merged enterprise was to be called, the British (Guest, Keen, Baldwins) Iron & Steel Co.[104] It comprised the Dowlais and Dowlais–Cardiff steelworks formerly belonging to GKN and the Port Talbot and Margam steelworks owned by Baldwins.[105]

GUEST KEEN BALDWINS IRON & STEEL CO: THE RE-BUILDING OF DOWLAIS–CARDIFF

In view of the scarcity of orders for steel plate it was decided to close East Moors and transfer its business to Port Talbot. Accordingly, the melting shop and rolling mills both closed in 1930, leaving only one blast furnace to continue in production.[106] If the Cardiff steelworks were to have a future, it would have to find a new market, which, in turn, would require a wholesale rebuilding with the very latest plant and equipment. Such a project would be immensely expensive and of necessity time-consuming in its execution. By creating a new company to embrace their heavy steel interests, GKN and Baldwins had increased their chances of obtaining external finance. If either group had applied individually to the banks for capital for re-investment in their respective steelworks, the lenders would have been entitled to reply that the scale of their operations and assets would justify a share issue, or that they should employ their own internally generated reserves. By setting up a joint enterprise, whose operations lay exclusively in steel, these arguments no longer applied. Guest Keen Baldwins (GKB) could not fund the reconstruction of its works either from reserves or by recourse to the stock market. In October 1930 negotiations were opened with the Bankers' Industrial Development Trust (BIDT)[107] for sufficient funds to rebuild Dowlais–Cardiff. The BIDT (later renamed the Bankers Industrial Development Company) had followed an initiative proposed by Montagu Norman, governor of the Bank of England, that the banking community should join in a co-operative venture to assist industrial re-organisation. In June 1930 he persuaded all the clearing banks and other financial institutions to form the BIDT. The Bank of England subscribed a quarter of the nominal share capital; the remainder provided by other institutions. As its priority was consultation and advice, direct finance was available only for a few projects.

While the scheme to re-build Dowlais–Cardiff had been well received, the BIDT requested that GKN and Baldwins should both guarantee the capital and interest of any monies raised. Since one of the reasons for forming GKB was to divorce GKN from direct responsibility for their steelworks, they refused to underwrite the loan in this way.[108]

Nevertheless, discussions continued. The accountants appointed by BIDT investigated the viability of the Cardiff reconstruction in December 1930,[109] but agreement was ultimately prevented by GKN and Baldwins withholding a guarantee on the loan. In its first year of operation GKB recorded a loss of £51,838, though, it was observed that 'but for the amalgamation, the individual losses of this company [GKN] and Baldwins Ltd on their heavy iron and steel plants would have been a considerably greater figure'.[110] In view of the continuing slump, no attempt was made during 1931 to re-open the melting shop or re-start the rolling mills, though £70,000 was authorised for the re-building of No. 4 blast furnace.[111] GKB moved into a small profit (£9,890) in 1931 (Table 4.3), but any plans for Cardiff were postponed in the summer of 1932 in view of the enduring depression and the decision to spend £90,000 at Port Talbot on gas by-product plant.[112]

During 1932 various ideas were floated for the revitalisation of Cardiff. They concluded the expenditure of £1 million on a plan for the production of 'semis' (steel in a semi-finished form to be sold to re-rollers who then rolled it down to a multitude of finished sizes and shapes)[113] which would involve the operation of two blast furnaces supplying hot metal to the steel plant,[114] and a scheme to erect a mill to roll billets and sheet bar.[115] The catastrophic state of the market prevented either of these from being considered too seriously. Rather as demand remained sluggish, thoughts of further amalgamations of steel interests in South Wales were considered. Sir Charles Wright held discussions with representatives of Richard Thomas & Co. (the owners of a steelworks at Llanelli and a large number of tin-plate mills situated throughout South Wales), it being suggested that the latter should join GKB along with John Lysaght and Henry Summers & Co.[116]

Throughout these difficult years, Dowlais–Cardiff remained an

Table 4.3   Output from GKN, Castle Works, Cardiff, 1939–48 (tons)

Year	Rod mill	Bar mill	Strip mill	Wire	Nails
1939	145,201	39,594	13,967	57,156	29,405
1940	141,234	55,933	12,323	59,179	24,465
1941	147,267	50,215	13,058	56,379	22,088
1942	158,060	60,959	18,331	66,782	25,627
1943	145,629	78,091	17,489	71,361	24,292
1944	141,197	77,980	11,684	75,907	24,570
1945	144,836	63,829	20,961	81,277	29,423
1946	154,286	88,122	30,829	91,568	35,486
1947	155,755	72,130	29,110	95,144	32,570
1948	167,607	85,872	32,933	102,049	32,763

Source: R.C.I. Guppy, 'GKN (South Wales) Limited' (typescript, 1967), p. 16.

iron-making plant. In December 1932 it was agreed that No. 2 furnace should be re-constructed at a cost of £13,000, while the improvement in the trade for hematite iron encouraged them to accelerate the rebuilding of No. 4 furnace.[117] In July 1933, as the outlook brightened, GKB produced a scheme to install a Morgan continuous mill, new coke ovens and other plant for Cardiff costing between £1.5 and £1.75

32   Dowlais–Cardiff after its re-construction, photographed in the late 1930s (*Welsh Industrial and Maritime Museum*).

million.[118] Approval was forthcoming from the GKN board in August[119] and the Bankers Industrial Development Company (BIDC), who were to provide the finance, followed suit in October.[120] By November 1933, when the market had improved to such an extent that GKB had to purchase ingots from other makers,[121] it was decided to proceed with all haste on the rebuilding of East Moors. Site clearance was well underway in December. By this time the estimate for the cost had risen to £2 million,[122] the BIDC granting their approval for the increase in January 1934.[123]

In the event, the BIDC agreed to loan GKB £2,032,000 for a maximum of three years at half a per cent over bank rate, with a minimum of four per cent, plus a commission of one-sixteenth per cent chargeable each quarter.[124] Whilst the GKN board thought these terms reasonable, they agreed that it would be unwise to 'conclude a contract with the BID Company until the government had definitely decided upon a continuance of the Iron and Steel tariffs which . . . terminate on 25 October [1934]'.[125] The *Western Mail* announced on 10 February that a delay in approving the re-construction of Dowlais–Cardiff had arisen because the Import Duties Advisory Committee refused to declare whether the 33.3 per cent duty on foreign steel was to be extended and quoted Sir John Field Beale, chairman of GKN, as saying,

> I would be subjecting our shareholders to a wholly unjustifiable risk if we were to commit them to the large expenditure involved while it remains the law that duties terminate in a little over nine months . . .[126]

Parliament voted on the prolongation of tariffs in May and in August the deal with BIDC was signed.[127] In the event, the cost of the reconstruction far exceeded the original figure, being put at £2,700,000 in April 1935,[128] and finally reached £3 million.

The new steelworks was designed and the rebuilding superintended by J.S. Hollings, joint managing director, with the assistance of GKB's engineering and operative staff, while the International Construction Co. were appointed as consultant engineers.[129] In essence, the plan consisted of erecting new coke ovens and by-product plant, a steel melting shop (comprising two open-hearth furnaces and three tilting furnaces each of 200 tons capacity), a cogging mill, a Morgan continuous sheet bar and billet mill, and a Lamberton 21in light bar mill.[130] Two of the three blast furnaces had been rebuilt over the previous three years and were considered to be sufficiently modern for the task. These two, with a combined output of around 50,000 tons per annum, were to provide molten metal for the steel furnaces while the third was to sell pig iron to other steelworks in South Wales.[131] Of crucial importance in the reducing costs was the coke-oven and by-product plant. The contract for these was won by the Woodall-Duckham Vertical Retort and Oven Construction Co. of London.[132] The regenerative ovens, heated by blast-furnace gas, had a weekly capaity of 6,000 tons of coke. The by-product plant removed the tar, ammonia and benzol before passing the purified coke-oven gas to the 1 million cubic feet gasholder which then supplied the open hearth furnaces and re-heating furnaces, the surplus being sold to supplement Cardiff's town gas supply. In addition, the slag produced by the blast furnaces was converted into tarmacadam for roads.

The East Moors steelworks came into production, as planned, on 2 January 1936 when the first ingots were rolled into billets by the Morgan continuous mill.[133] The Lamberton mill was employed in the production of colliery arches, pit props and light sections. With an output of around 400,000 tons of steel ingots a year, GKB's Cardiff Works could regard itself as one of the most modern medium-sized steelworks in Europe. Following the upturn in business experienced in the mid-1930s and the group's increased steel-making and rolling capacity, it soon became clear that there was insufficient iron-making capacity within GKB. Accordingly, in January 1937, at a cost of £190,000, the construction of two new blast furnaces, one at East Moors and the other at Margam, was authorised.[134] In fact, the building of the second was postponed in favour of erecting an additional open-hearth furnace at Cardiff.[135]

In February 1938, when S.R. Beale, chairman of GKN, was invited to address the Newport and District Metallurgical Society, worries about the future of the steel industry were raised. G.D. Latham, managing director of the Whitehead Iron & Steel Co. of Newport, observed,

> during the last few weeks orders booked by the steel trade as a whole have been less than the actual production of steel ... Pessimists have predicted that not only are we on the crest of a wave of prosperity but a slump is imminent.[136]

If the pattern of previous trade cycles had been allowed to continue then the industry would probably have slipped into another depression. In the event, East Moors and the other steelworks in the GKN group were protected by an influx of business occasioned by rearmament. During the period preceding the outbreak of war, Dowlais–Cardiff produced shell steel and a variety of structural steels required by the forces, together with arches for the construction of air raid shelters.[137]

CASTLE WORKS: TRANSFER FROM ROGERSTONE TO CARDIFF

The Castle Works, Rogerstone, laid down by Nettlefolds Ltd in 1886–87, was originally conceived as a small Bessemer plant for the production of steel ingots which could then be rolled to rod for consumption at the Heath Street screw mills.[138] Growing demand resulted in the two

33   The former Nettlefolds steelworks and rolling mills at Rogerstone in 1902 (*Allied Steel and Wire*).

Bessemer converters being unable to keep pace with orders and in 1912 plans were laid for the erection of Siemens–Martin open-hearth steel furnaces.[139] Delays resulted in the implementation of the scheme and in July 1914 Edward Steer and John Williams, general manager (1910–30), were finally able to travel to Germany to inspect the latest plant, their efforts forestalled by the imminent threat of war. The shortages experienced during the hostilities resulted in the installation of a Parson's turbine drive to power the finishing train on No. 6 mill, which raised the output of rod by about 30 per cent.

During the post-war boom, John Williams visited various steelworks
in America and Canada, and on his return in January 1920 recommended the installation of modern blast furnaces, coke ovens and new
rolling mills.[140] However, the slump of 1921 and the collapse in orders
for steel products killed the scheme. In addition, the clearing up of vast
quantities of scrap from the battlefields (including the salvage of the
German battle fleet) provided open-hearth steelworks with cheap raw
material. By contrast, prices for hematite pig iron remained high,
resulting in the closure of many Bessemer works, including the

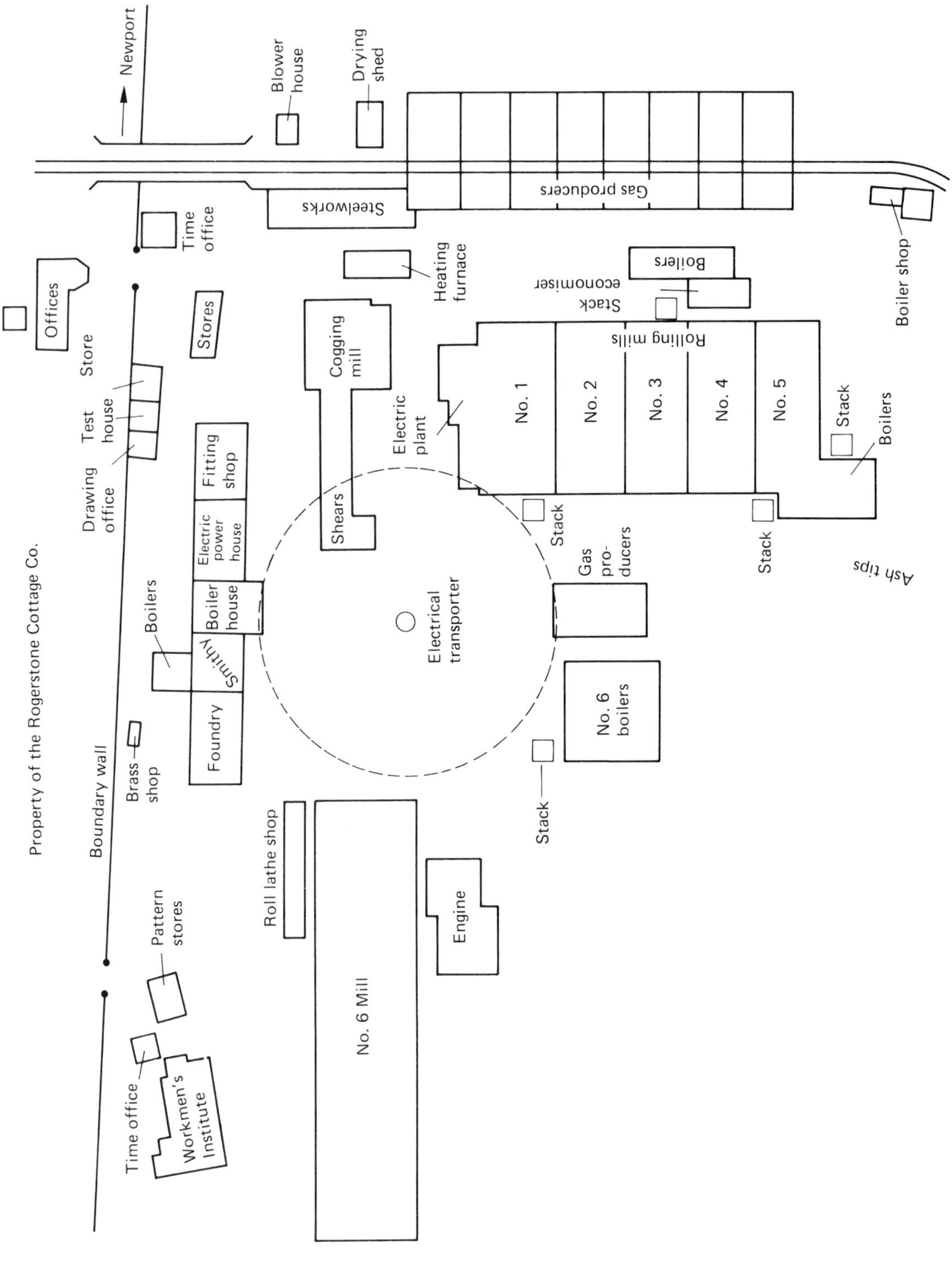

Property of the Rogerstone Cottage Co.

Newport →

Blower house

Drying shed

Time office

Steelworks

Gas producers

Boiler shop

Heating furnace

Stack economiser

Boilers

Offices

Store

Stores

Cogging mill

Rolling mills

Drawing office

Test house

Boilers

Fitting shop

Electric power house

Boiler house

Smithy

Shears

Electric plant

No. 1

No. 2

No. 3

No. 4

No. 5

Stack

Boilers

Boundary wall

Brass shop

Foundry

Electrical transporter

Stack

Gas pro- ducers

Stack

Ash tips

Pattern stores

Roll lathe shop

No. 6 boilers

Stack

Time office

Engine

Workmen's Institute

No. 6 Mill

Figure 6   Castle Works, Rogerstone, c. 1910

Rogerstone plant which ceased operations on 5 March 1921. The cogging and billet mill rolled down the accumulated stock of cold ingots and then this too ceased operations. Henceforth, billets were purchased from other steelworks including Dowlais, Pontymister, Pontardawe, Ebbw Vale and various Continental manufacturers. In effect, the Castle Works comprised a bar and hoop mills, together with No. 6 wire rod mill and the 'H.P.' (Hugget's Patent) nail works nearby at Tydu.[141]

Castle Works struggled through the 1920s and in an attempt to even out the fluctuations in orders by broadening the capabilities of the rod mill it was agreed in 1927 that a modern cooling bed should be installed.[142] Nevertheless, the expected upturn failed to materialise and Rogerstone remained under-employed until the early 1930s.[143] Whilst trying to find the works more orders, T.S. Peacock offered to place a contract for the supply of 10,000 tons of bars for the group's nut and bolt factories at Darlaston. The deal was contingent upon Rogerstone being able to persuade the railway companies who carried the steel from their mills to the Midlands to lower their rates as Peacock refused to pay more than £6 per ton for bars delivered to his factory.[144] In February 1928 it

34 The former Nettlefolds wire mill at Coverack Road, Newport in 1936 (*Allied Steel and Wire*).

35 Although this photograph is recorded as being of Castle Works, Rogerstone, it appears that this is Newport and the River Usk which would suggest that it depicts the Coverack Road Mills (*Welsh Industrial and Maritime Museum*).

was reported that the GWR's transport manager had agreed to a reduced freight charge of 10s 6d per ton and the arrangement could proceed.[145]

Being part of an integrated group also had its disadvantages: Rogerstone repeatedly complained of the obligation placed upon it to accept billets (used in the production of rod destined for the screw mills) from Dowlais at prices higher than could be obtained from other steelworks.[146] In the event, this matter was settled by the closure of Dowlais in 1930.

John Williams, who had managed the Castle Works for some thirty years, retired in April 1930.[147] Described by his personal secretary, Edgar Brown, as 'a fine manager, strong in character, generally of good humour and reasonably tolerant',[148] Williams was accused by some of having allowed Rogerstone to decline, though in view of the various schemes of modernisation which he had presented to the GKN board this seems to have been an unfair judgement.[149] His successor, Roland C. Harding, according to Brown, 'was intolerant and impatient, and imbued fear as his tremendous driving force'.[150] Yet his determination to succeed, together with the recovery evident in the economy, produced a short-lived revival in the fortunes of the Rogerstone Works.

By the purchase of more modern machines from the Continent[151] and a basic reorganisation, Harding revitalised the nail department at Tydu. Until his appointment all rod was sent from Rogerstone to the Imperial Mills, Coverack Road, Newport, to be drawn into wire, some being sent back to Tydu to be made into nails. The system was time-consuming and costly. Harding obtained permission for the installation of a wire-drawing machine at Tydu and arranged for nails produced there to be sold in conjunction with screws manufactured at Heath Street.[152] Nail output increased from 200 tons a month in April 1930 to 225 tons a week by April 1932, and reached 500 tons in 1934.[153]

The general upturn in the demand for steel, together with the success of the nail plant combined to put pressure on the out-dated Rogerstone mills. In March 1933, Harding was involved in discussions by which both Castle Works and the Whitehead Iron & Steel Co. of Newport would join the GKB combination,[154] Rogerstone having been omitted from the package of January 1930. Although the merger did not materialise, the talks between Harding and the executives of GKB were of importance in view of the planned reconstruction of Dowlais–Cardiff for the latter was to be laid out to roll billets and Rogerstone was regarded as a potential major customer. In October 1933 Harding was instructed by the GKN board to

> prepare a report generally on the policy to be adopted, expenditure and whether the works remained at Rogerstone or were transferred to Cardiff . . . When the Cardiff re-development was underway, the rod mill could be moved to Cardiff with substantial economies in production costs.[155]

The recommendations presented by Harding a month later favoured

36 The Castle Works, Cardiff, situated between Roath Docks and Dowlais–Cardiff Steelworks. This photograph was possibly post-1945 (*by permission of H. Tempest, Welsh Industrial and Maritime Museum*).

37 The general office at Castle Works, Cardiff, (c. 1940). The building was demolished in 1985 (*Allied Steel and Wire*).

the construction of a modern rod mill (with a capacity of 1,600–2,000 tons a week) at Cardiff, to be followed at later date by a light hoop mill and a small bar mill.[156] The first stage of the programme, estimated at £145,000, was designed to provide the works with the capability of rolling down to smaller gauges and in heavier coils. In February 1934 the scheme was approved in principle.

In the event, the Bankers Industrial Development Co. made it a condition of their loan to rebuild the East Moors steelworks that GKN confirm their intention to lay down a modern rod mill beside the Cardiff site.[157] On their part they promised not to grant funds to any proposed scheme of a similar nature.[158] In April 1934 GKN recorded that they had ordered a continuous mill from the Morgan Co. for £72,000.[159] The specification had been prepared by G.A. Phipps and when completed it was regarded as being the most modern of its kind, with a weekly capacity of 3,000 tons of rod.[160]

The Cardiff rod mill came into operation in July 1935,[161] the project having cost around £170,000.[162] Initially, shortages of both supplies of steel and orders prevented a second shift being employed despite there being the trained men available.[163] The first barrier to full production was removed in January 1936 when the first billet was rolled by the East Moors steelworks.

Shortly after the Cardiff rod mill began work, Roland C. Harding died. He was succeeded by H. Speed Peacock, who, according to Brown,

> brought with him the broader concept of co-operative management; he had a charm and magnetism that quickly welded the Rogerstone officials into a team . . . I shall ever remember the first days of his coming the realisation of a powerful mind that

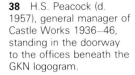

38 H.S. Peacock (d. 1957), general manager of Castle Works 1936–46, standing in the doorway to the offices beneath the GKN logogram.

absorbed and held information with the greatest possible ease and rapidity.[164]

In February 1936, W.A. Murray, formerly of Monks Hall Co., was appointed as works manager of Castle Works.[165]

Shortly after the arrival of H.S. Peacock, [Sir] N. Richard R. Brooke (b. 1910) was appointed to take charge of the accounting department at Rogerstone.[166] The son of W.R. Brooke, general manager of Normanby Park (p. 59), he had been educated at Charterhouse School and qualified as a chartered accountant with Carter & Co., GKN's auditors based in Birmingham.[167] Deciding that a career in industry would be more rewarding than remaining in practice, Brooke joined GKN and among his first duties at Rogerstone was the preparation of reports and estimates for the new plant and machinery at Cardiff.[168]

At the beginning of February 1936, a second shift was employed at the Cardiff rod mill.[169] With rolling firmly established beside the rejuvenated steelworks, it made sense to transfer the remaining manufacturing operations from Rogerstone. In April it was agreed that the

39 The entrance gates to Castle Works, featuring the Nettlefolds' 'Castle' emblem. They were probably manufactured by Bayliss, Jones & Bayliss (*Allied Steel and Wire*).

40 The entrance hall and reception area of the general offices (*Allied Steel and Wire*).

41 The board room at Castle Works (*c.* 1940). The walls were panelled in walnut (*Allied Steel and Wire*).

42 The general drawing office at Castle Works (*Allied Steel and Wire*).

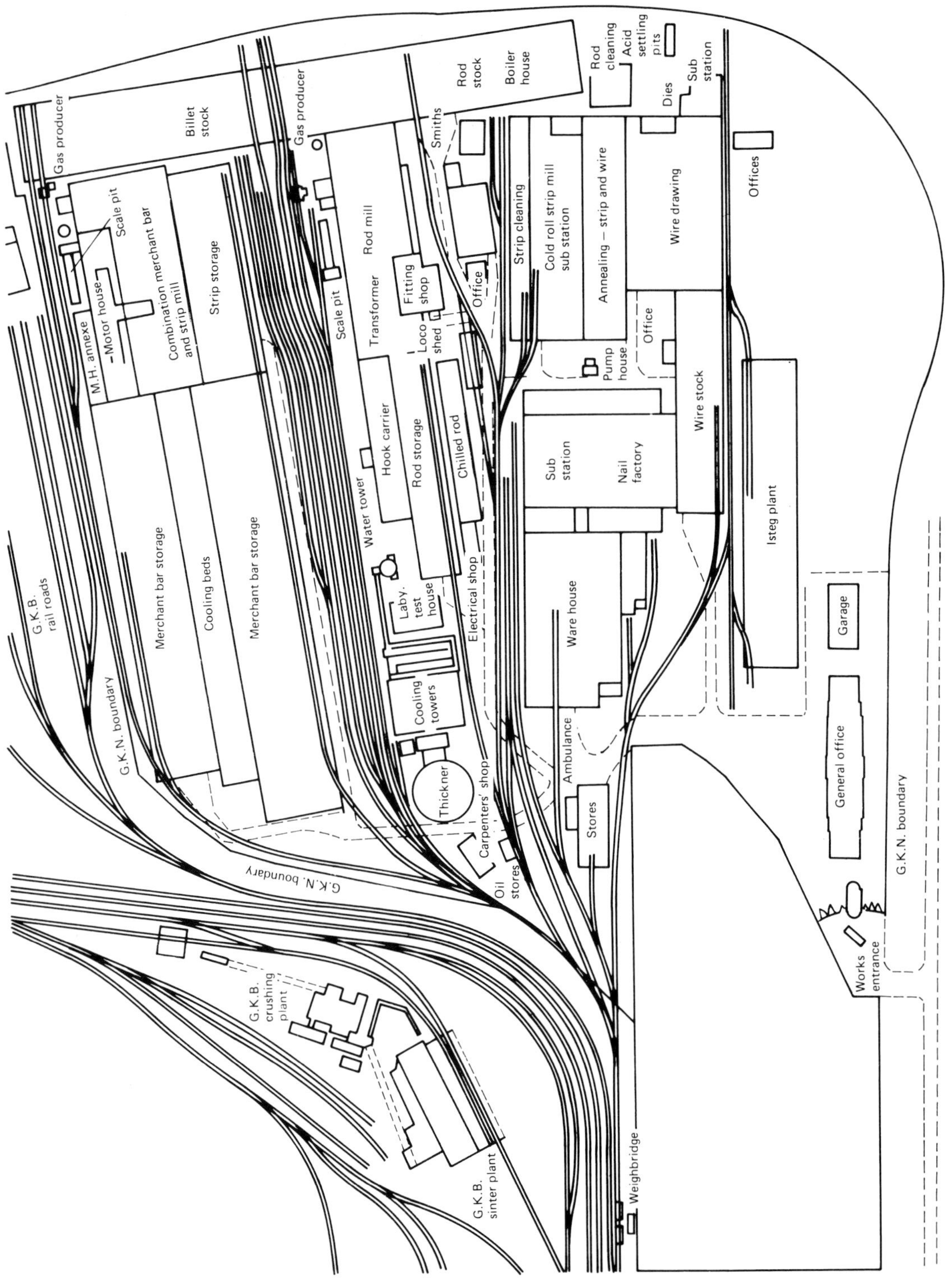

Gas producer

Billet stock

Gas producer

Rod stock

Boiler house

Rod cleaning

Acid settling pits

Sub station

M.H. annexe

Motor house

Scale pit

Combination merchant bar and strip mill

Strip storage

Strip storage

Scale pit

Transformer

Rod mill

Fitting shop

Office

Smiths

Strip cleaning

Cold roll strip mill sub station

Annealing – strip and wire

Dies

Sub station

Offices

Wire drawing

Water tower

Hook carrier

Loco shed

Rod storage

Chilled rod

Office

Pump house

Office

G.K.B. rail roads

Merchant bar storage

Cooling beds

Merchant bar storage

Laby. test house

Electrical shop

Sub station

Nail factory

Wire stock

G.K.N. boundary

Cooling towers

Carpenters' shop

Ware house

Isteg plant

Thickner

G.K.N. boundary

Oil stores

Ambulance

Stores

Garage

General office

G.K.B. crushing plant

G.K.N. boundary

Weighbridge

Works entrance

G.K.B. sinter plant

Figure 7   Plan of Castle Works, Cardiff, 1939

wire drawing at Newport and nail making department at Tydu should be relocated at a cost of £190,442,[170] and in May it was announced that the transfer had begun.[171] When completed, the nail plant achieved a capacity of 650 tons a week, while the wire drawing department had an output of 1,200 tons per week.[172]

Initially, it proved difficult to obtain sufficient orders to justify the second shift at Cardiff. As a result, GKN considered purchasing an interest in Frederick A. Power & Sons, whose wire mills in Adderley Road, Birmingham, consumed considerable quantities of rod.[173] In the event, a minority holding was obtained and a trading arrangement concluded and it was not until 1962 that the business was acquired by GKN.[174]

The contract to supply the new combined merchant and strip mill at Cardiff was won by the Morgan Construction Co., who had earlier agreed to install a bar and hoop mill.[175] The cost was estimated in September 1936 as being £397,493, this figure to include the provision of devices for precision rolling. The Morgan Co. also offered to place an

43 The Morgan rod mill, photographed shortly after its installation in 1935 (*Allied Steel and Wire*).

44   The roughing stands of the Morgan continuous rod mill (*Welsh Industrial and Maritime Museum*).

embargo on the sale of this equipment to any other British mill for a period of three years for a further payment of £6,000;[176] this proposal was rejected by GKN. The total estimated expenditure on the new Castle Works (rolling, nail and wire plant combined) amounted to £718,834, and represented a major capital investment for the group.

With the transfer of the nail and wire drawing plants from Rogerstone and Newport complete by the end of December 1937,[177] and the starting of the bar and strip mill and cold rolling plant in November 1938, growing numbers of workers moved to Cardiff, but for those who remained a special bus service was provided, operating at the three shift times each day, and continued until 1985. Many made the ten-mile relocation, but those elderly employees, who had completed thirty years service with the company and who were unlikely to obtain jobs elsewhere, were offered their pensions earlier than they would have normally expected.[178] GKN sold the Rogerstone site to the Northern Aluminium Co., who commenced the smelting of aluminium there

45 The installation of the merchant bar and strip mill at Castle Works (*Welsh Industrial and Maritime Museum*).

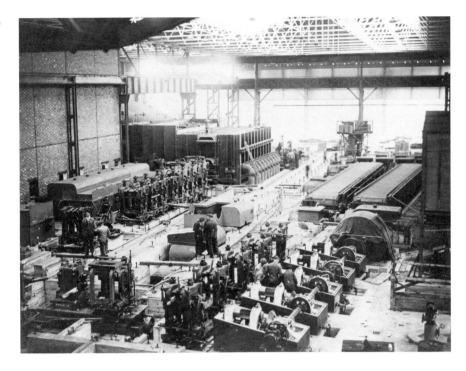

46 A GKN laboratory, either at Castle Works or Dowlais–Cardiff, showing rudimentary apparatus (*Welsh Industrial and Maritime Museum*).

47 The wire rod store at Castle Works. A sense of scale is provided by the small figure in the middle ground to the right (*Welsh Industrial and Maritime Museum*).

and took on some GKN workers who had been reluctant to move to Cardiff.

Thus, on the eve of the outbreak of the Second World War, the Castle Works at Cardiff could be described as comprising 'modern electrically-operated equipment for producing strip, bars, rods, wire'.[179] In essence, it comprised four mills: the rod mill (with a shift capacity of 220 tons); the combined merchant bar and strip mills (with an output of 1,500 tons per week, rising to 2,000 tons); and the wire mill.[180] In addition, the 126 nail-making machines were capable of turning out 800 tons of finished nails per week. A substantial two-storey brick office block had also been constructed, making for a compact and integrated layout. The various mills were linked by rail to both Roath Docks and Dowlais–Cardiff steelworks and had a connection to the G.W.R. main line. It was ironic, therefore, that the works should have been on the point of proving their business potential when war broke out.

48 Nail-making machines at Castle Works (*Welsh Industrial and Maritime Museum*).

CWMBRAN WORKS

Acquired by Arthur Keen as an ironworks for the Patent Nut & Bolt Co., the Cwmbran Works, being a small and not very modern plant, recorded declining outputs during the Edwardian period and Great War (Table 4.4). It comprised a blast furnace with Coppée coke ovens and a by-product plant, a foundry for the production of pot-sleepers, chairs, fishplates and general cast-iron work, and shops which turned out nuts, bolts and spikes for railway companies. A subsidiary operation, the Henllis Firebrick & Retort Works, was located nearby for the manufacture of firebricks and other refractories, its clay being supplied by the Viaduct Colliery.[181]

After the hostilities the furnace was blown out for alterations and relining. It was estimated that these improvements would raise output from 750 to 1,000 tons a week.[182] However the post-war depression prevented it from being blown in until June 1923. Although idle for most of 1925 and throughout 1926, the furnace remained in blast till January 1930. Most of the pig iron made at Cwmbran was sent to

49 The manufacture of nails at Castle Works (*Welsh Industrial and Maritime Museum*).

Dowlais–Cardiff Steelworks, though a little was sold to outside customers. The furnace was briefly blown in during 1934 but thereafter appears to have been unused. Table 4.5 demonstrates that the Cwmbran Works recovered gradually from the post-war slump but began to experience difficulties in the late twenties. Figures for the period 1929–38 have not survived, though it was clear that by 1939 the mills and foundry had experienced a revival.[183] In terms of products there was little change throughout the interwar years. In the late thirties, for example the mills rolled flats, clip and fang-nut bar, angles, nut and washer bar, while the foundry manufactured chairs, pole fittings, cable brackets and wagon castings all for railway companies.

50   A Weber nail-making machine, with wire being fed from the left (*Allied Steel and Wire*).

EXORS. OF JAMES MILLS: ACQUISITION AND OPERATION

In April 1929, Allan Macbeth, the managing director of Exors. of James Mills (EJM) approached GKN with a view to forming a closer association.[184] GKN and EJM had become acquainted with one another on a personal basis through their respective activities in India. During the spring of 1927, because of the volume of business they were conducting with Indian railway companies, Allan Macbeth had opened a branch office in Bombay.[185] His brother was a director of Macbeth Bros. & Co. Ltd, selling agents in India, whom GKN employed to handle their bolt and nut exports. As a result of visits by senior GKN managers, the Macbeths became known to the company and established cordial relations. As manufacturers of railway fixtures and fittings (chains, spikes, bolts, fishplates and crossings), EJM were in competition with both the Cwmbran Ironworks and F.W. Cotterill at Darlaston. Acquisition would, therefore, increase GKN's market share and provide its steelworks with one further captive outlet. The take-over was provisionally agreed in December, when it was arranged that GKN should exchange 130,000 of their ordinary shares for 100,000 in EJM.[186] Ratification followed in the spring of 1930,[187] and EJM became a wholly-owned subsidiary of GKN, Sir John Field Beale and T.S. Peacock being elected to the former's board,[188] while Allan Macbeth was appointed a director of GKN in July 1937.[189]

The business had been founded in 1850 at Stockport by James Mills (1827–69), who had opened a factory for the manufacture of engineers

Table 4.4   Cwmbran Works: 'Outputs from principal departments', 1906–21 (*tons*)

		Iron works (puddling and rolling)	Bolt works	Foundry	Total
to 30 June	1906	7,027	9,468	45,700	62,195
	1907	7,467	9,646	35,879	52,992
	1908	6,295	7,334	32,455	46,083
	1909	3,730	5,550	20,060	29,339
	1910	3,575	5,733	20,374	29,681
	1911	4,076	6,252	30,369	40,697
	1912	4,803	5,328	22,376	32,507
	1913	7,465	4,131	36,757	48,353
	1914	4,714	3,571	40,578	48,363
	1915	3,884	3,141	16,781	23,807
	1916	3,464	3,313	13,050	19,827
	1917	2,787	4,860	6,140	13,787
	1918	2,619	5,181	2,586	10,385
	1919	1,691	4,742	620	7,053
	1920	—	—	—	
	1921	1,613	2,882	22,752	27,246

Source: D.503, Cwmbran Works, Annual Output Statements, 1906–21.

Table 4.5   Output of Cwmbran Works, 1922–28 and 1939, (*tons*)

	Rolling mills	Bolt works	Foundry	Total
1922	511	2,491	11,294	14,296
1923	5,489	2,496	18,546	26,537
1924	6,232	4,221	19,209	29,662
1925	5,708	3,938	17,975	27,621
1926	5,086	3,336	11,619	20,041
1927	4,646	5,512	8,091	18,249
1928*	4,822	6,045	9,428	20,295
1939	29,291	4,064	13,260	46,615

Note: *10 months only

Source: GWRO, D.409.1 Monthly Output Figures and D.409.2; Cwmbran Works.

keys.[190] By 1874, when the firm moved to larger premises at Bredbury, Cheshire, it employed thirty workers. There, under the control of Tom Hampden Mills (1851–1916), son of James Mills, the production of cotter pins for railway companies was introduced, establishing a client connection that was to last until the mid-twentieth century. Shortly

51 An elaborate display of different types and sizes of nails and staples manufactured at Castle Works (*European Industrial Services*).

after becoming a private limited liability company in 1900,[191] a rolling mill was installed together with a draw bench for bright finished bar. In the 1920s, under the leadership of Macbeth, a re-organisation was implemented and the range of sizes, sections and quantities of bright steel bar increased greatly. The cotter department was extended and began to produce steel rail keys and jaws (to hold rails firmly on their sleepers), this proving to be a valuable diversification.

Early in 1935 it was decided to form a separate company to market the hire and sale of scaffolding,[192] EJM having become involved in the manufacture of the joints. A new organisation, Mills Scaffold Co., was established in which EJM held half the shares, the other half being owned by Col. Winby.[193] In April, GKN advanced the newly formed company £4,000, at 5 per cent, to accumulate the necessary stocks of steel tubing.[194] In October 1936, orders were reported as being 'very satisfactory' these including scaffolding employed for the construction of aerodromes occasioned by the preparations for war.[195]

52 The coke screening and ammonia sulphate recovery plant and coke ovens at Cwmbran (*Welsh Industrial and Maritime Museum*).

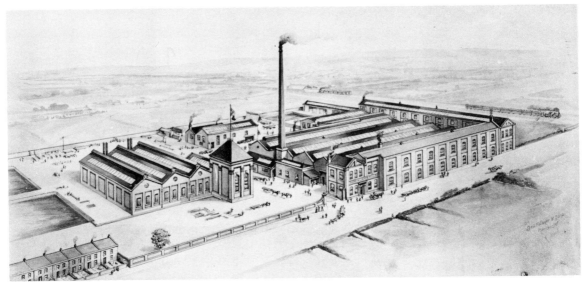

53 A Victorian illustration of Exors of James Mills at Bredbury by the Manchester publisher George Falkner & Sons.

MANAGEMENT AND ITS POLICIES

When H. Seymour Berry set about reorganising the highest levels of GKN's management in 1921, he created four new sub-boards: the Birmingham, Colliery, Investment Registration and Steel Committees.[196] The chairmanship of the last fell to W.R. Lysaght, and its other members comprised Edward Steer, F.W. Keen, H.S. Berry, T.S. Peacock, John Paton, D.C. Lysaght, Howell R. Jones, A.K. Reese and John Williams. With the replacement of Reese as general manager of Dowlais–Cardiff by William Simons in 1922, the composition of the Steel Committee remained unaltered until 1928.[197] Its membership can be divided into two distinct groups. First, there were the works managers, men who took daily responsibility for the group's various steelworks and these included D.C. Lysaght (Orb Works, Newport), Howell R. Jones (Dowlais Works), William Simons (Dowlais–Cardiff, East Moors) and John Williams (Rogerstone). Secondly, there were five GKN main board directors who were either non-specialist in steel or, in the case of John Paton, whose outside interests compelled them to take a non-executive stance. These were Steer, Berry, Peacock, Keen and Paton. W.R. Lysaght, the chairman, qualified for membership of both parties, being a director of GKN, and as joint managing director of John Lysaght Ltd, taking a particular interest in the fortunes of its Newport rolling mills, Bristol galvanising shops and Scunthorpe steelworks.

What, then, was the function and purpose of the Steel Committee? Appreciating that the merger between GKN and Lysaghts had created a group which could not be effectively managed by a single monthly meeting, the four sub-committees were designed to take direct responsibility for its principal areas of interest. They would, in effect, devise the strategic policy and implement decisions involving major capital expenditure, but report to the main board for ultimate approval. The chain of command worked as follows: the managers of a steelworks might conclude that they required a new piece of equipment. A report would be prepared outlining the cost of the improvements and the savings which might accrue over, say, a five-year period. The suggestion would then be taken by the general manager to the Steel Committee where the plan would be discussed in relation to the company's overall policy: would the innovation cause problems for other steelworks within the group; would it, indeed, produce the anticipated savings? If the scheme met with the approval of the Committee, it was then presented at the GKN main board by W.R. Lysaght, where, unless finances were particularly stretched, it could generally expect to be ratified. The Steel Committee was, therefore, a strategic and tactical policy-making body placed above individual operating companies but below the GKN board, and was, in effect, akin to the two steel 'subgroups' (GKN Steel and GKN Rolled & Bright Steel) created by the company in the early 1960s.

Whilst the membership of the Steel Committee remained remarkably constant during the early and mid-1920s, a number of changes occurred at the end of the decade. When Berry died in May 1928, his place was taken by the new GKN chairman, Sir John Field Beale; Howell R. Jones resigned as general manager of the Dowlais Works in October 1928 (being replaced by W. Simons) but retained his seat on both the Steel

Committee and the GKN main board until retirement in 1934.[198] During 1928–29, Beale, Keen and Peacock left and were succeeded by Charles H. Keen and I.F.L. Elliot.[199] Charles H. Keen (1899–1937), the son of A.T. Keen, had been educated at Rugby School and Trinity College, Cambridge, and on graduating with a degree in engineering, joined GKN to specialise in the steel industry.[200] He spent most of his working life at Dowlais–Cardiff where he became assistant general manager. In August 1932 he was appointed to the board of Guest Keen Baldwins[201] and in July 1933 became a GKN director.[202] Thus it was with considerable surprise that his death was recorded in December 1938 at the comparatively young age of thirty-eight.[203]

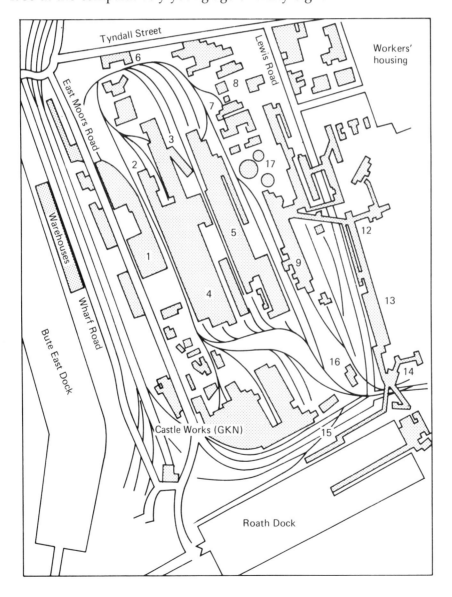

Figure 8 Dowlais–Cardiff Steelworks, East Moors (*c.* 1968)
1 Oil Tank Farm,
2 Colliery Arch Plant,
3 Rolling Mills,
4 Finishing Banks,
5 Mould Assembly,
6 General Office,
7 Steel Making,
8 Laboratories,
9 Blast Furnaces,
10 & 11 Coke Ovens,
12 Sinter Plant,
13 Ore Stocks,
14 & 15 Ore Handling Plant,
16 Vehicle Repair Shop,
17 Gasholders.

What brought the Steel Committee to an end was not the lack of any organisational effectiveness, but the decision to merge the company's heavy steel interests with those of Baldwins. The formation of GKB in January 1930, which removed Dowlais and Dowlais–Cardiff, together with their associated collieries, from GKN's direct control, made the Steel Committee somewhat redundant. Henceforth, the Normanby Park steelworks operated as an integral part of the Lysaght chain, supplying sheet bar to the Orb rolling mills and billets to Joseph Sankey; from 1924 the Cwmbran Ironworks became, in effect, a foundry and bolt producer (p. 149), while Rogerstone, which had ended steelmaking in 1921, transferred to the East Moors site as GKN Castle Works from 1935. The decision to hive off the group's two least profitable areas of operation (coal and heavy steel making) into subsidiary companies (Welsh Associated Colleries and GKB) resulted in the sub-board system being reduced by half, with only the Investment Registration and Birmingham Committees surviving into the 1930s.

SUMMARY

The British steel industry had experienced mixed fortunes during the interwar period, and GKN's circumstances mirrored the national trend. Expectations of plenty and booming profits had been raised by the shortages created during the Great War and for a brief spell these were fulfilled by the boom of 1919–20. Collapsing into the slump of 1920–21, it soon became clear that the old and least efficient steelworks could not survive long in the climate of reduced demand and falling prices. Cyfarthfa had been finally shut down in 1919, ironmaking ended at Cwmbran in 1924, and Dowlais remained poised on the brink of closure throughout the 1920s. The traditional industries, coal, ship-building, textiles and steel, suffered particularly hard during the depression of 1929–30. GKN had invested heavily in two of these activities. It was readily appreciated that the group needed to set those companies engaged in loss making to one side. Welsh Associated Colleries was formed to accommodate their colleries while a new enterprise, Guest Keen Baldwins, came into existence in January 1930 to run the heavy steel interests of GKN and Baldwins. Having ended steelmaking at Dowlais and backed by loans granted by the Bankers Industrial Development Co., GKB was able to rationalise production between its three remaining steelworks. Dowlais–Cardiff, rebuilt between 1934 and 1936, designed for the production of billets rather than slab or plate, was fortunate in that its re-opening coincided with a period of recovery. Whilst this reconstruction had been taking place, GKN had begun the transfer of production from the ageing plant at Rogerstone to a new site beside the East Moors steelworks. There a modern rod mill, and later a merchant bar and strip mill, were erected, together with a wire mill and a nail factory equipped with the latest American machines. Adversity had brought relocation and innovation. Before the Great War, it seemed as if the mighty Dowlais Ironworks could never fail and that its more modern namesake at Cardiff, laid out for the production of ships' plate, had a guaranteed future supplying the largest merchant navy the world had seen. Plans had been laid for installing blast furnaces and an open-hearth steelworks at Rogerstone. These never came to fruition. Ageing technology could not hope to compete in times of falling orders, and ultimately the works was forced to transfer to a site where it could be efficiently supplied with billets.

The management of GKN retained an adherence to steel in a way that they did not with coal. While Welsh Associated Colleries were sold to Powell Duffryn in 1935, the company persevered with its steelworks, continuing to invest considerable capital sums in them. In part, this was because their other activities (the manufacture of woodscrews, nuts and bolts, pressings, bright bar and so forth) required considerable quantities of steel, often of a specialised nature. Although this raw material could have been purchased from other UK producers, and in certain cases more cheaply from the Continent, GKN wished to safe-guard its supplies. However, steelworks were retained not solely to maintain a high level of vertical integration. Steel, or rather iron, had been at the root of GKN's prosperity for over a hundred years and was the one product which had run through the business without a break. To have surrendered the steelworks would have been to have abandoned the company's heritage, its *raison d'etre*, almost its philosophy. For its directors, many of whom had been brought up in the history of the great Dowlais ironmasters, it would have been unthinkable that GKN could exist without manufacturing steel.

References

1. GKN Minute Book, Vol. 3, March 1916–September 1922, 2 January 1919, item 3240.
2. Jones, *GKN, Vol. One*, op. cit., p. 385.
3. GKN Minute Book, Vol. 3, op. cit., 4 December 1919, it. 3426.
4. J.C. Carr and W. Taplin, *History of the British Steel Industry*, Oxford (1962), pp. 356–57.
5. GKN Minute Book, Vol. 3, op. cit., 1 January 1920, it. 3433.
6. Ibid., 1 April 1920. it. 3479.
7. Ibid., 3 June 1920, it. 3518.
8. Ibid., it. 3523.
9. B.W.E. Alford; *Depression and Recovery? British Economic Growth 1918–1939*, London (1972), p. 15.
10. Carr and Taplin, *British Steel*, op. cit., pp. 362–63.
11. GKN Minute Book, Vol. 4, October 1922–December 1923, 5 October 1922, it. 4120.
12. Ibid., it. 4123.
13. Ibid., 2 January 1923, it. 4186.

14. Jones, *GKN, Vol. One*, op. cit., p. 275.

15. Carr and Taplin, *British Steel*, op. cit., p. 365.

16. Ibid.

17. Alford, *Depression and Recovery?*, op. cit., p. 15.

18. GKN Minute Book, Vol. 4, op. cit., 1 February 1923, it. 4209.

19. Ibid., 4 January 1923, it. 4184.

20. *GKN Dowlais–Cardiff Works, Visit of HRH The Prince of Wales, February 22, 1918*, p. 7.

21. GKN Minute Book, Vol. 4, op. cit., 5 April 1923, it. 4252.

22. Ibid., 5 April 1923, it. 4254.

23. John A. Owen, *The History of the Dowlais Iron Works 1759–1970*, Risca (1977), pp. 101–2.

24. Ibid., it. 4253.

25. Owen, *Dowlais Iron Works*, op. cit., p. 103, it. 4254.

26. GKN Minute Book, Vol. 4, op. cit.

27. Ibid., 3 May 1923, it. 4265.

28. Ibid., 2 August 1923, it. 4335.

29. Ibid., 13 September 1923, it. 4357.

30. Ibid., 2 August 1923, it. 4335.

31. GKN Minute Book, Vol. 5, December 1923–February 1925, 3 April 1924, it. 4494.

32. Ibid.

33. Ibid., 1 May 1924, it. 4512.

34. GKN Minute Book, Vol. 5, December 1923–February 1925, 3 January 1924, it. 4434.

35. Ibid., 4 February 1925, it. 4671.

36. Ibid., 27 June 1924, it. 4547.

37. Ibid., November 1924, it. 4608.

38. Ibid., 4 December 1924, it. 4628.

39. GKN Minute Book, Vol. 6, February 1925–July 1926, 2 April 1925, it. 4698.

40. Ibid., August 1925, it. 4799.

41. Ibid., 3 December 1925, it. 4860.

42. Ibid., 5 November 1925, it. 4838.

43. Ibid., 4 March 1926, it. 4906.

44. Ibid., 8 April 1926, it. 4924.

45. Ibid., 16 April 1926, it. 4975.

46. GKN Minute Book, Vol. 7, September 1926–April 1928, 4 November 1926, it. 5032.

47. Ibid., September 1927, it. 5197.

48. Ibid., 3 November 1927, it. 5222.

49. Ibid., 1 December 1927, it. 5236.

50. Ibid., 5 January 1928, it. 5266.

51. Ibid., July 1928, it. 5350.

52. Interview E. Jones with W.F. Cartwright, March 1984.

53. GKN Minute Book, Vol. 7, op. cit., 2 August 1928, it. 5367.

54. Ibid., 4 October 1928, it. 5374.

55. Ibid.

56. Interview E. Jones with W.E. Simons, June 1984.

57. GKN Minute Book, Vol. 7, op. cit., 4 October 1928, it. 5374.

58. Ibid., it. 5384.

59. *Guest Keen Baldwins*, op. cit., pp. 38–9.

60. GKN Minute Book, Vol. 7, op. cit., 1 November 1928, it. 5404.
61. Ibid., 6 December 1928, it. 5420.
62. Ibid., 3 January 1929, it. 5436.
63. Ibid., 7 February 1929, it. 5449.
64. Ibid., 7 March 1929, it. 5462.
65. Ibid., 4 April 1929, it. 5485.
66. Owen, *History of Dowlais Iron Works*, op. cit., p. 105.
67. Jones, *History of GKN, Vol. One*, op. cit., p. 62.
68. GKN Minute Book, Vol. 7, op. cit., 6 June 1929, it. 5531.
69. Ibid., 3 October 1929, it. 5589.
70. Ibid., it. 5594.
71. Ibid., 2 January 1930, it. 5658.
72. Ibid., 1 May 1930, it. 5734.
73. Ibid., 2 October 1930, it. 5796.
74. Owen, *Dowlais Iron Works*, op. cit., p. 106.
75. R. Lyttleton's Newspaper Cuttings, Dowlais Works', 14 March 1934, p. 2.
76. Owen, *Dowlais Iron Works*, op. cit., p. 106.
77. R. Lyttleton's Newspaper Cuttings, *Merthyr Express*, 21 November 1936, p. 31.
78. Ibid., *Merthyr Express*, June 1936, p. 19.
79. P.B. Shelley, 'Ozymandias'.
80. This closed in December 1987, bringing to an end 228 years of manufacturing history. Much of the site has now been landscaped such that an uninitiated visitor would scarcely know that they were standing where once the greatest ironworks in the world operated.
81. Owen, *Dowlais Iron Works*, op. cit., p. 108.
82. GKN Minute Book, Vol. 5, op. cit., 4 December 1924, it. 4628.
83. Ibid., 15 January 1925, it. 4644; 4 February 1925, it. 4665.
84. GKN Minute Book, Vol. 6, op. cit., 5 November 1925, it. 4833.
85. GKN Minute Book, Vol. 8, May 1928–March 1931, 8 November 1930, it. 5815. *East Moors Album, Portrait of a Steelworks 1888–1978*, Cardiff (1978).
86. GKN Minute Book, Vol. 6, op. cit., 5 November 1925, it. 4838.
87. Ibid., 16 April 1926, it.
88. GKN Minute Book, Vol. 7, September 1926–April 1928, 9 September 1926, it. 4999.
89. Ibid., 3 March 1927, it. 5101.
90. Ibid., 7 April 1927, it. 5118.
91. Ibid., 4 May 1927, it. 5136.
92. Ibid.
93. Ibid., 7 July 1927, it. 5177.
94. Ibid., 3 November 1927, it. 5222.
95. Ibid., 1 December 1927, it. 5236.
96. Ibid., 2 February 1927, it. 5266.
97. Ibid., July 1928, it. 5350.
98. Ibid., 2 August 1928, it. 5367.
99. Ibid., 6 June 1929, it. 5531.
100. Ibid., 4 July 1929, it. 5523.
101. Ibid., 3 October 1929, it. 5594.
102. *DBB*, Vol. 5 (1986), Graeme M. Holmes, 'Sir William Charles Wright', pp. 906–7.
103. GKN Minute Book, Vol. 8, op. cit., 2 January 1930, it. 5644.

104. Ibid., 6 February 1930, it. 5667.
105. *Guest Keen Baldwins*, op. cit., pp. 35, 38–9.
106. *Guest Keen Baldwins*, op. cit., p. 55.
107. GKN Minute Book, Vol. 8, op cit., 6 November 1930, it. 5812.
108. Ibid.
109. Ibid., 4 December 1930, it. 5832.
110. Ibid., 5 February 1931, it. 5881.
111. GKN Minute Book, Vol. 9, op. cit., 5 November 1931, it. 6012.
112. Ibid., 2 June 1932, it. 6137.
113. W.K.V. Gale, *The British Iron and Steel Industry*, Newton Abbot (1967), pp. 113–14.
114. GKN Minute Book, Vol. 9, op. cit., 6 October 1932, it. 6181.
115. Ibid., 1 December 1932, it. 6219.
116. Ibid.
117. Ibid., it. 6221.
118. Ibid., 6 July 1933, it. 6345.
119. Ibid., 3 August 1933, it. 6364.
120. Ibid., 5 October 1933, it. 6384.
121. Ibid., 2 November 1933, it. 6402.
122. Ibid., 7 December 1933, it. 6422.
123. Ibid., 4 January 1934, it. 6443.
124. Ibid., 1 February 1934, it. 6457.
125. Ibid.
126. R. Lyttleton's Newspaper Cuttings, *Western Mail and South Wales Echo*, 10 February 1934, 'Tariffs Policy Uncertainty Delays operations at Cardiff-Dowlais Works'.
127. Ibid., 22 August 1934, it. 6564.
128. GKN Minute Book, Vol. 10, op. cit., 7 April 1935, it. 6687.
129. *Guest Keen Baldwins*, op. cit., p. 56.
130. *Guest Keen Baldwins Iron & Steel Co. Ltd* (reprinted from *The Iron & Coal Trades Review*, 16 October 1936), p. 3.
131. R. Lyttleton's Newspaper Cuttings, '£3 million spent on East Moors', January 1936, p. 15.
132. *The W-D Becker Coke Ovens and By-Product Plant, at East Moors Works, Cardiff, of Guest Keen Baldwins Iron & Steel Co. Ltd.* (Visit of the Iron & Steel Institute, 13 September 1939).
133. GKN Minute Book, Vol. 10, op. cit., 2 January 1936, it. 6794.
134. Ibid., 7 January 1937, it. 6941.
135. Ibid., 4 March 1937, it. 6967.
136. R. Lyttleton's Newspaper Cuttings, February 1938, p. 53.
137. *East Moors Album*, op. cit.
138. See Jones *GKN Vol. One*, op. cit., pp. 222–23.
139. 'Rogerstone Works' (typescript, n.d.), p. 3.
140. Edgar Brown, 'An Attempt at a Story' (typescript, June 1958), p. 8.
141. *An Outline History of GKN*, op. cit., pp. 36–7.
142. GKN Minute Book, Vol. 7, op. cit., September 1927, it. 5197.
143. Ibid., 3 November 1927, it. 5222.
144. Ibid.
145. Ibid., 2 Februry 1928, it. 5266.
146. Ibid., 7 February 1929, it. 5449; 6 March 1930, it. 5691.
147. Ibid., 3 April 1930, it. 5701.

148. Brown, 'Attempt at a Story', op. cit., p. 8.
149. Ibid., pp. 8–9.
150. Ibid., p. 9.
151. GKN Minute Book, Vol. 9, 3 March 1932, it. 6078.
152. Ibid., p. 10.
153. R.C.I. Guppy, 'GKN (South Wales) Limited', (typescript, 1967), p. 21.
154. GKN Minute Book, Vol. 9, 2 March 1933, it. 6285.
155. Ibid., 5 October 1933, it. 6381.
156. Ibid., 2 November 193, it. 6406.
157. Ibid., 1 February 1934, it. 6458.
158. Ibid.
159. Ibid., 12 April 1934, it. 6501.
160. Guppy, 'GKN (South Wales) Limited', op. cit., p. 21.
161. GKN Minute Book, Vol. 10, op. cit., 5 August 1935, it. 6739.
162. Ibid., 7 February 1935, it. 6654.
163. Ibid., 3 October 1935, it. 6754.
164. Brown, 'Attempt at a Story', op. cit., p. 12.
165. GKN Minute Book, Vol. 10, 6 February 1936, it. 6807.
166. Brown, 'Attempt at a Story', op. cit., p. 12.
167. Interview E. Jones with Sir Richard Brooke, December 1983.
168. Brown, 'Attempt at a Story', op. cit., p. 12.
169. GKN Minute Book, Vol. 10, op. cit., 5 March 1936, it. 6823.
170. Ibid., 2 April 1936, it. 6837.
171. Ibid., 7 May 1936, it. 6847.
172. Guppy, 'GKN (South Wales) Limited', op. cit., p. 21.
173. GKN Minute Book, Vol. 10, op. cit., 7 May 1936, it. 6847.
174. *Centenary Year, F.A. Power Ltd, 1874–1974.*
175. GKN Minute Book, Vol. 10, op. cit., 2 July 1936, it. 6868.
176. Ibid., 3 September 1936, it. 6885.
177. Ibid., 6 January 1938, it. 7085.
178. Ibid., 4 February 1937, it. 6955.
179. *Descriptive Article of Castle Works and Rolling Mills, Cardiff,* reprinted from *Iron & Coal Trades Review,* 20 October 1939, p. 2.
180. *GKN, Castle Works & Rolling Mills, Cardiff, Description of Works and Products,* December 1939.
181. *An Outline History of GKN,* op. cit., p. 39.
182. GwRO, D. 409.1 General Manager's Report, 1921–1929.
183. GwRO, D 409.1 Monthly output figures 1921–29; D 409.2 Monthly output figures 1938–43.
184. GKN Minute Book, Vol. 8, 2 May 1929, it. 5500.
185. Exors. of James Mills, Directors Minute Book, Vol. 1 (1900–1930), 18 March 1927, p. 169.
186. Ibid., December 1929, it. 5623.
187. Ibid., 3 April 1930, it. 5709.
188. Exors. of James Mills Minute Book, Vol. 1, 24 June 1930, p. 183.
189. 1 July 1937, it. 7009.
190. *The Executors of James Mills Limited 1850–1950,* Bredbury (1950), pp. 3–5; Robert Hunter, *A Short History of Bredbury and Romily,* Bredbury (1974).
191. Exors. of James Mills, Directors Minute Book, Vol. 1, December 1900–June 1930, 4 December 1900, pp. 1–2.
192. Exors. of James Mills, Directors Minute Book, Vol. 2, 1930–1948, 17 April 1935.

193. GKN Minute Book, Vol. 10, op. cit., 2 July 1936, it. 6869.
194. Ibid., 2 April 1936, it. 6833.
195. Exors. of James Mills Minute Book, Vol. 2, op. cit., 26 March 1936; 19 October 1936.
196. *GKN Annual Report and Accounts to 31 March 1921.*
197. *GKN Annual Report and Accounts 1922–1928.*
198. GKN Minute Book, Vol. 7, op. cit., 4 October 1928, it. 5374.
199. *GKN Annual Report and Accounts.*
200. Interview E. Jones with T.H. Keen, March 1984.
201. GKN Minute Book, Vol. 9, op. cit., 4 August 1932, it. 6150.
202. Ibid., 6 July 1933, it. 6330.
203. GKN Minute Book, Vol. 10, op. cit., 6 January 1938, it. 7077.

Part II

Engineering in the Midlands, 1918–45

5 Nettlefolds and the Woodscrew Trade, 1918–39

> Of the West the factory chimneys on sullen sentry
> will all night wait
> To call, in the harsh morning, sleep-stupid faces
> through the daily gate.
> Louis MacNeice, 'Birmingham' (October 1933)[1]

Speaking of the mid-1930s when he joined GKN, W.W. Fea, a chartered accountant later to become finance director, recalled,

> they had monthly accounts in those days and the Nettlefolds division [sic] was the real backbone of GKN, and my job was to take them up to Mr. [E.C.] Drake, who was the group secretary and chief accountant, and he would incorporate them in the group figures that he gave to the board . . . I got the impression from him that the Nettlefolds' profits were the most important, because they were stable. In fact the biggest shock they ever had was when I had to report a loss one month.[2]

Throughout the entire interwar period, when GKN's collieries and steelworks recorded losses, Nettlefolds remained within a surplus. In the decade of peace before the Great War, they consistently contributed around 35–40 per cent of the group's profits.[3] With its virtual monopoly of the British woodscrew trade and established reputation for quality and service, Nettlefolds constituted the dynamic element in GKN during the 1920s and 1930s. If this subsidiary failed then it was sure that the group as a whole would sustain a loss. That Nettlefolds were able to remain a viable commercial enterprise throughout the slump suggested either that it was particularly skilfully managed or that it occupied an advantageous position in the marketplace, or a combination of the two factors.

THE DIFFICULT YEARS 1919–31

During the five months ended 30 November 1918, 63 per cent of the profit (£200,313) earned by GKN in its manufacturing plant derived from Nettlefolds.[4] For the two months ended 31 August 1919, when the steel and coal interests of the company recorded a loss of £198,791 and London Works together with the other nut and bolt factories, were £6,988 in deficit, Nettlefolds achieved a surplus of £41,156.[5] The figures for the five months to 30 November 1919 were losses of £187,866 and £2,712, and a profit of £165,146[6] – a remarkable disparity of fortunes.

The loss or destruction of what were very detailed internal accounting and production records, has left the profit series for Nettlefolds incomplete (Table 5.1). It does, however, reveal that the screw works benefited from the post-war boom (£660,551 for 1920), but was then affected by the short depression. The business had recovered by 1923 and prospered until the slump of the early thirties when profits fell to a low, though the signs were that a recovery was established by 1934.

Although considerable sums were needed for new plant and machinery for GKN's steelworks, the requirements of its Heath Street and King's Norton screw mills were of a more modest nature. In October 1919, for example, £11,360 was authorised to be spent on a power station and boiler plant at the former[7] and in December 1919 £25,000 was allocated for a new fitting shop, smith's pattern shop, stores, offices and canteen,[8] this at a time when the cost of relining and reconditioning a single blast furnace was £39,475.[9] The replacement of

54   A late-nineteenth century display case of Nettlefolds' fasteners. Note the elaborate carving and decoration which contrasted with those of the interwar period.

Table 5.1 Pre-tax profits earned by Nettlefolds, 1901–34

		£	£ Adjusted			£	£ Adjusted
to 31 March	1901	119,694	217,625		1919	397,923	292,590
to 30 June	1902	176,724*	315,579		1920	660,551	418,600
	1903	186,411	330,516		1921	233,335	163,057
	1904	190,949	336,178	to 31 March	1922	173,747†	149,782
	1905	164,664	291,957		1923	415,166	372,013
	1906	159,884	283,482		1924	512,024	462,533
	1907	184,993	317,857		1925	508,804	455,918
	1908	201,644	338,329		1926	533,329	489,742
	1909	195,438	327,916		1927	369,173	347,620
	1910	213,325	355,542		1928	356,694	340,032
	1911	207,750	341,133		1929	387,412	372,512
	1912	214,484	339,911		1930	364,975	364,975
	1913	173,425	274,841		1931	230,618	245,600
	1914	198,317	316,295		1932	189,393	207,896
	1915	189,621	242,482		1933	146,939	166,221
	1916	302,416	327,290		1934	225,935	253,007
	1917	478,206	428,500				
	1918	537,210	418,387				

Notes: *15 months
    † 9 months
Figures adjusted by the Bank of England's Index of Consumer Prices 1930 = 100.

Source: BRL, 298/2 Nettlefolds Ltd. Annual Accounts General, 1893–1904; GKN, Nettlefolds Dept. Annual Accounts General, 1905–1920; 298/16 Nettlefolds Dept. Annual Accounts General, 1921–1934.

the worming machines at Heath Street was estimated at £20,000,[10] when £110,000 had recently been spent on a power house at Dowlais–Cardiff Steelworks and £75,000 at its Dowlais counterpart on a similar project.[11] Even the scheme to electrify the Heath Street mills was costed considerably lower at £20,536[12] than many of the extensions or renewals demanded by the group's steelworks. In the absence of cumulative figures, the impression given by individual decisions was that there existed a marked disparity between the contribution made by Nettlefolds to to the group's profits and the capital expenditure it incurred. In effect, the woodscrew business was subsidising both the steel and colliery interests of GKN throughout the 1920s.

Given that a major and positive imbalance existed between income and expenditure at Nettlefolds, it appeared curious that so little was spent on new technology. Although the original 'A' and 'B' machines, constructed to the Sloane patents of the 1840s, had been modified to run more efficiently,[13] the period to 1918 had seen no substantial investment in new technology. This was surprising as in 1911, P.J.

55 A GKN trade stand dating from the nineteen twenties featuring a complex arrangement of Nettlefolds' fasteners between its entrances.

Worsley, a gifted mechanical engineer employed at the works, had designed the 'C11' thread-cutting machine' which operated at twice the speed of the existing 'A' and 'B' versions. Although not a particularly expensive item to build, few of these had been introduced before the late 1930s, and most were installed during the Second World War (p. 312). Why, then, was comparatively little emphasis placed on manufacturing technology at Heath Street when so much capital was expended elsewhere in the group?

The answer appears to lie both within and without Nettlefolds. Exogenous factors related to the composition of the GKN main board and the strategy pursued by its protagonists. Following the merger with John Lysaght Ltd, H. Seymour Berry and his deputy, Sir David Llewellyn, became two of the most powerful directors. Their interest and involvement lay primarily in South Wales coal and steel, and naturally they placed considerable emphasis on the development of these two areas (p. 73). As a result, new directorial appointments tended to mirror this strategy (John Paton, T.J. Callaghan, Sir L.W. Llewelyn, E.A. Mitchell Innes and so forth). Capital followed in the same direction: many collieries were purchased and considerable sums spent in the rebuilding of the group's steelworks in Cardiff, Dowlais and Scunthorpe (p. 129). So long as Nettlefolds generated handsome profits, there seemed little point in diverting valuable capital resources

56   The GKN stand at the Engineering Trade Exhibition of February 1938 (*Allied Steel and Wire*).

to Heath Street, as it appeared that these funds were needed more urgently elsewhere. Until the mid-1930s, when the composition of the GKN board swung back to reflect the fastener interests (p. 288), substantial investment in plant and machinery at Heath Street and King's Norton would not have been a strategic priority.

The second explanation for the absence of major capital spending on plant and machinery may be found within Nettlefolds itself. The management preferred to concentrate its energies on marketing, sales and distribution. First, the existing and complex UK marketing scheme was revised and improved; secondly, an emphasis continued to be placed on the rapid delivery of any type of fastener from stock and thirdly, the company was instrumental in re-establishing and operating the International Woodscrew Union, a body which regulated conduct between national producers. Success in these three respects were major contributors to the company's profitability during the interwar period.

The company's marketing scheme, which governed its relations with British wholesalers or 'factors', had grown up partly by design and partly by trial and error during the nineteenth century.[14] In essence, Nettlefolds never sold direct to ironmongers, they dealt with wholesalers who in turn supplied retail outlets. Since the list price of woodscrews to the public did not alter during the nineteenth and mid-twentieth centuries, Nettlefolds responded to competition by

Table 5.2 GKN woodscrew sales, 1920–47 (in grosses)

		Total	Home	Export
Year ended June	1920	18,051,277	10,896,505	7,154,772
March	1923	15,681,804	9,702,634	5,979,170
	1925	17,015,382	11,156,434	5,858,948
	1927	16,717,879	10,904,888	5,812,991
	1929	18,245,808	12,250,465	5,995,343
	1931	14,805,432	11,456,846	3,348,586
	1933	15,657,490	11,569,038	4,088,452
	1935	21,197,146	14,715,311	6,481,835
	1937	25,111,101	18,530,184	6,580,917
	1939	20,022,586	14,700,116	5,322,470
	1941	29,530,239	23,041,223	6,489,016
	1943	33,354,609	29,792,081	3,562,528
	1945	33,859,597	27,704,830	6,154,767
	1947	29,336,813	23,647,806	5,689,007

Source: Working papers 'GKN Group Fastener Manufacturers and Traders' November 1975.

raising or lowering the discount rate which they offered to the wholesaler (see Table 5.3).

In the spring of 1922, it was decided to overhaul and standardise the system which had tended to develop in a piecemeal fashion as new factors were added and others had their arrangements modified.[15] Under the revised 'factors rebate scheme' wholesalers were asked to sign an agreement by which they were to stock all articles listed in the *Nettlefolds Catalogue* (an extremely extensive range) and to buy exclusively from them. In return, Nettlefolds undertook not to supply either ironmongers or consumers direct, apart from special exceptions which would be defined in advance. In addition, Nettlefolds signed an agreement with virtually every ironmonger in Britain which specified the factor or factors who were to supply them, and bound the retailer to purchase and stock only from Nettlefolds all items listed in the catalogue. On top of the published discount rate, factors were allowed an extra discount of 5 per cent. Further, a rebate system based on the loyalty agreement was introduced by which both wholesalers and retailers were rewarded.[16] Ironmongers received a 5 per cent rebate at the end of the year if their orders had exceeded £100, a target comparatively easy to meet, while the larger ironmongers could qualify for still higher percentages. The factor received a rebate in the form of a 10 per cent discount on all purchases from Nettlefolds and this was paid quarterly. Since, in practice, stock was often delivered direct from the factory to the ironmonger's shop, the factor could often win this rebate for little more than collecting the order from the ironmonger and passing it on to the screw manufacturer.

Table 5.3   Discounts on Nettlefolds steel woodscrews sold in Britain, 1918–45

Date		Discount (%)	Gross margin index (1853=100)
9 November	1918	25	133
23 December	1919	15	141
10 February	1920	5	147
13 April	1920	Net	150
8 June	1920	to size 8: Net	150
		size 9 & over: plus 15	157
15 January	1921	Net	150
1 March	1921	10	144
1 June	1921	25	133
2 January	1922	35	123
1 January	1927	45	109
1 April	1929	45	109
6 September	1932	50	100
22 March	1934	47½	105
18 March	1937	40	117
1 May	1937	37½	121
2 January	1939	40	117
1 November	1939	37½	121
1 February	1940	35	123
3 April	1940	32½	126
1 July	1940	30	128
15 August	1944	22½	136
31 December	1945	17½	140

Note: The Gross Margin Index is calculated on the following basis, assuming that the list price of one gross woodscrews was 100p and that the manufacturing cost was 25p, if a discount of 50 per cent were offered then the profit would be 25p (50p minus 25p cost) or 25 per cent of the list price. The margin would be 25 over 50 (the discounted price) which is then expressed as a percentage (50 per cent). 50 per cent has been used as a base because that was the discount operating in 1853 when the series began (see table 7.5, Jones *GKN, Vol 1*, op. cit., p. 209).

Comparatively small variations in the discount rate could, as the above table shows, result in quite large changes to the gross margin index. The manipulation of the discount, therefore, was a matter for judgement and experience.

Source: 'Woodscrew Discounts from 1853 to 1954' (typescript, May 1954), courtesy of Sela Fasteners Ltd, Leeds.

In June 1925, when competition from overseas manufacturers encouraged the company to consider cutting the list price of screws, an alternative policy was proposed: that of giving factors and large ironmongers an additional rebate on their purchases of Nettlefold screws.[17] At a meeting, the extra payment was accepted by the wholesalers, allowing 'the home price of screws [to] be maintained for the second half of 1925'.[18]

Why, then, in circumstances of increased competition in the UK from American and Swedish exporters did Nettlefolds choose to leave the retail price of woodscrews unchanged and reward intermediaries rather than fight off rivals by price cutting? In a sense, Nettlefolds adopted a form of protectionism. They chose to try to stifle competition rather than enter into combat. Having a virtual monopoly of the UK market and having concluded loyalty agreements with both factors and retailers they could prevent rivals from gaining any substantial share of the market by ensuring that the middlemen refused to accept orders from overseas. By offering the wholesalers and shops an additional rebate they were, in effect, rewarding their loyalty, and ensuring that they would lose financially if they decided to sell woodscrews made elsewhere. Unless American or Swedish manufacturers set up their own sales and distribution networks, they would find it difficult to compete on any scale with Nettlefolds.

Moreover, there were more general reasons why Nettlefolds were reluctant to enter into a price-cutting war with imports to Britain. In a depressed economy characterised by rising unemployment, they believed that cheaper woodscrews would not necessarily result in vastly increased sales, and certainly not of the order to fund the price reduction. Unlike certain non-essential items of food such as beer, woodscrews were relatively price inelastic; the handyman's decision, whether or not to build a garden shed would have been based upon the total expenditure on the project. Since the cost of woodscrews would be a minor consideration within this calculation, he would purchase them

57 A GKN display at a Glasgow trade fair in May 1938, flanked by two gimlet pointed woodscrews (*Allied Steel and Wire*).

according to how many he needed rather than their retail price. In the absence of cheaper alternatives (such as plastic fasteners or powerful adhesives) the same considerations also applied to the two major trade consumers, builders and the furniture makers. Nettlefolds could reasonably safely assume, therefore, that considerations other than price (such as the general state of the economy, exchange rates and so forth) were more important in determining levels of consumption. Further, as a result of the arrangements concluded by the International Woodscrew Union (p. 182), the customer would have found it difficult, if not impossible, to purchase cheap imports. The factors and the ironmongers were those who suffered most from the slump in trade and since they were Nettlefolds' natural customers, rather than the public, it made commercial sense to offer them some form of compensation.

A further reason why technical innovation was not given the highest priority in the twenties and thirties concerned the nature of demand. Although price was a consideration, in the absence of cheaper alternatives, it was not uppermost in the consumer's mind. Both the trade customer and the handyman wanted quality, immediate delivery and the ready availability of all sizes and types of woodscrew. By careful control over their raw material inputs and scrupulous checks during manufacture, Nettlefolds ensured that their screws were always of the best quality. In order to guarantee the rapid despatch of orders, Nettlefolds maintained an extensive warehouse which stocked every type of fastener. Tiers of bins were served by an overhead crane and manhandled on platforms by a semi-mechanised system. Orders in hand were never permitted to exceed two weeks production and the most popular sizes were never allowed to run out of stock.

Factors and ironmongers knew from experience that they could rely on the prompt delivery of any Nettlefold product. In order to maintain such levels of supplies considerable amounts of capital had to be tied up in the business; one of the reasons for the failure of the English Wood Screw Co. (p. 192) was the promoters' under-estimate of the financial provision for stock. Given that the cost of woodscrews in any item of furniture of building project was of minimal importance, but any delay in obtaining them could prove expensive, it was essential that Nettlefolds maintain their reputation for reliability and speed of supply.

Having said that there was little technical innovation at Heath Street during the 1920s, it would be wrong to assume that there was none. In October 1924, for example, the decision was taken to electrify the mill at a cost of £20,536 to be spread over two and a half years.[19]

A review of productive processes at Heath Street was carried out in January 1927 when the question of changing from acid to basic steel was considered. The latter, being cheaper and in plentiful supply, could have been obtained from the group's steelworks at Cardiff or Scunthorpe. However, acid Bessemer billets had superior machining qualities and produced a better quality woodscrew. Concerned that their reputation might suffer, Nettlefolds decided to continue purchasing acid steel from Dowlais even though this was more expensive.[20] When this works closed three years later, GKN could no longer supply the screw works with its acid steel and billets were purchased from the Workington Iron & Steel Co[21] to be sent to Castle Works, Rogerstone (later Cardiff) where they were rolled into rod and then drawn into various gauges of wire. In an attempt to consume GKN-made steel, experiments were conducted on billets made at Normanby Park in 1932 but proved unsatisfactory.[22]

Unfortunately, the loss or destruction of production and profit records for Nettlefolds has created considerable scope for guesswork. Received opinion suggests that output rose to a peak in 1914.[23] The disruption caused by the Great War, the immediate post-war depression and the era of competition which followed, culminating in the slump of the early 1930s, combined to suppress any growth (Table 5.2). In fact, total production was down on the 1920 figure every year except for 1929.

Despite these disappointing results the Heath Street works made sound profits each year. Although it was a proud boast that the woodscrew business never made an annual loss throughout the interwar period, this was not true of every month.[24] One way of obtaining an indication of changes in levels of profits is an examination of the discount rate. By contrast to the nineteenth century when discounts of 30 to 60 per cent were standard and those of 60 to 75 per cent not uncommon,[25] the years 1918 to 1939 did not witness the discount rate rise above 50 per cent (Table 5.3). In the period to January 1927, the discount attained a maximum of 35 per cent and was briefly abandoned during the harsh post-war depression. Sales appear to have fallen to marginal levels such that Nettlefolds had little surplus to pass on to their factors. Paradoxically, the increase in the discount rate from 45 to 50 per cent in 1927–32 probably reflected even tighter conditions as prices were, in effect, cut to stimulate trade during the slump. When the economy recovered during the mid-thirties the discount generally remained in the 35–40 per cent region, lower than in the prosperous Victorian era but higher than the 1920s. Output rose accordingly, peaking at around 25 million gross in 1937 (Table 5.2).

Why, then, were the twenties such difficult years in comparison with the late nineteenth century? The answer lay principally with the growth of competition abroad. Woodscrew manufacture was not technologically difficult to master – the machines in operation in the interwar period were not so remarkably different from those devised in the 1840s – and the financial barriers to entry were not high. A businessman who decided to establish a woodscrew factory would not have to raise the considerable capital sums required of, say, a steelworks, or pharmaceutical plant, nor would he need to employ as many specialist engineers, while most of the machinery could be attended by semi- or unskilled workers. Hence, by 1919 the main industrial nations of

Europe and America had a number of woodscrew makers. So long as markets had continued to expand at rapid rates during the nineteenth century they could satisfy a growing number of producers. In the interwar period when demand either stagnated or increased at a slower rate, companies could find themselves in difficulties. In September 1926, for example, Kenneth Peacock complained of heightened competition within the UK, particularly from Swedish exporters, sufficient for him to consider revising the discount rate.[26] Although the Germans and Belgians remained Nettlefolds' principal competitors, American makers also proved 'troublesome', especially Reed & Prince.[27] At the beginning of August 1930, T.S. Peacock reported orders had fallen off to such an extent that he was contemplating reducing the working week to three days.[28] By November 1930, Heath Street operated at 75 per cent of its capacity.[29] While the home trade held up reasonably well, exports suffered during the slump[30] – in 1937, 3,348,586 gross woodscrews were sold abroad in comparison with 7,154,772 gross in 1920.

RECOVERY AND GROWTH 1932–39

In March 1932, the Nettlefold directors were able to report an improvement in export orders but acknowledged that these had been taken at low prices because of the continuing high levels of competition.[31] The rise in overseas sales was sustained through the summer[32] but often at the expense of taking orders at or about cost price.[33] In November 1932, T.Z. Lloyd, general manager at Heath Street, observed that 'as the foreign stocks in this country were gradually decreasing more orders were coming forward for Nettlefold screws',[34] in other words as markets recovered prices tended to rise, eliminating any cost differences between home and imported woodscrews.

In September 1932, meetings with the Import Duties Advisory Committee had resulted in the imposition of tariffs designed to protect the home trade.[35] On their side, Nettlefolds had introduced a discount of 50 per cent and refunds had been made to stockholders on their August purchases. It was estimated that an increase in sales of about one million gross was needed to recoup the amount given away in discounts. Figures were produced in February 1933 to show the continuing decline in the number of imported woodscrews since the imposition of duties and a greater proportion of the home trade being attracted by Nettlefolds. Whilst competition in export markets remained fierce, the company held little hope of increasing overseas sales, though low prices were quoted to try to re-establish a substantial footing in Japan.[36] In May 1933, turnover for the past year was reported as being up and imports to the UK were lower, though showing a small upward trend.[37] The latter half of 1933 saw a sustained increase in fastener sales as the British economy as a whole recovered. By January

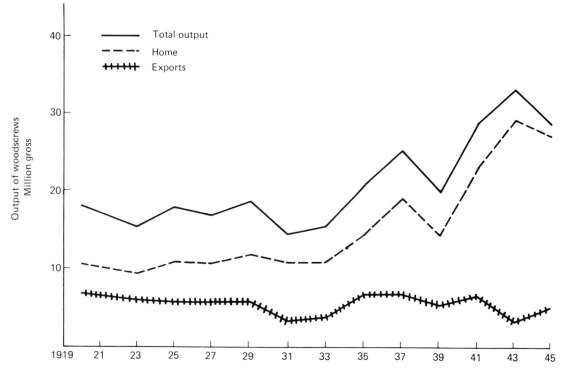

Figure 9 Woodscrew Sales by Nettlefolds, 1920–45

1934, the factors and retailers were expecting Nettlefolds to announce a price rise, and, so as not to disappoint them, the discount rate was cut by 2½ points from 22 March.[38]

With markets returning to a reasonable level of commercial prosperity, GKN were surprised to discover that Reed & Prince Manufacturing Co., an American rival, were planning to set up a screw works on a site they had leased in Glasgow.[39] In response to this obvious threat, GKN devised a four-point response: first, that they leave Nettlefold discounts unchanged and meet the competition with their various woodscrew subsidiaries; two, that they come to an arrangement with Reed & Prince by which they offer them a quota; third, that the Nettlefold discount be substantially increased; and fourth, that the new Reed & Prince be offered a compensatory payment not to proceed with their factory.[40] The GKN main board considered options one and two to be unsatisfactory as in both eventualities their competitor would be able to establish themselves. The cost of effecting the third approach was viewed as being too high, leaving them no choice but to adopt the fourth course of action. A meeting was held on 3 December 1935 with Alden and Winsor Reed at which Reed & Prince agreed not to manufacture in the UK for a period of ten years in exchange for £7,500 per annum; GKN were also to purchase the Scottish plant, valued at £28,070, and refund the Americans' expenses of £9,500. The arrangement was formally approved in January 1936.[41]

58 To encourage the consumption of Australian products, this display of groceries and wines was arranged in the Heath Street Mills (*European Industrial Services*).

Given that the trade recovery had shown itself to be sustained and that investment on plant and machinery was due, the GKN board agreed in March 1936 to the expenditure of £39,233 over the next two years.[42] In the following year it was reported that all of the group's fastener factories were 'fully occupied and working sectional overtime'.[43] In May 1937, the screw works found it difficult to keep pace with demand and a general shortage of steel was interfering with their supply of wire rod.[44] Average weekly sales in February 1937 reached £39,475 (in contrast to £35,573 for the corresponding month in 1936), while output rose to 660,000 gross a week. Exports advanced by 86 per cent in volume on the previous year and were up 40 per cent in value.[45] In such an obvious sellers' market and in view of higher steel prices, Nettlefolds reduced the discounts for both home and overseas customers.[46] However, the boom was not to last. In November it was apparent that the volume of new orders had fallen in comparison with the previous annual period.[47] Exports during the month of August 1937 were down by 30 per cent,[48] while iron woodscrew sales by Nettlefolds and GKN'S other subsidiaries to the UK totalled 1,461,000 gross in October, as against 1,797,000 gross in 1936.[49] By December, the falling off in trade was sufficient to demand for cuts in production[50] and from January 1938 Saturday mornings were no longer to be worked.[51] By

59 The heading department at St. George's Works. The wire (seen coiled on the right-hand side) was cut to the required length and a head forged at one end of these machines (*c.* 1925).

60 The bar shop at Imperial Mills, Cranford Street, Smethwick, adjacent to the Heath Street Mills. These machines mass produced bright goods from bar (*c.* 1920).

61 The screw mill at King's Norton Works (*European Industrial Services*).

March, as the British economy slipped into recession, the home trade lost its buoyancy, while exports had also fallen despite considerable price reductions.[52] To prevent the Heath Street warehouse becoming overly congested, the works was closed for three days and further periods of rest were contemplated. It has been suggested that it was only the stimulus provided by rearmament which prevented the British economy from entering another devastating depression in 1938–39. For whatever the reason, Nettlefolds experienced a slight improvement in screw orders towards the end of September 1938,[53] though the works' output for 1939 remained considerably down on that for 1937 (Table 5.2). The outbreak of war and enormous demand that this created for fasteners of every form, resulted in Heath Street returning to full-time operation with extra shifts and much overtime.

Having concentrated so much energy and capital into marketing and sales agreements (involving the acquisition of numerous subsidiaries both at home and abroad, pp. 187), it may be that Nettlefolds had understandably neglected technical innovation. Some evidence for this fell within 1937 when K.S. Peacock went on a fact-finding tour of America. He returned with two agreements.[54] The first concerned an arrangement with the Parker–Kalon Corporation under which GKN were licensed to produce self-tapping screws in Britain and the Empire (with the exception of Canada), and the second was a licence from the Phillips Screw Co. to produce their patented design. The latter,

62 K.S. Peacock (the tallest in the picture) making a presentation to long-service employees.

distinguished by the reset cross in the head, (requiring a special screw-driver), rather than the traditional slot, had made 'great headway in the US market'. None was then on sale in the UK and if GKN were to maintain their licence, Peacock noted the Phillips screw would have to be actively promoted.[55] This innovative design (which was subsequently developed by Nettlefolds under various names including 'pozidrive', 'supadriv' and latterly 'supascrew') implied that some American manufacturers had placed greater emphasis on technical innovation than GKN or had been more fortunate in their experiments.

THE INTERNATIONAL WOODSCREW UNION

Feeling the force of competition from German producers, in May 1886 Nettlefolds had approached their rivals with a view to forming a cartel. Discussions continued until June 1888 when Edward Steer succeeded in arranging a meeting of French, Belgian and German makers in Brussels which resulted in an experimental International Union being set up. The parties agreed to sell at the English price (72½ per cent discount), and a system of fines was arranged for those who transgressed this limit. The International Woodscrew Union, which continued to meet on average twice a year until the outbreak of war in 1914, remained the prime regulator of competition between the leading European manu-facturers.[56]

The Union appears to have resumed its activities in 1919 with the return to peacetime conditions of business, that is with the exception of German manufacturers who were excluded from its membership.

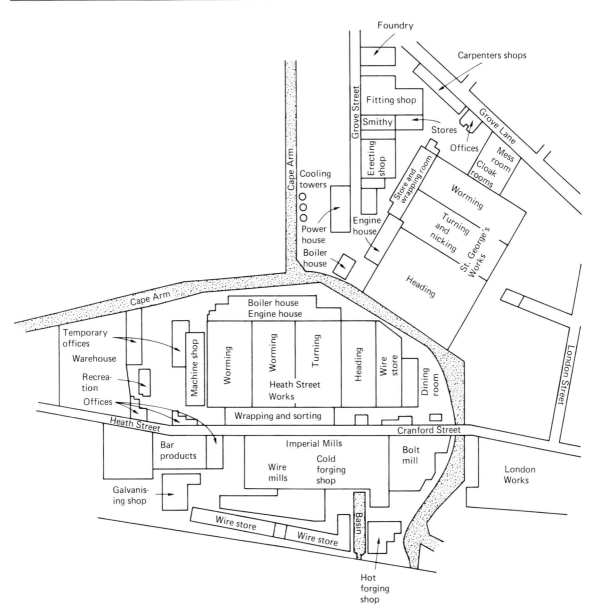

Figure 10 A plan of Heath Street Mills, *c.* 1930

Doubtless, feelings of hostility contributed to this policy and it may also have been thought that a war-ravaged Germany was no longer a match for its competitors. However, the limitations of a trade regulatory body which excluded one of the principal manufacturing nations became apparent, particularly as the German economy recovered. Accordingly, in May 1922, under the presidency of Edward Steer, it was proposed that the Germans be readmitted.[57] The suggestion was defeated. The effectiveness of the International Woodscrew Union was further reduced by the inability of the Americans to join (prevented by their

63 An advertisement for self-tapping screws made by Nettlefolds under licence from Parker-Kalon of New York (*European Industrial Services*).

anti-trust laws) and by the expulsion of the Swedes, who had not abided by its rules. With this in mind, the November 1924 meeting in Paris considered means by which the Germans and the Swedes might be readmitted and a special arrangement concluded with the United States.[58]

In the event, the two woodscrew makers in Sweden turned down the Union's overtures because a third competitor, Aug. Stenman AB, would not agree to the terms. They believed, however, that the company might agree to a sale and T.S. Peacock was instructed to investigate the possibility of GKN acquiring a foreign subsidiary (p. 194).[59]

As international rivalry stiffened during the mid 1920s, so the incentives for an all-embracing trade association increased.[60] In June 1925, when national members conceded the value of re-admitting the Germans, the only barrier that remained was the refusal of two companies to agree to the scheme.[61] In conditions of ruinous competition, the outstanding manufacturers capitulated and on 13 July 1925, at the Lucerne meeting, the Germans were readmitted to the International Union.[62]

In December 1925, it was decided to revise the Union's rules. Henceforth, certain export markets would be 'reserved' for particular producers, while members were commanded to respect the integrity of each other's home markets. Each country was given a quota and penalties were introduced in cases of over production.[63] Nevertheless, the Swedes, who had been admitted, remained argumentative and American manufacturers still refused to join the cartel. The cost of shipping woodscrews across the Atlantic made it difficult for European producers to penetrate the United States at a profit, while the Americans, with a large and protected home market, could always export surplus production to Britain and the Continent if prepared to sell at very low margins. In April 1926, a deputation, including T.S. Peacock, was sent by the Union to try to discover whether American makers might be able to accept membership.[64] The discussions proved fruitful as it was reported that should Reed & Prince, large exporters to Britain, be 'brought into line', there was a favourable prospect of coming to an arrangement'.[65]

The major weakness of any trade association (one that had revealed itself in the eighteenth century when groups of ironmasters had gathered together to protect values in times of low demand),[66] was that any member who broke the rules could, if the others held firm to price and quota deals, win potentially vast orders. In July 1926, it was reported that the French were refusing to pay the penalty due on their over production, while the Germans, whose home consumption was poor, had begun to export to America, the latter retaliating by cutting the price of their screws destined for the English market.[67] In these circumstances, T.S. Peacock observed 'it would be very difficult to keep the Union together'.[68] In September, the German members gave notice of their decision to resign, which, if it were carried through, Peacock believed, could result in a severe price-cutting war.[69] In October, at the Paris meeting, the refusal of both the French and Belgians to pay the compensation due to the Germans precipitated the resignation of the latter.[70] Anticipating the reductions in price that this would entail, Nettlefolds decided to introduce a discount of 45 per cent as from 1 January 1927 (Table 5.3). At the November 1926 meeting, the withdrawal of the Germans and disobedience of the French and Belgians was recognised as having brought the Union's existing rules to an end. For the future, it was agreed that members would respect the sovereignty of each other's home markets and not seek to export to them; under this system, Australia was deemed to be part of the UK.[71]

Almost in abeyance from November 1926, it appears that deepening depression was responsible for the resurrection of the International Union in the late 1920s. Elected president in December 1927,[72] T.S. Peacock succeeded in settling a long-standing dispute among French makers as regards values and output, the result of which was a rise in their prices by 25 per cent.[73] Tougher rules of conduct were passed at the October 1928 meeting, when the possible membership of the German and Swedish makers was also discussed.[74] With the readmission of the former, the representatives of the Swedish manufacturers attended the gathering in May 1929, agreeing to re-apply should both the United States and Canada be included within the Union's boundaries.[75] In the event, the problem of Swedish membership was solved by the acquisition of Aug. Stenman, the country's largest maker, by GKN in 1930 (p. 195), while North American manufacturers never in fact joined.

In the spring of 1930, at the nadir of the slump, GKN considered circumventing the Union by the creation of a major Continental subsidiary. In the process of acquiring Stenmans, Nettlefolds investigated the possibility of purchasing an interest in the Brussels screw works, Visserie Belge, managed by Paul Defize, encouraged by the low costs of production there.[76] The depression had also resulted in amalgamations amongst German makers and if one of these groups were to be taken over, GKN believed it could form an 'international company, having in turn, its separate national companies'.[77] Should this merger be concluded, Nettlefolds might be able to 'attain a pre-eminent and controlling position in the European screw trade, stabilise prices, and to a large extent to enable the financial requirements to be provided without calling on GKN alone'.[78] This bold strategy was not pursued, possibly because it would have aroused the opposition of other Continental makers.

So long as conditions remained depressed, the various nationalities co-operated over price and output. In July 1931, Lt. Col. Guest, who had succeeded T.S. Peacock as president in January 1930,[79] reported that 'various difficulties were being experienced in keeping the members together' but that most 'realised that conditions in the trade would be far worse without the Union'.[80] Nevertheless, the breakup of the cartel was avoided in September 1931 only by a relaxation of its rules as trade conditions improved. Members agreed to respect each other's home markets, subject to certain payments for under and over production.[81]

Ironically, having been the founding and organising force behind the International Union, Nettlefolds were the ones to leave in December 1931. They resigned their membership not because of disillusionment with the organisation or a disagreement over its policies, but because of adverse economic circumstances. The abandonment of the Gold Standard leading to 'uncertainty in regard to fiscal policy of the country and the variations in exchange' had placed them in a difficult situation.[82] Imports of cheap woodscrews had increased dramatically at the end of 1931. In view of GKN's failure to secure protective measures or Anti-Dumping Orders from the government, it was thought that the only alternative was to withdraw from the International Union in order to be able to increase discounts and therefore compete with low-price rivals.

The introduction of protective duties and the consequent gradual recovery of Nettlefolds' business from September 1932 led to fresh suggestions for an international cartel. Since GKN had been the driving force behind the Union, their departure in 1931 had heralded its collapse. Accordingly in the latter months of 1932 they contacted the leading European and American screw makers to discover whether they were willing to re-establish the association. With the exception of the Swedes, most agreed.[83] However, in the three months that it took to arrange a meeting (held in Paris on 21 February 1933) the markets collapsed and this instability precluded any deal; opposition arose chiefly from certain Belgian producers.[84] By July, both the German and French makers had become keen to set up a system of national quotas, but agreement could not be reached on actual numbers.[85] A further assembly held in June 1934 at Dusseldorf failed to resolve the impasse and plans to re-constitute the Union were postponed.[85] There was little incentive for manufacturers to join a cartel during the lush years of 1936 and 1937 as markets boomed and prices recovered. When, however, difficulties arose during 1938, K.S. Peacock suggested that some arrangement had to be concluded with the Continental markers if the export trade were 'to be in any way remunerative'.[87] 'There seemed no hope', he observed,

> of reconstituting the old International Union, and he had been considering whether some Central Selling Organisation could not be formed to handle the whole of the sales of screws for the export market ... Certain of the Continental makers were definitely interested in the scheme, although others, including the Swedish group, had not yet been approached.[88]

In the event, this plan was prevented from coming to fruition by the outbreak of war and it was a revival of the International Union which followed the return to peace rather than the introduction of a central-ised selling organisation.

SUBSIDIARY ACQUISITIONS

In the period up to 1914, GKN had two woodscrew factories in the Midlands (Heath Street, Smethwick, and the King's Norton Works at Stirchley which specialised in the smaller gauges of woodscrew, though concentrated on cotter pins, screw hooks and eyes) together with one subsidiary, the British Screw Co. in Leeds. During the interwar period, occasioned partly by the tough competitive con-ditions, a number of smaller Midlands screw businesses either offered themselves for sale or were taken over by GKN to form a satellite group around the principal works at Heath Street.

64   Thomas P. Hawkins & Son of Balsall Heath, manufacturers of cotter pins, chains and staples, taken over by GKN in 1938. Depicted here in 1935 shortly before the acquisition.

65   The loop and staple shop at Hawkins.

The first companies to be acquired were Henry Cox Screw Co. Ltd. and A. Stokes & Co. Ltd, both taken over in the spring of 1923.[89] In June 1927 Thomas Haddon & Co. was purchased,[90] and in 1938, in view of the congested nature of their factory, it was decided to merge this company with that of Stokes. Brought together under a single management, at a cost of £62,000, new mills, a warehouse and offices were constructed alongside the existing factory of Stokes at Deritend.[91] Both companies had pioneered the production of machine screws with rolled threads, and in Haddon's case had also made cold, forged bolts. The merged enterprise was styled Thomas Haddon & Stokes.[92]

In the spring of 1925, the chairman of Recess Screws of Gillingham approached GKN, suggesting a possible sale. After an inspection of the plant and their accounts, T.S. Peacock recommended that £25,000 be offered for the business as a way of reducing competition.[93] Recess Screws then raised the price to £35,000 and GKN withdrew from negotiations.[94] The company then went into voluntary liquidation and the receiver was reported as having obtained a higher price than GKN was prepared to pay.[95] The new company, Recess Screws (1926) Ltd, was acquired by the Distillers Co. through one of their subsidiaries but in February 1927, disappointed by its results, they offered the business for sale to GKN.[96] T.S. Peacock estimated that it might cost up to £40,000 to purchase the business but the board 'considered that it would be policy to deal effectively with this company, which had been a source of trouble for many years'.[97] In the event, the purchase was completed for £29,000 and the factory at Gillingham closed.[98]

Nettlefolds obtained the bulk of their wire from their own plant,

66 The cotter pin shop of Hawkins.

Imperial Mills, Coverack Road, Newport, which, in turn, was provided with rod by Castle Works, Rogerstone. However, this was of the steel variety and since Heath Street made considerable quantities of brass screws it was considered prudent to obtain closer control over all their supplies of wire. In March 1922, T.S. Peacock opened negotiations with the United Wire Works Ltd (UWW), an Edinburgh enterprise which in 1916 had set up a branch factory in Birmingham manufacturing brass and copper wire.[99] Peacock proposed that a new company, to be called United Wire Works (Birmingham) Ltd, be formed to run the Birmingham plant and that the share capital be subscribed equally by GKN and UWW. The cost to GKN of implementing this scheme was about £15,000 for the investment, together with a payment of £5,000 as an entry fee. In January 1928, GKN suggested to UWW that they might like to sell their holding in the wire factory.[100] The purchase was completed by June, when Peacock announced the acquisition of the outstanding 12,500 preference and 12,500 ordinary shares for £50,000.[101]

At the depth of the depression, in October 1930, the directors of

67 The Hawkins warehouse where women alone seem to be employed.

Frederick Mountford (Birmingham) Ltd approached GKN with a view to the latter taking them over.[102] At their Moseley Street works they made taper pins, machine keys and special repetition parts. Since they were in competition with various companies, the GKN group decided to take advantage of this offer, acquiring Mountfords in exchange for 10,000 second preference shares in GKN.

In April 1932 a firm of stockholders posted a circular to selected factors and ironmongers informing them of plans to form a new company to manufacture and sell woodscrews and encouraged them to subscribe to the enterprise.[103] Concerned that a major competitor might be about to enter the UK market, GKN asked Exors. of S. Berger, one of their distributors, to acquire 500 £1 shares, for which they were reimbursed and the shares assigned to GKN under a deed of trust. In this way, GKN were able to obtain a copy of the English Wood Screw Co.'s (EWS) articles of association. This revealed that it had been set up by the directors of the Central Iron & Metal Co. in conjunction with a Dutch woodscrew business run by P. Van Thiel.

In February and March 1933, while their Croydon factory was being

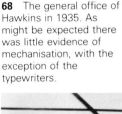

68 The general office of Hawkins in 1935. As might be expected there was little evidence of mechanisation, with the exception of the typewriters.

equipped, EWS approached GKN with proposals for market sharing, all of these, however, were rejected. In June, when EWS began production,[104] samples of their screws were obtained and tests revealed that though their standard was not as high as Nettlefold's best, they were certainly saleable.[105] During the summer and autumn of 1933, EWS sold woodscrews at around 20 per cent below Nettlefold prices. However, the Croydon enterprise fell into difficulties during September; EWS had been under-capitalised, insufficient funds had been provided to finance the large quantities of stock demanded by the business.[106] Accordingly, the balance sheet for the first year of operation revealed a loss of £7,111. The directors of EWS quarrelled among themselves, which allowed GKN to acquire the company through Van Thiel in January 1934.[107]

GKN did 'not expect to get anything like the value in plant and stocks for the money expended' but viewed the acquisition 'in the nature of an insurance against the market price of screws being disturbed as, if that happened, the loss to the company would be considerably more than the cost of the shares in question'.[108] Nevertheless, GKN kept their interest a secret and retained Van Thiel as chairman and managing director.[109] They appointed Mr. R.D. Sherbrook-Walker of Carter & Co., GKN's auditors, and [Sir] Anthony Bowlby, then a manager at Heath Street, as directors. The latter, in effect, ran the works at Croydon and under his leadership its 100 employees eventually produced a profit of £4,796 in 1935 and subsequently regularly generated a surplus of £2,000 a month. Bowlby was instructed not to poach Nettlefolds' established customers but to target those factors and ironmongers who were already buying cheap imported woodscrews, particularly Belgian and Japanese makes. Just as customers in the Edwardian period and later did not realise that the British Screw Co. in Leeds was a subsidiary of GKN, so the true owners of the English Wood Screw Co. remained concealed. Austin Motors, for example, had concluded contracts with both Nettlefolds and EWS during the 1930s and attempted to play one off against the other. However, in August 1935 it was decided to wind up EWS; the machines were to be sent to GKN's screw factory at Santa Rosa, Brazil, and in June 1937 the site was sold to the Southern Galvanising Co. for £6,200.[110]

Other acquisitions undertaken in the 1930s included the Birmingham Wire Work Co., described as a 'keen competitor in the cotter [pin] trade', which was purchased in the spring of 1935 for £15,000.[111] The company had also been taken over to provide a modern works for David Powis & Sons Ltd (established 1864), manufacturers of copper rivets and nails and zinc nails and tacks, who had been bought by GKN during the twenties.[112] It was planned that the Birmingham Wire Work Co. would close and Powis move to the former's site in Golden Hillock Road, Sparkbrook, during 1936.[113] In September 1938, GKN acquired Thomas P. Hawkins & Sons of Balsall Heath for £25,000. As a Birmingham cotter pin company dating back to 1786, which had earned 'satisfactory profits' over the last few years, it was thought advisable that GKN should obtain control 'rather than it should fall into the hands of competitors'.[114]

In October 1938, K.S. Peacock signed an arrangement with the Bradshaw Patent Screw Co. by which Nettlefolds were licensed to manufacture a patent tamper-proof screw for use in the motor car trade.[115] While the screw was believed to have some merit, 'the real purpose of arriving at an agreement had been to prevent Mr. J.W. Gibson [chairman of] ... Acton Bolt & Fine Threads Ltd. from commencing to manufacturing woodscrews there'.[116]

The final fastener acquisition effected by GKN before the outbreak of war was that of George Goodman Ltd. Established as needle makers in 1810, they had won a gold medal at the Great Exhibition of 1857 for the quality of their steel pins but from 1892 the safety pin became the business' principal product, diversifying into blanket, hat and collar pins. Because the company was considering making brass woodscrews,

69 The offices and showrooms constructed on the Euston Road for Nettlefolds and Sons. The ironwork to the first-floor windows and the shields above the doorways featured the initial 'N' (*Author*).

GKN decided to suggest a takeover. Initially, in October 1938, the company refused GKN's offer of £240,000 for the 40,000 ordinary shares,[117] though the improved price of £7 per ordinary share and 25 shillings for each £1 preference share (total cost £330,000) won acceptance.[118] In order that GKN's identity be kept from public knowledge, the takeover was conducted through Bishopsgate Nominees. As in the case of the British Screw Co. and the English Wood Screw Co., the fact that the enterprise in question had passed into the hands of GKN was not revealed. The Goodman board of directors remained largely unaltered, though GKN appointed W.L. Barrows, senior partner of Howard, Smith, Thompson & Co., chartered accountants, as their representative.[119] In March 1939, the GKN board approved Goodman's proposal to acquire J.W. Broughton & Co. of Smethwick, makers of safety and hair pins, for £15,000, who were also contemplating the manufacture of woodscrews.[120]

THE ACQUISITION OF AUG. STENMAN AB

During the 1920s, Swedish makers of woodscrews had been a considerable problem for Nettlefolds. They were reluctant and only occasional members of the International Union, but as manufacturers of high quality screws were able to export to Britain.[121] As early as December 1924 the notion of acquiring Aug. Stenman, one of the leading Swedish firms and possibly also the least co-operative, was discussed by the GKN board.[122] Established in 1881 at Eskilstuna as a hinge-making business, it expanded and, having introduced self-acting machinery, entered the fastener trade. Given the limitations of the Swedish home market, the company was compelled to concentrate on exports, so that by 1930 about four-fifths of the factory's entire output was sold overseas. The death of the founder, August Stenman in 1920, had precipitated the firm into crisis as the only heir was his daughter, Baroness Elise Åkerhielm, who in 1921 arranged to float Stenmans as a joint stock company with a share capital of one million kronor.[123]

In September 1926, the level of Swedish exports to Britain had reached such levels that T.S. Peacock proposed the raising of discounts on both steel and brass woodscrews.[124] Because Swedish manufacturers continued to remain outside the International Union and sell aggressively into the UK, in December 1927 the GKN board considered purchasing three small screw-making plants there, 'for the purpose of breaking up their trade'.[125] In May 1928 the notion was taken further when T.S. Peacock was sent to visit the premises of the nation's largest maker, Aug. Stenman, provided with plenary powers to negotiate a purchase.[126] However, his visit proved abortive as the price asked was, in his judgement, 'prohibitive'.[127]

In January 1929 when the Falu Screw Works in Sweden was offered for sale, GKN sent a deposit of 175,000 kronor to Aug. Stenman who would then handle the transaction. In addition, it was intended that Stenman acquire the Prior Works. These two small screw factories would then be broken up, thereby considerably simplifying the Swedish market and 'it was hoped would facilitate the entrance of the two big Swedish firms into the Union'.[128] The final purchase price of the Falu Works (which came to around £13,000)[129] was to be found by members of the Union according to their percentage sales. In the event, however, they refused to make any contribution.

When Mr Diedrichs of Uddeholms informed them that they wished to acquire the Eskilstuna Works of Stenmans but needed either GKN or the Union to provide one-third of the purchase price (about £11,000), the board approved the expenditure.[130] In 1928, Baroness Åkerhielm had sold the company to a syndicate headed by the Swedish banker, Jacob Wallenberg. The largest shareholder, with 50 per cent of the stock, was Mr Sixten Nilsson. Rather than let Uddeholms acquire the company, GKN then decided to take over Stenman itself and in November 1929 T.S. Peacock and Sir John Field Beale opened negotiations with Captain Rudberg, the chairman, Wallenberg and Nilsson.[131] Price Waterhouse & Co., the City firm of chartered accountants, were instructed to investigate the company's financial situation,[132] and on receipt of a satisfactory report the purchase was completed in June

70 Sixten Nilsson, general manager of Aug. Stenman AB.

1930. For £783,700, GKN obtained 1,000 'A' shares (of a total 5,000) and all 30,000 'B' shares.[133] Although this gave GKN a controlling interest, the acquisition had been governed by the condition that Stenmans would remain under Swedish management and retain a degree of autonomy. Profits were never transferred to Britain, although this would have been permissible under Swedish law. The takeover did not entirely solve GKN's problems for Nilsson, who remained as general manager, continued to sell Stenman screws to British factors,[134] and at the October 1931 meeting of the International Union declared that he would export in contravention of its rules.[135] Given that 80 per cent of Stenman's output was sold overseas, tight cartel arrangements could spell financial ruin for such a company.

In the spring of 1935, Uddeholms themselves offered their business for sale to GKN. The asking price was 6 million kronor. At a meeting with their managing director, Mr Troili, GKN offered 5.5 million kronor as it was estimated that £25,000 would have to be spent in proving a further factory.[136] In the event, the acquisition was completed for 5 million kronor, 2 million being provided by Stenmans, 1.5 million by John Lysaght and 1.5 million by GKN.[137]

Although Stenman and Uddeholms were owned by GKN they were allowed a considerable measure of independence and did not always behave as subservient subsidiaries. In the autumn of 1938, for example, when export market contracted, Nilsson, who relied on overseas sales for profitability threatened to reduce his selling price to Britain. Since the Swedes were then selling in the region of 4,400,000 gross wood-screws to Britain and Ireland,[138] this policy could have damaged Nettlefolds' home business. Accordingly, after negotiations Nilsson agreed to accept compensatory payments to adhere to existing arrangements.[139] In November 1938, he obtained GKN's permission to acquire the business of a Mr Thulin who had successfully established a lock and window fastener factory at Eskilstuna in direct competition with Stenman.[140]

NETTLEFOLDS IN AUSTRALIA

Traditionally, Nettlefolds had supplied Imperial territories from Heath Street and in the past had succeeded in keeping the Australian market largely to themselves despite tough competition from German manu-facturers.[141] Accordingly in 1922, when the Burgess Screw Co. decided to set up a screw works there,[142] GKN initially decided to acquire the business, agreeing a price in August of £11,500.[143] In the event, the deal was not concluded, GKN withdrawing from the purchase.[144] Neverthe-less, it may have been this episode which encouraged the board to consider manufacture themselves in Australia. The Federal Govern-ment, often with the threat of import duties, was putting pressure on British exporters to establish an industrial base in the subcontinent. If

GKN were to set up a screw works in Australia it would have virtually excluded any other manufacturer from doing so given the vast geographical size but comparatively low volume of the fastener market there. In September 1924 GKN approved the formation of a new company, Nettlefolds Proprietary, to take charge of the works and the company's existing distribution networks. Its chairmanship fell to H.R. Lysaght, while Messrs. Merritt, T.S. Peacock, Lightfoot Walker, Nichol and Brookes were appointed directors.[145]

The contracts for the construction of a factory, totalling £22,389, were approved in October 1924.[146] The works, in the town of Sunshine, near Melbourne, were largely complete by the summer of 1925:[147] Mr Kelly, the manager sent from Heath Street, had arrived, the machinery had been shipped during March and the buildings finished by the end of April.[148] The site had been chosen for two reasons. First, it was close to the main railway lines between Melbourne, Ballarat and Bendigo, though little use was made of this facility until after 1940. Secondly, though land prices were low, it was thought that the district would develop as the industrial centre of Victoria.[149] Once in production, output soon rose to around 8,000 gross per week,[150] and in December 1928 had attained 20,000 gross.[151] With the extensions that were then underway, it was calculated that the Sunshine Works would be able to satisfy the entire Australian demand by February 1929. Annual profits were recorded as being around £16,000 before tax.[152] In December 1934, following a visit by T.Z. Lloyd, a further expenditure of £9,275 was authorised to increase the plant's capacity.[153] In 1937 Nettlefolds Proprietary was judged to be too successful by the Federal Government (its profits being disproportionately large in relation to its capital) and they reduced the tariffs charged on woodscrews imported into Australia.[154] Despite this adjustment the company remained highly successful and recorded a profit of £44,900 for 1937–38.[155]

MANAGEMENT

Thomas Zachary Lloyd (1872–1939) was the general manager of Heath Street throughout the interwar period. Educated at Clifton College and as a student of mechanical engineering at King's College, London, he had joined Nettlefolds in about 1892 and became general manager in 1906 on the death of Charles Steer. Sir Anthony Bowlby (b. 1906), who entered Heath Street from New College, Oxford, in April 1929 and himself subsequently took charge of the screw business, recalled that Lloyd appeared to him as

> a studious and academic type, a sort of introverted person. He was highly intelligent, a very well qualified engineer and a cultured man and seemed to me to be someone I could get on with.[156]

71 T.Z. Lloyd (1872–1939), general manager of Heath Street Mills.

Lloyd was not, however, an autocratic figure. 'He would take an awful lot', observed Bowlby, 'but he would be very patient and very persistently resistent'.[157] Whilst he was responsible for the operation of the works, T.S. Peacock, as managing director of GKN, took the overall strategic decisions. The fact that Peacock, whose industrial experience was in bolts and nuts at Darlaston, tended to involve himself in the running of Nettlefolds may have delayed Lloyd's appointment to the main board until August 1930.[158] Peacock was, for example, responsible for appointing N.B. Rosher, an electrical engineer, as general works manager at Heath Street. Rosher had originally supervised the conversion of the Heath Street mills from steam to electrical power and given that he had no experience of mechanical engineering or of fastener production, his subsequent appointment seemed to many to have been inappropriate.[159]

When Rosher died in September 1936,[160] he was succeeded as general works manager by his assistant, [Sir] Anthony Bowlby, who had returned to Birmingham in that year, having spent several years in Croydon running the English Wood Screw Co. When T.Z. Lloyd retired at the end of March 1939 (and sadly died shortly afterwards following a lifetime's work at Heath Street),[161] his position as general manager passed to Maurice Tollit, who, together with Bowlby, ran the screw works throughout the war years. In May 1935, Stephen Lloyd had joined Heath Street as an assistant to his father, T.Z. Lloyd. Educated at Oxford University, he had entered the Indian Civil Service but having contracted polio in Benares was forced to return to England.

The sales and marketing departments were the responsibility of E.C.B. Rowley. A former schoolmaster, he was recruited from a firm of consultants and with imaginative flair revitalised Nettlefolds' marketing plan (p. 172). Rowley, in turn, had two assistants both of whom were to rise to high office within GKN, Kenneth Peacock and Maurice Tollit.

It was a measure of the importance of the Heath Street Works that the ablest young men were offered position here, and if they fulfilled their potential could eventually be offered main-board appointments. Kenneth Peacock, Maurice Tollit, [Sir] Anthony Bowlby and Stephen Lloyd all became directors of GKN and owed their promotion to an involvement with the woodscrew business.

As regards its management within the GKN group, representatives from Heath Street originally sat on the Nettlefolds Committee. Formed in October 1902, it continued to supervise the affairs of the various screw works until 1921, when the meeting was re-named the Birmingham Committee.[162] As woodscrew subsidiaries were acquired in the interwar period, so their directors were appointed to the Birmingham Committee. In May 1923, for example, all board members of both Henry Cox Screw Co. and A. Stokes & Co. took their places at the gathering.[163] As the number of fastener subsidiaries increased during this period, so its membership must have become quite large. Perhaps this constitution proved unworkable, for by the mid-1930s full membership of the committee had been reduced to: T.S. Peacock (chairman), S.R. Beale, T.Z. Lloyd, K.S. Peacock, Lt. Col. C.H.C. Guest, J.H. Jolly, W.R. Lysaght and the secretary, H.N. Briggs; also in attendance were E.C. Drake, M.H. Tollit, H.S. Peacock, [Sir] Anthony Bowlby and W.W. Fea.[164] Executive directors of subsidiaries were asked to attend when their company was the subject of discussion.

The paternalistic attitude of management at Nettlefolds established during the nineteenth century endured throughout the 1920s and 1930s. Because a high proportion of the workforce lived locally in settlements of red-brick, terraced houses, a continuity and loyalty to the Heath Street works was maintained. Generations of the same families were employed there and often completed lengthy periods of service. In April 1936, K.S. Peacock and T.Z. Lloyd persuaded the GKN board to introduce a contributory pension scheme which could then be adopted by any works or subsidiary within the group. Arranged with the Prudential, workers were asked to contribute one shilling a week, while staff paid 5 per cent of their pensionable salary. At Heath Street around 90 per cent of all male employees joined the scheme (women were not included for many years). Early in 1941 Nettlefolds took the then uncommon step of appointing their first full-time medical officer, Dr W.J. Lloyd, then a general practitioner in Suffolk. Soon afterwards he took responsibility for the health care of employees at the nut and bolt works in Darlaston and the group's other fastener factories.

SUMMARY

During the interwar years the Heath Street Works of Nettlefolds was the crucial profit earner within the GKN group. Although it went through difficult times, particularly between 1929 and 1931, earnings from woodscrews were less subject to violent fluctuations than those from the company's coal, steel or nut and bolt interests. With the re-organisation of their UK marketing plan and leadership of the International Woodscrew Union, Nettlefolds were able to retain their dominance of home customers and secure some safeguards against ruinous competition overseas. Should a new screw-making enterprise be mooted then Nettlefolds either compensated its proposers (as in the case of Reed & Prince's Glasgow plan) or an outright, though often concealed, acquisition was arranged (as in the case of Recess Screws and the English Wood Screw Co.). The company also took advantage of depressed periods to take over a number of smaller, Midlands competitors including Henry Cox Screw Co., A. Stokes & Co., the Haddon group, David Powis & Sons, T.P. Hawkins & Son, George Goodman, and J.W. Broughton & Co., while licensing arrangements were concluded with the Bradshaw Patent Screw Co., Parker–Kalon Corporation and the Phillips Screw Co.

For the first time, and largely as a defensive operation to protect their UK market, Nettlefolds acquired several foreign subsidiaries – all in Sweden, a source of vigorous competition. The acquisition of Aug. Stenman in 1930 was followed by that of Uddeholms in 1935 and three years later by Thulin's fastener business. In response to the Australian government's wish to encourage domestic industry, GKN established a screw works at Sunshine, near Melbourne, under the style, Nettlefolds Proprietory.

For management purposes the screw works came under the overall authority of T.S. Peacock, one of the joint managing directors of GKN, but because his own expertise lay in the related bolt and nut trade and being based at Cotterills in Darlaston, in practice, executive authority fell to T.Z. Lloyd, as general manager of Heath Street. The sales and marketing departments were the initial responsibility of E.C.B. Rowley and subsequently were taken over by Kenneth Peacock and Maurice Tollit. Sir Anthony Bowlby, who had joined GKN in 1929 after a period running the English Wood Screw Co. in Croydon, returned in 1936 to become general works manager in place of N.B. Rosher, while in 1935 T.Z. Lloyd was joined by his son, Stephen Lloyd. W.W. Fea, another Oxford graduate and a chartered accountant, joined GKN in March

1935 and, reporting to Kenneth Peacock, was responsible for taking a financial overview of the Heath Street operations.

In so far as there were problems at Nettlefolds, they concerned the plant and machinery. Employing some 4,390 workers in 1937,[166] and in the light of post-war cuts, the works were over-manned (in 1936 when Sir Anthony Bowlby visited Germany he discovered that twenty machines fitted with feeders could be looked after by one woman, while at Heath Street, where the plant was less advanced, the figure was fifteen to each operator), but the unions fiercely resisted attempts to obtain reductions. Although a programme of capital investment in plant had been initiated in March 1936, the replacement of the modified 'A' and 'B' machines really began in earnest during the Second World War. New types of self-tapping and 'Phillips' screws were introduced in the late 1930s but under licence from American makers. However, machine screws, used in vehicles, white goods and tools, were of subsidiary importance.

Despite the upheavals of the interwar period, the woodscrew remained the principal device for assembling pieces of wood. Consumed in its millions by builders, the furniture trade and the handyman, no acceptable substitute was discovered. With the development of powerful adhesives, plastic fasteners, metal staples in the 1960s, it may be judged that the woodscrew had reached maturity, and may perhaps have been entering old age in the product cycle by the end of the interwar period. The fact that it, as an item of consumption, had ascended to an apogee was one of the factors responsible for the success of Nettlefolds.

References

1. Michael Longley (Editor), *Louis MacNeice, Selected Poems*, London (1988), p. 17.
2. Interview J. Cockcroft with W.W. Fea, December 1972, p. 3.
3. Jones, *GKN, Vol. One*, op. cit., Table 11.2, p. 371.
4. GKN Minute Book, Vol. 3, op. cit., 2 January 1919, it. 3226.
5. Ibid., 2 October 1919, it. 3393.
6. Ibid., 1 January 1920, it. 3433.
7. Ibid., 2 October 1919, it. 3400.
8. Ibid., 4 December 1919, it. 3426.
9. Ibid.
10. Ibid., 1 March 1922, it. 3956.
11. Ibid., 6 May 1920, it. 3501.
12. GKN Minute Book, Vol. 5, op. cit., 2 October 1924, it. 4584.
13. Jones, *GKN, Vol. One*, op. cit., pp. 160, 210.
14. See Edgar Jones 'Marketing the Nettlefold Woodscrew by GKN 1850–1939' in R.P.T. Davenport-Hines (Editor), *Markets and Bagmen, Studies in the History of Marketing and British Industrial Performance 1830–1939*, Aldershot (1986), pp. 131–45.

15. GKN Minute Book, Vol. 4, op. cit., 29 June 1922, it. 4046.
16. Plan outlined in a letter from Sir Anthony Bowlby, December 1985.
17. GKN Minute Book, Vol. 6, op. cit., May 1925, it. 4744.
18. Ibid., 26 June 1925, it. 4763.
19. GKN Minute Book, Vol. 5, op. cit., 2 October 1924, it. 4584.
20. GKN Minute Book, Vol. 7, op. cit., 13 January 1927, it. 5065; GKN Minute Book, Vol. 8, op. cit., 6 March 1930, it. 5691.
21. Interview J. Cockroft with Sir Anthony Bowlby, 25 April 1972, pp. 12–13.
22. GKN Minute Book, Vol. 9, op. cit., 4 August 1932, it. 6160.
23. Interview J. Cockroft with Sir Anthony Bowlby, 25 April 1972, p. 13.
24. Interview J. Cockroft with W.W. Fea, 8 December 1972, p. 3.
25. Jones, *GKN, Vol. One*, op. cit., p. 209.
26. GKN Minute Book, Vol. 7, op. cit., 9 September 1926, it. 4997.
27. GKN Minute Book, Vol. 8, op. cit., 4 April 1929, it. 5482.
28. Ibid., 7 August 1930, it. 5772; 6 November 1930, it. 5810.
29. Ibid., 4 December 1930, it. 5828.
30. Ibid., 8 January 1931, it. 5855.
31. GKN Minute Book, Vol. 9, op. cit., 3 March 1932, it. 6078.
32. Ibid., 7 April 1932, it. 6096.
33. Ibid., 2 June 1932, it. 6135.
34. Ibid., 3 November 1932, it. 6198.
35. Ibid., 6 October 1932, it. 6177.
36. Ibid., 2 February 1933, it. 6256.
37. Ibid., 4 May 1933, it. 6322.
38. Ibid., 1 March 1934, it. 6478.
39. GKN Minute Book, Vol. 10, op. cit., 7 November 1935, it. 6765.
40. Ibid., 5 December 1935, it. 6779.
41. Ibid., 2 January 1936, it. 6793.
42. Ibid., 5 March 1936, it. 6823.
43. Ibid., 4 March 1937, it. 6968.
44. Ibid., 6 May 1937, it. 6992.
45. Birmingham Committee Minute Book, Vol. 5, April 1937–January 1939, 6 April 1937, it. 3464.
46. Ibid., 4 May 1937, it. 3474.
47. GKN Minute Book, Vol. 10, op. cit., 4 November 1937, it. 7061.
48. Birmingham Committee Minute Book, Vol. 5, op. cit., 5 October 1937, it. 3526.
49. Ibid., 30 November 1937, it. 3557.
50. GKN Minute Book, Vol. 10, op. cit., 2 December 1937, it. 7073.
51. Ibid., 6 January 1938, it. 7085.
52. Ibid., 3 March 1938, it. 7114.
53. GKN Minute Book, Vol. 11, op. cit., 3 November 1938, it. 7179.
54. GKN Minute Book, Vol. 10, op. cit., 2 December 1937, it. 7070.
55. Ibid.
56. Jones, *GKN, Vol. One*, op. cit., pp. 230–1.
57. GKN Minute Book, Vol. 3, op. cit., 17 May 1922, it. 4007.
58. GKN Minute Book, Vol. 5, op. cit., 6 November 1924, it. 4603.
59. Ibid., 4 December 1924, it. 4625.
60. GKN Minute Book, Vol. 6, op. cit., 5 March 1925, it. 4689.
61. Ibid., 5 June 1925, it. 4744.
62. Ibid., 6 August 1925, it. 4776.

63. Ibid., 3 December 1925, it. 4858.
64. Ibid., 8 April 1926, it. 4922.
65. Ibid., 3 June 1926, it. 4966.
66. Jones, *GKN, Vol. One*, op. cit., pp. 81–2.
67. GKN Minute Book, Vol. 6, op. cit., 22 July 1926, it. 4980.
68. Ibid.
69. GKN Minute Book, Vol. 7, op. cit., 9 September 1926, it. 4997.
70. Ibid., 4 November 1926, it. 5029.
71. Ibid., 2 December 1926, it. 5048.
72. Ibid., 5 January 1928, it. 5251.
73. GKN Minute Book, Vol. 8, 3 May 1928, it. 5310.
74. Ibid., 1 November 1928, it. 5403.
75. Ibid., 6 June 1929, it. 5529.
76. Ibid., 3 April 1930, it. 5708.
77. Ibid., 3 April 1930, it. 5708.
78. Ibid.
79. Ibid., 6 February 1930, it. 5674.
80. GKN Minute Book, Vol. 9, op. cit., 2 July 1931, it. 5956.
81. Ibid., 1 October 1931, it. 5997.
82. Ibid., 3 December 1931, it. 6029; 7 January 1932, it. 6049.
83. Ibid., 1 December 1932, it. 6217.
84. Ibid., 2 March 1933, it. 6282.
85. Ibid., 3 August 1933, it. 6362.
86. Ibid., July 1934, it. 6539.
87. GKN Minute Book, Vol. 10, op. cit., 7 April 1938, it. 7125.
88. Ibid.
89. GKN Minute Book, Vol. 4, op. cit., 3 May 1923, it. 4274, 4275.
90. GKN Minute Book, Vol. 7, op. cit., 7 July 1927, it. 5166.
91. GKN Minute Book, Vol. 10, op. cit., 3 February 1938, it. 7099.
92. GKN Minute Book, Vol. 11, op. cit., 3 November 1939, it. 7179.
93. GKN Minute Book, Vol. 6, op. cit., 26 June 1925, it. 4756.
94. Ibid., 6 August 1925, it. 4773.
95. Ibid., 4 February 1926, it. 4884.
96. GKN Minute Book, Vol. 7, op. cit., 3 February 1927, it. 5076.
97. Ibid., 3 March 1927, it. 5094.
98. Ibid., 7 April 1927, it. 5111.
99. GKN Minute Book, Vol. 3, 1 March 1922, it. 3973.
100. GKN Minute Book, Vol. 7, op. cit., 5 January 1928, it. 5248.
101. GKN Minute Book, Vol. 8, op. cit., 7 June 1928, it. 5328.
102. GKN Minute Book, Vol. 8, op. cit., 6 November 1930, it. 5807.
103. 'The English Wood Screw Company History, or the Record of an Undercover Operation' (typescript n.d.).
104. GKN Minute Book, Vol. 9, op. cit., 3 August 1933, it. 6326.
105. Ibid., 5 October 1933, it. 6380.
106. Interview J. Cockroft with Sir Anthony Bowlby, 25 April 1972, p. 6.
107. GKN Minute Book, Vol. 9, op. cit., February 1934, it. 6459.
108. GKN Minute Book, Vol. 10, op. cit., 1 August 1935, it. 6739.
109. GKN Minute Book, Vol. 9, op. cit., 1 March 1934, it. 6476.
110. Birmingham Committee Minutes, Vol. 5, op. cit., 29 June 1937, it. 3495.
111. GKN Minute Book, Vol. 10, op. cit., 7 April 1935, it. 6685.
112. *The GKN Group of Companies, A Handy Group to Know*, Birmingham [n.d.].

113. GKN Minute Book, Vol. 10, op. cit., 1 August 1935, it. 6471.

114. GKN Minute Book, Vol. 11, op. cit., 1 September 1938, it. 7166; 6 October 1938, it. 7180.

115. Ibid., 6 October 1938, it. 7183.

116. Ibid.

117. GKN Minute Book, Vol. 11, op. cit., 3 November 1938, it. 7196.

118. Ibid., 1 December 1938, it. 7210.

119. Ibid., 2 March 1939, it. 7257.

120. Ibid., 2 March 1939, it. 7257.

121. Interview J. Cockroft with Sir Anthony Bowlby, 25 April 1972.

122. GKN Minute Book, Vol. 4, op. cit., 4 December 1924, it. 4625.

123. 'GKN Stenman AB' (typescript history, n.d.); G.G. Jones (Editor), *British Multinationals* Aldershot (1986), Edgar Jones, 'Steel and Engineering Overseas: GKN's Multinational Growth 1918–1965', p. 177.

124. GKN Minute Book, Vol. 7, op. cit., 9 September 1926, it. 4997.

125. Ibid., 1 December 1927, it. 5234.

126. GKN Minute Book, Vol. 8, op. cit., 3 May 1928, it. 5310.

127. Ibid., 2 August 1928, it. 5365.

128. Ibid., 3 January 1929, it. 5434.

129. Ibid., 7 March 1929, it. 5460.

130. Ibid., 7 March 1929, it. 5460.

131. Ibid., December 1929, it. 5622; 6 March 1930, it. 5686.

132. Ibid., 6 March 1930, it. 5686.

133. Ibid., 5 June 1930, it. 5754.

134. GKN Minute Book, Vol. 9, op. cit., 6 August 1931, it. 5979.

135. Ibid., 1 October 1931, it. 5996.

136. GKN Minute Book, Vol. 10, op. cit., 6 June 1935, it. 6718.

137. Ibid., 1 August 1935, it. 6740.

138. Birmingham Committee Minutes, Vol. 5, op. cit., 1 February 1938, it. 3596.

139. GKN Minute Book, Vol. 11, op. cit., 1 September 1938, it. 7170.

140. Ibid., 3 November 1938, it. 7195; 1 December 1938, it. 7214.

141. Jones, *GKN, Vol. One*, op. cit., p. 230.

142. GKN Minute Book, Vol. 3, op. cit., 17 May 1922, it. 4008.

143. Ibid., 3 August 1922, it. 4046.

144. GKN Minute Book, Vol. 4, op. cit., 5 October 1922, it. 4116.

145. GKN Minute Book, Vol. 5, op. cit., 4 September 1924, it. 4571.

146. Ibid., 2 October 1924, it. 4584.

147. Ibid., 4 December 1924, it. 4625.

148. GKN Minute Book, Vol. 6, op. cit., 5 March 1925, it. 4689.

149. 'Guest Keen & Nettlefolds (Aust) Ltd., Nettlefolds Division' (typescript, n.d.).

150. Ibid., 8 April 1926, it. 4922.

151. GKN Minute Book, Vol. 7, op. cit., 6 December 1928, it. 5418.

152. Ibid.

153. GKN Minute Book, Vol. 10, op. cit., 6 December 1934, it. 6624.

154. Ibid., 2 September 1937, it. 7028.

155. GKN Minute Book, Vol. 11, op. cit., 1 December 1938, it. 7213.

156. Interview J. Cockroft with Sir Anthony Bowlby, 25 April 1972, p. 2.

157. Ibid., p. 3.

158. GKN Minute Book, Vol. 8, op. cit., 7 August 1930, it. 5763.

159. Interview J. Cockroft with Sir Anthony Bowlby, op. cit., p. 4.

160. GKN Minute Book, Vol. 10, op. cit., 1 October 1936, it. 6891.
161. GKN Minute Book, Vol. 11, op. cit., 5 October 1939, it. 7329.
162. GKN Minute Book, Vol. 3, op. cit., 3 March 1921.
163. GKN Minute Book, Vol. 4, op. cit., 3 May 1923, it. 4274, 4275.
164. Birmingham Committee Minute Book, Vol. 5, op. cit., 1937–39.
165. Information provided by Mr Stephen Lloyd and Mr W.A. Smyth.
166. Birmingham Committee Minute Book, Vol. 5, op. cit., 1 January 1938, it. 3598.

6 Fasteners and Forgings, 1918–45

Machines and rolling-mills with pleasure view;
Whilst sturdy Cyclops, anvils ranged around,
With thund'ring hammers made the air resound.

James Bisset (1762?–1832)
'Ramble of the Gods through Birmingham'[1]

In contrast to its woodscrew operations, which were concentrated at the Heath Street mills (albeit with a growing number of smaller satellite factories), GKN never sought to focus the production of nuts and bolts into a single site or company. This reflected, in part, the diversity of the market as the range of bolts was far broader and their uses greater. Further, there were many more manufacturers so that GKN could never hope to dominate this sector of the fastener market as it had that of the woodscrew. In essence, the group relied upon four, and later two mills to produce its nuts and bolts. Originally, the London and Stour Valley Works (formerly belonging to the Patent Nut & Bolt Co.) were its principal enterprises. However, little capital had been spent on them over the twenty years preceding the Great War and, having been worked to capacity throughout the hostilities, they fell into a state of disrepair and obsolescence. Francis Keen, the GKN board member responsible for their operation, realised that up-to-date technology could be acquired more simply by taking over an existing producer rather than by revitalising these ailing works. Accordingly, in 1919 GKN bought F.W. Cotterill, the Darlaston maker of nuts and bolts, together with its subsidiary, John Garrington & Sons, drop forgers to the automobile, tube engineering and electrical trades.[2] Shortly afterwards in 1920 the group took over Bayliss, Jones & Bayliss, the Wolverhampton manufacturers of fencing, ornamental gates, spikes and railway fasteners.[3] Thus, within two years of the armistice GKN had both strengthened and broadened its position within the fastener market in, what was for the company, a novel strategy of innovation by acquisition.

DECLINE OF LONDON WORKS AND CLOSURE OF STOUR VALLEY

Although the London and Stour Valley Works when visited by a reporter from *The Engineer* in 1865 could be regarded as embodying the latest technology,[4] by 1918 this was no longer the case. Little had been spent on new plant and machinery from the 1880s, Arthur Keen tending to invest surplus capital in the stock market.[5] As a result, they remained wedded to wrought iron, rather than steel, production methods; they duplicated several functions, each having their own puddling furnaces and rolling mills, and were differentiated by product; the Stour Valley Works concentrated on the manufacture of railway fasteners, while London Works turned out engineer's bright and black bolts and nuts, coach screws, rivets and washers together with those fasteners used by shipbuilders, agricultural engineers and railway carriage and wagon builders.[6] In the immediate post-war boom, when demand outstripped supply, the two were able to earn reasonable profits: in the ten months to 30 April 1919 they, together with the Cwmbran Ironworks, produced a surplus of £34,058,[7] though this remained meagre in contrast to the £342,468 generated by Nettlefolds. The railway strike in the summer of 1919 was sufficient to push the three works into the red and for the two months to 31 August a loss of £6,988 was recorded.[8] Being able to return only modest profits in lush years, London and Stour Valley Works were doomed in periods of depression, and when the harsh slump of 1920–21 took its toll the former PNB works fell further into deficit. For the eight months to 29 February 1920 a loss of £21,969 accrued.[9]

Subsequent accounting details no longer survive, though general statements about the bolt and nut trade suggested that London and Stour Valley Works endured increasingly difficult commercial conditions. They continued to manufacture their established products, the former under its famous 'Globe and Lion' trademark. However, in view of the group's overall difficulties in this area, T.S. Peacock was asked in the spring of 1924 to prepare a strategy for the future.[10] By this time Cotterills had become GKN's major nut and bolt producer and a policy of rationalisation (p.212) was initiated in its favour, part of which involved the closure of Stour Valley Works and the sale of the site in 1925.[11]

F.W. COTTERILL OF DARLASTON

It was not recorded why GKN selected F.W. Cotterill of all the Black Country nut and bolt manufacturers for acquisition. They were, nevertheless, among the largest producers having been established in the first decade of the nineteenth century by Alexander Cotterill,[12] who in 1818 was listed as a 'sett [tool] maker' at Bur Croft[13] (subsequently written as Butt Croft Works). Under his son, Frederick, the firm developed rapidly following the introduction of self-acting machinery. By 1850 their range of products had broadened and they were recorded as being bolt and latch makers.[14] In 1861 they included the 'manufacture of machines' in their activities.[15] In 1874 it was decided to move to

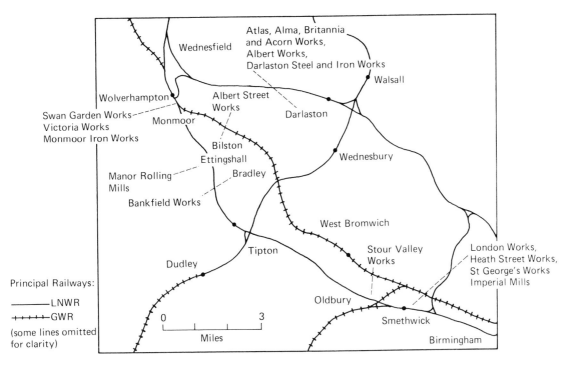

Principal Railways:

———— LNWR

+++++ GWR

(some lines omitted for clarity)

Figure 11 GKN Works in the Black Country, *c.* 1920

a new and larger site at Darlaston, where the Atlas Works were laid down having an entrance in Station Street[16] – the company's trade mark depicted Atlas standing on a nut and bolt, holding the world on his shoulders.

That they decided to remain in Darlaston was understandable. 'The principle articles made here', reported *Kelly's Directory* for 1880

> are iron and wood screws, railway screws, screw bolts, shoe tips, files, latches, wire gauges and hand rails; a large amount of railway ironwork is also manufactured. There are iron foundries, steel works, malt kilns and brick fields'.[17]

A pool of skilled labour and established networks of suppliers and customers would have resulted from this industrial specialisation. Following the bolt forgers' strike and the recession of the late 1870s, the firm installed more automatic machinery. In 1880 it became a private limited liability company,[18] and in 1912 took over John Garrington & Sons, stampers and drop forgers, also of Darlaston, in a strategy of cautious diversification (p. 217).

Whether the Cotterill management, fearing difficult trading conditions, approached GKN about an acquisition, or whether the latter simply decided to advance on a profitable and respected company has not been discovered. In August 1919 the GKN directors examined the current accounts of both Cotterills and Garringtons and the purchase

72 The Atlas Works at Darlaston belonging to F.W. Cotterill (possibly pre-1914) (*Walsall Local History Centre*).

had been completed by October when T.S. Peacock, the latter's chief executive, was appointed to the main board.[19] Peacock had joined Cotterills in 1892 as the company secretary, becoming the general manager in the following year and managing director in 1900.[20] He must have played a crucial role in the negotiations surrounding the acquisition and perhaps the offer of a directorship of GKN was crucial in obtaining his consent to the scheme. His position was soon re-inforced as in 1920, after the merger with Lysaght, Peacock was elected a joint managing director. At a time when the group would have considered the manufacture of fasteners (subdivided between wood-screws and nuts and bolts) one of its principal activities, it was appropriate that the manager selected to oversee these operations should occupy a senior position on the board.

Unfortunately for Peacock his promotion coincided with the begin-nings of the post-war slump and a decade of adverse trading con-ditions. In October 1921 he was having to report a scarcity of orders and a price-cutting war,[21] and by November 1922 the 'heavy losses' which had accrued prompted Peacock to suggest 'joint action with the other larger makers to prevent the price falling so much below the cost of production as at present.'[22]

It was in this atmosphere that GKN attempted to protect itself further by acquisition. They bought the neighbouring Vulcan Works in order that the screwing shop at Atlas Works could be extended and in 1923 took over the Alma Works of Horton & Son.[23] Shortly afterwards two

73   The screwing shop,
Atlas Works, July 1928.
These machines cut the
threads on to forged bolts
(*Walsall Local History
Centre*).

74   The upper part of the
hot forging shop at Alma
Works, Darlaston in June
1932. On the floor are
piles of blank bolts on to
which heads have been
forged (*Walsall Local
History Centre*).

75 The finishing shop, Atlas Works, July 1928. Here the thread was cut into the forged nuts (*Walsall Local History Centre*).

more Darlaston manufacturers were purchased – the Britannia Works of Enoch Wilkes & Co., and the Acorn Works of James Simpson & Sons (Bolts and Nuts) – in an attempt 'to concentrate the operations of the bolt and nut trade'.[24] By this they meant the imposition of price and output controls, rather than the elimination of competition as these anciliary works continued to operate for several years, apparently being closed in the slump of 1929–30.

Nevertheless, the bolt and nut companies belonging to GKN continued to record losses despite the formation of a trade association whose regulatory efforts proved 'unsuccessful owing to the jealousy of one or two firms'.[25] In these circumstances Peacock concluded that the only solution was to allow competition to eliminate surplus capacity through the bankruptcy of weaker producers. It became imperative, therefore, that a new plan of campaign be organised. In April 1924 Peacock asked to be released from 'the detailed supervision of the screw works' in order that he could focus his activities. The board readily assented and granted him 'absolute control of the bolt and nut and railway fastening departments in the Midlands and at Cwmbran, with power to make drastic changes at, or to close if need be, any of the works'.[26]

In July 1924 Peacock presented the report which would decide the fate of the fastener companies.[27] His wide-ranging recommendations fell into three main categories: centralisation of head office functions and distribution systems, a greater measure of autonomy in purchasing,

76 The warehouse at
Atlas Works, July 1928,
staffed in part by women
(*Walsall Local History
Centre*).

and the rationalisation of production. He had identified a lack of unity
and coherence among GKN's various nut and bolt producers. To
provide an external sign of integration it was suggested that individual
company names (F.W. Cotterill, Bayliss, Jones & Bayliss, Horton &
Son) be abandoned and that the factories should trade under the name
'Guest, Keen & Nettlefolds'. Atlas Works was selected as the site for a
head office and instead of the five existing estimating departments, one
was to be established there, divided into sections representing each
class of business. Similarly, Peacock advocated the creation of a central
sales department which would then allocate orders to the individual
works. Distribution networks, he believed, could also be profitably
merged. A new warehouse to be erected at Atlas Works, costing an
estimated £40,000, would accommodate the combined output of Cotterills, Hortons and London Works. This, when completed, would enable
London Works to be diverted to other uses and its machinery transported to Darlaston. The Stour Valley Works was recommended for
closure as soon as its business could be transferred to other mills,

77 The despatch area of the warehouse with trucks from various railway companies about to be filled with bags of fasteners, July 1928 (*Walsall Local History Centre*).

thereby enabling the 'whole of the engineering and general bolt and nut trade . . . [to] be concentrated at Darlaston'.[28]

Finally, in order to reduce costs, Peacock argued 'that the combine should be permitted to purchase its iron and steel from the cheapest suppliers', rather than offer GKN steelworks preference. Much of their high tensile steel was bought from Dowlais which in the twenties was far from being the most efficient producer. Their other internal source was the Darlaston Steel and Iron Works, which had been recently acquired from Tolley, Sons & Bostock, in order to have closer control over their raw material inputs. Being of Victorian age and limited size, it was difficult for such a steelworks to earn a profit in the deflationary 1920s, and Peacock recommended its temporary closure.

Almost all of these recommendations were accepted by the GKN board, though some took several years to implement. By October 1924 plans were well advanced for the construction of the new Atlas Works warehouse, and some manufacturing capacity had already been transferred to Darlaston from London Works.[29] Steps were also taken to reduce the numbers of staff, many long-service employees being made redundant.[30] In order that London Works could be closed as a bolt and nut producer on completion of the warehouse at Darlaston, many workers there had been given retirement allowances.[31] By September 1925 puddling and rolling were due to cease when stocks of iron were exhausted, these operations to be taken up by Tolley, Sons & Bostock at Darlaston to reduce transport charges.[32] In the meantime, the Stour Valley Works had been emptied of all plant and machinery and the site put up for sale.[33]

78 Atlas Works (*c.* late 1930s) after the construction of the new offices, canteen and works institute (*Walsall Local History Centre*).

Although Bayliss, Jones & Bayliss and Horton & Son continued to use their original company names, it was agreed that F.W. Cotterill be put into voluntary liquidation and its assets be incorporated within GKN in order that the group's bolts and nuts could be marketed under the 'Guest, Keen & Nettlefolds' style.[34] Under the valuation, performed on 31 May 1925, the company was classified as follows:

	£
Freehold land, buildings	155,279
Plant, machinery and rolling stock	83,250
Stock-in-trade	47,758
Investments (marketable securities)	130,316
John Garrington & Sons (2,500 shares)	125,000
Tolley, Sons & Bostock (shares and loans)	25,000
Debtors	82,764
Cash at bank	26,923
Less Creditors	(78,635)
Total	£600,655[35]

It was not recorded whether the board granted Peacock permission to obtain his supplies of steel in the market place without reference to GKN suppliers. Given the difficulties experienced by Dowlais, it seems unlikely that such a concession was made. During the General Strike, for example, he was at liberty to purchase from the Continent, though found it difficult to transport the orders to Darlaston.[36]

Throughout this period of rationalisation and re-organisation, competition within the bolt and nut trade remained 'severe'.[37] No sustained or dramatic recovery occurred; in November 1928 business was reported as being 'slack'.[38] Particular problems resulted in February 1929 because one of their principal customers, the railway wagon builders, under the impact of deepening worldwide depression, were suffering from reduced orders.[39] By March Peacock observed that trading conditions had never been so poor,[40] and short-time working was introduced at Darlaston.[41] As a defensive measure (an attempt to control output and prices through market dominance), GKN suggested to Sir John Hunter, chairman of the Rivet, Bolt & Nut Co., another major producer, that they merge their interests; the proposal was, however, declined.[42]

The slump and the problems which it created enabled GKN to buy out some of their smaller less efficient rivals. In June 1929 they acquired the Staffordshire Bolt, Nut & Fencing Co.,[43] and in October 1930, for £3,750, purchased the plant, machinery and goodwill of Barwells, who had decided to abandon the manufacture of nuts and bolts.[44]

Trading conditions became so severe in the spring of 1931 that T.S. Peacock considered the temporary closure of one of the Darlaston works.[45] Matters began to ease in the autumn when orders picked up but not to the extent of advancing prices.[46] In December Peacock reported 'that competition was still exceptionally keen, and that it was hoped that the reduced value of sterling would help in shutting out some of the cheap Continental material that had been coming in'.[47] Yet eleven months later the rivalry appeared just as intense and the problem was expected to be resolved by the impending bankruptcy of several producers.[48] These continuing difficulties prompted the calling of a trade meeting at which it was agreed to increase prices by 10 per cent.[49] This arrangement appears to have held, for a year later GKN put an additional £1 per ton on its bolts and nuts.[50]

In step with the economy as a whole the trade revived throughout 1933,[51] and in March of the following year Peacock was able to announce 'a moderate general improvement'.[52] In April, Atlas Works was busier than for some time past, though not yet fully employed.[53] By the summer Peacock felt sufficiently confident about trading conditions to recommend the expenditure of £40,000 on a new cold forging shop.[54]

By the winter of 1936–7 the recovery was virtually complete and Peacock reported that the busy Atlas Works was 'well supplied with orders'.[55] Prices for black nuts and bolts were raised by a further £1 per ton in the spring of 1936 at a time when sales to South Africa were rising dramatically.[56] In October the construction of a new hot press shop, costing an estimated £30,393, was approved.[57] By January 1937 sectional overtime was necessary to satisfy demand,[58] Atlas Works finding it difficult to keep pace with orders in a context of steel shortages.[59]

Whether Atlas Works was affected by the pre-war slackening of peacetime demand has not been recorded, though it was decided in May 1939 to spend £60,000 on modernisation.[60] The principal expenditure (£46,356) was on four National bolt making machines and two open die headers.[61] In December it was decided to construct a new fitting shop and central toolroom to enable the demolition of the existing antiquated shops.[62]

During the Second World War, the consumption of munitions and the mechanised character of the conflict combined to exert great demand on GKN's fastener factories. In November 1942 the Ministry of Supply approached the Atlas Works to ask them to double their output of cold forged nuts and bolts.[63] This request was answered by double shifting and the construction of a further building for forging nuts, half the £29,000 cost to be paid by the government.

In the absence of detailed profit records, it is impossible to tell whether the former Cotterill company proved a wise acquisition for GKN over the twenty-six years from 1945. The period from the summer of 1935 through to the end of the war was a successful one, but whether it compensated for the difficult years of the 1920s and early 1930s cannot be calculated. Had there been a net deficit GKN might still have concluded that the takeover was justified, for it maintained the group in a market in which it was traditionally established and provided its steelworks, rolling mills and wire works with a constant source of employment in what, for them, had been traumatic years.

JOHN GARRINGTON & SONS OF DARLASTON

It is believed that John Garrington set up a small stampings business at Catherine's Cross, Darlaston, in 1830,[64] producing gun cocks and other forged components for military and sporting rifles,[65] but by 1851 his Old Phoenix Works was also making bolts, nuts and bed screws.[66] These items were typical of Darlaston's industry which was described as long being 'famous for the manufacture of gunlocks, stirrups, buckles, nails, bed and woodscrews, bolts, latches, cast-iron articles, etc'.[67]

On the death of John Garrington in 1877 the firm was carried on by his two sons, Richard and Benjamin. Two years later they moved the works to a larger site, the Albert Works, Willenhall Road, Darlaston, situated beside the Wyrley and Essington Canal.[68] On the retirement of the two brothers, Bertram Garrington, the son of Richard, became the senior partner and it was his trustee, in 1912, who sold the business to F.W. Cotterill. When the new owners decided to float the concern as a limited liability company, it became a wholly-owned subsidiary.

By the time that GKN had acquired Garringtons, through their takeover of Cotterills, the scope of their manufacture had narrowed to drop forging, excluding the production of fasteners; the company supplied

79 GKN products at a British Empire Trade Exhibition, Buenos Airies, 1931. In the foreground is a display case containing forgings manufactured by John Garrington & Sons. To the left is a Sankey copper lifebuoy (*Allied Steel and Wire*).

the automobile, agricultural, aircraft, tube engineering and electrical trades with a variety of forged components. Garringtons, too, experienced difficulties during the post-war slump, though seem not to have suffered to the same extent as Cotterills in the mid and late 1920s. In July 1927, for example, the company reported a 'great pressure of orders', which occasioned the extension of the drop-forging shop at a cost of £13,000.[69]

The slump affected the company adversely. A scarcity of orders combined with low prices conspired to reduce profits to a minimum (Table 6.1).[70] In the spring of 1933 'a fair volume of enquiries' was received though competition remained 'terrifically keen, and the prices quoted made it very difficult to secure a remunerative business'.[71] By July matters had eased as a considerable proportion 'of the orders given out for next season's requirements in the motor trade' had been won by Garringtons.[72] Once the depression had been negotiated, A. Beech, the general manager, proposed, 'as little capital expenditure had been made for some years', that the works be both reconstructed and

Table 6.1   John Garrington & Sons gross profits, 1932–38

		£	£ Adjusted*
12 months to 31 December	1932	5,538	6,079
	1933	4,643	5,252
	1934	11,697	13,099
	1935	16,442	18,128
	1936	24,606	26,487
	1937	33,440	34,368
	1938	26,901	27,255

Note: *Figures adjusted by Bank of England's Index of Consumer Prices, 1930 = 100.

Source: John Garrington & Sons Minute Book Vol. 3, August 1932–March 1940.

extended.[73] Having won the approval of K.S. Peacock, as chairman, and other members of the Garrington board the proposals were submitted to GKN for ratification. The expenditure of around £100,000 for an extra battery of stamps, heat treatment plant, a warehouse and siding accommodation was authorised in February 1936.[74]

With these improvements completed in the summer of 1939, GKN considered selling a majority interest in Garringtons to John Harper Bean, a car manufacturer.[75] An agreement had been signed between Bean and GKN that for one year from 1 August he had the option of purchasing the group's shareholding in Garringtons.[76] Under this arrangement Bean was elected to a directorship and subsequently T.S. Peacock resigned as chairman so that the former could take his place.[77] The circumstances surrounding this event remain unclear. It is possible that Bean, wishing to obtain closer control over forged components, approached GKN as part of a strategy of vertical integration. More mysterious is perhaps why the group would consider disposing of a profitable subsidiary (a surplus of £24,000 was earned in the year to December 1940).[78] Since forging was not a core activity, and much of the plant and machinery was Victorian, GKN may have thought that in the medium term the company would require considerable capital expenditure to keep it in business. Under the terms of the negotiations, J.H. Bean would have become chairman, though Jolly and K.S. Peacock would have remained on the Garrington board.[79]

With the outbreak of war the Albert Works, became a 'controlled undertaking', by which its commercial activity was closely regulated by the government. Having attracted the attention of the Admiralty, anxious to raise the output of munitions, it was agreed in July 1940 to construct a shell forging plant at Garringtons, costing around £100,000.[80] In these circumstances it became unlikely that Bean would exercise his option to acquire the company, and he had failed to do so by the September 1940 deadline.[81] Nevertheless, the GKN board felt it desirable that a businessman of his experience not be lost to them. Accordingly, in November GKN bought 5,000 5s. ordinary shares in Beans Industries for £30,000 on the understanding that Bean would continue to manage Garringtons for four years from 1 January 1940.

In February 1940 Albert Beech, a director and general manager of Garringtons, announced his retirement. He was to be succeeded in June 1941 by Raymond P. Brookes and J.C. Beech who would serve as joint general managers.[82] Although at the time not considered a portentous appointment, the promotion of Brookes was to prove of great significance in the history of GKN since he was later to become chairman and developed the group as one of the country's principal suppliers of automotive components.[83]

When the war drew into its final phase, GKN negotiated with the Ministry of Supply to purchase the hammers, presses and other plant installed by the government.[84] They secured favourable terms: £261,433 worth of equipment being obtained for £104,573. It was also agreed that Garringtons could buy the building erected by the Admiralty at 40 per cent of its cost. The adjacent land, belonging to Tildsleys, was bought in order to provide despatch facilities and room for expansion. In addition, the GKN board authorised the installation of automatic Massey hammers to replace plant which had been in operation for 30 to 50 years.[85] They also explored the possibility of selling the company but no other drop forgers had expressed an interest,[86] and, therefore, concluded that 'if John Garrington wished to retain its interest in the trade the expenditure appeared to be inescapable'.[87]

In September 1944, when many of these improvements had been effected, contributing to a major increase in turnover and profits, J.H. Bean asked the GKN board to clarify their intentions once the hostilities had ended.[88] It was decided not to dispose of the company and with this in mind Bean was offered a directorship of GKN,[89] his election following on 2 November.[90] At about the same time both R.P. Brookes and J.C. Beech were appointed to the Garrington board,[91] and the company was poised to enter one of its most expansive and successful periods.

BAYLISS, JONES & BAYLISS OF WOLVERHAMPTON

The circumstances surrounding the take-over of Bayliss, Jones & Bayliss (BJB) by GKN have not been firmly established. It was suggested that William Bayliss, the then chairman and son of the founder, had diverted capital from the business into a country estate and had speculated unsuccessfully on the Birmingham stock exchange, drawing the company into debt.[92] Taking advantage of the post-war slump and fears of a lengthy recession, GKN acquired what was a well-established business, which could also serve as a consumer of steel billets since BJB

80 Sketches of the founders of Bayliss, Jones & Bayliss: William Bayliss (1803–1878), Moses Bayliss (1816–1894) and Edwin Jones (1833–1904).

The Founders of

BAYLISS , JONES and BAYLISS

WILLIAM BAYLISS

1803 - 1878

MOSES BAYLISS

1816 - 1894

EDWIN JONES

1833 - 1904

specialised in the manufacture of iron fencing and gates; in addition, its bolt and nut section supplied railway companies, traditional customers of the ailing London Works. Once a subsidiary, the company was permitted to retain its original name and its management remained in the hand of the Bayliss family: William Bayliss (d. 1925) continued as chairman, while Samuel (d. 1932), his younger brother, and Horace W. Bayliss were directors. P.S. and F.W. Bayliss, the sons of Samuel, were appointed to the board in 1921 and 1925 respectively, and became joint managing directors in 1928.[93]

The business had been founded by William Bayliss (1803–78), who in 1825 inherited his father's smithy.[94] In 1839, following several success-ful land deals, he was able to buy the property in Cable Street, Monmoor Green, which was constructed the Victoria Works. This enabled him to diversify into chain-making (for mines and shipping) and iron fencing.[95] Originally he had done little more than shoe horses and repair colliers' picks; now, however, he was able to make iron sheep hurdles, railings, gates, stable fittings and ornamental ironwork. The first appears to have been a new and growing market, for *Slater's Staffordshire Directory* (c. 1850) listed only two makers for Wolverhampton, neither being Bayliss.[96] He appears to have entered into a partnership but in 1853 a disagreement led to its dissolution and William Bayliss continued alone.[97] Becoming ill, he was advised to move to the fresher atmosphere of Wolverhampton. His departure heralded the arrival of his brother, Moses Bayliss (1816–94), a nut and bolt maker of Darlaston. The two firms combined under the style of W. & M. Bayliss of Victoria Works, Monmoor Green, and Providence Works, Darlaston, with a London office at 43 Fish Street Hill, Eastcheap.[98] When they were joined in 1859 by Edwin Jones (1833–1904), who had married William Bayliss's daughter, Jane, the partnership became Bayliss, Jones & Bayliss.[99]

By 1870, with his health continuing to deteriorate, William Bayliss relinquished his managerial responsibilities, his two sons, William and Samuel taking a greater share of executive authority. Moses Bayliss retired in 1880 by which time the firm had been floated as a private limited liability company. His son [Sir] William Maddock Bayliss became a distinguished physiologist but was also a non-executive director of BJB.[100]

Throughout the latter third of the nineteenth century the Victoria Works continued to expand, and by 1880 were also making 'fish bolts, chair spikes, railway fastenings and nuts'.[101] In 1896 they purchased North & Wright's Monmoor Ironworks nearby in Cable Street, which provided them with their own puddling furnaces and rolling mills. The business was floated on the Stock Exchange in 1901 under the chair-manship of William Bayliss, who was succeeded by Samuel in 1925. The business was then taken over by GKN in 1920.

In common with Cotterills, BJB found themselves in difficulties during the early 1920s; in March 1922, for example, the GKN board

81 'How Wrought Iron was Wrought', a group of three sketches by W. Heath Robinson commissioned by Bayliss, Jones & Bayliss to illustrate manufacturing processes and the qualities of their product.

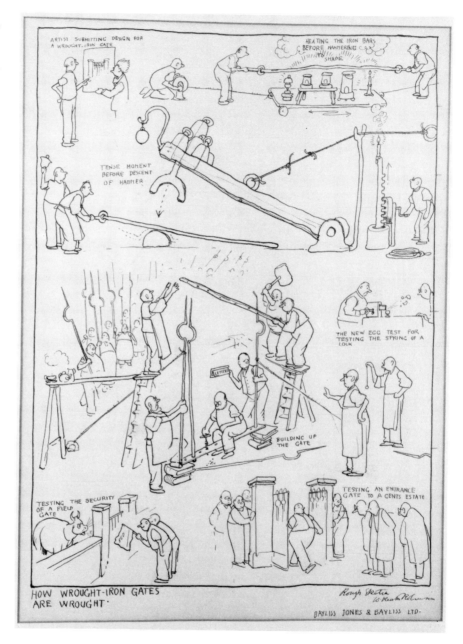

informed the latter's executives that 'the company's affairs need[ed] to be improved'.[102] Their manufacture of spikes, fish bolts, lock nuts and fasteners for the railways suffered more acutely than their fencing business. Accordingly, under T.S. Peacock's plan a new 'screw rolling shop' was equipped and their bolt works reorganised to bring them to a state of technical proficiency.[103] In an effort to reduce costs a new mill (for the conversion of billet into bar) was installed at the Monmoor Iron

81   *cont.*

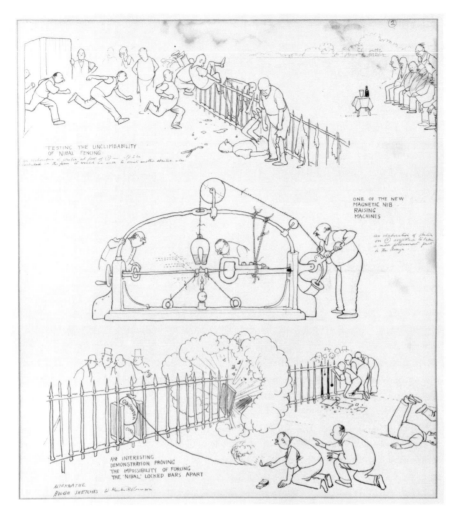

Works in 1927–28.[104] Being a traditional industry using established methods of productivity, it is difficult to see how BJB could have escaped the force of the slump. Orders fell dramatically from 1930 and recovered only in the mid-1930s.[105]

The published profit figures of BJB (Table 6.2) revealed a remarkable continuity. With the exception of the slump of 1929–30, and the payment of an unusually high dividend (60 per cent) on the 100,000 ordinary shares in 1936 (the previous three years being 45, 40 and 30 per cent respectively), the level remained around £20,000, though advanced beyond £40,000 only during the Second World War with the help of inflation. If the figures are adjusted for the effects of price movements, then the mid-1930s appear as BJB's most successful years.

As the illustrations show (83–85), BJB produced ornamental iron-work (gates, fences, brackets, balustrading, tree guards, and railings) of

81 *cont.*

the very highest quality, either to standard patterns or to designs specified by an architect. Although this work may have held up better in recession than the fastener trade, it, too, would have declined in step with the fortunes of the construction industry.

GKN IN SOUTH AFRICA

In the autumn of 1933 negotiations were held between GKN and the Union Steel Corporation of South Africa with a view to setting up a

joint company for the manufacture of nuts and bolts.[106] The venture was costed at around £30,000, the capital to be provided equally by the two parties. Agreement was reached in April 1934 to form the South African Bolts & Nuts (Proprietory) Ltd.[107] The plant for the works, valued at about £8,200, was to be supplied by GKN and the buildings were to include a warehouse so that orders could be despatched from stock.[108] Since it was planned to manufacture clips, sleeper and fish bolts, spikes and nuts, the country's railways were expected to be major customers. The existence of such a scheme enabled GKN to win large export orders from South Africa.[109] However, the joint venture proved short-lived as in October 1937 the group agreed to sell its shareholding in South African Bolts & Nuts (Proprietory) for 17s 6d per share to the Union Steel Corporation.[110] GKN believed that the planned development of the works on a new site would not prove profitable and calculated that it would cost £40,000 to gain control of the

83   Gates and fencing manufactured by Bayliss, Jones & Bayliss.

84   Barrier railings in front of Kingston Station produced by Bayliss, Jones & Bayliss for the Southern Railway.

Table 6.2 Profits of Bayliss, Jones & Bayliss, 1923–46

	£ Profits	£ Adjusted*
1923	35,147	31,494
1924	19,544	17,700
1925	32,635	29,243
1926	30,422	27,936
1927	29,156	27,454
1928	12,802	12,204
1929	13,011	12,511
1930	20,413	20,413
1931	27,241	29,197
1932	29,049	31,887
1933	29,061	32,874
1934	33,756	37,801
1935	39,479	43,527
1936	39,456	42,471
1937	3,897	4,005
1938	19,175	19,428
1939	23,364	23,364
1940	25,905	22,255
1941	30,777	24,387
1942	34,955	27,589
1943	41,105	32,571
1944	44,870	35,303
1945	47,354	36,880
1946	45,992	35,680

Note: *Figures adjusted by the Bank of England's Index of Consumer Prices, 1930 = 100.

Source: Folder of typewritten minutes for Bayliss, Jones & Bayliss, 1921–48, pp. 110, 142, 206, 264, 313, 361, 405, 456, 500, 554, 629, 666, 706.

enterprise.[111] For the moment at least, the group relinquished its interest in the enterprise.

SUMMARY

When Arthur T. Keen became chairman of GKN in 1915, his younger brother, Francis Watkins Keen, a joint managing director, apparently took overall responsibility for the group's nut and bolt factories. However, both London and Stour Valley Works were in need of modernisation and Keen, in his mid-fifties, had not the inclination to carry this through. The take over of F.W. Cotterill, one of the largest bolt makers in Darlaston, and the recruitment of their managing

85   The assembly of gates at Bayliss, Jones & Bayliss.

director, the tough and determined T.S. Peacock, proved the answer to GKN's needs. Peacock was given overall responsibility not only for the company's bolt works but also the screw mills at Heath Street, and it was his scheme of reorganisation which in 1924 led to the closure of Stour Valley Works, the cessation of bolt manufacture at London Works, the incorporation of Cotterills and rationalisation of BJB. Having implemented these changes no further attempt was made to centralise fastener production. BJB, for example, was allowed to retain its name, board of directors and trading policies. So long as one man, Peacock, was capable of overseeing the affairs of the former Cotterill works, Garringtons and BJB, GKN remained content to exercise authority through the holding-subsidiary company structure. When F.W. Keen died in April 1933, after an extended period of illness, he was succeeded as deputy chairman by Peacock.[112]

The style of management remained paternalistic. Peacock was re-nowned for possessing a tough, sometimes tempestuous nature, but on

86 Machining components at Bayliss, Jones & Bayliss (*c.* 1950).

occasion could be forgiving (p. 284). In 1926, for instance, he personally purchased a plot of land which was then donated to GKN on condition that it be converted into a recreation ground for the employees of Atlas Works.[113] Shortly afterwards Peacock persuaded the company to install a heating system, together with improved lavatories in the bolt mills.[114]

Cotterills, Garringtons and BJB were companies with a strong local identity, often recruiting several generations of workers from the same family; long-service awards were common.[115] As established Victorian businesses, each had a well-known name and identity maintained by the physical presence of the works, which often dominated the neighbourhood (the repetitive thud of the Garrington hammers was a feature of their part of Darlaston). Within these communities they were major employers of labour so that periods of short time working could have dramatic repercussions for the immediate economy, while times of plenty were equally influential.

87 At work in the forge,
using centuries-old skills –
pre-heating ornamental
sections of fencing.

References

1.   Quoted from Roger Lonsdale (Editor), *The New Oxford Book of Eighteenth Century Verse*, Oxford (1987), p. 838.
2.   *An Outline History of GKN*, op. cit., pp. 53–5.
3.   Ibid., pp. 58–9.
4.   *The Engineer*, Vol. XX, 15 September 1865, 'Visits to the Provinces', pp. 161–2.
5.   Interview J. Cockroft with J.H. Jolly, 25 July 1972, p. 2.
6.   Jones, *GKN, Vol. One*, op. cit., p. 171.
7.   GKN Minute Book, Vol. 3, op. cit., 5 June 1919, it. 3310.
8.   Ibid., 2 October 1919, it. 3393.
9.   Ibid., 1 April 1920, it. 3479.
10.   GKN Minute Book, Vol. 5, op. cit., 10 July 1924, it. 4559.
11.   GKN Minute Book, Vol. 6, op. cit., 5 November 1925, it. 4840.
12.   *An Outline History of GKN*, op. cit., p. 53.
13.   *Staffordshire General & Commercial Directory*, Manchester (1818), p. 298.
14.   *Slater's Staffordshire Directory* [*c.* 1850], p. 22.
15.   *Directory and Gazetteer of Staffordshire*, London (1861), p. 151.
16.   *Kelly's Directory of Staffordshire*, London (1880), p. 98.
17.   *Kelly's Directory of Staffordshire*, London (1880), p. 97.
18.   *Kelly's Directory of Staffordshire*, London (1912), p. 162.
19.   GKN Minute Book, Vol. 3, op. cit., 28 August 1919, it. 3367.
20.   *DBB*, Vol. 4 (1985), Edgar Jones, 'K.S. Peacock', p. 570.
21.   GKN Minute Book, Vol. 3, op. cit., 6 October 1921, it. 3846.
22.   GKN Minute Book, Vol. 4, op. cit., 2 November 1922, it. 4150.

23. Ibid., 7 June 1923, it. 4295.
24. Ibid.
25. GKN Minute Book, Vol. 5, op. cit., 3 April 1924, it. 4491.
26. Ibid.
27. Ibid., 10 July 1924, it. 4559.
28. Ibid.
29. Ibid., 2 October 1924, it. 4587.
30. Ibid., 6 November 1924, it. 4605.
31. Ibid., 4 December 1924, it. 4626.
32. GKN Minute Book, Vol. 6, op. cit., 11 September 1925, it. 4795.
33. Ibid., 5 November 1925, it. 4840.
34. Ibid., 4 March 1926, it. 4903.
35. Ibid.
36. GKN Minute Book, Vol. 7, op. cit., 9 September 1926, it. 4997.
37. Ibid., 7 October 1926, it. 5014.
38. Ibid., 1 November 1926, it. 5403.
39. GKN Minute Book, Vol. 8, op. cit., 7 February 1929, it. 5447.
40. Ibid., 7 March 1929, it. 5460; 5 March 1931, it. 5902.
41. Ibid., 6 November 1930, it. 5810.
42. Ibid., 6 June 1929, it. 5524.
43. Ibid., 2 May 1929, it. 5499; 6 June 1929, it. 5525.
44. Ibid., 2 October 1930, it. 5792.
45. GKN Minute Book, Vol. 9, op. cit., 4 June 1931, it. 5939.
46. Ibid., 1 October 1931, it. 5997.
47. Ibid., 31 December 1931, it. 6032.
48. Ibid., 3 November 1932, it. 6198.
49. Ibid., 1 December 1932, it. 6220.
50. Ibid., 2 November 1933, it. 6400.
51. Ibid., 7 December 1933, it. 6419.
52. Ibid., 1 March 1934, it. 6478.
53. Ibid., 12 April 1934, it. 6500.
54. Ibid., 22 August 1934, it. 6561.
55. GKN Minute Book, Vol. 10, op. cit., 2 January 1936, it. 6793.
56. Ibid., 5 March 1936, it. 6823.
57. Ibid., 1 October 1936, it. 6896.
58. Ibid., 7 January 1937, it. 6939.
59. Ibid., 6 May 1937, it. 6992.
60. GKN Minute Book, Vol. 11, op. cit., 4 May 1939, it. 7287.
61. Ibid., 1 June 1939, it. 7300.
62. Ibid., 7 December 1939, it. 7362.
63. Ibid., 5 November 1942, it. 7821.
64. *An Outline History of GKN*, op. cit., p. 55.
65. *Directory and Gazetteer of Staffordshire* London (1861), p. 152.
66. William White, *History, Gazetteer of Staffordshire*, Sheffield (1851), pp. 599, 602.
67. Ibid., p. 598.
68. *Kelly's Directory of Staffordshire*, London (1880), p. 99.
69. GKN Minute Book, Vol. 7, op. cit., 7 July 1927, it. 5179.
70. John Garrington & Sons Minute Book, Vol. 3, August 1932–March 1940, 30 August 1932, p. 1.
71. Ibid., 2 May 1933, p. 22.
72. Ibid., 4 July 1933, p. 27.

73. Ibid., 5 March 1935, p. 81.
74. GKN Minute Book, Vol. 10, op. cit., 2 January 1936, it. 6795; 6 F-bruary 1936, it. 6808.
75. GKN Minute Book, Vol. 11, op. cit., 3 August 1939, it. 7323.
76. Garrington Minute Book, Vol. 3, op. cit., 1 August 1939, p. 233.
77. Ibid., p. 234.
78. GKN Minute Book, Vol. 11, op. cit., 7 March 1940, it. 7408.
79. Ibid., 4 July 1940, it. 7463.
80. Ibid., 3 October 1940, it. 7484.
81. Ibid., 4 October 1940, it.
82. Ibid., 6 February 1941, it. 7549.
83. DBB, Vol. 1 (1984), op. cit., Edgar Jones 'Lord Brookes', pp. 463–8.
84. GKN Minute Book, Vol. 12, op. cit., 3 February 1944, it. 8040.
85. Ibid.
86. Ibid., 2 December 1943, it. 8009.
87. Ibid., 3 February 1944, it. 8040.
88. Ibid., 7 September 1944, it. 8130.
89. Ibid., 5 October 1944, it. 8149.
90. Ibid., 2 November 1944, it. 8158.
91. Ibid., it. 8167.
92. Interview E. Jones with Mr George Moore, July 1984.
93. Dora Ware, 'A History of Bayliss, Jones & Bayliss Limited' (typescript, 1950), pp. 29–30.
94. 'The Autobiography of William Bayliss' (typescript), pp. 1–2; Victoria County History of Stafford, Vol. II, Oxford (1967), p. 149.
95. Ibid., p. 10.
96. Slater's Staffordshire Directory, (c. 1850), p. 151.
97. Ware, 'A History', op. cit., p. 21.
98. Directory and Gazetteer of Staffordshire, London (1861), p. 27.
99. Ibid., pp. 22–23.
100. Ibid., p. 27.
101. Kelly's Directory of Staffordshire, London (1880), p. 391.
102. GKN Minute Book, Vol. 3, op. cit., 1 March 1922, it. 3966.
103. GKN Minute Book, Vol. 5, op. cit., 4 December 1924, it. 4626.
104. GKN Minute Book, Vol. 7, op. cit., 4 April 1928, it. 5296.
105. GKN Minute Book, Vol. 9, op. cit., 2 June 1932, it. 6136.
106. Ibid., 5 October 1933, it. 6376.
107. Ibid., 3 May 1934, it. 6517.
108. Ibid., 1 February 1934, it. 6454.
109. GKN Minute Book, Vol. 10, op. cit., 5 March 1936, it. 6823.
110. Ibid., 7 October 1937, it. 7041.
111. Ibid., 2 September 1937, it. 7027.
112. GKN Minute Book, Vol. 9, op. cit., 4 May 1933, it. 6309; 6 July 1933, it. 6329.
113. GKN Minute Book, Vol. 6, op. cit., 3 June 1926, it. 4958.
114. GKN Minute Book, Vol. 7, op. cit., 7 April 1927, it. 5116.
115. Interview E. Jones with Mr H. Anthill, general works manager, Albert Works, August 1983.

7 *Joseph Sankey & Sons*

> I felt that I was not looking at this place and that, but at the
> metallic Midlands themselves, at a relief map of a heavy industry,
> at another and greater exhibition of the 'fifties'.[1]
>
> J.B. Priestley, *English Journey* (1934)

PART I 1854–1918

JOSEPH SANKEY FOUNDS THE BUSINESS

The business of Joseph Sankey & Sons, hollow-ware manufacturers of
Bilston in Staffordshire, owed its existence to a partnership formed
between Samuel Jackson and Joseph Sankey in 1854, for the production
of blank trays from tinplate.[2] Joseph Sankey himself had not been
overly blessed with good fortune in his early life. Born at Bilston in
1827, the son of William Sankey (b. *c.* 1776) and his wife Elizabeth, he
was left an orphan in the summer of 1836 when his father, a potter,
died prematurely. The latter had possibly been weakened by the Asiatic
cholera which had swept through the town in the previous year, when
it had killed Joseph's mother.[3] Brought up as a Wesleyan Methodist,
the young Sankey was adopted by 'a substantial tradesman' called
Jackson. The Bilston register of 1836 contains only one Jackson who
might fit this description and he was a cooper, with a beer house as a
side line, though in 1818 a Samuel Jackson of 88 Church Street had been
listed as being a japanner.[4] For the next four to five years Joseph
attended the Royal Orphanage School in Wolverhampton, and at the
age of fourteen was apprenticed to John Duncalfe, tray blank maker of
Hall Street, Bilston, where he received instruction in design and mechanical drawing. A letter written by Duncalfe to his pupil in February
1846 not only praised Joseph's fidelity and good behaviour, but also
recorded the presentation of the master's own instruments, including a
'T' square and a drawing board.[5] If this represented a parting testi-
monial, Joseph Sankey would have completed his training when
nineteen. His first employers were the Birch brothers who fashioned
tinplate trays which were then 'japanned', that is applied with thick
japan varnishes as both protection and decoration.

Although Birmingham and Wolverhampton were the principal Midlands towns where japanning developed, the trade had begun about a
quarter of a century earlier in Bilston, Joseph Allen and Samuel Stone

88   Joseph Sankey
(1827–86), founder of the
business.

being listed as japanners in the parish registers of 1718–19.[6] Neverthe-less, it probably remained a subsidiary activity to toymaking and metal working in these early years. By the second half of the eighteenth century it had become a recognised trade in its own right and among those firms of japanners listed in 1781 were Homer, Bickley & Sons, John Hartill, John Simmons, and Hanson & Jackson,[7] and by 1818 some fifteen firms of japanners were listed in the local trade directory.[8] Because Bilston provided for the lower end of the market, it rarely produced wares to rival those of Birmingham or Wolverhampton, concentrating on tin rather than papier-mâché objects. Two reasons were given for this market division. First, articles made in Bilston were for export to Spain and South America 'where brilliance of colour and cheapness is preferred to quality',[9] and secondly because 'labour is cheaper here than anywhere else, the manufactories do a large business with the Birmingham merchants who run the prices down when they get a chance during a bad time of trade'.[10] As a result, the Bilston japanners were affected far less by changing tastes and fashions, and several of them outlived their more prestigious rivals in Birmingham and Wolverhampton.[11] By 1834, when William, White compiled his

Gazetteer of Bilston, he was able to conclude that the chief manufactures of the town were 'iron and tinplate japanned and enamelled goods'.[12]

When the japanning and tinplate business belonging to the Birch brothers failed, two of the senior workmen, Charles Harthill and Samuel Jackson, decided to set up their own firm in Middlefield Lane.[13] With Joseph Sankey as the leading hand and around half a dozen workmen, they subsequently acquired premises in Dudley Lane (now Street). For the Great Exhibition of 1851, they produced a magnificent japanned tray, nearly four feet in diameter (colour plate five), this said to have been hammered by Joseph Sankey.[14] A piece of considerable craftsmanship, the central area depicts the discovery of Moses in the bulrushes by the Pharaoh's daughter.[15] Despite the skills evident in the workforce, the business did not flourish and when Charles Harthill died in 1854, the firm owed John Bates, a sheet iron merchant, eight hundred pounds.[16] In part, this may have been a reflection of the general decline which the japanning trade entered in the 1850s. Changing tastes, the rise of electro-plating, aluminium wares and the manufacture of vitreous enamelled hollow-ware had combined to undermine its traditional markets.

John Bates secured possession of the plant and stock-in-trade ('tools implements and effects') of the firm as security for the outstanding debt.[17] In Joseph Sankey he had perceived both talent and determination and he persuaded Jackson to take him into partnership in 1854. The two became great friends, Sankey serving as Bates' best man in 1864, and Joseph having named a daughter after his benefactor's surname. The admission of Sankey to the ranks of management corresponded with the decision to abandon japanning and to concentrate on the production of blank trays. These were stamped cold from tinplate (sheet wrought iron given a thin coat of tin) before being sold to japanners, originally most went to Bilston but, as the business grew, greater numbers were dispatched to Wolverhampton and Birmingham. By specialising in the metal side of tray manufacture, Jackson & Sankey could produce a considerable variety of shapes and sizes, amongst their best-selling lines were the 'Elgin', 'Climax' and the 'Blondin', the last suggesting properties of balance.[18] To finance expansion, Joseph Sankey repeatedly mortgaged the premises in Dudley Street, though expansion enabled him to repay the loans within several years.

In 1867, Joseph Sankey purchased land in Albert Street contiguous to the rear of the Dudley Street workshop. He had paid Samuel Jackson £500 for his share of the partnership in August 1861,[19] but the latter remained with the firm for a further seventeen years as a foreman in the blank tray shop. Larger workshops capable of housing the latest technology were constructed in Albert Street. Steam-powered drop stamps were installed, enabling Sankey to fashion the heavier gauges of metal as used for frying pans. This trade was a novelty in Bilston so that experienced men had to be recruited from Birmingham. A kettle shop was also erected and as these, too, were products not normally made in the district, workers were sought from Wolverhampton.

In order to obtain closer controls over supplies of tinplate and sheet iron, Joseph Sankey, in partnership with Richard Chambers and John Page, bought a small rolling mill and ironworks at neighbouring Stonefield in 1862 or 1863. Each of the partners put up £500 and the business was renamed the Bilston Iron Co. Its success may be judged by the fact that within twenty years, the value of these original investments had each risen to £16,000.[20]

In 1870 sales by the firm totalled over £6,500, of which almost £4,000 derived from tray blanks, the original product made by Harthill & Jackson. Four years later, when the workforce had reached 65, the business generated sales worth £11,000, of which £5,000 came from tray blanks.[21] From 1874, sales of tray blanks declined and hollow-ware items multiplied, these ranging from dish covers, tin boxes, trunks, lamps and lanterns, milk churns and chocolate moulds stamped with the name Cadbury.[22] A catalogue issued in January 1905 listed no less than 250 stamped or pressed metal products, including corrugated metal life buoys, bath tubs, fire shovels, jelly moulds, candlesticks, egg poachers and fender stands.[23] A considerable export business developed: Cassada pans (shallow utensils in which coffee beans are dried) were exported to Brazil in large quantities, rice bowls were shipped to India and Ceylon, and cash bowls to China.[24] Speaking of the Cassada pans. W.H. Fellows, who completed over fifty years service with the company, recalled in December 1950 that

> Sankeys had a monopoly of this trade for many years, and there was an enormous trade very lucrative to the firm. Quite a lot of business was done through German merchants, our agent being Herm Holm of Hamburg ... Sizes varied from 14ins to 72ins normally, and I remember the largest size ever made was 120ins diameter. The plates for the medium sizes were usually obtained from British mills, but the very large size plates came from Krupps, Germany, through our London agent, Robert Jenkins ... Two firms in this country tried to produce Cassada pans, but had to abandon the ideas as Sankeys with their knowledge and long-experienced workmen held the field.[25]

Until the late 1860s, in typical entrepreneurial style, Joseph Sankey did most of the firm's book-keeping and paid the wages himself. However, in 1871 his eldest son, John William Sankey (1855–1913)[26] left Wolverhampton Grammar School to work in the offices, where he took on these accountancy roles. In 1878 J.W. Sankey became a partner, and as the effort required to build up the business began to affect Joseph's health, the former assumed a greater share of the executive burden. A second son, George H. Sankey (1865–1934), joined the firm in 1884. His younger brother, Frederick E. Sankey (d. 1931), had spent several months in the office during 1882 but left to enter the engineering

5 The japanned tray which depicts Moses being discovered in the bulrushes by the Pharaoh's daughter. Nearly four feet in diameter, it was reputedly hammered by Joseph Sankey, and was displayed at the 1851 Great Exhibition.

department of Thos. Perry & Sons of Bradley, and subsequently spent four years with Taylor & Challen, pressmakers. A fourth son, Harry, came for a brief course of clerical work in 1888 but later took up farming (see Figure 12).[27]

Table 7.1 Joseph Sankey & Sons net profits, 1902–18

		£	Adjusted* £
12 months to 31 March	1903	11,620	16,841
	1904	14,541	21,074
	1905	24,415	34,879
	1906	24,151	33,543
	1907	37,032	48,094
	1908	24,097	30,121
	1909	8,924	12,225
	1910	19,732	26,665
	1911	34,059	43,665
	1912	10,420	13,025
	1913	26,619	31,316
	1914	33,770	39,729
	1915	30,895	36,347
	1916	66,668	61,730
	1917	40,505	29,783
	1918	39,103	21,845

Note: *Figures adjusted by the Sauerbeck – *Statist* index of prices, 1867–77 = 100.

Source: Joseph Sankey & Sons Ltd Directors Minute Books, Vol. 1, September 1902–August 1912; Vol. 2, September 1912–November 1916; Vol. 3, January 1917–December 1921.

Joseph Sankey had many of the qualities of the classic Victorian entrepreneur. He rose from humble beginnings and personal hardship through determined hard work; he learned a wide range of tasks, took calculated risks (to the point of mortgaging his own property) and strove for success. Like so many of this class, he was a Non-conformist, and served from 1856 as trustee of the Bilston chapel funds. Sankey led and inspired his workforce through the strength of his personality. A sheet roller at the Bilston Iron Co. recalled that Joseph Sankey was

> the best man I ever worked for. He used to bring baskets of fruit and vegetables from his garden at Goldthorn Hill and distribute them among the work people.[28]

The force of his character and the scale of the business which he had created were both indicated by the attendance of over 200 workmen at his funeral service in Bilston. Although he originally appears to have

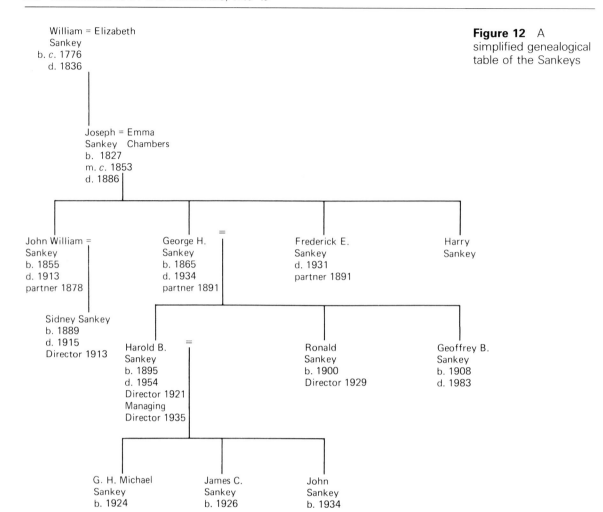

Figure 12 A simplified genealogical table of the Sankeys

lived on the premises, in the early 1860s Sankey commissioned a new home, Goldthorn House, on the top of Goldthorn Hill, near Wolverhampton,[29] where the sons that were to carry the business into the twentieth century were brought up.

In his sixtieth year on 1 April 1886, Joseph Sankey died from a severe bronchial attack. In his will he left £17,010 gross,[30] a sum which would have marked him out as a wealthy man but which also suggested that a considerable proportion of the firm's profits had been ploughed back into the business to generate expansion.

JOSEPH SANKEY & SONS: ELECTRICAL LAMINATIONS

It was under the auspices of J.W. Sankey in December 1886 that a fortuitous turn of events led to the firm becoming the largest producer of electrical laminations in Britain. A London iron merchant, Robert Jenkins, whilst visiting King Brown & Co. of Edinburgh, was shown a disc of charcoal sheet iron with the comment that in future dynamo armatures would be made from these instead of iron wire wound in bobbin fashion. Realising that Sankeys possessed machines which might be adapted to produce these discs, he broke his return journey at Bilston to tell John and George Sankey of the development.[31] Back in London, Jenkins consulted a Mr Leukert of Siemens, the electrical engineers, who confirmed the opinion he had received in Edinburgh. He persuaded Siemens to make an order and early in 1887 Sankeys received their first request for electrical stampings through the merchants, Harold & Jenkins.[32]

The volume of work grew rapidly and within three years contracts had been concluded with, among others, Cromptons, Allen, and Brush. When the Admiralty showed an interest, Sankeys decided that they needed to deal directly with the customer rather than through an intermediary and in 1887 the goodwill of Harold & Jenkins was purchased for 500 guineas, Harry Harold and Robert Jenkins being appointed Sankey's selling agents on a commission basis.[33] In 1893, the partnership of Jenkins & Harold dissolved, with the former continuing to work for Sankeys and the latter setting up on his own account as a merchant in electrical fittings. The extrovert Jenkins, it was said, was largely responsible for enabling Sankeys to build up and retain their monopoly of lamination manufacture in the UK by convincing customers of the quality of the Sankey product and the cost factors involved in entering this market themselves.

From the mid-1890s onwards, the development of alternating current using transformers demanded stampings of more complicated shapes and higher quality. The principal problem was the rapid ageing of material once in operation. Tests were conducted on various grades of iron and steel. As a result, Sankeys abandoned charcoal iron in favour of a particular metal steel sheet which they gave the brand name 'Lohy', a contraction of the words 'low' and 'hysteresis', the latter referring to the time lag between magnetic effects and their causes.[34]

The continued expansion of the business led John William Sankey to admit his two younger brothers, Frederick Ernest and George Herbert Sankey, to the partnership in July 1891.[35] The style of the firm was altered to 'Joseph Sankey & Sons'[36] and the profits were to be divided accordingly: John William Sankey (one-half), Emma Sankey, widow of the founder Joseph (one-quarter), and F.E. and G.H. Sankey (each one-eighth).[37]

Not only did the firm diversify into the manufacture of electrical laminations, it also succeeded in developing its traditional pressing and stamping business. During the 1890s, Joseph Sankey & Sons acquired a number of smaller concerns which had become uncompetitive; these included Edward Morris & Sons (sugar-making utensils), Huttons (nickel plated trays), the Sanitary Bath Co. (copper-clad steel) and, most important, the established firm of J.H. Hopkins & Sons of Granville Street, Birmingham. The latter, a hollow-ware and japanning company, possessed the 'Sphinx' trademark which Sankeys subsequently adopted. The japanning side of Hopkins' business was sold in line with Sankeys' policy, and the remaining stamping and pressing operations concentrated within the Albert Street Works.[38]

In 1890, Sankeys patented a process under the name of 'Neptune Ware'. Rather than stamp or press a particular object and then apply a design, the tinplate was run through colour rollers to undercoat both sides. Having been embossed and then painted in the required decoration (either floral Japanese or imitation crocodile hide), the ware was blanked out to the final shape.[39] This manufacturing technique had been borrowed partly from America by John Sankey who had introduced it with help from a diemaker called Stone, whom he had met while on a visit to the United States.[40] Although not aesthetically of the highest quality, Neptune Ware proved an immediate success with the consumer and parts of the Albert Street Works had to be extended to cope with growing demand. Besides 'waiters' (small trays), the technique was used for ash-trays, cups, children's money boxes, cake baskets, curry bowls and other small articles.

During the 1890s, Sankeys made more kettles than any other British company. Fashioned from Staffordshire wrought iron, they were coated inside with tin and japanned outside in black; the bottoms, sides and shoulders were brazed in place by craftsmen but, it was said that these men, who were 'jealously possessive of their trade and craftmanship', would 'not have any learners or apprentices'.[41] Accordingly, John Sankey decided to make kettles with pressed bodies in one piece with beaded shoulders which gradually replaced the harder wearing brazed version. Their manufacture was cheapened in the last quarter of the nineteenth century by the substitution of steel, which could be pressed into shape more easily, increasing the speed of production.[42]

In 1900 the continued expansion of the business encouraged the purchase of a derelict iron and tinplate works across the canal at Bradley. It had been established in 1833 by Thompson, Hatton & Co.,[43] but the collapse of prices following the protection of the American market (caused by the introduction of the McKinley tariff) led to the closures of the works, though it subsequently re-opened in an attempt to produce tinplate profitably.[44] Failure to do so resulted in the Bradley Iron Works falling into the hands of the Capital and Counties Bank as mortgages for sale in two lots. In June, Sankeys bought the new site of the works (8,516 sq yds) for £2,600, and in October acquired the remaining 6,083 sq yds for £1,550.[45] Most of the existing buildings were demolished and new shops were constructed to accommodate fifteen slotting machines and eight keyway cutters, in order that the manufacture of electrical laminations could be transferred to the renamed Bankfield Works from Albert Street.

To meet the rising sheet requirements of the Bankfield Works, in 1904

89 Employees of Joseph Sankey & Sons, possibly at the Bankfield Works when war had encouraged the recruitment of female workers.

the Manor Rolling Mills at Ettingshall were bought from Stephen Thompson Ltd for £10,570.[46] The two plants, though several miles distant, were connected by the Shropshire Union Canal, the waterway continuing to be used well into the twentieth century.[47] Fortunately, for Sankeys, the Thompson Company had won orders to supply electrical sheets to the Electrical Construction Co. of Wolverhampton and had converted some of their mills to this end. The acquisition was well conceived, for in May 1907 Sankeys were able to report that

> the Manor Works have proved a most satisfactory addition to the operations of the company. In addition to providing a profit of £6,227 18s 7d [for 1906–07] . . . they proved a great convenience to the other branches of the company's interests, especially since the recent boom in iron and steel, when it would have been very difficult to get the supplies needed for the Albert Street and Bankfield Works.[48]

In April 1906, Sankeys and the Hadfield Steel Foundry Co. of Sheffield entered into an arrangement by which the former were granted an exclusive licence to obtain or manufacture special electrical steel henceforth referred to as 'stalloy'. Sankeys agreed to pay

Hadfields a royalty of £1 per ton up to a maximum annual payment of £12,500 on all ingots which they purchased or made themselves.[49] In 1909, Sankeys sub-licensed John Lysaght to roll sheets under the Hadfield patents at their Orb Works on a royalty of £1 10s per ton. The Lysaghts, who had rolling mills nearby in Wolverhampton (the Swan Lane and Osier Bed Works), were friends of the Sankeys, a connection which was later to lead to a more formal association (p. 5). In the same year Sankeys granted the Brymbo Steel Co. near Wrexham a licence to make steel bars and blooms under the Hadfield patents, on condition that these would then be sold to Lysaghts alone for rolling into sheet. In this fashion, without incurring great capital expenditure, Sankeys were able to increase their control over the supply and quality of their raw material inputs.

Much of this growth and diversification had been made possible by resort to limited liability. In September 1902, Joseph Sankey & Sons was floated with an authorised capital of £200,000 divided into 10,000 ordinary shares of £10 each and 10,000 5½ per cent preference shares of £10 each.[50] John (with 3,395 ordinary shares), George (1,250) and Frederick Sankey (1,250) were each appointed directors, together with John Chambers,[51] the latter having been employed in the offices from his youth and risen to be, in effect, the company secretary. John Sankey became chairman, a post which passed in 1913 to George when the former died.[52] Subsequent appointments to the board included Sidney Sankey (1889–1915) in June 1913,[53] Harry Thomas Sankey in May 1915[54] and Robert Arthur Dawbarn, a professional engineer, in October 1915.[55] The death of the last resulted in the election of J. Falshaw Watson in June 1917.[56]

John Sankey, like his father, exhibited a commitment to the management of the family business. He, like his younger brother George, worked a twelve-hour day and was intimately involved in the practical operation of the various works. A formidable figure, the story had been recounted that in the early days of Bankfield somebody mistakenly let off the steam hooter to indicate the end of the day an hour early. John Sankey looked at his watch and shouted at his employees 'Get back to your machines all of you. Take your hands out of my pockets!' At Christmas he would stand by the pay office and give half a crown to each boy and five shillings or a brace of ducks to each man. Being a fervent teetotaller, like his brother George, John would advise every man to take the money home to his wife and not waste it on drinks.[57]

W.H. Fellows, who knew George Sankey well, described the latter as being 'rather austere and exacting though perfectly just' at business, while outside the works could be 'perfectly charming'.[58] Both he and his younger brother, Frederick, took a paternalistic interest in their workforce. Annual outings were organised, the first being to Arley which included dinner at the Valencia Arms Hotel. In 1892, following their admission to the partnership, a store-room at Albert Street was cleared and converted to serve as a canteen so that employees no longer had to eat meals beside the machines, the food being sent from their homes. In addition, a sick benefit club was set up to which the firm contributed £25 a year.[59]

SUPPLIERS TO THE AUTOMOTIVE TRADE

In 1902, George Sankey had been persuaded by his friend and fellow Liberal, Sir Henry Newman M.P., to purchase a simple and relatively inexpensive American car, an Oldsmobile.[60] Wishing to increase its carrying capacity, he extended the body of his car but found that this put too much strain on the six horse-power engine and in due course exchanged the Oldsmobile for a De Dion four-seater. Whether this personal involvement with the automobile inspired Sankey to believe that there was a commercial future in their manufacture has not been recorded. Nevertheless, when his friend Herbert Austin (1866–1941)

90 Sankey wheels manufactured at the Handley Castle Works during the Great War.

approached Sankeys in 1904 about pressing metal body shells for wooden frames, he agreed to take on the work. Austin had originally been employed by the Wolseley Sheep Shearing Machine Co. based at the Sydney Works in Alma Street, Birmingham but, on his own initiative, diversified into the manufacture of motor cars. In 1901, he had set up the Wolseley Tool & Motor Co. to concentrate his energies solely on their production.[61] This initial order for pressed body panels was followed by many more as Austin's cars became increasingly popular. From these beginnings, Sankeys began to supply Daimler, Humber, Rover and Argyle.[62] In addition, the company started to produce both wood and iron coachwork which necessitated the construction

91 The pressed Sankey wheel – product of considerable commercial success.

of wood-working body shops at Albert Street. An export trade also developed, one of their first customers being Vederin et Cie of Paris. By November 1906, unpainted and untrimmed body panels were being sold to Edward E. Cary Inc. of 159 Park Place, New York.[63]

In 1908, largely due to the ingenuity of Wingfield Burton, then works manager at Albert Street, Sankeys developed and patented the first pressed and welded, detachable motor car wheel.[64] Orders for other automotive components (clutches, fans, step brackets and so forth which demanded pressings) also increased rapidly and it soon became evident that the Bilston Works could no longer accommodate this additional demand. As the directors reported in May 1906, 'the increase in the Albert Street business is largely due to motor car stampings, the manufacture of which is now well established and promises to be a permanent and remunerative branch of business'.[65]

Towards the end of 1909, when the depression of 1908 had passed,[66] and 'a general improvement was experienced',[67] Sankeys decided to look for new premises. At Hadley Castle, near Wellington, Shropshire, they discovered the former factory of the Castle Car Co., manufacturers of tramcars, who had supplied 150 of these to the London County Council.[68] Some of the equipment, woodworking machinery and a large press, which would prove suitable for body panels, was intact. As well as being situated on an arm of the Shropshire Union Canal, the works also possessed a railway siding from the LNWR. They had, in fact, belonged to Nettlefold & Chamberlain during the 1860s at which time they comprised a blast furnace, puddling furnaces and rolling mills, though they had been sold in 1886 when the Castle Works was transferred to Rogerstone.[69]

Before making an offer for the works, Sankeys commissioned a report from Morley & Dawbarn, consulting engineers, who concluded in August 1910 that

> the place is in excellent order and the tools are driven periodically in order to keep the motors etc. in good condition . . . Money had not been spared in any way in the construction of these works. The works are all brick built with excellent top lights throughout.[70]

92 A charabanc whose coachwork had been supplied by Sankeys.

93   Sankey wheels fitted to a pre-war family saloon.

They discovered that the 33½ acres had cost £5,713, the buildings a further £72,622 and the plant and machinery £39, 387, making a total of £112,009.[71] Morley & Dawbarn suggested that the entire premises and their contents could be obtained for around £35,000 or possibly less. Accordingly, Sankeys opened negotiations and concluded the purchase in December 1910 for the sum of £30,000.[72] Taking possession of the factory in January 1911, the transfer of the body shop from Bankfield proceeded forthwith, and in May the wheel shop moved from Albert Street. By June the relocation of Sankeys' automotive business had been accomplished under the supervision of the new works manager, S.L. Brunton, an austere graduate engineer of King's College, London, who had previously been employed by Cromptons.[73]

   The success of the Hadley Castle project appears to have been achieved, initially at least, at the expense of the Albert Street Works. The directors' report for 1911–12 observed,

> the disappointing results at Albert Street are also in part due to the removal of the wheel and body panel work and the consequent transfer of a remunerative department to Hadley with the subsequent rearrangement of shops and machines here. This was to some extent anticipated though it was hoped that the transfer would prove less costly .. The Hadley Works are now in working order and the output is steadily increasing.[74]

The new works did not confine its activities to bodies, wheels and

94 A convoy of lorries loaded with Sankey wheels about to leave the Hadley Castle Works.

stampings. Amongst other components it was soon manufacturing a steel piston turned from a weldless tube. In addition, a limited degree of diversification resulted in the production of steel barrels for palm and other oils collected in East Africa.[75]

At one point Sankeys almost entered into an agreement with Thomas Tilling of Peckenham, and W.A. Stevens of Maidstone, which, had it come to fruition, would have brought them to the point of making omnibuses and lorries.[76] Under the proposed scheme, Sankeys were to sell the Hadley Works and its patents for £105,000 to the new merged business, which would be called the Hadley Engineering Co. Ltd.[77] A prospectus was prepared and shares offered to the public but the minimum subscription was not met, whereupon Sankeys withdrew from the project much to the disappointment of George Sankey. Tilling and Stevens persevered and for several decades made a success of manufacturing the Tilling–Stevens lorry and omnibus.

One of the most profitable products turned out from Hadley Castle was the Sankey wheel. The original design almost certainly belonged to Wingfield Burton, the Albert Street works manager, who also undertook the development work. One story related that he had been inspired by the stamped wheel of a child's toy and another that George Sankey, dissatisfied with the wooden wheels on his car, set Burton to devise a steel version in conjunction with Arthur Clews, his chauffeur. The prototype set made with a cast-iron punch and leaden die were tested on his automobile, and are reported to be those preserved in the Science Museum.

The Sankey wheel was formed of two sheets or discs of steel, in which holes were punched to correspond with the openings between the spokes. By sucessive operations, the spokes and rim were pressed into shape and then the two halves welded together.[78] Using this manufacturing technique, wheels could be produced in a variety of sizes.[79] In addition, the company made brass hubs with a circular ring or lock nut which enabled the wheel to be easily detached.

The Sankey wheel was sold extensively to British car makers, notably to the larger producers, such as Herbert Austin and William Morris. In February 1913, George Sankey was empowered to license the E.G. Budd Manufacturing Co. of Philadelphia to make Sankey wheels for an annual royalty of not less than £3,000.[80]

The other area of great development at Hadley Castle comprised the production of car and charabanc bodies, pressed from sheet steel. It is said that George Sankey and Sir Richard Paget between them evolved a system of body design which, in essence, remained in use well into the 1950s. Sankey provided a model, about a foot long, indicating the size and position of the vehicle's essential parts while Paget moulded an envelope around it.[81] Further, by 1912 the works had begun to press chassis frames, though their production in large quantities did not follow until the 1920s.[82]

PROFITS AND PERFORMANCE

The annual profits of Joseph Sankey & Sons during the Edwardian period revealed a consistently successful company. Nevertheless, both the reported figures and those adjusted for price movements (Table 7.2) showed that their surpluses in 1913–14 were of the same order of those achieved in 1905–7, and the effect of the Great War was to trim back results as the 1917 and 1918 figures demonstrated.

In more detail, Sankeys grew steadily between 1902 and 1907 achieving progressively higher profits in both real and cash terms. In December 1907, however, the market turned against them and they faced 'a considerable diminution in the amount of orders', and prices fell 'very materially'.[83] The depression experienced throughout 1908 continued into the following year and Sankeys calculated that the turnover for 1908–9 was about two-thirds of that for 1907–8.[84] 'It is satisfactory to note', the directors added, 'that there has been no falling off in the percentage of gross profit but it is impossible to reduce the working expenses proportionately to the reduction in the volume of business',[85] an observation which implied that economies of scale were lost at an increasing rate beyond a certain point and when fixed costs assumed a growing importance. A recovery began in August 1909 and was maintained throughout the year such that by May 1910 Sankeys could report turnover up by one quarter on the previous twelve months.[86] The upswing in business was sustained in 1910–11, turnover increasing by one-third in 1909–10, which represented an increment of 70 per cent on 1908–9 figures[87] – a trend that revealed itself in the company's reported profits.

The poor results recorded in 1911–12 were not entirely of Sankeys' making, as they reflected the railway strike of August 1911 and coal strike of March 1912 both of which reduced output, though the transfer of the automotive business from Bilston to Hadley Castle also affected the company's profitability.[88] Recovery was well underway when the outbreak of war disrupted progress. The flood of orders presented by the Ministry of Munitions (below) initially boosted the company's fortunes such that in 1916 a record surplus was attained.[89] Although Sankeys earned £40,505 in 1917, this was a period of high inflation and the indexed results for that year and for 1918 were £29,783 and £21,845 respectively. However, these figures took account of allowances for anticipated Excess Profits Duty. For the two years ended 31 March 1918, Sankeys had put aside £95,000 to settle their tax demands, but in January 1919 found themselves presented with a request for £110,000.[90] While appealing against this figure the company agreed to a takeover by John Lysaght. The reduced level of profit and pressing claim from the revenue may well have been significant factors in the Sankey family's decision to sell the business (p. 253). On balance, therefore, the Great War was not of particular commercial benefit to Sankeys.

THE GREAT WAR

The immediate effect of the outbreak of hostilities was the loss of workers, whether skilled or otherwise, to the armed forces. In August 1914, for example, 342 employees were called to serve with the colours, the company having encouraged enlistment in the Territorial Army by granting full pay to those engaged on the two weeks of summer training.[91] This produced a fall in output which, in turn, was reflected in the published profits for 1915 (Table 7.2).[92] The company allocated £2,000 in June 1915 to a Bonus and Benevolent Fund to be distributed to the dependents of employees killed or wounded in the fighting;[93] by 1918 the total had risen to nearly £5,000.[94]

While several branches of Sankeys' business were brought to a virtual standstill, the enormous demands of the mobilised economy resulted in substantial orders for war material.[95] From November 1915, the Albert Street Works became a Controlled Establishment under the authority of the Ministry of Munitions.[96] This factory, together with Hadley Castle, produced field kitchens, mine hemispheres, paravanes, aeroplane parts and bombs, rifle grenades, mortar bombs, anti-submarine devices and their largest single order, 4.5 ins. H.E. shell bodies,[97] though perhaps their greatest contribution was the manufacture of the steel helmet. A number of Sheffield companies had suggested that steel sufficiently tough to resist a revolver bullet fired at close range could not be pressed into the shape of a helmet. The War Office reluctantly concurred with their opinion and specified mild steel as an advance on the cloth cap as worn in 1914–15. George Sankey, whose eldest son was at the front and whose nephew had been mortally wounded, determined not to be beaten and after many disappointments, succeeded in discovering a method of pressing such resistant sheet. In the event, Sankeys supplied five and a half million manganese steel helmets to the troops, almost the entire requirement of the British Army.[98]

In order to cope with the vast quantities of war material that they were requested to manufacture and yet handicapped by having so many employees away in the forces, Sankeys took on increasing numbers of women. This, in turn, created some ill-feeling amongst those skilled men who remained at their jobs. Under union-negotiated wages for setting up lathes and machines, they earned around £4 a week, while both men and women operating the machinery on piece work rates could accumulate from £12–16 a week. The problem was solved at a stroke when the war ended, orders were rapidly curtailed and some 1,150 temporary employees made redundant.[99]

Sixty-nine employees lost their lives in the war. Of particular importance for the future of the company was the death of Captain Sidney Sankey (1889–1915) killed in France.[100] The eldest son of John William Sankey entered the Albert Street Works to begin his training, and completed his industrial education in Canada. He began to attend board meetings in 1911 and was made a director in June 1913.[101] Reported as being a skilful engineer and talented administrator, Sidney Sankey had been marked out as a potential future chairman.[102] In view of the takeover of Sankeys by John Lysaght (p. 253), his premature demise appeared to have been of even greater significance than the loss of an able manager.

SUMMARY

Thus it was on the end of hostilities in November 1918, Sankeys found themselves reasonably placed to compete in the peacetime economy. Their involvement in both the motor car trade (through the supply of body pressings and wheels) and the electrical industry (in the production of laminations) would prove fortunate indeed, as these were to prove growth areas during the interwar period. Not so successful would be their traditional manufacturing base – hollow-ware items of daily consumption – as other materials such as plastics increasingly entered the market.

The small Bilston business which Joseph Sankey had joined in 1854 had expanded dramatically and now embraced four separate works: Albert Street and Bankfield (both in Bilston), the Manor Rolling Mills, Ettingshall, and the Hadley Castle Works, near Wellington. Floated as a public limited liability company in September 1902, the business had flourished in the six years to 1908 when a trade depression interrupted growth until 1911. If problems existed in 1918, then they were of a managerial nature rather than technical or commercial. Overly reliant upon family members to run the business, few managers had been recruited to board level. The death of John William Sankey in 1913, who had served as chairman since 1886, produced a crisis of executive authority as his younger brother George, who temporarily accepted the chairmanship, had no continuing desire to run the company. Sidney Sankey, the most promising of the younger generation, had been killed in 1915, while Harold B. Sankey's entry to the business had been postponed by war service. In such circumstances, George Sankey considered selling the company to John Lysaght with whom there were strong business and social ties, and in doing so altered the course of the Sankey history.

PART II, 1918–1945

TAKEOVER BY LYSAGHTS

On 19 November 1919 George H. Sankey, chairman of Joseph Sankey & Sons, announced to his fellow directors that at a meeting called by John Lysaght and held in their offices in the Orb Works, Newport, H. Seymour Berry had 'made a firm offer to purchase all the ordinary shares in this company at the price of £27 10s 0d per share and for acceptance within seven days'.[103] The board, which comprised Frederick S. Sankey, Harry T. Sankey and James Felshaw Watson, together with the secretary, Edgar J. Budd, agreed to the offer and it was arranged that Berry, chairman of Lysaghts, would acquire 8,200 of the 10,000 £10 ordinary shares in two ways: 4,040 shares would be bought by a combination of cash and shares in John Lysaght (then valued at £2 10s) in the proportion of one-third and two-thirds respectively; 2,165 would be purchased entirely in cash, and for the remaining 1,995 payment would be made one half in cash and one half in Lysaght ordinary shares of £1 each, valued at £2 10s.[104]

It remains something of a mystery why such a well-established and profitable company (surpluses of £39,103 and £37,055 had been earned in 1918 and 1919)[105] should have allowed itself to be taken over with virtually no resistance. The role of George H. Sankey as chairman was crucial in the decision to sell. Anecdote suggests that he believed economic conditions would worsen and that a family business, albeit one quoted on the Stock Exchange, would find it difficult to weather the impending commercial storm. The death of Sidney Sankey in the war had removed the one obvious candidate to succeed George H.

Sankey, now fifty-four. Although Sankeys were a public company, the majority of the shares were owned by the family and an increasing proportion of these belonged to female members,[106] who may have had no direct interest in the running of the enterprise. The Sankeys and the Lysaghts had long been acquainted, an association which had arisen because the latter had supplied the former from their Swan Garden and Osier Bed Ironworks at nearby Wolverhampton. On commercial grounds, the takeover would have the advantage of providing Sankeys with a guaranteed supply of steel from Lysaghts' Normanby Park Works and an alternative source of sheet from their Orb Mills, Newport. Perhaps the notion that Sankeys and Lysaghts might combine had long been around but it took the determination and buccaneering spirit of H. Seymour Berry to pull the deal together.

The result of the takeover was that George H. Sankey surrendered the chairmanship in favour of Berry.[107] Harry Sankey, who as a farmer had occupied a non-executive seat on the board, retired, but Frederick E. Sankey and J. Felshaw Watson retained their directorships.[108] Representing Lysaghts, D.R. Llewellyn, Sir Leonard W. Llewelyn and D.C. Lysaght were elected to the Sankey board. Shortly afterwards, J. Gomer Berry and William Trimmer, both of Lysaght, were also appointed directors.[109] Not many months later, Lysaghts and GKN merged under the latter's mantle and Sankeys found themselves responsible to yet one more layer of authority.

THE ALBERT STREET WORKS

In the nineteenth century the manufacture of hollow-ware at Albert Street had formed the core of Sankeys' business. In the immediate post-war slump it was this market which experienced greatest difficulties. In these circumstances, George H. Sankey was asked to prepare a report on the future on the works. 'The hardware and enamel trades', he observed in July 1921,

> were at the present time in a deplorable condition. The complexity of manufacture involving many separate departments running on a low output made economic production almost impossible ... Many of the articles produced were likely in future to be subject to even keener foreign competition ... He had reluctantly come to the conclusion that the possibility of replacing the present range of manufactures with some standard article, for which the buildings were suitable, should be seriously considered as he was doubtful whether any considerable outlay in reorganisation and reconstruction for the existing trade would be justified.[110]

Much of the plant at Albert Street was in poor condition having been run at capacity through the war years.[111] Because the works had been extended piecemeal on the back of expanding demand, the buildings lacked a coherent plan comprising separate departments on different levels linked by narrow passages and stairways. It was difficult, therefore, to envisage a rapid revitalisation in the works' fortunes.

For a short period the Albert Street Works was in effect closed, and in February 1922 the board considered selling the factory.[112] Perhaps because the matter had been placed in George H. Sankey's hand, an effort was made to retain the business and minimise redundancies. Although trade revived slightly, it never recovered to pre-war levels and in April 1924 Sankeys agreed to cease enamelling hollow-ware in favour of Messrs. Macfarlane & Robinson of Bushbury, Wolverhampton, who contracted to purchase all stampings in excess of their existing output from Albert Street.[113]

A few of the traditional lines maintained their profitability following improvements in manufacturing methods. Cassada pans sold to Brazil, for example, were now spun on a lathe rather than stamped from hot sheet steel[114] – a technique which during the Second World War proved its worth in the production of aircraft spinners. New pressed products introduced at Albert Street during the mid-1920s included casings for petrol pumps (supplied to W. & T. Avery for the Shell company) and vending machines, together with welded motorcycle tanks. The first two lines dried up following the Hatry financial crash of 1930, while the production of fuel tanks ceased on the winding-up of the A.J.S. Motor Cycle Co. in 1933–34.

The association with Shell brought Sankeys into contact with the Asiatic Petroleum Co., which, in turn, was attempting to promote the consumption of paraffin in domestic heaters.[115] They had encouraged the Florence Stove Corporation America of Gardner, Massachusetts, to set up a UK subsidiary. The abandonment of the Gold Standard in 1931 made the import of American-made stoves uneconomic, and Sankeys were able to sign agreements with both the Asiatic Petroleum Co. and the Florence Stove Co. of England to make paraffin-burning heaters for the latter to sell. In this way, Albert Street entered the market for oil heating and cooking stoves. In the spring of 1938 Sankeys acquired a one-third interest in the English subsidiary by purchasing 333 ordinary shares of £1 each at £8 per share.[116] The agreement also included the option of buying a further third at a similar price in four years time – of which Sankeys duly availed themselves in 1942.[117] Finally they obtained the outstanding interest and, having changed the name of the company to the Florence Stove & Hardware Co., the production of paraffin heaters grew to represent a substantial proportion of Albert Street's output during the 1950s.

In April 1929 Sankeys purchased the neighbouring Bath Street Works, formerly occupied by Holcrofts Steel Foundry Co. and more recently by the Staffordshire Stainless Iron Co., for £20,000 and converted the buildings into a press shop and tool room.[118] The space thereby made available at Albert Street was diverted to the manufacture of steel wheelbarrows – a most successful product, with a considerable export trade.[119]

The general recovery in the nation's economic fortunes evident by the mid-1930s encouraged Sankeys to undertake a partial reconstruction of the Albert Street Works, the plans being approved in January 1934.[120] A further expenditure of £17,500 was authorised in May 1936, principally to be spent on extending the warehouse, plating and paint department and re-establishing an enamelling shop,[121] while in April 1937 £6,000 was allocated for new presses.[122] However, the largest programme of expenditure followed in May 1940 when a new boiler house and plant to heat the Albert Street and Bath Street Works was approved, the scheme having been devised in June 1938 but not effected on grounds of cost. This modernisation, together with the provision of replacement machinery, amounted to £23,000.[123]

BANKFIELD AND MANOR ROLLING MILLS

Given the difficulties experienced by Albert Street in trying to maintain its hold over a declining market in traditional products, it was wisely concluded that any profits available for re-investment should be concentrated in the Bankfield Works, then enjoying a monopoly in the manufacture of electrical stampings, and its supplier, Manor Rolling Mills, which with Lysaghts' Orb Mills at Newport were the two principal producers of electrical sheets.[124] Accordingly, in June 1920 it was agreed that the 'alterations and renewals recommended in respect of Bankfield be carried out as soon as possible' at an estimated cost of £45,000 to £50,000.[125] The scheme involved the complete reconstruction of the main shops, a task undertaken by Lysaghts' structural department at Netham. Subsequently, a gantry was built across the canal to facilitate the unloading of narrowboats carrying sheet from Manor Mills, and in November 1921 the Great Western Railway agreed to provide a siding into the works,[126] in order that sheet could be transported by rail from Lysaghts' Orb Works at Newport.

Appointed general manager at Bankfield in March 1922,[127] E.W. Richmond presided over rising outputs as the electrical industry expanded. He was successful in convincing electrical engineering companies, who made their own laminations, that this was a specialised operation and that they would be better served by obtaining their components from Sankeys. In 1933, for example, he arranged with Crompton Parkinson to take over their presses and supply them with stampings, such that they became Bankfield's largest customer.[128] Crompton Parkinson being a major consumer of slotted washers, they decided in March 1937 to spend £15,000 on machines for their manufacture.[129] Another area of rising demand was provided by the increasing popularity of the wireless which needed stampings for transformers, chokes and so forth.

The association Sankeys had formed with the electrical trade proved fortunate during the depression, for in the early 1930s when the government decided to establish a national grid, involving the construction of a number of major power stations, the company tendered successfully for the laminations required by their dynamos and transformers.[130] In view of the importance of this business, Sir John Field Beale suggested that Ronald Sankey visit America and Canada during the autumn of 1934 in order to study alternative methods of manufacturing electrical steel sheet.[131] Reporting on his tour of steelworks there, he was instructed to pass on his discoveries to the managers at Orb Works, Newport.[132] Large orders for high silicon electrical steels were completed by Manor Mills and then sent along the Shropshire Union Canal from Ettingshall to Bankfield. In order to cope with this growing volume of business a transformer strip shop was erected on the west side of the Bankfield Road, at an estimated cost of £20,000.[133] From 1936 part of this building was occupied by the company's training school run by a full-time superintendent. Before 1937 the Bankfield general manager and his staff were accommodated within the Albert Street offices but as their numbers grew it became imperative that they be housed on site, rather than half a mile away. A group of old stoves and workshops were demolished in order that a new office building could be constructed.[134]

Since the Manor Rolling Mills had been acquired by Sankeys in 1904 (p. 243), there had been little investment in new plant and machinery.[135]

95 A works outing to Goldthorn House, near Wolverhampton, the home of George H. Sankey (1865–1934) on 28 July 1934.

The mills were hand-operated and driven by steam engines rather than electric power. However, with improvements in rolling mill technology, largely pioneered in America, and the electrical industry's demand for greater quantities of high quality sheet, it became essential that Sankeys introduce a programme of mechanisation. In June 1935, Ronald Sankey reported that the cost of 'roof extensions, cranes, furnace, producer plant, electric drive, mechanised mill, housings etc' totalled £25,000.[136] The expenditure was authorised in November, as was the purchase of 8,000 square yards of land adjoining the Manor Works from Messrs. J. Hanson & Sons in order that the warehouse could be extended.[137]

One of the most important processes in the manufacture of electrical sheets was annealing after rolling. This was carried out in old and rather crude furnaces fired either by coal or producer gas. Pyrometers purchased from the Cambridge Instrument Co. helped to determine the temperatures, though it remained largely a matter of personal judgement how long sheets were treated.[138] Smoke from the furnaces was so thick that one end of the annealing bay was invisible from the other. In the mid-1930s the first electric annealing furnace was installed on an experimental basis and when in October 1938 its operation was reported as a success, the board agreed to the introduction of two further furnaces.[139] Despite these improvements, Manor Mills had difficulty in satisfying the requirements of the highest grade of transformer sheet. Ronald Sankey, supported by Sir David Llewellyn, urged the need for reorganisation of the plant.[140]

Whilst all rolling mills of any size had laboratories to test the quality of their product, the scientific demands on electrical steels were probably higher than on others. When Ronald Sankey joined Manor Mills in 1921 he was placed in charge of the testing department. Questioning the reliability of the traditional magnetic test, he devised alternative methods of assessing the characteristics of the various grades and gauges of electrical sheet.[141] As investigations became increasingly technical and science-based, plans were laid in November 1943 for the construction of a new laboratory at Manor Works,[142] though approval for this and the appointment of a research team was not granted until July 1945.

HADLEY CASTLE WORKS

Having established themselves in the Edwardian period as suppliers of wheels, chassis frames and car bodies, Sankeys were able to take advantage from the growth in the number of automobile manufacturers which followed the cessation of hostilities in 1918. This period of prosperity proved short-lived and soon Hadley Castle had the problem of collecting debts from unpaid orders. S.L. Brunton, the general manager, ruled that no chassis on which coachwork had been assembled could be driven away before the account had been settled.[143] Even the

Austin Motor Co. fell into difficulties and in July 1920 it was resolved that should their account not be settled by 15 August, they were to be sued and no further deliveries were to be made except for cash.[144] In these circumstances, chassis for the Austin 20 kept mounting up at Hadley, gradually filling up the body shop while attempts were made to conclude a financial arrangement. In the event, Sankeys accepted 4 per cent debentures in Austins to the value of the debt, these being sold when the company had recovered.

The automotive industry did not experience easy trading conditions during the 1920s. The motor car remained a luxury item and many manufacturers were forced into liquidation, including Clement Talbot, Arrol Johnson, Argyle, Star, Belsize and Clyno, to whom Sankeys had supplied wheels and parts from the earliest days.[145] However, the company's expertise and reputation for quality was such that they established close trading links with the Ford Motor Co. and Vauxhall Motors for the supply of wheels and chassis frames. In January 1932, Col. Harold B. Sankey persuaded the board to approve the expenditure of £25,000 on the reconstruction and re-equipping of the chassis frame press plant.[146]

Sankeys were determined to maintain their leading position as a components supplier to the automotive trade and having endured the difficulties of the 1920s were able to reap the benefits which accrued in the expansive 1930s. In November 1935, for example, it was agreed to spend £5–6,000 on three rim-making machines in order that Hadley

96 A display stand of Sankey–Sheldon steel furniture at the British Industries Fair of 1930.

97 A full range of Sankey products, including a variety of cooking utensils and two Belisha beacons at the British Industries Fair of 1937 held at Castle Bromwich.

Castle could compete with the Light Easy Clean Motor Car Wheel.[147] The importance of this business was emphasised in September 1936 when a further investment of £30,000 was authorised 'in connection with the wheel, general engineering and steel furniture departments'.[148] Shortly afterwards, S.L. Brunton retired after twenty-six years service with the company.[149] When he had first taken charge at Hadley Castle in 1910 the plant had been standing idle for several years, but by 1936, through the success of its products, the labour force had risen to nearly 1,500. During the Second World War, the insatiable demand for mechanised vehicles prompted much overtime. In August 1939, Lysaghts' Constructional Department was contracted to extend the wheel department.[150]

A further product range, pioneered at Hadley Castle, was also to prove commercially successful – the manufacture of steel furniture. As experts in the rolling of sheet and able to press steel into a variety of shapes, it was not surprising that Sankeys considered entering this market. In 1912 George Sankey had discussed such a venture with E. Wentworth Smith, who had some experience in steel furniture design,

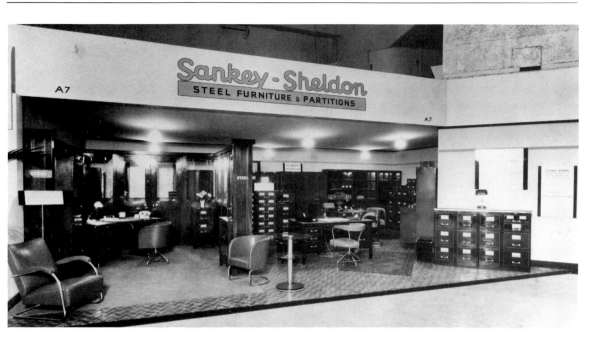

98 Filing cabinets, desks, shelving, partitions and doors manufactured from steel sheet by Sankey–Sheldon on display at the British Empire Exhibition of 1937.

but in the summer of 1914 as their plans were finalized the outbreak of war prevented implementation.[151]

In 1918, George Sankey found himself chairing a committee set up by the Minister of Reconstruction to investigate the hollow-ware trade, one of its members being T.E. Sellers, a director of Harris & Sheldon, shopfitters of Birmingham.[152] The latter was concerned to find an alternative use for a factory that had been established during the war to make small metal pressings for aeroplanes. He, too, was considering the production of steel furniture. The upshot of his discussions with George Sankey was that Harris & Sheldon entered into arrangements with both Sankeys and E. Wentworth Smith to undertake the marketing of the product under the brand-name 'Sankey-Sheldon', though manufacture would be exclusively performed at Hadley Castle. The first sales office was opened in March 1919 in a side street in the City of London, but moved in the summer of 1920 to GKN's office at 66 Cannon Street.

Initially the business developed slowly as there was a reluctance to change from wooden to steel furniture. In July 1920 Sankeys were offered the rival company, Crittals of Braintree, for £20,000, which they purchased[153] after having obtained a reduction of £8,000.[154] In November 1926 Harris & Sheldon invited Sankeys to acquire an interest in their company, and the latter agreed to purchase 10,000 ordinary shares at 23s 10½d from John H. Sheldon, part of the arrangement being that George H. Sankey be elected to the Sheldon board.[155] By March 1929 the steel furniture business had become sufficiently well established to justify an extension to the works, costing £12,000.[156] The trade flourished in the mid-1930s and in April 1937 Col. H.B. Sankey reported that it had become necessary 'to ask for [an] additional expenditure up to £10,000 on welding equipment, conveyors, ovens and miscellaneous plant'.[157] Besides wheels, chassis frames and steel furniture, Hadley Castle Works developed a number of subsidiary product lines during the thirties, including steel barrels for the palm oil trade in Africa, steel roofing sheets supplied to the Ruberoid Co. for decking, radiators, metal trim, bath panels and steel pulleys.

PROFITS AND PERFORMANCE

As Table 7.2 demonstrates, with the exception of the 1920–21 slump, Sankeys proved to be an extremely profitable business. It enjoyed two periods of particular success, 1924–27 and 1934–39, these being interrupted by a worldwide depression. If the series is adjusted for the effects of inflation, then the peak in the mid-to-late 1920s is smoothed out in favour of a slightly more dramatic rise in the mid-1930s, and the high figures generated during the Second World War have to be tempered in the light of price rises caused by high demand and restricted supply. Had the company not possessed its own captive steelworks, then it might have encountered raw material difficulties such that customers would have complained of late deliveries and a sub-standard product.

MANAGERS AND MANAGEMENT

Although Joseph Sankey & Sons was a subsidiary of John Lysaght, which, in turn, was a subsidiary of GKN, it retained a high degree of autonomy in the practical running of the business. After the takeover various Lysaght and GKN directors sat on the Sankey board, notably H. Seymour Berry, Sir David Llewellyn, W.R. Lysaght, D.C. Lysaght and S.R. Beale. However, the production of strategic plans lay for the most part with various members of the Sankey family and senior managers who had been appointed to directorships, these then requiring the approval of their colleagues. The scheme to modernise the Manor Rolling Mills in 1935, for example, would have been discussed by Ronald Sankey, the general manager, with his assistants and then presented by him to the board where it was formally ratified by W.R. Lysaght as chairman, Sir John Field Beale (chairman of GKN) and D.C. Lysaght representing Lysaghts, Sir David Llewellyn being absent from that particular meeting.[158]

The chairmanship of Sankeys remained, in effect, a non-executive position throughout the interwar period. When, for example, Lord Buckland was killed whilst riding, he was succeeded by W.R. Lysaght,[159] who retained the post until his death in April 1945.[160] In June 1945 Sir

Table 7.2   Joseph Sankey & Sons net profits, 1918–43

		£	£ Adjusted*
to 31 March	1918	39,103	30,454
	1919	37,055	27,246
	1920	26,952	17,080
	1921	3,011	2,104
	1922	73,375	63,254
	1923	84,844	76,025
	1924	162,273	146,588
	1925	141,428	126,728
to 31 December	1925†	103,391	92,644
	1926	129,550	118,962
	1927	144,669	136,223
	1928	79,273	75,570
	1929	77,993	74,993
	1930	83,260	83,260
	1931	112,637	120,726
	1932	73,497	80,677
	1933	74,048	83,765
	1934	138,380	154,961
	1935	164,931	181,842
	1936	166,493	179,217
	1937	150,728	154,911
	1938	156,980	159,047
	1939	160,331	160,331
	1940	154,147	132,429
	1941	251,678	199,428
	1942	202,999	160,220
	1943	181,376	143,721

Notes: *Figures adjusted by the Bank of England's index of consumer prices, 1930 = 100.
†Nine Months.

Source: Joseph Sankey & Sons Ltd Minute Books, Vols 3–8 (1917–45).

Samuel R. Beale, who had been deputising for Lysaght during his long illness, was formally confirmed as chairman.[161]

The senior managers of Sankeys during the nineteen-twenties can, in effect, be divided into two groups – a distinction which tended to blur in the 1930s. First, there were the family directors comprising George H. Sankey, Frederick E. Sankey and Harry T. Sankey. George H. Sankey (1865–1934), who had served as chairman from 1913 until the takeover in 1919 when he became managing director, remained the effective head of the business until his death.[162] Described in the company's unpublished history as a 'very strong character' and a 'tremendous worker', his fault was an inclination to be intolerant of other people's ideas, and this was not an encouragement to his younger lieutenants. One had to be very sure of one's facts and conclusions before putting up a proposition to George Sankey ... His passing might be said to be the end of a benevolent autocracy. George Sankey could, however, be very kind to anyone in trouble and rarely would he allow anyone to be sacked.[163]

Frederick Sankey (d. 1931), the second son of Joseph, had joined the family business in 1884 after a short period in America to gain engineering experience;[164] having become a partner in 1891, he was appointed a director on the flotation of the firm in 1902. Frederick Sankey was somewhat eclipsed by his elder brother, George H., but remained a 'wise councillor and well-loved by the workpeople and staff'.[165] The Sankeys were teetotallers, and no alcoholic drinks were seen in the directors' dining room until Harold Sankey succeeded his father as managing director in 1935.

The third generation of Sankeys recruited by the business included Harold B. Sankey (1895–1954), George Ronald Sankey (1900–) and Geoffrey B. Sankey (1908–83), all three being sons of George H. (Figure 12). Educated at Wolverhampton Grammar School, Harold Bantock Sankey enlisted in the Field Artillery on the outbreak of war and served in France and Italy winning the Military Cross for laying a telephone line under heavy shell fire to a forward position at Thiepval;[166] he subsequently became a Brevet Colonel in the Territorials, retiring in 1934,[167] but always employed his Army title in business. At Trinity College, Cambridge, between 1919 and 1921, he obtained a degree in mechanical science and after a short period at Orb Works, Newport, joined Sankeys as a resident director and assistant to S.L. Brunton at Hadley Castle Works.[168] On the death of his father, he became managing director, the executive head of the company, and moved to the head office at Albert Street.[169] From 1942 to 1944 Harold Sankey was appointed by the Ministry of Production as Regional Controller for the Midlands, which necessitated him relinquishing temporarily the post of managing director in favour of Ronald Sankey. He continued to serve as managing director until shortly before his death at sixty-one in 1954, having succeeded Sir Samuel R. Beale as chairman in 1951.

Ronald Sankey, second son of George H., joined the family business after taking a degree in mechanical engineering from Cambridge, and went to work as assistant to Messrs Nock and Aston at Manor Rolling Mills.[170] He was elected to the board in 1929,[171] though did not become general manager at Manor Works until 1941 when Joshua Nock retired. Two years later, Ronald Sankey took on the management of Bankfield Works, a post he retained until his retirement.[172]

Geoffrey B. Sankey, having trained as a barrister, originally worked at the Bilston head office but when George H. Sankey became ill in December 1934 was transferred to Hadley Castle so that Harold B.

Sankey could move from there to the Albert Street headquarters to take command.[173] In June 1937 he was appointed a director.[174]

Other important figures included James Felshaw Watson (d. 1937), an engineer who had joined the company in 1916 and was responsible for the reconstruction of both Manor and Bankfield Works.[175] Elected to the board in June 1930,[176] S.L. Brunton had presided over the rise of Hadley Castle Works as a major supplier of automotive components and manufacturer of steel furniture. Walter van Helden, appointed general manager of Albert Street Works in 1929, helped to revitalise this factory through his forceful personality, drive and enthusiasm.[177] E.W. Richmond, who for eleven years had served as general manager of Bankfield, became a director in February 1932 and continued as such until retirement in 1943.[178] Of significance for the future was the recruitment in March 1936 of H.F. Hodgson as assistant to the works director at Hadley Castle.[179] A Canadian national formerly employed by Briggs Motor Bodies of Dagenham and with experience in the American automobile industry, he had been selected as a potential successor to Brunton.[180] Hodgson ultimately served eighteen years as general manager of the works and in January 1941, along with W. van Helden, was elected a director of Joseph Sankey & Sons.[181] Subsequently, Hodgson also rose to the chairmanship of Sankey and accordingly took his seat on the GKN board.

Like Nettlefolds at Heath Street, or Garringtons at Darlaston, Sankeys built up powerful links with the communities of Bilston and Wellington. Several generations of the same families worked for the company, achieving lengthy service records. In June 1921 Sankeys purchased the Barborsfield estate, some twenty acres of land,[182] and in 1935 when the workforce numbered 3,100[183] it was decided to level this land between Albert Street and Bankfield Works in order to lay out a sports ground complete with pavilion to house the newly formed Sankey Sports & Social Club,[184] at an estimated cost of £4,000.[185]

From January 1938 a contributory staff pension scheme was established in conjunction with the Prudential Assurance Co.[186] Of the 199 eligible male and 106 female employees, 180 and 34 respectively joined on its formation.[187]

THE SECOND WORLD WAR

Sankey's manufacturing plant soon found itself in the front line of industrial production. A number of extensions were made to the buildings and plant, much of the cost being provided from government funds. Early during the hostilities, two new bays were built at Albert Street in response to the enormous demand for aeroplane spinners by De Havilland and Rotol (used in the assembly of Mosquitos and Spitfires), and later the former Brookside shop and warehouse were demolished in order that a new factory could be erected for the secret fabrication of parts used in jet engines for the De Havilland DH1.[188] At Hadley Castle, extra shops were constructed for both spinner production (at an estimated cost of £48,000)[189] and the complete assembly of Spitfires.[190]

By the end of 1940, 85 per cent of the company's output was directed to war work.[191] The labour force increased dramatically in size, with many men being retained under 'reserved occupation' regulations and large numbers of women being recruited. As a result, the canteen at Hadley Castle, constructed during the First World War, proved inadequate and a modern canteen and assembly rooms, with ornamental gardens and sports grounds, were completed in 1940.[192] Improved catering facilities were provided at Albert Street and Bankfield and, for the first time, a purpose-built canteen was installed at Manor Works.

The following list provided an indication of the variety and intensity of Sankeys' contracts for the government:

Heavy wheels for army vehicles	2,079,108
Ammunition boxes	5,520,591
Steel helmets	4,205,212
Bombs, explosive, 250lb	16,470
Bombs, explosive, 500lb	37,610
Bombs, explosive, 2000lb	21,448
Bombs, explosive, 4000lb	29,454
H.E. and smoke bombs	1,990,000
Mines	60,658
Mines, mechanic	35,704
Depth charge cases, charges & throwers	85,382
Spinners for aircraft	115,134
Floats for Admiralty	562,435
Complete Spitfires	868
Bailey Bridge sections	10,010[193]

In addition, Sankeys manufactured electrical stampings for wireless sets, radar, asdic anti-submarine apparatus, gyro compasses, and portable power stations destined for the USSR. Steel furniture was supplied to the Royal Navy and the merchant service, together with shelving, bins and racks for shadow factories, stores and stations.[194]

The directors' report for the year 1944 observed that Sankeys had been engaged to their maximum capacity on war work; however, once the hostilities in Europe ended in May 1945, orders began to fall off. Whilst plans had been laid for the transition to normal peacetime conditions, continuing military demands for the Far East theatre, shortages of labour, the need to develop prototypes, and the slowness of the authorities to approve schemes for rehabilitation would of necessity hamper the changeover and retard the recovery in output.[195] Some assistance was provided in May 1946 by an agreement to employ German prisoners-of-war on the night shift at Bankfield Works.[196]

99 A visit by the Rt. Hon. Oliver Lyttleton, the Minister of Production, to Bankfield Works, Bilston, on 29 January 1943. Front row, left to right, E.W. Richmond (general manager, Bankfield Works), G. Ronald Sankey (managing director), Rt. Hon. O. Lyttleton, Col. H.B. Sankey (regional controller Ministry of Production), the Earl of Dudley, J. Wills Pearson (Mayor of Bilston), and Councillor E. Allen. Fifth from left in the back row was W. van Helden (general manager of Albert Street Works) and sixth, G.B. Sankey.

INDIA: SANKEY ELECTRICAL STAMPINGS LTD

Early in 1941, Harold Sankey was approached by Frank Parkinson of Crompton Parkinson to ask whether Sankeys would consider establishing a factory in India to supply them with electrical sheets and stampings.[197] GKN having granted their approval for such a scheme, it was decided to occupy a vacant building at Worli, Bombay, on a site rented from Crompton Parkinson. By July 1943, two consignments of plant from Bankfield had arrived in India, and K.C. Maitra, the technical and commercial manager (acting general manager from December 1945), together with three mechanics, were on the point of departing from England.[198] The new company, Sankey Electrical Stampings Ltd, had an authorised capital of 2,000,000 rupees. The following had been asked to serve as directors: A.H. Bishop (chairman), J. Leisk, A.J. Taylor (of Sandersons & Morgan, solicitors), Ronald Sankey and Allan Macbeth; the first two were on the board of GKW and as a result had considerable experience of Indian business. The Tata

Iron & Steel Co. (who became minority shareholders) agreed to supply the new enterprise with steel,[199] though the initial orders had to be placed in America because of indigenous shortages. The works began operations in January 1944 following the arrival of 150 tons of sheet steel from the United States.[200] Brisk business justified the expenditure of a further £60,000 in August 1945 on a second factory at Shalimar on the outskirts of Calcutta,[201] the site having been cleared and construction underway by December.[202] Completion was delayed by the transfer of the Bombay factory from Worli to GKW's site at Bhandup in 1946.[203]

SUMMARY

Of all the acquisitions made by GKN in the interwar period, that of Joseph Sankey & Sons proved to be among the most successful, though in reality it had been H. Seymour Berry who had seized the opportunity presented by George B. Sankey's forebodings for the company's future prosperity and taken over the business for John Lysaght. Whilst much of the GKN group in the 1920s was associated with Britain's traditional industries (in particular coal and steel), which were notoriously poor performers in depression years, Sankeys had the foresight and good fortune to have become leading suppliers to both the electrical and automotive trades. Two of the growth sectors in the UK economy during the 1920s and 1930s, they were almost sure to pull their commercial elements into profitability. Once the post-war slump had been negotiated, Sankeys entered on a twenty year period of sustained expansion, a trend interrupted only by a slump from 1928 to 1933.

While Bankfield, supplied from the Manor Rolling Mills, flourished by supplying the ever increasing demand for electrical stampings, and Hadley Castle could provide wheels, chassis frames and body pressings for the car makers and help to generate a widening market for steel furniture, Albert Street was forced by adversity to discover new products. Its success in the Victorian period was founded on cheap consumer goods such as kettles, trays, metal boxes and sundry other items of hollow-ware. Cheap imports and changing fashions cut the ground from under the company's feet in the early twenties. Short-time working, redundancies and the search for alternative products followed. Petrol pump casings, cooking and heating stoves, and barrels were among the solutions generated as the Albert Street Works gradually came back to commercial prosperity.

Despite being a subsidiary, albeit a major one, in a large manufacturing group, the Sankey family were able to retain a considerable measure of managerial autonomy. First, George H. Sankey and then Harold B. Sankey occupied the post of managing director taking *de facto* reponsibility for the operation of the four works and having the final say in the preparation of strategic plans before they were submitted to GKN for ratification. The directors on the Sankey board comprised selected general managers of the three factories and rolling mills, together with other members of the family, and representatives from GKN and Lysaghts.

Sankeys' very success as a supplier of war material created problems when the hostilities ended. Having expanded and diverted their factories to make what were now unwanted products, a period of adjustment and rationalisation was needed.

References

1. J.B. Priestley, *English Journey*, London (1934), Harmondsworth (1977), p. 109.
2. *DBB*, Vol. 5 (1986), Edgar Jones, 'Joseph Sankey', p. 63.
3. [Compton McKenzie], 'The Sankey Story' (typescript, *c.* 1958), p. 1.
4. *Staffordshire General & Commercial Directory for 1818*, Third Part, Manchester (1818), p. 290.
5. 'Sankey Story', op. cit., p. 2.
6. Yvonne Jones, *Georgian and Victorian Japanned Wares of the West Midlands*, Wolverhampton (1982), p. 24.
7. *Victoria County History of Stafford*, Vol. 2, Oxford (1967), p. 178.
8. *Staffordshire General & Commercial Directory for 1818*, Third Part, Manchester (1818), p. 290.
9. Samuel Griffiths, *Guide to the Iron Trade of Great Britain*, London (1873).
10. Ibid., p. 84.
11. Jones, *Japanned Ware*, op. cit., p. 25.
12. William White, *History, Gazetteer & Directory of Staffordshire*, Sheffield (1934), p. 221.
13. William White, *History, Gazetteer & Directory of Staffordshire*, Sheffield (1857), among the twenty two japanning firms listed was Harthill & Jackson, p. 151.
14. 'Sankey Story', op. cit., p. 3.
15. *Midlands Survey (Part One) 1960*, 'The Story of Joseph Sankey & Sons Ltd. of Bilston', p. 1.
16. 'An Agreement made the thirtieth day of October 1854 between Samuel Jackson of Bilston . . . and John Bates of Bilston aforesaid iron merchant'.
17. Ibid; *Lysaght Review*, No. 9, June 1936, Col. H.B. Sankey 'Joseph Sankey & Sons Ltd', p. 8.
18. 'Sankey Story', op. cit., p. 4.
19. 'An Agreement made and entered into this 19th day of August 1861 between Samuel Jackson of Bilston . . . blank tray maker and Joseph Sankey of Bilston'.
20. 'Sankey Story', op. cit., p. 5.
21. Ibid., p. 8.
22. Joseph Sankey Product Ledger 1865–1879, Baths, pp. 53–8; Boxes and Trunks, pp. 94–95; Lamps and Lanterns, pp. 17–26; and Dish Covers, pp. 137–42.
23. *Joseph Sankey & Sons Ltd, Bilston, Stamped & Pressed Hollow-ware*, January 1905.
24. 'Sankey Story', op. cit., pp. 9, 10.
25. W.H. Fellows, 'Reminiscences of Joseph Sankey & Sons Ltd, Bilston', (typescript, December 1950), p. 4.

26. *DBB*, Vol. 5 (1986), Edgar Jones, 'John William Sankey', p. 59.
27. 'Sankey Story', op. cit., p. 7.
28. Ibid., p. 9.
29. Ibid., p. 5.
30. *DBB*, Vol. 5, op. cit., p. 64.
31. 'Sankey Story', op. cit., p. 11.
32. 'The Sankey Story 1854–1966' (typescript, n.d.).
33. Ibid.
34. 'Sankey Story', op. cit., p. 12.
35. Articles of Partnership, dated 11th July 1891.
36. Ibid., item 2.
37. Ibid., item 9.
38. 'Sankey Story', op. cit., p. 13.
39. Ibid., p. 13.
40. W.H. Fellows, 'Reminiscences', op. cit. p. 2.
41. Ibid., p. 3.
42. *Victoria County History of Stafford*, Vol. 2, op. cit., p. 183.
43. E.H. Brooke, *Chronology of Tinplate Works of Great Britain* (1944), p. 138.
44. *Victoria County History of Stafford*, Vol. 2, Oxford (1968), p. 175.
45. 'Sankey Story', op. cit.
46. Ibid., p. 23.
47. *DBB*, Vol. 5, op. cit., p. 60.
48. Joseph Sankey & Sons Ltd, Directors Minute Book, Vol. 1, September 1902–August 1912, 14 May 1907.
49. 'Sankey Story', op. cit. p. 24.
50. 'Sankey Story', op. cit., p. 23.
51. Joseph Sankey & Sons Ltd, Directors Minute Book, Vol. 1, September 1902–August 1912, 19 September 1902.
52. Joseph Sankey & Sons Ltd, Directors Minute Book, Vol. 2, September 1912–November 1916, 20 September 1913.
53. Ibid., 2 June 1913.
54. Ibid., 10 May 1915.
55. Ibid., 29 October 1916.
56. Joseph Sankey & Sons Ltd, Directors Minute Book, Vol. 3, January 1917–December 1921, 21 June 1917, p. 22.
57. 'Sankey Story', op. cit., p. 15.
58. W.H. Fellows, 'Reminiscences', op. cit., p. 9.
59. 'Sankey Story', op. cit., p. 13.
60. Ibid., p. 16.
61. *DBB*, Vol. 1, London (1984), Roy Church, 'Herbert Austin', p. 80.
62. 'Sankey Story', op. cit., p. 17.
63. Ibid.
64. Ibid., p. 18.
65. Sankey Minute Book, Vol. 1, op. cit., 14 May 1906.
66. Ibid., 2 June 1909.
67. Ibid., 24 May 1910.
68. Ibid., 19 October 1910.
69. Jones, *GKN, Vol. One*, op. cit., pp. 143–4, 222–3.
70. 'Notes on Visit to the Castle Works, Hadley, near Wellington, Shropshire' by Morley and Dawbarn, 31 August 1910.
71. Ibid.

72. Sankey Minute Book, Vol. 1, op. cit., 18 May 1911.
73. 'Sankey Story', op. cit., p. 19.
74. Sankey Minute Book, Vol. 1, op. cit., 30 May 1912.
75. 'Sankey Story', op. cit., p. 20.
76. Sankey Minute Book, Vol. 1, op. cit., 27 October 1912.
77. Sankey Minute Book, Vol. 1, op. cit., 19 December 1911.
78. *Sankey Patent Steel Wheels* (n.d.), p. 3.
79. *Sankey Patent Steel Wheels, List No. 2*, October 1913.
80. Sankey Minute Book, Vol. 2, op. cit., 26 February 1913.
81. *The Motor*, D.B.T., 'Edwardian Logic, and a design thirty years ahead of its time', 29 August 1956.
82. 'Sankey Story', op. cit., p. 21.
83. Sankey Minute Book, Vol. 1, op. cit., 25 May 1908.
84. Ibid., 2 June 1909.
85. Ibid.
86. Ibid., 24 May 1910.
87. Ibid., 29 May 1911.
88. Ibid., 21 May 1912.
89. Sankey Minute Book, Vol. 2, op. cit., 22 June 1916.
90. Sankey Minute Book, Vol. 3, op. cit., 30 January 1919.
91. 'A Works Manager's Experiences from . . . July 1914 to the End of the Great War', (typescript, n.d.), p. 2.
92. Sankey Minute Book, Vol. 2, op. cit., 15 June 1915.
93. Ibid.
94. 'Sankey Story', op. cit., p. 28.
95. Sankey Minute Book, Vol. 2, op. cit., 15 June 1915.
96. Ibid., 29 October 1915.
97. 'A Works Manager's Experiences', op. cit., pp. 5–6.
98. 'Sankey Story', op. cit., p. 28.
99. 'A Works Manager's Experiences', op. cit., p. 18.
100. Sankey Minute Book, Vol. 2, op. cit., 1 October 1915.
101. Ibid., 2 June 1913.
102. 'Sankey Story', op. cit., p. 25.
103. Sankey Minute Book, Vol. 3, op. cit., 19 November 1919, pp. 130–1.
104. Ibid., p. 131.
105. See Table 7.2, p. 7–41.
106. Interview: E. Jones with J.C. Sankey, 25 September 1984.
107. Sankey Minute Book, Vol. 3, op. cit., 3 December 1919, p. 136.
108. Ibid.
109. Ibid., 4 February 1920, p. 142.
110. Ibid., 20 July 1921, pp. 236–7.
111. 'Sankey Story', op. cit., p. 31.
112. J. Sankey & Sons Minute Book, Vol. 4, January 1922–December 1925, 23 February 1922, p. 10.
113. Ibid., 8 April 1924, p. 151.
114. 'Sankey Story', op. cit., p. 35.
115. Ibid.
116. Joseph Sankey Minute Book, Vol. 7, May 1936–July 1941, 5 May 1938, p. 85.
117. Joseph Sankey Minute Book, Vol. 8, August 1941–May 1945, 3 September 1942, p. 62.
118. Sankey Minute Book, Vol. 5, op. cit., 16 April 1929, p. 179.

119. 'Sankey Story', op. cit., p. 36.
120. Joseph Sankey & Sons Minute Book, Vol. 6, May 1930–April 1936, 4 January 1934, pp. 158–59.
121. Joseph Sankey & Sons Minute Book, Vol. 7, May 1936–July 1941, 7 May 1936, p. 2.
122. Ibid., 7 April 1937, p. 40.
123. Ibid., 4 April 1940, p. 173.
124. 'The Sankey Story', op. cit., p. 32.
125. Sankey Minute Book, Vol. 3, op. cit., 30 June 1920, p. 174.
126. Ibid., 1 November 1921, p. 252.
127. Sankey Minute Book, Vol. 4, op. cit., 26 January 1922, pp. 2–3.
128. 'Sankey Story', op. cit., p. 37.
129. Sankey Minute Book, Vol. 7, op. cit., 4 March 1937, p. 38.
130. Ibid.
131. Sankey Minute Book, Vol. 6, op. cit., 2 August 1934, p. 183.
132. Ibid., 1 November 1934, p. 191.
133. Sankey Minute Book, Vol. 6, op. cit., 7 February 1935, p. 204.
134. 'Sankey Story', op. cit., p. 37.
135. Ibid., p. 39.
136. Sankey Minute Book, Vol. 6, op. cit., 6 June 1935, p. 217.
137. Ibid., 7 November 1935, p. 235.
138. 'Sankey Story', op. cit., p. 40.
139. Sankey Minute Book, Vol. 7, op. cit., 6 October 1938, pp. 107–8.
140. Ibid., 4 May 1939, pp. 137–38.
141. 'Sankey Story', op. cit., p. 39.
142. Sankey Minute Book, Vol. 8, op. cit., 4 November 1943, p. 130.
143. 'Sankey Story', op. cit., p. 32.
144. Sankey Minute Book, Vol. 3, op. cit., 29 July 1920, p. 179.
145. 'Sankey Story', op. cit., p. 41.
146. Sankey Minute Book, Vol. 6, op. cit., 1 January 1932, p. 71.
147. Ibid., 7 November 1935, p. 235.
148. Sankey Minute Book, Vol. 7, op. cit., 3 September 1936, p. 20.
149. Ibid., 1 October 1936, pp. 24–5.
150. Ibid., 3 August 1939, p. 154.
151. 'Sankey Story', op. cit., p. 32.
152. Ibid., p. 33.
153. Sankey Minute Book, Vol. 3, op. cit., 29 July 1920, p. 172.
154. Ibid., 30 September 1920, p. 186.
155. Sankey Minute Book, Vol. 5, op. cit., 18 November 1926, p. 48.
156. Ibid., 27 March 1929, p. 174.
157. Sankey Minute Book, Vol. 7, op. cit., 4 March 1937, p. 41.
158. Sankey Minute Book, Vol. 6, op. cit., 6 June 1935, pp. 215, 217.
159. Sankey Minute Book, Vol. 5, op. cit., 26 June 1928, p. 136.
160. Sankey Minute Book, Vol. 8, op. cit., 2 May 1945, p. 234.
161. Sankey Minute Book, Vol. 9, op. cit., 6 June 1945, p. 1.
162. Ibid., 3 January 1935, pp. 196–97.
163. 'Sankey Story', op. cit., p. 42.
164. Sankey Minute Book, Vol. 6, op. cit., 4 February 1931, p. 36.
165. 'Sankey Story', op. cit., p. 42.
166. 'Sankey Story', op. cit., p. 28.
167. Who's Who, London (1947), p. 2437.

168. Sankey Minute Book, Vol. 3, op. cit., 20 July 1921, p. 235; 'Sankey Story', op. cit., p. 42.
169. Sankey Minute Book, Vol. 6, op. cit., 3 January 1935, p. 198.
170. 'Sankey Story', op. cit., p. 34.
171. Sankey Minute Book, Vol. 4, op. cit., 25 October 1929, p. 203.
172. 'Sankey Story', op. cit., p. 40.
173. Sankey Minute Book, Vol. 6, op. cit., 1 November 1934, p. 191.
174. 'Sankey Story', op. cit., p. 43; Sankey Minute Book, Vol. 7, op. cit., 23 June 1937, p. 48.
175. 'Sankey Story', op. cit., p. 43.
176. Sankey Minute Book, Vol. 6, op. cit., 4 June 1930, p. 6.
177. 'Sankey Story', op. cit., p. 36.
178. Sankey Minute Book, Vol. 6, op. cit., 4 February 1932, p. 73.
179. Ibid., 5 March 1936, p. 263.
180. 'Sankey Story', op. cit., pp. 41–2.
181. Sankey Minute Book, Vol. 7, op. cit., 2 January 1941, p. 206.
182. 'Sankey Story', op. cit., p. 32.
183. Sankey Minute Book, Vol. 7, op. cit., 2 July 1936, p. 16.
184. 'Sankey Story', op. cit., p. 43.
185. Sankey Minute Book, Vol. 6, op. cit., 7 November 1935, p. 235.
186. Sankey Minute Book, Vol. 7, op. cit., 4 November 1937, pp. 65–6.
187. Ibid., 3 March 1938, p. 78.
188. Sankey Minute Book, Vol. 8, op. cit., 3 September 1942, p. 59.
189. Ibid., 1 October 1942, p. 65.
190. 'Sankey Story', op. cit., p. 45.
191. Sankey Minute Book, Vol. 7, op. cit., 5 June 1941, pp. 237–8.
192. Ibid., p. 46.
193. Quoted from 'Sankey Story', op. cit., p. 47.
194. Ibid., p. 48.
195. Sankey Minute Book, Vol. 9, op. cit., 4 July 1945.
196. Ibid., 1 May 1946.
197. Sankey Minute Book, Vol. 7, op. cit., 6 March 1941, pp. 218–19.
198. Ibid., 1 July 1943, p. 108.
199. Ibid., 2 September 1943, p. 116.
200. Ibid., 4 January 1944, p. 139.
201. Sankey Minute Book, Vol. 9, op. cit., 1 August 1945.
202. Ibid., 5 December 1945.
203. Ibid., 6 November 1946.

8 The Management and Organisation of GKN

What were the struggles of his youth, what acts
Made him the greatest figure of his day:
Of how he fought, fished, hunted, worked all night...[1]

W.H. Auden, 'Who's Who' (1933–38)

Thus far, this history has been concerned in the main with companies, products or manufacturing processes and has attempted to show the reasons why particular businesses succeeded or failed. Reference has been made to those individuals who exercised a crucial influence over specific strategies (H. Seymour Berry and Sir David Llewellyn, for example, in the acquisition of collieries in South Wales) or who shaped the fortunes of one enterprise (H.R. Lysaght's chairmanship of John Lysaght (Australia) Pty.). However, it is important to recognise that the course GKN took during the interwar period, whether for good or ill, was not solely determined by market forces (the price of steel, exchange rates), government decisions (the level of import duties, the return to the Gold Standard) or the application of technical innovations to steelworks and factories (the reconstruction, for instance, of East Moors in 1934–36 at a cost of almost £3 million). The calibre of the directors and senior managers responsible for devising the group's policy and its implementation must, to a degree, have been reflected in GKN's record of profits and performance. In times of slump they sought to mitigate the effects of reduced demand, low prices and short-time working, while during the mid-1930s they took advantage of new orders and rising values. The interwar years were, in general, hard times for British industry, in particular for its traditional trades, and therefore represented a special challenge to managerial skills and acumen. The personalities of the company's leaders and the organisational structures which they devised form the central themes of this chapter.

THE DYNASTIC SUCCESSION

Appointed chairman in July 1918 following the sudden and unexpected death of Arthur T. Keen (1861–1918),[2] Edward Ponsonby, eighth Earl of Bessborough (1851–1920), broke a tradition which had existed from the foundation of the various businesses which came together to form GKN.[3] He was the first 'non-executive' head of the company. Until his appointment, every leader (whether as a senior partner or chairman) had been schooled in the practical management of the business. Often joining the company at an early age, gaining a technical education in the works, the senior managers of the Dowlais Ironworks, the Patent Nut & Bolt Co.'s various mills or the Heath Street Screw Works of Nettlefolds were all men who possessed an intimate knowledge of their respective businesses. The first two chairmen of GKN, Arthur Keen and his eldest son, Arthur T. Keen, had both acquired a long experience of the manufacturing industry. By contrast, the Earl of Bessborough, an Irish aristocrat, had originally joined the Royal Navy, but retired in 1874 with the rank of Lieutenant to pursue a career in law.[4] Called to the Bar in 1879, he served as secretary to the Speaker of the House of Commons from 1884 to 1895. As Viscount Duncannon (subsequently succeeding to his father's title in 1906),[5] he became vice-chairman of the Dowlais Iron, Steel & Coal Co. on its formation in 1899 having become a close adviser of Lord Wimborne, its chairman and principal proprietor. Their friendship had arisen following Bessborough's marriage to Blanch Vere Guest, daughter of Sir John Guest, and younger sister of Lord Wimborne. Bessborough also served as secretary to the Caledonian Canal Commissioners (1896–99) and as chairman of the London, Brighton & South Coast Railway.[6] He was, therefore, a member of the landed aristocracy with important business interests, rather than an industrialist or career manager who had been rewarded with a title for his endeavours.

The appointment of a non-executive chairman at the head of GKN was not the result of a conscious policy; rather, it was an expedient adopted in response to unforeseen circumstances. Arthur T. Keen, who had succeeded to the chairmanship in 1915, was only fifty-seven when he died whilst suffering from endogenous depression.[7] This left only five main-board directors (the Earl of Bessborough, F.W. Keen, Edward Steer, E. Windsor Richards and Sir John Field Beale), and each had reasons for not taking the post of chief executive. F.W. Keen (1863/4–1933), a qualified mechanical engineer who had spent most of his working life divided between managing the nut and bolt mills at Stour Valley Works and the Cwmbran Ironworks[8] and who appeared to be a natural successor to his elder brother, preferred not to accept the responsibilities of high office. Arthur Keen, as Jolly recalled, considering his eldest son to be the heir apparent, had not pushed F.W. Keen and as a result the latter never became an ambitious man.[9] In the event, this proved to have been a fortunate decision as ill health during the 1920s compelled his absence from many board meetings.[10]

E. Windsor Richards (1831–1921), though a steelmaker of considerable experience and a recipient of the prestigious Bessemer Gold Medal,[11] was in retirement after a managerial career culminating at Bolckow, Vaughan & Co. He had never taken full-time responsibilities at GKN, having acted as a non-executive adviser to Arthur Keen.[12] Sir John Field Beale (1874–1935), the senior partner in London of the solicitors, Beale & Co., had an indirect family connection with the

Nettlefolds which had resulted in his election to the board in 1918 to replace Godfrey Nettlefold (1874–1918) who had died in office. The involvement of Sir John with GKN was therefore too brief for consideration as the leader.

Given the reluctance of F.W. Keen to accept the chairmanship,[13] the age of E. Windsor Richards and the lack of experience possessed by Sir John Field Beale, Edward Steer (1851–1927) was the obvious choice as successor to Bessborough. The son of Charles Steer (husband to Martha Nettlefold), he had entered Nettlefolds in 1868 and having gained considerable experience in the Heath Street mills, in 1882 was appointed a director. Subsequently, he was entrusted with the task of finding a site for a steelworks (Rogerstone) to which the Castle rolling mills could be transferred.[14] Steer supervised their construction during 1887–88 and became the general manager when they opened. In 1902, after the acquisition of Nettlefolds, Steer was elected to the merged GKN board and continued to take responsibility for the Rogerstone operations, living at 'Woodlands', Malpas, near Newport. Why Lord Bessborough was preferred to Steer as chairman in 1918 has not been recorded. It may have been that the former sought the post while the latter, who lived in South Wales, had no compelling desire to succeed Arthur T. Keen. Both Steer and F.W. Keen were both appointed joint deputy chairman and managing director, which suggested that daily executive authority had been divided between them, leaving Lord Bessborough

100 Edward Steer (1851–1927), chairman of GKN from 1920 to 1927, the last of the Victorian managers.

as a figurehead to oversee operations and maintain cordial relations with the City and government.

In the event, Lord Bessborough's period in office proved short-lived for on 1 December 1920, whilst attending a dinner in Birmingham for directors and senior managers of GKN, he collapsed and died.[15] To what extent he had been instrumental in negotiating the merger with John Lysaght Ltd it is difficult to judge. In resisting the claims of Lysaghts to take over GKN, Lord Bessborough may have played an important part maintaining the group's share price by encouraging investor confidence. As a result of the union, H. Seymour Berry was appointed a third deputy chairman, while T.S. Peacock also became a third managing director.

The debate over who should succeed Lord Bessborough was settled within a few weeks of his death and on 15 December 1920 Edward Steer was proposed as chairman by F.W. Keen and seconded by H. Seymour Berry.[16] A little of Edward Steer's biography has been mentioned (p. 277). His father, Charles Steer (1824–58), had been educated at University College School in Gower Street, then a leading educational establishment for Dissenters and where Joseph Chamberlain had studied, leaving aged fifteen to work in the publishing business of Mr Knight, a friend of his mother.[17] Shortly afterwards he joined Letts, the stationers, as a partner and from there set up his own firm in Long Acre, Covent Garden, making cardboard playing cards and mottled covers for exercise books. Charles Steer earned sufficient to enable him to marry at the age of twenty-three. For his wife he selected Martha Nettlefold (1822–1905), daughter of John Sutton Nettlefold, founder of the woodscrew business. The premature demise of her husband left Martha Steer with five children to bring up.

At the time of his father's death Edward was aged seven. His mother's two elder brothers (presumably Edward John and Joseph Henry Nettlefold) undertook the management of the stationery firm in Long Acre, but the family's reduced financial circumstances compelled a move to a smaller house in Beresford Terrace, Highbury, where a restrained, Unitarian regime prevailed.[18] Any notions of further education or professional training for the sons appear to have been abandoned and both Edward and his elder brother, Charles, each entered the Covent Garden business on reaching fourteen. Having worked there for about three years, in 1868 both brothers were offered what would now be termed 'trainee management posts' by Nettlefold & Chamberlain. In view of the profitable nature of the Smethwick woodscrew enterprise and perhaps because they feared that the youthful Steers would eventually oust them from the stationery firm, their uncles advised the brothers to take the new career opportunity. Accordingly, they sold their shareholding to the Willises, and in later life Edward asserted that they would have done far better financially to have refused the Nettlefold & Chamberlain offer. Having moved to Birmingham, their salaries were impounded by their uncles towards payment for shares in Nettlefold & Chamberlain that they, as partners, were obliged to take.[19] Charles was twenty-five when at last he was granted a salary of £1,000 per annum and a like sum was offered to Edward a year or two later. Shortly after their move, Charles and Edward left the Unitarians to attend St Augustine's Church, Edgbaston, where they were baptised and confirmed.[20]

Edward Steer worked at the Heath Street mills for some eighteen years before he moved to the Rogerstone steelworks and rolling mills. Both appear to have been popular managers at Heath Street and Charles, being affectionately known as 'the Uncle', was instrumental in the provision of a works canteen.[21] They were each appointed directors of Nettlefolds in 1882, two years after its flotation as a public limited liability company, and in 1891 on the departure of Frederick Nettlefold to work full-time for Courtaulds, Charles Steer became managing director, a post he retained after the takeover by Guest, Keen & Co. in 1902.[22] It was said that anxiety over the future of Nettlefolds and the worry that resulted when the merger was impending contributed to Charles Steer's failing health, and his death followed shortly afterwards in April 1906 whilst serving as joint managing director of GKN.[23]

Although happy with the notion of being second-in-command, Edward Steer may not have relished the post of leader. Throughout the greater part of his managerial career he had been deputy to his older brother, Charles, to whom he was devoted.[24] The move to Rogerstone would have provided Edward with his first taste of independence, though the operations there remained subsidiary to the Heath Street headquarters. Steer was sixty-nine when in December 1920, he became chairman of GKN. However, the fact that he retained the post of managing director (when Lord Bessborough had been chairman alone) implied that he was no figurehead leader. Despite progressively ailing health, Edward Steer continued as the executive head of GKN until 7 April 1927 when he retired in favour of H. Seymour Berry.[25] Throughout the 1920s Berry, in conjunction with Sir David Llewellyn, had been the dynamic figure on the GKN board. If the latter represented change, then Steer stood for continuity. With his family connections and deep personal involvement with the Nettlefold elements of the group, he would have defended the interests of the fastener companies and, in view of its historical association as a supplier of acid steel, may have favoured the retention of the Dowlais steelworks. Steer remained a director after his chairmanship though his office was brief, as he died of a stroke on 29 October 1927.[26]

A self-effacing man and devout Christian, Edward Steer fell into the mould of the paternalistic businessman. Committed to one company for the greater part of his working life, he took a sustained interest in the welfare of his employees and became a respected manager. Amongst his pastimes was the composition of light verse, which he then read to his family. Edward Steer was, in effect, the last of the Victorians to manage GKN.

A full description of H. Seymour Berry, Lord Buckland, the fifth chairman of GKN, will be found in the chapter dealing with the group's colliery interests (pp. 76ff). Suffice it to say that Berry was an astute businessman, an organiser rather than a technician, a dealer rather than a manager of men, an individual who saw commercial possibilities where others would have no inkling; by his ability to arrange mergers and takeovers, he was able to assemble major industrial groups within a comparatively short space of time. How GKN would have developed under Berry's chairmanship it is interesting to speculate, as his period of executive authority lasted for just over one year, his death caused by a riding accident in May 1928 occurring at a crucial point in the group's history.

Together with Sir David Llewellyn, Berry had been responsible for extending the group's holding of South Wales collieries, entering the anthracite market and becoming involved in the sale and distribution of coal. Alas, these decisions could not have been worse timed as world prices tumbled. His successor, Sir John Field Beale, backed the board's decision to create a subsidiary company, Welsh Associated Collieries, which could then either fend for itself or be sold. To what extent Berry would have concurred with this plan had he remained chairman it is difficult to tell. As a businessman who placed a premium on profits and growth, it is unlikely that he would have opposed a scheme designed to extricate GKN from an awkward financial position.

Following in the tradition established by Lord Bessborough, the chairmanship of Sir John Field Beale assumed a non-executive character. Educated at Harrow School, Beale entered Trinity College, Cambridge, where he earned a rowing blue in 1898.[27] His father, James Samuel Beale (d. 1912), a solicitor, was evidently a wealthy practitioner who also held several industrial directorships, including from 1882 the chairmanship of L. Sterne & Co. Ltd., manufacturers of refrigerating equipment, railway springs, emery wheels and grinding machines.[28] Sir John Field Beale qualified as a solicitor and joined the London office of the family firm, Beale & Co. As partner-in-charge of the Westminster office, he was elected to the GKN main board in May 1918[29] as a replacement for Godfrey Nettlefold who had died unexpectedly in office.[30] Having no direct industrial experience, Beale was appointed to represent the Nettlefold interest, for his father had married a member of the Field family who had been owners of the Birmingham Screw Co. which in 1880 had been absorbed within the Heath Street mills. In addition, his father's Birmingham practice had served as the Patent Nut & Bolt Co.'s legal advisers, and became GKN's joint solicitors with Ryland, Martineau & Co. on its formation in 1902.[31]

Sir John Field Beale may also have owed his election to his connections with government, having served as chairman of the Wheat Executive during the Great War and vice-chairman of the Royal Commission on Wheat Supplies. In September 1918 he became First Secretary to the Ministry of Food (a post rewarded by a knighthood)

101   Sir John Field Beale (1874–1935), chairman of GKN from 1928 to 1935.

and in January 1919 was appointed with Lord Reading to represent Britain on the Allied Supreme Council of Supply and Relief. During the ten years of his directorship of GKN from 1918, Sir John continued to live in London, initially at 49 Porchester Terrace, Paddington. Although he took the additional post of joint managing director in June 1929,[32] his principal role within the group was as chairman of the influential Investment Registration Committee,[33] which handled the group's reserves placed in stocks and securities.

The two other candidates for the chairmanship in 1928 were the joint managing directors, F.W. Keen and T.S. Peacock (p. 284). The former had no interest in the post and his fluctuating health probably removed any possibility of his candidature.[34] Nothing has been discovered of Peacock's claim. Age would not have ruled him out and he had an extensive experience of the GKN group. Perhaps his ambitions did not extend to the highest office and he remained at his happiest running the company's nut and bolt factories in Darlaston (p. 210).

On 9 December 1935, Sir John Field Beale died while chairman.[35] He had suffered increasingly from a debilitating illness and much of the responsibility for guiding GKN must have fallen to T.S. Peacock, deputy chairman, and J.H. Jolly, joint managing director from August 1934 (p. 286). Beale had presided over one of GKN's least successful periods as it suffered during the 1931–33 depression, but saw the company recover during the early 1930s. However, since he was a non-executive leader not too much importance should be attached to his contribution in either of these episodes. Further to his legal practice and GKN involvement, Sir John Beale was a director of the London, Midland & Scottish Railway, the Midland Bank and L. Sterne & Co., and served as chairman of the Legal Insurance Co. Among his interests was sailing and he became a member of the Royal Cruising, Leander, and Royal Norfolk and Suffolk Yacht Clubs.

Elected a director of GKN in November 1929,[36] [Sir] Samuel Richard Beale (1881–1964) was not an obvious candidate to succeed his elder brother. Educated at Marlborough, he had taken an engineering degree from Trinity College, Cambridge, and in 1903, like Sir John before him,

102 Sir Samuel R. Beale (1881–1964), chairman of GKN from 1935 to 1947.

represented the university in the boat race.[37] Leaving Cambridge in
that year, he moved to Glasgow to become a trainee in his father's
company, L. Sterne & Co. S.R. Beale began by working in the pattern
shop at the company's headquarters, the Crown Ironworks in North
Woodside Road.[38] A conservative management had resulted in falling
profits creating opportunities for reforms. In 1905, only two years after
his arrival, Beale became commercial manager, and despite resistance
from his father and other directors, had a new machine shop built. He
also improved the design of the company's refrigerators and in 1912
Beale joined the board as the general manager. When the chairmanship
fell vacant in 1924 on the death of Louis Sterne, Sir John Field Beale was
appointed, Samuel becoming managing director.[39] In 1935, however,
the latter suggested that he should be chairman and asked his brother
to resign. Before this could be accomplished Sir John had died, whereupon S.R. Beale moved south to take the former's place as chairman of
GKN.[40]

Why, then, was S.R. Beale, a comparative outsider, elected to the
highest office in GKN? First, he was virtually the only candidate on the
board. J.H. Jolly (p. 286), who had only just been appointed managing
director in August 1934, C.H. Keen and K.S. Peacock (who had both
been elected in July 1933)[41] would all have been considered too young
for such responsibilities. J.G. Berry, and Lord Kemsley, and William E.
Berry, Lord Camrose, Lord Buckland's younger brothers, were non-
executive insofar as they were fully committed to building up their
newspaper and periodical publishing businesses. I.F.L. Elliot, who was
GKN's representative in London, was shortly to depart in March 1936
to become commercial director of the British Iron & Steel Federation's
commercial department,[42] while Lt. Col. C.H.C. Guest was a serving
Member of Parliament and on the board to represent his family's
interests. This left two directors of considerable industrial experience
and ability, Sir David Llewellyn and W.R. Lysaght, aged 56 and 77
respectively. Each had their own particular specialist commitments: the
former was deeply involved with the South Wales coalfield and the
latter had accepted the chairmanship of John Lysaght. Perhaps neither
had the ambition to seek the most senior post in the GKN group. This
left S.R. Beale who had a number of recommending factors: he was an
engineering graduate with extensive managerial experience and his
family had a long-standing connection with GKN. Ambitious and able,
Beale was an obvious candidate for the chairmanship.

Taking command in at the beginning of 1936, S.R. Beale had little
time to alter the shape and direction of GKN before the outbreak of war.
The re-opening of the Dowlais–Cardiff steelworks and the completion of
the transfer from Rogerstone to East Moors were projects initiated and
implemented during the chairmanship of his elder brother. There were no
major acquisitions nor any fresh capital-intensive projects in the UK
during this three year period. S.R. Beale led GKN throughout the Second
World War, being knighted in 1942, and continued in office until 1947,

when compelled to retire under a new company rule that chairmen should resign at sixty-five.

Sir Samuel Beale remained a director of GKN until 1957. His commercial expertise encouraged invitations to serve on the boards of Thomas Cook & Son and the Scottish Amicable Life Assurance Society to add to his long-standing connection with the Union Bank of Scotland. He retired as chairman of L. Sterne & Co. in 1960.[43]

A Conservative Unionist, Sir Samuel Beale served for a time as president of the St. Rollox Unionist Association, though he does not appear to have harboured any serious political ambitions. Giving generously to the Glasgow Chamber of Commerce, Beale became a director in 1925 and its president in 1929–30. From 1934–36 he was president of the Association of British Chambers of Commerce. A man with a sense of humour, Beale adopted an uncomplicated lifestyle and had the ability to make quick decisions. His interests were recorded as shooting and gardening, while he was a member of the Junior Carlton, Leander and Western Clubs. With a town house in Campden Hill, and a country home, Drumlamford, Barrhill, Ayrshire, Beale divided his time between London and Scotland.

DIRECTORS OF INFLUENCE

If a number of the GKN chairmen during the interwar period were of a non-executive character, this implies that other members of the board were active in running the business, making major policy decisions and overseeing their implementation. Who, then, were these influential managers? From 1920 until his retirement in July 1941,[44] Thomas Swift Peacock (d. 1946) served as joint managing director of GKN (retiring as such in 1941), being appointed, in addition, as deputy chairman from July 1933 in succession to F.W. Keen,[45] a post which he retained until his death. Like Edward Steer he was, in a sense, a Victorian manager – a man who had completed a lengthy apprenticeship in the business, rising to board level in a subsidiary organisation and then being promoted to a post of authority in the holding company. In 1892, Peacock had joined F.W. Cotterill, manufacturers of nuts and bolts established in the first decade of the nineteenth century (p. 210), and was employed as company secretary at their Darlaston works.[46] He became general manager in the following year and managing director in 1900.[47] Jolly observed that Peacock was 'a very shrewd man' and

> the building up of Cotterills was ... entirely due to him. He was very hard-working, very thorough and interested in his workpeople ... My own criticism of Tom Peacock would be that although a very likeable man, the course of his own career had made him give too much attention to detail, rather than very broad policy ... he had not what I call that vision of group development as distinct

103 T.S. Peacock (d. 1946), joint managing director of GKN from 1920 to 1946. Lord Camrose recalled that the directors requested Peacock to succeed Sir John Field Beale in 1935 but that, on advice from his doctors, the latter had declined the post.

from development of one side of it . . . I think his success was very largely due at Cotterills to the same kind of thing as the success at Nettlefolds was due to the Steer family.[48]

It was said that the gentlemanly behaviour of his son, [Sir] Kenneth Peacock (p. 288), contrasted with the sometimes brusque and forceful demeanour of T.S. Peacock. Several have described him as being 'a rough diamond'[49] but also recorded a paternalistic interest in the workforce. Sir Anthony Bowlby recalled that having fired an employee he would instruct him to report to his home which was situated near the works. Peacock would then offer the man his job back, spend the morning taking him round the garden, stand him a pint of beer and send him back to the factory. He could be 'very tough and yet very generous; he was very unpredictable'[50] and to those who encountered his moods could present a terrifying figure.

The key position occupied by Cotterills within the group resulted in T.S. Peacock's appointment to the GKN board when it acquired this fastener business in 1919. His star was truly in the ascendant, for in the following year the union with John Lysaght resulted in Peacock's promotion to joint managing director, presumably to represent former GKN interests with the merged company.

Based at Cotterills' head office in Darlaston and living at 'Bescot House', Walsall, Peacock continued to oversee the group's nut and bolt factories and took overall responsibility for their screw works through his membership of the Birmingham Committee. Although also seated on the Steel Committee, he was a manager concerned with the practicalities of business, a technician rather than a strategist such as H. Seymour Berry or G.T. Clark.

Much of the head-office planning and vital liaison work that this entailed would have fallen to James Hornby Jolly (1887–1972), GKN's company secretary from 1918 and managing director from August 1934.[51] A Lancastrian, educated at Baines's Grammar School, Poulton Le Fylde, he had qualified as a chartered accountant with the Blackpool practice of Bowman & Grimshaw in 1909. Having moved to Cardiff to work for W.B. Peat & Co., Jolly was sent to compile a report on the Blaenavon Co., a steelworks with colliery interests, and having recommended managerial changes asked Peats whether he could leave to carry them into effect. The request was granted and Jolly remained at Blaenavon until 1918 when Edward Steer, mindful that GKN's current company secretary, H. Probyn (d. 1926),[52] suffered from poor health, suggested that he join the group.[53] Accordingly, Probyn was made a director and Jolly took his place as company secretary,[54] having been provided with a reference by John Paton. Surprised by the company's

104 J.H. Jolly (1887–1972), who trained as a chartered accountant, joined GKN as company secretary in 1918. He became a joint managing director in 1934, deputy chairman in 1943 and chairman four years later.

antiquated methods of keeping financial records, Jolly, as the first professionally qualified accountant to be employed by GKN, insisted that he be appointed chief accountant as well as secretary.[55] He proceeded to recruit a small number of qualified assistants in order that the accounting methods could be reorganised (p. 295).

After twelve years as company secretary, in October 1930 Jolly was elected to the GKN board,[56] and four years later, at the comparatively young age of forty-seven, he became a joint managing director,[57] continuing in this office until October 1947 when Jolly succeeded Beale as chairman, having been appointed a joint deputy chairman in April 1943. The central role played by Jolly throughout the interwar period needs to be related to GKN's organisational structure.

The group (Figure 13) comprised GKN, the holding company (which also embraced the former Nettlefolds and Patent Nut & Bolt factories), and around a dozen principal subsidiaries. Commonly, two or three GKN directors were appointed to the boards of the subsidiary companies to maintain a working or advisory brief. Sir John Field Beale, for example, sat on the boards of Bayliss, Jones & Bayliss, John Garrington, Exors. of James Mills, Aug. Stenman, and John Lysaght.[58] As a result, the performance of subsidiary companies were monitored in two ways: by attendance at their board meetings, and by scrutiny of their annual accounts. In both respects, Jolly was of importance. His directorships included Welsh Associated Collieries (and subsequently Powell Duffryn), Guest Keen Baldwins, Exors. of James Mills, and Bayliss, Jones & Bayliss. Because of his accountancy expertise, he was required to analyse the balance sheets of GKN-owned companies and report on their performance. Not trained in the intricacies of engineering or steel-making technology, Jolly wisely avoided becoming enmeshed in the production side of GKN. He remained, in the words of Nicol, 'a

Figure 13 GKN in 1935

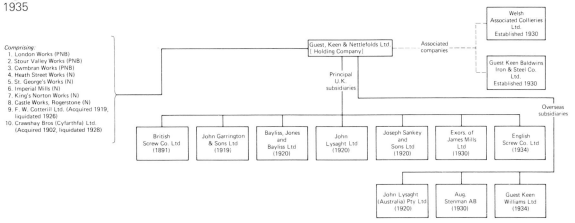

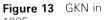

Note: Unless otherwise stated, dates refer to the year of acquisition by GKN. F. W. Cotterill Ltd, taken over by GKN in 1919, was liquidated in 1926.
Abbreviations: PNB – a former Patent Nut & Bolt Co. factory; N – a former Nettlefold Co. factory.

finance and administration man but very clear headed in the way in which things should go'.[59] His intimate understanding of the group acquired during the 1920s and 1930s made him a natural successor to Beale as chairman.

An austere man of few methods, J.H. Jolly's taciturn nature concealed a decisive mind and a determination to solve problems. A conservative businessman who believed in the value of economy, he would offer unswerving support to a project once convinced of its value. Jolly was straight-forwardly honest and resolute in board-room debate with an integrity to match his words. W.A. Nicol, one of the qualified accountants whom Jolly had recruited as an assistant, recalled that the latter had

> no time for detail; he liked to be very correct in the way he approached subjects; he was very good in the way in which he harnessed his facts and the way he put things together; he did not propose to write a lot of matters into his letters but they were clear, very concise and right to the point.[60]

When asked, on retirement, what he felt his achievements at GKN had been, Jolly replied that he might go down as being someone who had created a certain order out of chaos.[61] Jolly was perhaps too austere to be a charismatic leader or public figure which may explain why titles which were awarded to both his predecessors and successors eluded him. For recreation he walked the fells of the Lake District, often accompanied by E.C. Lysaght, a pastime reflected in the name of his home, 'Langdale', Barnt Green, near Bromsgrove.

In 1912 Jolly, then a Wesleyan Methodist, married Elizabeth Parkinson, the daughter of a corn merchant; they had one son, who having become a Flying Officer in the RAF, was killed in 1944 (his death prompting Jolly's interest in spiritualism) and a daughter. His brother, Thomas Jolly, entered GKN in the early 1920s direct from school and, having spent some time in America and been employed at the Port Talbot steelworks, rejoined the company in 1942 when he was appointed general manager of East Moors steelworks, later rising to become its joint managing director. Another brother, W.A. Jolly, served as managing director of a further GKN subsidiary, W.A. Bonnell (1924), London timber importers, from April 1938 to March 1958.

The other director of influence and who later was to rise to the chairmanship was [Sir] Kenneth Swift Peacock (1902–68). Born at Walsall, Staffordshire, the only son of T.S. Peacock and his wife Elizabeth Amy, nee Richards, he was educated at Oundle School and on leaving there in May 1920 joined GKN.[62] He entered the Heath Street mills of Nettlefolds to learn about the fastener business. There, under T.Z. Lloyd, the general manager, Peacock worked in various departments but eventually specialised in sales and marketing. At the age of twenty-three he was made assistant to his father who was

105   K.S. Peacock (left) at the wheel of a racing car. From 1929 to 1934, he competed in the RAC Tourist Trophy in Ireland and was a member of the Lea-Francis, Riley and Aston Martin teams.

responsible for all the GKN fastener factories. In this position he encouraged the employment of several young graduates including [Sir] Anthony Bowlby, who later became general manager at Heath Street and joined the GKN board. At the comparatively young age of thirty-two, K.S. Peacock became a director of GKN in July 1933, a reflection not only of his abilities, but also the importance of sales departments within Nettlefolds, then the group's principal source of profits.[63] In January 1936, when still in his early thirties, Peacock became a joint managing director of GKN.[64] With the gradual withdrawal of T.S. Peacock from the business, his son took increasing responsibility for the fastener factories. During the Second World War, to all practical intents, he and Jolly ran the business, the latter being the senior of the two.

In character, K.S. Peacock was quite unlike his father. He possessed an extraordinary charm, great ability and an elephantine memory.[65] A humane man, Peacock won the affection and regard of the workforce and managers alike. Without a university, professional or technical training, he relied on his natural intelligence and an intuitive under-standing of problems, a favoured expression being 'you have got to have the feeling in your water'.[66] Peacock, the extrovert, was tempera-mentally distinct from the introverted Jolly; while the former was favourably disposed towards capital spending, the latter placed an emphasis on economy and cost-effectiveness. When disagreements arose, Sir Samuel Beale often employed humour as a way of diffusing tension.

In his youth, K.S. Peacock was a keen amateur racing driver and from 1929 to 1934 competed in the RAC Tourist Trophy races in Ireland and the 24-hour competition at Le Mans as a member of the Lea-Francis, Riley and Aston Martin teams. He won the Rudge–Wentworth Cup and was awarded the 'Index of Performance' at Le Mans in 1934. An enthusiastic horse rider, he hunted with the North Cotswold Hounds, the Devon and Somerset Stag Hounds and the Exmoor Foxhounds. His first marriage in 1925 to Hilaria (d. 1926), daughter of Sir Geoffrey Syme of Melbourne, and by which they had a daughter, was distressingly short because of her sudden death. In 1934 Peacock married Norma Rigby and they had two sons.

106 Sir Kenneth Peacock (1902–68) photographed after he had succeeded Jolly as chairman of GKN.

Excepting the chairmen of GKN, who were the directors of influence during the interwar period? The names which stand out were: T.S. Peacock, Sir David Llewellyn (p. 79), W.R. Lysaght (p. 23), J.H. Jolly and K.S. Peacock.

If the boards of the immediate post-war years (1919–21) are compared with those of the last three years of the Second World War (1943–45), a number of contrasts emerge. In the former period, the general managers of the five principal works (Dowlais, Cardiff, Smethwick, Cwmbran and Rogerstone) were excluded from the main board. This would have been inconceivable by the nineteen-forties, when an executive sufficiently senior to be running a major factory would automatically be involved in strategic decision-making. This, in part, reflected the reduced emphasis given to the committee system; those formed to oversee coal and steel had been superseded, though the Investment Registration and Birmingham Committees continued to perform their specialised roles. In 1921, five (Sir William E. Berry, T.J. Callaghan, Lt. Col. C.H.C. Guest, M.P., H.G. Hill and John Paton) of the twelve directors could be classified as non-executive,[67] a proportion which had scarcely altered by 1943 when four (Sir Maurice Denny, Lt. Col. C.H.C. Guest, M.P., Edmund L. Hann and Lord Hyndley) of the twelve board members were without operational position within GKN.[68] Important areas of the group were represented by the most recent appointments: E.C. Lysaght (Orb Mills, Newport), Allan Macbeth (Exors. of James Mills), Col. H.B. Sankey (Joseph Sankey & Sons). Non-executive directors were elected for a variety of reasons; either their wealth of industrial experience qualified them to offer sound advice as Edmund L. Hann or Sir Maurice E. Denny (1886–1955). The former was chairman of Powell Duffryn to which WAC had been sold, and the latter, appointed to the GKN board in February 1939,[69] a marine engineer, was chief executive of the family business, William Denny & Brothers, shipbuilders. He was also chairman of the Irrawaddy Flotilla Co. and the British & Burmese Steam Navigation Co. Denny owed his introduction to GKN to W.R. Lysaght, whose daughter, Marjorie, he had married.[70] Other non-executive directors were appointed because of a particular connection with government or a public body rendered the connection useful (Lord Hyndley), or a powerful historical link provided a reason (Lt. Col. C.H.C. Guest, Conservative MP for the Drake Division of Plymouth from 1937 to 1945).

ORGANISATIONAL STRUCTURE

In common with Britain's other leading industrial groups, GKN exhibited all the features of the holding-subsidiary company model during the interwar period (Figure 13). Although this organisational structure was, in essence, devised in the twenties, a number of elements dated from the pre-war years. The pattern in the nineteenth century had been for acquired companies to be incorporated within their new owner's corporate body. When the four elements merged to form Nettlefolds in 1880, each lost their former name as a sole all-embracing company was created. The same pattern was true of the two mergers which created GKN. Rather than keep either the Dowlais Iron, Steel & Coal Co. or the Patent Nut & Bolt Co. as a holding company and add subsidiaries such as Nettlefolds, the various elements were incorporated within a single new identity.[71] This was typical of the Edwardian era when a number of major enterprises emerged – Imperial Tobacco, Dunlops and Vickers.[72] In 1914, GKN possessed only three subsidiaries and there were special reasons for each of them; the British Screw Co., acquired in 1891, was run as if it were an autonomous company to create the illusion of competition within the UK; Crawshay Bros (Cyfarthfa) was retained as a separate identity because of its particular problems and historical importance; and the Orconera Iron Ore Co. of Bilbao was owned jointly by GKN, the Consett Iron Co. and Krupp of Essen.

The acquisition of F.W. Cotterill and John Garrington & Sons in 1919 marked the proper beginning of the holding-subsidiary company structure. Both were wholly-owned by GKN but initially retained their names and boards of directors – Cotterills being put into voluntary liquidation in 1926 so that it could be subsumed within GKN. The merger with John Lysaght and its subsidiary, Joseph Sankey & Sons, in the following year added considerably to the group's scale. Further subsidiaries were taken over during the interwar period, including Bayliss, Jones & Bayliss (1920), A. Stokes & Co. (1923), Henry Cox Screw Co. (1923), Thomas Haddon & Co. (1927), Exors. of James Mills (1930), English Screw Co. (1934), and Thomas P. Hawkins & Sons (1938), together with three overseas companies, John Lysaght (Australia) Pty (1920), Aug. Stenman AB (1930) and Guest Keen Williams (1934).

The management of GKN, therefore, was of a highly decentralised nature. Although ultimate authority for capital investment or senior appointments remained with the main board, the directors of the individual subsidiaries retained considerable independence of action. As Jolly recalled, this constituted a deliberate policy:

> We encouraged them to go ahead with their own schemes and finance themselves if they could but if not we would help them . . . If a company 'X' wanted to spend, shall we say, a million pounds (a big sum in those days) . . . they would have their own board meeting and would make their case, and their representative would come to the GKN board. If we had the money and approved the principle we would tell them to go ahead and if we had not got the money, we would find it . . . But beyond that our line was (and it paid off handsomely) let them go ahead on their own. . .[73]

The advantage of this arrangement, to which Jolly alluded, would have included pooled overheads, risk spreading, the interchange of commercial and industrial methods, collusive pricing and sales policies, and a degree of co-ordination for new investment. However, head-office functions (internal accounting, legal advice, marketing, research and development) were comparatively undeveloped during the inter-war period, expertise often being sought from external consultants. Hence, opportunities to centralise these roles remained comparatively limited.

Nevertheless, by virtue of its growth through acquisition, GKN found itself with a number of comparatively small-scale office buildings attached either to works or set up in London to co-ordinate sales. The head office for GKN had been established in the entrance building to London Works for purely historical reasons. This was where Arthur Keen, as chairman of the Patent Nut & Bolt Co., was based and he saw no reason to move after the formation of GKN. The two-storey block with its central archway into the works formed an unpretentious edifice for a major industrial group. By 1939 it had fallen into some disrepair, with the original timber guttering hanging from the eaves in places.[74] After the Second World War the interior was re-built to provide additional accommodation.[75]

It had not been necessary to spend money on the head office during the interwar years, as it had few roles. The main board never met there; either they assembled in the Queens Hotel, Birmingham, in the new London offices at 66 Cannon Street, or they met at the Spa Hotel in Bath, which was equidistant from South Wales and Birmingham. The premises in Cannon Street, a four-storey building, five bays in width, housed a board room (finished in mahogany to the designs of Mr Pemberton of the architects, Osborne, Pemberton & White) on the second floor, and had been purchased in December 1918,[76] and was extended in 1923–24 when two storeys were added to accommodate as many of the London offices of subsidiary companies as possible.[77] Accordingly, the head office at Smethwick simply accommodated the chairman and a few senior directors together with the company secretary and chief accountant (this post not being divided again until 1948 when W.A. Nicol and W.W. Fea respectively were appointed) and his small staff. Early in 1923, it was decided to transfer to smarter premises in central Birmingham, the board having decided that this city should continue to be 'the location of the head offices of the company'.[78] When another bidder succeeded in topping GKN's offer the deal fell through and no further attempt was made to move.

Until the extension of 66 Cannon Street in 1923–24, the various elements of GKN continued to occupy their existing London offices (Nettlefolds at Fen Court, Fenchurch Street, Guest & Co. at King William House, 2A Eastcheap, and Lysaghts at Swan House, near London Bridge).[79] The additional two floors allowed many of these to move under one roof. Nevertheless, in January 1925, John Lysaght staff

107 The GKN boardroom at 66 Cannon Street as re-furbished to the designs of Osborne, Pemberton & White.

in London requested that they be allowed to move to Australia House in the Aldwych, as the vast bulk of their business was with Australian customers.[80] In the event, their request was refused given the 'distinct advantages of having all the London staffs of the group housed in one building'.[81]

During the interwar years, the London office of GKN assumed an importance it had not occupied before. With the rise of organisations such as the Federation of British Industries and the increasing need to negotiate with bodies such as the Bankers Industrial Development Co. and government departments over tariffs or subsidies, it became increasingly necessary to have a London representative. The post fell to I.F.L. Elliot, who forged important links with the National Federation of Iron & Steel Manufacturers, resigning from the GKN board in January 1935 to become the former's first director of their newly created commercial department.[82]

Having a decentralised system by which individual subsidiaries, to a large extent, ran their own affairs – to the extent of having their own individual staffs in London, albeit grouped under a single roof – there was little reason why GKN should set up a large head office. With the exception of a small accountancy staff, there were virtually no centralised functions. In common with the other industrial corporations of the period, there was, for example, no legal department (the group's first qualified member of staff, J.F. Howard, a barrister, was not appointed until December 1949), no public relations and no economic or marketing departments, whilst personnel, health matters and industrial relations were managed on a plant basis. If any specialist advice were needed, then outsiders were called upon in a consultative fashion. In times of economic hardship when retrenchment was the order of the day, it would have seemed extravagant to have bought larger premises and recruit staff to undertake tasks which were being performed in an unstructured way by those working within subsidiaries. The arrival of specialists from head office would, in many cases, have been treated with suspicion by operating companies with a defined personal style and high degree of autonomy.

ACCOUNTING POLICIES

In one area some steps were taken towards greater uniformity and a degree of centralised control – accountancy. The creation of an increasingly complex holding-subsidiary company structure created a need for accurate and standardised financial information. Since senior directors could no longer take an intimate interest in all the group's subsidiaries, they required the provision of clear annual returns. Jolly was the first chartered accountant to be employed by GKN, ostensibly as company secretary, but when he discovered the poor state of financial reporting, insisted on being made chief accountant as well. In October 1921 he relinquished the latter post, having persuaded the board to appoint another professionally qualified accountant, E.C. Drake, F.C.A., though the latter in August 1934 took on the post of company secretary as well.[83]

Whilst much improvement was made to the group's internal reporting procedures, the same was not true of its published accounts. In common with most large industrial companies, the directors' report and balance sheet presented by GKN remained vague and imprecise throughout the interwar period.[84] From 1908, as obliged by the Companies Act, a balance sheet was filed by GKN with the Registrar of Companies, though no directors' report was included.[85] Typed balance sheets were submitted from 1908–17, in 1920 and from 1930–40, leaving significant gaps. For shareholders, printed balance sheets with a brief directors' report were supplied from 1907 and profit and loss account added from 1930, as encouraged by the 1929 Companies Act.

Whilst GKN exhibited a considerable reluctance to provide information for the Registrar of Companies (in 1918–19 and 1922–29, for
example, they pasted the printed accounts over the annual return so
that only the side containing the balance sheet and audit report
remained visible),[86] they were also unwilling to include anything but
the statutory minimum of information in the published accounts. Until
compelled to do so by the 1929 Act, for instance, GKN provided no
indication of how their investments had been valued, despite the fact
that these were a major balance sheet item[87] – this in common with
most leading manufacturers in the UK.

The group set up a secret reserve fund in 1902 on its formation using
this to even out swings in profitability throughout the Edwardian
period. Swelled by generous provisions for Excess Profits Duty to be
levied after the war had ended, this internal reserve had amounted to
£900,729 by 1919,[88] when its disclosure was probably related to the
threatened takeover by Lysaghts. Given that the two companies were
of apparently similar value, the revelation of such a large fund could
have been of crucial importance. Having thus published the existence
of the fund, the group continued this practice throughout the 1920s and
1930s.

In two areas Jolly, an otherwise enlightened accountant, may be seen
to have fallen behind the most up to date practice – the provision of
sums for depreciation and the production of consolidated accounts.
The former, although introduced in the mid-1930s,[89] were recorded
only from 1940 and the latter were assembled merely when compelled
to do so by the 1948 Companies Act. A few groups (notably Dunlop
from 1934 and Distillers from 1945)[90] perceived the value of devising
accounts which documented fully the holding-subsidiary company
relationship. Given the size and diversity of the GKN group during the
1930s, some form of consolidation would have been necessary to obtain
a precise and detailed understanding of its overall financial performance. Jolly had not been opposed to the principle of consolidation but
gave it a low priority, preferring to concentrate upon improving GKN's
management and internal reporting policies by recruiting a number of
qualified accountants to work both at head office and in the major
manufacturing units.[91]

During the interwar years, Carter & Co., the Birmingham chartered
accountants, served as auditors to GKN. The annual fee, which was
agreed at around a thousand guineas throughout the period,[92] made
the company one of Carter & Co.'s leading clients. In May 1936 the
group's accounts had reached sufficient complexity for an audit committee (comprising Jolly, Lord Camrose and T.S. Peacock) to be
formed.[93]

SUMMARY

The period 1919 to 1945 witnessed a major change in the organisation and structure of GKN. In the twenty years from its formation in 1900–2, the group operated as a single company, newly acquired companies being incorporated within the existing entity. The problems of managing such a large and diverse manufacturing body were resolved by the creation of a succession of committees. Initially there were Nettlefolds, Works, Colliery and Finance Committees on whom sat mainboard directors.[94] When Lord Bessborough became chairman, the first non-executive head of the company, a new gathering, the Executive Committee, was set up composed of the general managers of the principal works and selected directors. In May 1920, a South Wales Committee was formed,[95] and continued to meet at Dowlais until March 1921 when H. Seymour Berry was largely responsible for revising the system with the creation of the Birmingham, South Wales, Colliery, Steel and Investment Registration Committees.[96]

With the gradual growth in the number of subsidiary companies, which were no longer incorporated within the GKN style but retained their legal identity and separate boards, the role of the committees diminished. The formation in 1930 of Guest Keen Baldwins Iron & Steel Co. and Welsh Associated Collieries brought about the end of the Steel and Colliery Committees almost at a stroke. Henceforth, the limited attempts to centralise the group by using the committee structure were abandoned in favour of maximum devolution to semi-autonomous subsidiaries and a minimalist head-office which functioned, in essence, as a central accounting department.

It is difficult to say whether the calibre of senior management improved throughout the 1920s and 1930s. There were able men in executive positions at the beginning of the period (notably Edward Steer, H. Seymour Berry, Sir David Llewellyn, W.R. Lysaght and T.S. Peacock) and in the forties (Sir Samuel Beale, J.H. Jolly, K.S. Peacock and E.C. Lysaght). An attempt had been made in the 1930s to recruit bright graduates (notably [Sir] Anthony Bowlby and Stephen Lloyd) and professionally-qualified accountants (W.W. Fea, W.A. Nicol, and [Sir] Richard Brooke). Whether the broad sweep of middle management or the directors of subsidiary companies became more skilful in their decision-making and innovative in their policies, it has not proved possible to judge. Doubtless, GKN suffered from the effects of the 'lost generation' (those talented and motivated young leaders who, as junior officers and NCOs, were slaughtered in the Great War),[97] as many potentially valuable managers and foremen had been denied to them. Nevertheless, it remained the case that the GKN group retained an ability to evolve in response to changing economic circumstances and continued to produce a number of talented leaders.

References

1. W.H. Auden, *Collected Shorter Poems 1927–1957*, London (1966), p. 78.
2. GKN Minute Book, Vol, 3, op. cit., 4 July 1918, it. 3102.
3. Jones, *GKN, Vol. One*, op. cit., p. 391.
4. *WwW*, Vol. II, op. cit.
5. GKN Minute Book, Vol. 2, 1905–1916, 9 March 1906, it. 1254.
6. Sir John Ponsonby, *The Ponsonby Family*, London (1929), p. 155.
7. R. Lyttleton's 'Newspaper Cuttings', op. cit., 4–5 July 1918.
8. Jones, *GKN, Vol. One*, op. cit., p. 189.
9. Interview, J. Cockroft with J.H. Jolly, 12 May 1972.
10. GKN Minute Book, Vol. 9, op. cit., 3 March 1932; 4 May 1933, it. 6309.
11. *DBB*, Vol. 4, London (1985), p. 897.
12. Jones, *GKN, Vol. One*, op. cit., p. 320.
13. *The Engineer*, Obituary F.W. Keen, 21 April 1933.
14. Jones, *GKN, Vol. One*, op. cit., p. 222.
15. GKN Minute Book, Vol. 3, op. cit., 4 December 1920, it. 3623.
16. Ibid., 15 December 1920, it. 3626.
17. Elsa Steer, *Threads from the Family History*, Moulsford (1957), p. 5.
18. Ibid., p. 8.
19. Ibid., p. 9.
20. Ibid.
21. Ibid., p. 14.
22. Ibid., p. 20; C. Anthony Crofton, *The Nettlefolds*, Lewes (1962), p. 30.
23. GKN Minute Book, Vol. 2, op. cit., 3 May 1906, it. 1288.
24. Steer, *Threads from the Family History*, op. cit., p. 27.
25. GKN Minute Book, Vol. 7, op. cit., 7 April 1927, it. 5108.
26. GKN Minute Book, Vol. 7, op. cit., 3 November 1927, it. 5213.
27. *WwW 1929–1940*, Vol. III, London, p. 81.
28. Anthony Slaven and Sydney Checkland (Editors), *Dictionary of Scottish Business Biography 1860–1960, Vol. 1, The Staple Industries*, Aberdeen (1986), Charles W. Munn, 'Sir Samuel R. Beale', p. 156.
29. GKN Minute Book, Vol. 3, 1916–1918, 2 May 1918.
30. Ibid., 11 April 1918, it. 3049.
31. *GKN Annual Report and Accounts*, (1902).
32. GKN Minute Book, Vol. 8, op. cit., 6 June 1929, it. 5516.
33. *GKN Annual Report and Accounts*, (1921); Ibid. (1928).
34. GKN Minute Book, Vol. 8, op. cit., 7 June 1928, it. 5321.
35. GKN Minute Book, Vol. 10, op. cit., 18 December 1935, it. 6785.
36. GKN Minute Book, Vol. 8, op. cit., 7 November 1929, it. 5598.
37. *Who's Who*, London (1947), p. 179.
38. *DSBB*, Vol. 1, op. cit., C.W. Munn, 'Sir S.R. Beale', p. 156.
39. Ibid., p. 157.
40. GKN Minute Book, Vol. 10, op. cit., 18 December 1935, it. 6785.
41. GKN Minute Book, Vol. 9, op. cit., 6 July 1933, it. 6330.
42. GKN Minute Book, Vol. 10, op. cit., 5 March 1936, it. 6813.
43. *DSBB*, Vol. 1, op. cit., C.W. Munn, 'S.R. Beale', p. 157.
44. GKN Minute Book, Vol. 11, op. cit., 7 August 1941, it. 7641.
45. GKN Minute Book, Vol. 9, op. cit., 6 July 1933, it. 6329.
46. *DBB*, Vol. 4, London (1985), Edgar Jones, 'Sir Kenneth Peacock', p. 570.
47. Typewritten notes [n.d.].

48. Interview, J. Cockcroft with J.H. Jolly, 12 May 1972, pp. 5–6.
49. Interview, J. Cockcroft with W.A. Nicol, 25 July 1973, p. 8.
50. Interview, J. Cockcroft with Sir Anthony Bowlby, 25 April 1972, pp. 27–28.
51. GKN Minute Book, Vol. 9, op. cit., 22 August 1934, it. 6549.
52. GKN Minute Book, Vol. 7, op. cit., 9 September 1926, it. 4997.
53. DBB, Vol. 3, London (1985), Edgar Jones, 'James Hornby Jolly', pp. 523–24.
54. GKN Minute Book, Vol. 2, op. cit., 22 August 1918.
55. Interview, J. Cockcroft with J.H. Jolly, 12 May 1972, pp. 4–5.
56. GKN Minute Book, Vol. 8, op. cit., 2 October 1930, it. 5787.
57. GKN Minute Book, Vol. 9, op. cit., 22 August 1934, it. 6549.
58. GKN Minute Book, Vol. 10, op. cit., 2 January 1935, it. 6792.
59. Interview, J. Cockcroft with W.A. Nicol, 25 July 1973, p. 9.
60. Interview, J. Cockcroft with W.A. Nicol, 25 July 1973, p. 2.
61. Ibid., p. 17.
62. DBB, Vol. 4 (1985), Edgar Jones, 'Sir Kenneth Peacock', p. 570.
63. GKN Minute Book, Vol. 9, op. cit., 6 July 1933, it. 6330.
64. GKN Minute Book, Vol. 10, op. cit., 2 January 1936, it. 6788.
65. Interview, J. Cockcroft with Sir Anthony Bowlby, 25 April 1972, p. 28.
66. Interview, J. Cockcroft with W.A. Nicol, 25 July 1973, p. 15.
67. GKN Annual Report and Accounts (1921).
68. GKN Annual Report and Accounts (1943).
69. GKN Minute Book, Vol. 11, op. cit., 2 February 1939, it. 7249.
70. Who's Who, London (1947), p. 724.
71. Jones, GKN, Vol. One, op. cit., pp. 361–65.
72. Leslie Hannah, The Rise of the Corporate Economy, London (1976), p. 25.
73. Interview, J. Cockcroft with J.H. Jolly, 12 May 1972, p. 14.
74. Interview, J. Cockcroft with W.A. Nicol, 25 July 1973, p. 2.
75. The building was finally demolished in 1986.
76. GKN Minute Book, Vol. 3, op. cit., 2 January 1919, it. 3236.
77. GKN Minute Book, Vol. 4, op. cit., 13 September 1923, it. 4360.
78. GKN Minute Book, Vol. 5, op. cit., 1 February 1923, it. 4206.
79. Post Office London Directory 1923, p. 1640.
80. GKN Minute Book, Vol. 5, op. cit., 15 January 1925, it. 4655.
81. Ibid.
82. Carr and Taplin, British Steel, op. cit., p. 522.
83. GKN Minute Book, Vol. 3, op. cit., 6 October 1921, it. 3852; ibid., Vol. 9, 22 August 1934, it. 6550.
84. J.R. Edwards, Company Legislation and Changing Patterns of Disclosure in British Company Accounts 1900–1940, London (1981), pp. 7, 13, 73–77.
85. Ibid., p. 13.
86. Ibid., p. 15.
87. Ibid., p. 30.
88. Ibid., p. 39.
89. GKN Minute Book, Vol. 10, op. cit., 4 June 1936, it. 6855.
90. Edgar Jones, Accountancy and the British Economy 1840–1980, The Evolution of Ernst & Whinney, London (1981), p. 154; Sheila Marriner (ed.), Business and Businessmen, Liverpool (1978), T.A. Lee, 'Company Financial Statements: An Essay in Business History, 1830–1950', p. 255.
91. Interview, E. Jones with W.W. Fea, 1 February 1984.
92. GKN Minute Book, Vol. 9, op. cit., 6 August 1931, it. 5970.
93. GKN Minute Book, Vol. 10, op. cit., 7 May 1936, it. 6845.

94. Jones, *GKN, Vol. One*, op. cit., p. 392.
95. GKN Minute Book, Vol. 3, op. cit., 6 May 1920, it. 3503.
96. Ibid., 3 February 1921.
97. John Stevenson, *The Pelican Social History of Britain, British Society 1914–45*, Harmondsworth (1984), pp. 331–2.

9 GKN at War, 1939–45

None are exempt from service in this hour;
And vanquished in ourselves we dare not be.
                    Siegfried Sassoon, 'Silent Service' (23 May 1940)[1]

A pamphlet compiled by the Iron and Steel Federation recording their contribution to the war effort emphasised the industrial nature of the conflict in 1939–45. A Lancaster bomber, it observed, though constructed of light metals and alloys, also contained around four tons of steel (for engine parts, airscrew hubs, mountings and armament) and could carry eight tons of bombs, most of the weight being derived from the steel casings.[2] To bring one aircraft factory into production no fewer than thirty to forty types of tool steel were needed. Further, by the end of 1943 some 83,000 tanks and armoured cars had been manufactured in Britain, together with over a million other military vehicles. If any single substance could be described as the material of war, then it was steel. In its various forms it became ammunition, weaponry, helmets, warships and a means of transporting troops. To convert such a basic raw material into so many different objects, each with their own characteristics and qualities, demanded an organisation and manufacturing capacity of great complexity. GKN, being a primary producer (with, in effect, two medium-sized steelworks) and possessing a variety of works concerned with the fashioning of steel objects, found itself in the front line of industrial warfare. In addition, the company had to earn profits and satisfy the expectations of its shareholders. How the group coped with the dual needs of the nation's desperate demand for munitions and its own commercial considerations form the central themes of this chapter.

THE WAR EFFORT

With the experience of the Great War only some twenty years distant, both government and industry were able to respond swiftly to the embracing demands of modern warfare. Indeed, to a much greater extent than in the period preceding 1914, there had been a degree of planning and anticipation. From around 1937, the British people had prepared themselves and their economy for combat. Workers and managers joined local territorial units or were enlisted into the militia for basic military training, some continuing to be paid by their employers when absent from the factory or office.[3] Manufacturers responded to the needs of re-armament – perhaps more enthusiastically because normal peacetime demand had fallen off.[4] The various steelworks belonging to GKN, for example, tendered for shell and constructional steel (p. 53), while from February 1939 Lysaghts rolled the vast quantities of corrugated sheet needed for air-raid shelters (p. 113) and, as in the Great War, Sankeys pressed millions of steel helmets required by the mobilising armies (p. 266). Hence, war was greeted in September 1939 not with the wild patriotism of 1914 but with stoicism, the mood being one of 'release from unbearable tension, of slightly fearful determination and of grim resignation'.[5]

Managers too took a more realistic view about the course and duration of war than in 1914. 'In view of rising prices', recorded the GKN board in November 1939,

> and the uncertainty of trade after the present exceptional demands have been satisfied, it was highly desirable that special [capital] expenditure at all works throughout the group should, before sanction, be very closely scrutinised in regard to its urgency.[6]

So that quick decisions could be made in an emergency (the main board meeting only once a month), a committee comprising the four managing directors (S.R. Beale, T.S. Peacock, J.H. Jolly and K.S. Peacock) under the chairmanship of Beale was set up in October 1939 to act for the holding company and its subsidiaries.[7] In fact, responsibility for strategic planning was soon taken out of the hands of the directors, as in July 1940 GKN and most of its subsidiary companies were declared 'controlled undertakings' by the Ministry of Supply.[8] At the company's annual general meeting in June 1940, Samuel R. Beale observed,

> war meant control – control of supplies, control of production, control of the destination of products and of the price at which they were sold.[9]

The Ministry of Supply became involved in all major decision-making: its representatives, concerned to maximise output while keeping costs within reasonable limits, monitored raw material inputs, costed the various manufacturing processes, discussed prices and determined questions of capital expenditure. In a controlled economy, peacetime considerations of competition and autonomy were sacrificed in favour of pooled productivity and centralised direction.[10] As Table 9.1 shows, although not successful in raising the output of steel, the government's role was in essence to increase the manufacture of weapons, munitions and the growing array of vehicles, ships, aircraft and machinery employed in war. To do this it was not only necessary to

108 A morale-boosting inspection by King George VI to Atlas Works, Darlaston, escorted by Sir Samuel R. Beale (middle) and T.S. Peacock (right).

divert engineering works from their peacetime roles (the Morris plant at Cowley, for instance, stopped making cars to concentrate on the production of tanks) but in certain cases to boost their capacity. To this end, the government invested huge sums in new industrial plant. By 1944–45, for instance, spending on defence, £5,125 million, represented 82.94 per cent of total state expenditure.[11] Never before had so many public funds been committed to manufacturing.

GKN benefited considerably from the government's need to raise output. Early in 1940 the works of John Garrington & Sons were selected by both the Admiralty and Ministry of Supply for investment. During peacetime the company had provided forged shells and bullets for the Army and sporting use,[12] but their capacity fell far short of war-time consumption. After negotiations, it was agreed that a new shell-forging plant be laid down at a cost of around £180,000, this to be paid for by the Admiralty.[13] The demand for forgings of every kind was so consuming that the Ministry of Supply decided to fund in part a further scheme of extensions,[14] and provided half of the £325,000 expended.[15]

In November 1942, the Iron and Steel Control (a part of the Ministry

Table 9.1   Output of selected industrial goods in Britain, 1939–45

Goods	Unit of measurement	1939	1940	1941	1942	1943	1944	1945
Steel	000 tons	13,221	12,975	12,312	12,764	13,031	12,142	11,824
Coal	000 tons	231,338	224,299	206,344	204,944	198,920	192,746	182,773
Total aircraft	number	14,486	17,702	18,974	19,906	18,494	15,472	14,175
Bomber aircraft	number	7,940	15,049	20,094	23,672	26,263	26,461	n.a.
Bombs	short tons	758	1,967	3,275	5,439	7,352	7,903	n.a.
		n.a.	51,093	147,848	211,048	233,807	309,366	n.a.

Note: n.a. – not available.

Source: United Kingdom, Central Statistical Office, *Statistical Digest of the War*, London, H.M.S.O. (1951).

of Supply) requested that Castle Works, Cardiff, increase its capacity for cold-rolled strip by 300 tons a week.[16] The cost of additional plant was estimated at £216,000, the Ministry agreeing to provide half. The arrangement was confirmed in May 1943.[17]

A further way of raising output was to concentrate production among the largest or most efficient makers to enable them to achieve the greatest economies of scale. Accordingly, in May 1942, the Iron and Steel Control suggested that if the light bar mill belonging to Guest Keen Baldwins were closed, rolling could then be concentrated at the under-used Cwmbran mill.[18] GKN agreed to pay GKB £4,000 a year compensation for the loss of business from the time of the closure until the end of the hostilities, when the latter was at liberty to re-enter the bar trade.[19]

The need to rationalise production and raise output also encouraged GKN to acquire a number of companies which would offer them a greater degree of vertical integration. For example, in December 1942 it was announced that GKN had obtained 5,600 £1 ordinary shares in the Somerset Wire Co., the purchase involving a promise from the latter that henceforth they would buy all their supplies of wire rod from Castle Works, Cardiff.[20] In September 1944 a further 2,000 shares were acquired, bringing GKN's holding to 40 per cent,[21] the remaining 60

109 A specialised tank assembled by Lysaghts at Bristol for the invasion of Europe (*Rheemco*).

per cent being obtained in 1950. The Uskside Engineering Co. at Newport was also taken over by John Lysaght in the same month at a cost of £42,500.[22] In September 1940, GKN had acquired 85 per cent of the shareholding in United Hinges for £28,288.[23] Although majority shareholders of Twisteel Reinforcement, the group decided, in view of the former's importance as a consumer of rod and situation adjacent to London Works, to purchase the outstanding 49 per cent.[24] By July 1944 their offer of 69 shillings a share had been accepted and the 21,983 shares were bought for £75,841.[25] During March 1945, following a policy of vertical integration, Twisteel itself acquired 80 per cent of the capital in Ferrocon Engineering Ltd. Not only would the takeover save Twisteel expenditure and 'have other technical advantages', Ferrocon also agreed to buy their steel supplies from Castle Works.[26]

Further, the acquisition of Nettlefold & Sons, a major wholesale fastener business based in London (founded, like Nettlefolds, by John Sutton Nettlefold but never incorporated within the Smethwick manufacturing business), opposite Euston Station, may be viewed within a policy extending into strategically important areas. Hitherto GKN had not entered the distribution market, preferring to supply the factors 'en masse'. The decision to take over Nettlefolds was partly to obtain a related, profitable business, but was also influenced by the desire to secure control over the name 'Nettlefolds'.[27]

Although this rationalisation of production appears, on balance, to have acted in GKN's favour, it did involve some losses. Given the heavy expenditure that would have been involved in modernising the roll foundries of John Lysaght and Bayliss, Jones & Bayliss, GKN agreed to sell both to the British Rollmakers Corporation for £120,000, to be settled by the grant of shares (the equivalent of 35.25 per cent) in the new merged company.[28] In the event, the £1 shares were allocated by Carter & Co., GKN's auditors, as follows: 52,500 to BJB and 67,500 to Lysaghts.[29]

GOVERNMENT CONTROLS

Having been responsible for placing major orders with companies, and on occasion having provided much of the finance necessary for new plant, the Ministry of Supply was concerned to check that it was not being charged excessively for products. In addition, if savings could be made by altering existing work patterns so much the better. Accountants, a 'reserved occupation', were recruited in large numbers to monitor government contracts, and their deployment in factories and mills resulted on occasion in the adoption of cost accounting regimes or improvements to existing financial systems. However, these new techniques were not always welcomed. In April 1942, following the introduction of 'time study methods' the workers in the bolt mill, Heath Street, decided to strike, the whole factory eventually coming out in sympathy.[30] Although the action did not win recognition from the operatives' union, it was not until 5 May that work resumed pending arbitration. In the discussions which followed the principle of using time study methods to determine wage rates was conceded by the workforce in return for various concessions on time allowances.[31]

110 Three posters designed by the workers of St. George's Works to boost output of Nettlefolds' fasteners.

"TRYING"
WORK NEEDS TRYING WORKERS

Nº 401. H.G PITT. Sᵀ GEORGES SORTING ROOM.

YOUR MACHINE STANDING
DELAYS ALLIES LANDING

Nº 29 G. PRICE. Sᵀ GEORGES HEADING DEPT

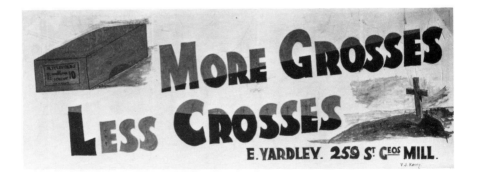

MORE GROSSES
LESS CROSSES

E. YARDLEY. 259 Sᵀ Gᴱᵒˢ MILL.

As in the Great War, when the government introduced an Excess Profits Duty of 50 per cent rising to 80 per cent, to prevent fortunately-placed businesses from benefiting excessively from the urgent needs of a nation at war, an Excess Profits Tax (EPT) of 60 per cent was imposed in 1939, this being raised, almost by popular demand, to 100 per cent in 1940.[32] Companies were able to select a benchmark profit level from their peacetime accounts and any additional sums earned above this

Table 9.2   GKN profits and equity interest, 1938–47

		Profits (£000s)	Adjusted*	Equity interest (£000s)	Adjusted*
to 31 March	1938	1,075	1,089	16,880	17,102
	1939	986	986	16,907	16,907
	1940	1,003	862	17,164	14,746
	1941	868	688	16,730	13,257
	1942	859	678	16,918	13,353
	1943	904	716	17,144	13,585
	1944	965	759	17,692	13,920
	1945	1,059	825	18,049	14,057
	1946	1,145	888	18,370	14,251
	1947	1,385	1,067	23,412	18,037

Note: *Figures adjusted by the Bank of England's index of consumer prices, 1930 = 100.

Source: *GKN Report and Balance Sheets*, 1938–47.

figure were then subject to EPT. This may well explain why GKN's published profits (Table 9.2) throughout the war remained static (and in real terms fell below their peacetime levels), as any extra gains that the group might have made would immediately have been lost to the new tax. However, due to the complexities of its calculation, EPT was paid considerably in arrears, companies having to make provision each year for what they believed was a realistic liability. As these totals were often large, they could have a major impact on a particular set of annual accounts. For the twelve months to 31 March 1940, Carter & Co., GKN's auditors, advised that £50,000 be set aside for EPT payments at a time when the group's income tax amounted to £275,000.[33] In the following year, when the EPT calculation was described as being 'an intricate matter',[34] provision ran at £800,000, double the sum for income tax.[35] In 1942 the respective figures were £762,000 and £400,000[36] and in 1943 reached £1 million and £425,000.[37] As the war drew to a close, so EPT payments fell (£750,000 in 1944[38] and £250,000 in 1945, the latter at a time when income tax liability was assessed at £560,000).[39]

The practical question of profits became a difficult issue in a government-controlled economy. Having powers to govern the flow of raw materials and capable of placing enormous orders, the Ministry of Supply could indirectly determine the commercial fate of an enterprise. By 1944 prices, for example, charged by the Heath Street woodscrew business had fallen behind the rate of inflation.[40] In peacetime, Nettlefolds would simply have informed their factors that the discounts were to be reduced and recoup their lost earnings. But as a Controlled

Establishment, any adjustment required the permission of the Iron & Steel Control. A statement demonstrating 'only a moderate return on the capital employed' at the works was presented by Carter & Co., the company's auditors, though it was recognised that 'concessions would have to be made in respect of aircraft products resulting in a lowering of the screw works profits'.[41] In the event, the Ministry were convinced and Nettlefolds allowed to decrease the discounts on iron woodscrews by 7½ points and on brass by 5 points.[42]

The degree to which the state intervened in the ordering of the economy may be illustrated by reference to the following request made of GKN by the Ministry of Information in April 1941: 'that drafts of the company's accounts, and of the chairman's speech should be submitted to the censorship division of the Ministry ... for consideration before issue'.[43] The company conceded and in his report of July 1942 to the shareholders, S.R. Beale wrote,

> Once again I have to ask you to accept a rather brief letter instead of the longer review of the activities of the G.K. & N. group that was the pre-war custom ... Pressure of demand has, of course, been heavy on all departments, and the only wish of everyone is to continue to contribute to the limits of their individual capacity.[44]

It is difficult to imagine what value an enemy agent might have gleaned from these documents, though the volume of government investment in GKN might have confirmed a suspicion that the group was engaged on important war work.

THE IMPACT OF WAR

Initially the greatest effect of the war was to create a problem of personnel: considerable numbers of men and managers were recruited by the armed forces. In September 1939, it had been agreed that those called up belonging to territorial or reserve units would have the difference between their standard rate of pay and their military pay provided by the company; militiamen were not to receive this allowance, though GKN offered to subsidise their contribution to the company pension fund.[45] Given that both groups of servicemen were likely to face equal dangers, this distinction was dropped for all members of staff in October when it was agreed that all married men were to be paid the difference between their GKN pay at September 1939 and their war service pay, less 10 shillings a week; and single men were to receive one-third of the difference between their salary and war pay.[46] As from December 1939, employees were offered a single payment a week: 10 shillings for married men and 5 shillings for unmarried.[47] These allowances continued for those called up during war-time until they were demobilised, but were not granted to those enlisted in the post-war period.[48] In the Great War it appears that around £150,000 was paid by GKN to the dependents of those serving in the forces,[49] whether this sum was exceeded during the Second World War has not been recorded.

Having lost both managers and skilled men in this process of recruitment, a considerable effort was made to have them recalled from military or government service. For example, E.C. Lysaght and [Sir] N.R.R. Brooke, both later to become directors of GKN, had volunteered for military service in 1940 when they were asked to return to Orb and Castle Works respectively.[50] When W.J. Brooke, general manager of Normanby Park Steelworks, retired in December 1943, GKN persuaded the RAF to demobilise his other son, Joe Brooke, in order that he could succeed him. Stephen Lloyd, also to become a director of GKN, spent a period working for the Steel Control before returning in March 1945 to supervise the group's various fastener subsidiaries in the Midlands.[52]

GKN suffered its share of bomb damage. Air raids in the Great War had been of a very limited nature and had not affected industrial output. With the technical development of aircraft and a strategic decision to bomb Britain into submission, the Midlands became a prime target for German attacks. The first hits on GKN factories occurred in October 1940, though the damage was reported as being 'slight'.[53] For the first time in the history of warfare, civilians en masse were considered a legitimate target and could expect to be killed or have their homes destroyed. GKN decided to offer employees grants in such eventualities, and the Necessitous Cases Fund (to which both workers and the company subscribed) already established at the Heath Street Works was empowered to act for the group as a whole.[54] By July 1945 the Fund had reached 'a very substantial amount' and it was agreed to reduce both employee and company contributions to three farthings a week for the year to June 1946 whilst ways were explored of distributing the surplus.[55]

Throughout the war property belonging to GKN was at risk from enemy action: in March 1941 the Liverpool offices and warehouse of Mosers were destroyed in an air raid;[56] the mills of the Henry Cox Screw Co. in Birmingham were seriously damaged in April 1941 and such plant as could be salvaged was transferred to a temporary building of tubular scaffolding erected in the grounds of London Works, Smethwick.[57] On the night of 29 July 1942, the city was the subject of a particularly heavy raid when some 150 incendiaries fell on the Heath Street Works, one member of staff being killed whilst trying to deal with a bomb.[58] The head office of Mosers in Borough High Street, Southwark, suffered a direct hit in January 1945, resulting in a large loss of life and many injuries.[59]

Although further from German-held aerodromes, Cardiff, too, was not immune from attack and the East Moors Steelworks became a prime target. A raid in May 1943 caused damage to the ingot stripping bay and adjoining buildings, though prompt repairs soon brought production back to normal.[60]

As well as having to spend capital and divert labour to reconstruct damaged buildings and machinery, GKN, in common with other major companies, was called upon to make donations to help the war effort. Towards the end of 1940, before the economy had become fully geared to the hostilities and when losses incurred in the fall of France and Battle of Britain had yet to be made up, 'Spitfire Funds' were established. The workforces at the various factories and works of GKN subscribed a total of £1,700 to which the company itself added £800.[61] In a 'Wings for Victory Week' during 1943, GKN agreed to give £50,000, John Lysaght offering a further £10,000.[62] Subjected to attack from the air and liable to have their homes or workplaces destroyed by bombing, these appeals provided everyone with an opportunity to feel that they were participating in an offensive action.

Where industrial production was concentrated in a few key sites, the risk of disruption by bombing was clearly great and the Ministry of Supply took steps to ensure a measure of dispersal. In July 1940, for example, K.S. Peacock was asked to provide emergency stocks of about one million gross woodscrews which could then be housed in various parts of Britain to minimise problems should Nettlefolds' Heath Street warehouse receive a direct hit. At that time, 500,000 gross had already been housed in five centres througout the UK.[63] In December, aware that Birmingham was a target area, the Ministry of Aircraft Production requested that Nettlefolds move some of those machines making screws and bolts required for aeroplanes to a safer district.[64] Since a number of the company's employees were travelling from the Cannock area, Peacock set in train plans to erect a small factory there at an estimated cost of £20,000.[65] After negotiations, it was agreed that 75 per cent of this expenditure would be borne by the government.[66] Construction proceeded swiftly and by April 1941 it was anticipated that the Cannock plant would be in operation within three months.[67] In addition, the Ministry of Aircraft Production requested that part of the tool room plant and bar products department also be dispersed from the Smethwick site. At a cost of around £17,000 a temporary building, paid for by the government, was erected on the company's sports ground at Thimblemill Lane to house this machinery.[68] Whilst the dispersal of plant made sense from a military standpoint, it was not conducive to manufacturing efficiency, and the dis-economies involved doubtless would have exercised a limited impact on GKN's profitability.

Because of the genuinely worldwide nature of the conflict in 1939–45, the conduct of the war could have an adverse effect on those companies with overseas subsidiaries. Despite the disruption caused by the Spanish Civil War, GKN had retained its shareholding in the Orconera Iron Ore Co. The Fascist government of General Franco, although ostensibly neutral, favoured Germany rather than Britain, which, in turn, undermined GKN's ground when negotiating with national regulatory bodies. In August 1941 the board acknowledged that the Orconera accounts revealed a loss primarily because the Spanish authorities had decided to favour local consumers by fixing ore prices at a low level.[69] In these circumstances, GKN considered an offer made by Spanish interests to purchase the Santander mines, though this appears to have been rejected, the group retaining its shareholding throughout the war years.

The other difficulty for GKN arose over their ownership of Aug. Stenman AB, makers of hinges and woodscrews, based at Eskilstuna, Sweden.[70] In 1930 the group had acquired a 91 per cent holding in the venture, but continued to allow the business a major degree of autonomy, including the retention of profits. Although Sweden was not invaded by the Axis powers, its neighbours, Norway, Denmark and Finland were fought over. Because Stenman and its subsidiary Uddeholms sold its products throughout Scandinavia, this was conceived as being an infringement of British Trading-with-the-Enemy regulations. The matter was first raised in July 1943, and in March 1944 the government threatened to put Stenman and Uddeholms on a black list to be effected once peacetime conditions had resumed.[71] In response to a letter from J.H. Jolly and an interview with Mr. H.W.A. Waring, HM Commercial Counsellor, Mr. Nilsson, chief executive of Stenmans, gave an 'assurance that he would cease all exports to enemy or enemy occupied territory, and place no more orders for material from these countries without prior permission'.[72]

However, the impact of the war on GKN was not all negative. As has been recorded, the government provided considerable funds for investment in new plant and machinery. Garringtons benefited greatly in this respect. Under the stimulus of voracious war demand, capital expenditure at Heath Street was both substantial and sustained though most was internally generated: in January 1943, a survey of the screw making machines revealed that most were outdated and their replacement at a cost of £322,257 was authorised by GKN to be spread over five years.[73] Similarly, the nail machines at Castle Works, Cardiff, were examined in September 1944 and found to be in 'a very bad condition' because having been installed in 1932–34 they had 'since been operating regularly three shifts per day and for the period of the war a number of these machines have operated as many as 160 hours per week'.[74] Their replacement was costed at £14,000, this being granted forthwith.

Not only had the war underlined the importance of cost accounting and financial controls, it had also emphasised the need for research and the application of new technology. Accordingly, in October 1944 the managing director of GKN, taking into account that the existence of a number of laboratories attached to various works within the group, concluded that

> these should be continued, but that for research in the widest sense of the term it might be advisable to equip a central laboratory which could be located away from the works. Whoever

was appointed to carry out research would also co-ordinate the activities of the works laboratories.[75]

Although their search for a scientist was diligently pursued and several highly qualified individuals were interviewed, none appeared suitable.[76] By June 1945 the project was no further advanced.[77] Presumably the most able candidates had already been recruited by either the government or were employed by the scientific industries, such as pharmaceuticals or aeronautics. Finally, in December 1945, Dr. B. Matthews was approached,[78] and in January 1946, after visiting some of GKN's Midland works, he accepted the post of chief scientific advisor,[79] though he was not able to join the group until the following September.[80] He was asked to submit requirements for a central laboratory. These specifications, together with the nucleus of the Sankey research laboratory (established at Manor Works in 1945), eventually formed the basis for the GKN Technical Centre set up in Birmingham New Road, Wolverhampton, in 1947.

It does not seem that the war years produced dramatic change in the composition of GKN's highest rank of management. Of the ten directors who sat on the main board in March 1939, six remained in March 1946: four of these were actively involved in the management of the group (Sir Samuel R. Beale, J.H. Jolly, K.S. Peacock and Allan Macbeth) and two were, in effect, non-executive, Lt. Col. C.H.C. Guest M.P., and Sir Maurice E. Denny.[81] The principal changes resulted from the deaths of W.R. Lysaght (April 1945),[82] T.Z. Lloyd (who had only recently retired from Heath Street before his demise in September 1939),[83] Sir David Llewellyn (December 1940)[84] and T.S. Peacock (February 1946).[85] The first had been unwell for some time and was scarcely able to attend a single meeting during the war; Lloyd, Peacock and Llewellyn also suffered periods of poor health which necessitated their absence from the board. T.S. Peacock had retired as managing director in July 1941, (his many directorships of subsidiary companies were re-allocated among other board members),[86] though he continued as a deputy chairman until his death. New elections included John Scott Hindley, Viscount Hyndley (1883–1963), then managing director of Powell Duffryn and chairman of Stephenson Clarke who retired in 1946 to become the first chairman of the National Coal Board, and Edmund L. Hann who joined the board in February 1940.[87] Both were principally involved in the coal industry and were non-executive so far as GKN was concerned. Following the death of Sir David Llewellyn, both Colonel H.B. Sankey and E.C. Lysaght became directors.[88] The former had been chairman of Sankeys, while the continuing illness of W.R. Lysaght required that another senior manager of John Lysaght attend meetings to represent that company.

The appointment of J.H. Jolly as deputy chairman in April 1943 was to name him (from the senior board members) as the successor to Sir Samuel R. Beale.[89] Older and more experienced than K.S. Peacock, the other managing director, he was possibly without rival in having some twenty five years of accumulated knowledge of GKN.

In January 1944, Maurice H. Tollit became a director of GKN.[90] A relative, by marriage, of the Peacock family, M.H. Tollit had occupied various managerial positions for GKN in the Birmingham district, including sales at Heath Street. Having been chairman of John Garringtons for some years (p. 219), on 2 November John Harper Bean, a former car manufacturer (Bean Cars), was also elected a director of GKN.[91] Sir Charles Bruce-Gardner (1887–1960) became a member of the board in April 1946, a vacancy occurring as a result of the death of T.S. Peacock.[92]

111 At Melbourne airport in September 1957, from left to right, Sir Charles and Lady Bruce-Gardner, R. Parry-Okeden and J.H. Jolly.

Having worked for the steelmakers, John Summers & Sons at Shotton, served on the board of the Bankers Industrial Development Company, and in 1943 become Controller of Labour Allocation and Supply at the Ministry of Aircraft Production, he gained considerable insight into the structure of the British steel industry and the workings of government departments. Bruce-Gardner was, therefore, a useful ally for a major manufacturing group to possess.

In practice it appears virtually impossible to measure the impact of the war on GKN's business fortunes. Certainly the group's profits suffered during the war years (Table 9.2). It would have been surprising if it had been otherwise: the loss of managers and men to the forces, the destruction of plant and buildings by raids and the dispersal that this entailed, the diversion of manufacturing to produce the material of war and the ceiling placed on surpluses by the imposition of a tough Excess Profits Tax, all conspired to ensure that there would be no gains on the pre-war figures. The advantages conferred on GKN by the war were of less immediate consequence. The introduction of cost accounting and financial reporting schemes, heavy capital expenditure in plant and machinery, the acquisition of related subsidiaries and the realisation that scientific research was of increasing importance were all factors which would take some years to yield results. Whilst the losses created by the hostilities had an immediate impact, it appears that the gains of the Second World War revealed themselves in the 1950s rather than the 1940s.

Whilst the end of the war was greeted by all with relief and rejoicing, the change of government created by the overwhelming Labour victory of July 1945, having been elected on a manifesto which included the nationalisation of steel,[93] presented GKN with a dilemma. Any capital they expended on their steelworks could shortly be lost. Accordingly, in August the board agreed to continue to invest in 'finishing departments' but that a 'go slow policy' should be adopted with regard to their steelworks and rolling mills at Scunthorpe, Cardiff and Newport.[94] The uncertainty which surrounded the government's intentions made it impossible for GKN to plan long term with reference to its iron and steel interests.[95]

SUMMARY

The picture of GKN at war presents two apparently opposed developments. On the one hand, the need to regulate the economy resulted in a greater level of government controls: the company was told which products it should manufacture, in what quantities and with specified margins of profit. Much of the funding for new plant and machinery came from the Ministry of Supply which, in turn, had indicated the areas where increased output was needed. Managers and workers who had not enlisted in the armed forces were, on occasion, recruited by the government to perform specific tasks. Even the group's annual report was subject to censorship by the Ministry of Information. The Second World War saw the imposition of the most authoritarian controls that Britain has ever experienced. Freedom of economic manoeuvre, in a strategic sense, was severely limited for GKN and other major manufacturing groups.

Paradoxically, at the tactical, shop floor level, there appears to have been a greater flexibility and an inspired determination to make-do in adversity. When factories were bombed, they came back into production, often using prefabricated structures, in remarkably quick time. If new products were needed for which purpose-built machinery was lacking, ingenious modifications or deals with competitors resulted in substitute methods. In an effort to increase output, restrictive practices, sometimes rigidly observed in peacetime, were waived. Adversity encouraged inspired qualities of coping and powers of recuperation which thrived in spite of conditions of greater state control.

The war years for GKN, in common with industry as a whole, had a topsy-turvy character, in which the normal rules of competitive business were turned upside down. Company priorities were, to a degree, sacrificed in favour of the national war effort. When peace was restored toward the end of 1945, the election of a Labour government committed to nationalisation and the maintenance of so much government machinery resulted in the creation of a mixed economy rather than the predominantly free-market of the 1930s. Six years of war, therefore, had effected major and lasting change to the business environment in which GKN and other major industrial groups had to operate.

References

1. Siegfried Sassoon, *Collected Poems 1908–1956*, London (1961), p. 257.
2. The Iron and Steel Federation, *The Battle of Steel, A Record of the British Iron and Steel Industry at War* (n.d.), pp. 1–2.
3. John Lysaght Minute Book, Vol. 7, op. cit., 7 December 1939, pp. 303–4.
4. GKN Minute Book, Vol. 10, op. cit., 3 June 1937, it. 7004; 3 February 1938, it. 7099.
5. Arthur Marwick, *The Home Front, The British and the Second World War*, London (1976), p. 20.
6. GKN Minute Book, Vol. 11, July 1938–January 1943, 2 November 1939, it. 7352.
7. Ibid., 5 October 1939, it. 7333.
8. Ibid., 4 July 1940, it. 7462.
9. *The Iron & Coal Trades Review*, Vol. CXL, 28 June 1940, p. 954.
10. John Stevenson, *British Society 1914–45*, Harmondsworth (1984), pp. 445–47; Alan S. Milward, *War, Economy and Society 1939–1945*, London (1977), pp. 91–92.
11. Central Statistical Office, *Statistical Digest of the War*, London HMSO (1951), p. 195.
12. *GKN, An Outline History*, op. cit., p. 55.
13. GKN Minute Book, Vol. 11, op. cit., 7 March 1940, it. 7408.
14. Ibid., 6 February 1941, it. 7549.
15. Ibid., 6 March 1941, it. 7571.
16. Ibid., 5 November 1942, it. 7820.
17. GKN Minute Book, Vol. 12, February 1943–June 1947, 6 May 1943, it. 7914.
18. Ibid., 7 May 1942, it. 7750.
19. Ibid., 5 November 1942, it. 7883.
20. GKN Minute Book, Vol. 11, op. cit., 3 December 1942, it. 7837.
21. Ibid., 7 September 1944, it. 8136.
22. Ibid., it. 7836.
23. Ibid., 3 October 1940, it. 7486.
24. Ibid., 1 June 1944, it. 8106.
25. Ibid., 6 July 1944, it. 8121.
26. Ibid., 5 April 1945, it. 8236.
27. Ibid., 5 April 1945, it. 8234; 3 May 1945, it. 8254.

28. GKN Minute Book, Vol. 12, 6 January 1944, it. 8025; 6 April 1944, it. 8075.
29. Ibid., 4 May 1944, it. 8090.
30. Ibid., 7 May 1942, it. 7754.
31. Ibid., 2 July 1942, it. 7782.
32. W.K. Hancock and M.M. Gowing, *British War Economy*, London HMSO (1949), p. 163.
33. GKN Minute Book, Vol. 11, op. cit., 6 June 1940, it. 7444.
34. Ibid., 5 June 1941, it. 7611.
35. Ibid., 3 July 1941, it. 7623.
36. Ibid., 2 July 1942, it. 7777.
37. GKN Minute Book, Vol. 12, op. cit., 1 July 1943, it. 7941.
38. Ibid., 6 July 1944, it. 8114.
39. Ibid., 4 July 1945, it. 8280.
40. GKN Minute Book, Vol. 12, op. cit., 6 April 1944, it. 8078.
41. Ibid.
42. Ibid., 1 June 1944, it. 8108.
43. GKN Minute Book, Vol. 11, op. cit., 3 April 1941, it. 7585.
44. *GKN Forty-Second Report and Balance Sheet* (1942).
45. GKN Minute Book, Vol. 11, op. cit., 5 October 1939, it. 7335; 2 November 1939, it. 7349.
46. Ibid.
47. Ibid., 7 December 1939, it. 7363.
48. GKN Minute Book, Vol. 12, op. cit., 4 October 1945, it. 8315.
49. Jones, *GKN, Vol. One*, op. cit., p. 397.
50. Interview Edgar Jones with E.C. Lysaght, December 1983.
51. GKN Minute Book, Vol. 12, op. cit., 4 March 1943, it. 7882.
52. Ibid., 1 March 1945, it. 8224.
53. GKN Minute Book, Vol. 11, op. cit., 7 November 1940, it. 7504.
54. Ibid., it. 7522.
55. GKN Minute Book, Vol. 12, op. cit., 4 July 1945, it. 8288.
56. GKN Minute Book, Vol. 11, op. cit., 3 April 1941, it. 7588.
57. Ibid., 1 May 1941, it. 7602.
58. Ibid., 3 September 1942, it. 7797.
59. GKN Minute Book, Vol. 12, op. cit., 1 February 1945, it. 8211.
60. Ibid., 3 June 1943, it. 7934.
61. GKN Minute Book, Vol. 11, op. cit., 2 January 1941, it. 7538.
62. GKN Minute Book, Vol. 12, op. cit., 4 March 1943, it. 7893.
63. GKN Minute Book, Vol. 11, op. cit., 4 July 1940, it. 7466.
64. Ibid., 5 December 1940, it. 7522.
65. Ibid.
66. Ibid., 6 March 1941, it. 7576.
67. Ibid., 3 April 1941, it. 7859.
68. Ibid., 3 July 1941, it. 7625.
69. GKN Minute Book, Vol. 11, op. cit., 7 August 1941, it. 7640.
70. G.G. Jones (Editor), *British Multinationals*, op. cit., Edgar Jones, 'Steel and Engineering Overseas', pp. 177–8.
71. GKN Minute Book, Vol. 12, op. cit., 2 March 1944, it. 8060.
72. Ibid., 6 July 1944, it. 8120.
73. GKN Minute Book, Vol. 11, op. cit., 7 January 1943, it. 7852.
74. GKN Minute Book, Vol. 12, op. cit., 5 October 1944, it. 8147.
75. Ibid., 5 October 1944, it. 8150.

76. Ibid., 1 March 1945, it. 8223.
77. Ibid., 7 June 1945, it. 8267.
78. Ibid., 6 December 1945, it. 8359.
79. Ibid., 3 January 1946, it. 8376.
80. Ibid., 3 October 1946, it. 8375.
81. *GKN, Thirty-Ninth Report and Balance Sheet* (1939); *GKN, Forty-Sixth Report and Balance Sheet* (1946).
82. GKN Minute Book, Vol. 12, op. cit., 3 May 1945, it. 8244.
83. GKN Minute Book, Vol. 11, op. cit., 5 October 1939, it. 7329.
84. Ibid., 2 January 1941, it. 7526.
85. GKN Minute Book, Vol. 12, op. cit., 7 March 1946, it. 8396.
86. Ibid., 7 August 1941, it. 7641.
87. GKN Minute Book, Vol. 11, op. cit., 1 February 1940, it. 7388; *DBB*, Vol. 3 (1985), J. Davenport, 'Viscount Hyndley', pp. 256–7.
88. GKN Minute Book, Vol. 11, op. cit., 6 February 1941, it. 7542.
89. Ibid., 1 April 1943, it. 7897.
90. GKN Minute Book, Vol. 12, op. cit., 6 January 1944, it. 8018.
91. Ibid., 2 November 1944, it. 8158.
92. Ibid., 4 April 1946, it. 8413; 7 March 1946, it. 8396.
93. Walter Gumbel and Kenneth Potter, *The Iron and Steel Act, 1949*, London HMSO (1951), p. xi; Sir Norman Chester, *The Nationalization of British Industry, 1945–51*, London HMSO (1975), pp. 149–50; A.J.P. Taylor, *English History, 1914–1945*, Oxford (1965), p. 597.
94. GKN Minute Book, Vol. 12, op. cit., 2 August 1945, it. 8299.
95. Ibid., 7 February 1946, it. 8390.

Part III
GKN Overseas to 1945

10 *John Lysaght (Australia) Pty, 1919–45*

> Galvanised iron is undoubtedly the best material yet produced for
> many purposes, particularly use in rural and mining industries.
> Its strength, light weight, lasting qualities, adaptability for erec-
> tion and fabrication and the low costs for transport place it in a
> field without any serious competition and there must be an ever-
> increasing demand to extend the area of water-proof covering for
> stock implements, plant stores, etc., and to extend house accom-
> modation to fabricate tanks, troughing and utensils.[1]
>
> Australian Tariff Board Report, 1932

In 1913 when John Lysaght Ltd achieved record outputs from its rolling
mills at Newport and galvanising works in Bristol, ninety per cent of its
galvanised sheet was sold overseas, and of this two-thirds (approximately 85,800 tons) were purchased by Australia.[2] This connection
between company and country, albeit stretched over eleven thousand
miles, was crucial in understanding the events of the interwar period.
Just as Australia was the principal market for the company's product,
so Lysaghts were the leading exporter to the subcontinent; in 1902, for
example, they supplied 64 per cent of all galvanised sheet consumed in
Australia.[3]

THE PRE-MANUFACTURING PHASE

As has been seen, the rising volume of business which John Lysaght
had been conducting with Australia had led to the company setting up
its own sales organisation and thereby reduce the large number of
direct sales to merchants. In 1879 the Victoria Galvanised Iron & Wire
Co., with a headquarters in Melbourne, was established.[4] Re-named
Lysaght's Galvanised Iron Pty Ltd in 1899, it supervised a growing
number of distribution depots opened throughout Australia (see
p. 35). Until the construction of the company's rolling mills and
galvanising pots at Newcastle, New South Wales in 1919–21, Lysaghts
operated a major export business without ever having to undertake any

heavy capital expenditure in the continent. A general debate has arisen surrounding the reasoning behind the decisions by British companies to set up manufacturing plant in overseas territories.[5] Their motives can, in effect, be divided into two major categories: either to improve efficiencies by reducing shipping costs and shorten delivery times; or because the imposition of tariffs, designed to encourage domestic production, increasingly made it uneconomic to supply customers from home.[6]

Tariffs on galvanised products had been in existence during the 1880s (being £3 per ton, or about 18 per cent, in New South Wales, and twenty five per cent in Victoria)[7] to encourage the development of industry in Australia and, in its absence, to serve as a source of revenue. However, because no steelworks then existed to supply slabs or billets for re-rolling into sheet, there was no prospect of any foreign company, whether British or otherwise, setting up galvanising plant. Since the tariff applied to exporters from all nations it had no real impact on whichever manufacturer won orders in Australia. Yet import duties were not without their influence on Lysaghts' thinking. In August 1907, for example, when the Federal Government considered raising the levy on foreign galvanised sheet from 15s a ton to around £3 per ton (or 20 per cent ad valorem), it was suggested that the company would have to set up a galvanising works in Australia. For they calculated that black sheets could be imported from Europe and galvanised in Sydney for about £1 per ton below the cost of those paying the new tariff.[8] With this eventuality in mind they decided to purchase 47 acres of land at Sandown, near Parramatta, adjoining the river and the Great Western Railway for £12,500. The plot was considered 'good value for the money ... even if we should not ultimately require it and wished later on to sell the whole or a portion of it'.[9] As matters turned out, Lysaghts did not need to construct a works as the government decided to reduce the proposed ad valorem duty on corrugated sheet from £3 5s 0d per ton to £1 per ton, and that on plain galvanised sheet from £2 10s 0d to 10s per ton. In addition, they favoured British manufacturers by charging them 10s a ton less than other overseas producers.[10]

In essence, the hold exercised by John Lysaght over the Australian market in the decade before the Great War was a secure one. In a report prepared by Thomas Davey, managing director of Lysaghts Galvanised Iron Pty, and read to the board in July 1912, the efforts of both British and American competitors to poach their customers had failed.[11] This, despite the fact that during 1908 and 1909 their loyalty had been stretched 'almost to breaking point owing to the shortness of supplies'.[12] With the continuing influx of immigrants from Europe, a movement encouraged by the Federal Government, the demand for galvanised iron, one of the principal materials used in the construction of new houses, was set to continue rising. This fact, combined with the inflexible delivery system resulting from the large distances involved, created a major opportunity for a manufacturer prepared to invest capital in an Australian works.

Table 10.1   Total sales of galvanised sheet in Australia by Lysaghts in 1911 and 1913 (tons)

State (or region) and port	1911 galvanised	1913 galvanised	1913 black
NSW and Fiji			
Sydney and Newcastle	24,415		
Sydney, forwarded to Suva	286		
Sydney and Suva		22,434	4,084
Newcastle		5,255	
Total	24,691	27,689	4,084
Other States			
Victoria (Melbourne)	18,804	17,924	381
South Australia (Adelaide)	10,335	10,092	13
South Queensland (Brisbane)	13,600	14,431	300
Central Queensland (Rockhampton)	1,514	1,885	
North Queensland (Townsville and Cairns	1,747	2,043	
Western Australia (Fremantle)	6,825	7,354	11
Tasmania (Hobart and Devonport)	1,436	1,762	18
Total	78,962	83,180	4,807

Source: BHP Central Library, typewritten sheets dated 18 March 1912 and 24 March 1914, re-arranged by Alan Stein.

In January 1894 a sheet mill had, in fact, come into production at the Eskbank Iron Works, Lithgow, NSW, and from 1900 was turning out small quantities of galvanised sheet from steel bars.[13] Its output of galvanised sheet in 1901 was 2,500 tons. In 1906–7, when a blast furnace was constructed, the Lithgow Works comprised a steel furnace, six puddling furnaces, a ball furnace, two mill furnaces, a steam hammer and an 18-inch mill.[14] William Sandford, the owner, had originally been in Lysaghts employment travelling to Australia in 1883 as the first manager of Lysaght Bros. wire netting factory at Five Dock on the southern shore of the Parramatta River (p. 35). Having failed to interest John Lysaght in the notion of manufacturing iron in Australia, Sandford resigned from the company in around June 1886 to take over the management of the Lithgow Works (founded in 1874), which was then producing rails and permanent way spikes.

Sandford did not abandon the idea of co-operation with Lysaghts and wrote in April 1906 to H.R. Lysaght to suggest that they might wish 'to form an alliance for our mutual advantage'. When the cost of the blast furnace rose beyond the estimate the company reached its overdraft limit, prompting Sandford to issue a prospectus. Negotiations with both Thomas Davey and H.R. Lysaght continued and on 7 June 1907 a draft agreement was drawn up whereby Lysaghts would purchase shares to the value of not less than £10,000 in Wm. Sandford Ltd in return for which the company was to appoint two Lysaght executives as directors. Sandford was to set up a separate business which undertook not to make iron or steel in Australia, or to acquire an interest in any company in this business, for ten years. John Lysaght, however, was to be allowed to manufacture in Australia or acquire a holding in a firm producing black or galvanised sheet, provided that the billets or other raw material were supplied by Wm. Sandford Ltd. The proposals were rejected by Sandford, and Lysaghts withdrew, precipitating the sale of the Lithgow Works to G. & C. Hoskins in December 1907. Assisted by the Commonwealth Bounties Bill of 1909, the enterprise returned to profitability, continuing in operation until 1928 when re-formed as the Australian Iron & Steel Co.; it moved to Port Kembla (p. 333), and was known as Hoskins Kembla Works.

Given the specialised nature of sheet rolling and galvanising and the strong demand for steel products of a less sophisticated nature, the Lithgow Works showed no signs during the decade preceding the Great War of expanding their operations to compete overtly with Lysaghts.[15] In effect, the rolling of sheet on a large scale could only become a profitable business when Australia possessed its first integrated steelworks.[16] Rumours spread in late 1911 that The Broken Hill Proprietory Co. (BHP), a mining enterprise (silver, lead and zinc) incorporated in Victoria with smelting interests at Port Pirie, South Australia, were considering laying down blast furnaces and steel-making plant ultimately with a view to rolling and galvanising sheet.[17]

LYSAGHTS' FIRST VENTURE: THE NEWCASTLE WORKS

During 1913, BHP decided to put into effect their plans for building an integrated iron and steelworks. The election of a Labour Government in Australia in the autumn of 1914 was a fillip to BHP as the party was known to favour the imposition of protective duties to encourage domestic industry. The first blast furnace was blown during March 1915, and the works officially opened on 2 June.[18] Situated beside the Hunter River at Newcastle, NSW, shipments of iron ore could be conveniently delivered and bulky consignments despatched.

As early as September 1899 H.R. Lysaght, then recently appointed manager of Lysaghts' NSW office, had been engaged in informal discussions to select a site in the Hunter Valley for a galvanising and rolling works. Writing to his superior, Thomas Davey, he observed

> Mr Capper, in the course of conversation, mentioned that if ever it was necessary for us, driving to Federation, to manufacture out here, he considered Greta [a mining township] would be the most suitable place to put down a works. It is on the Northern [Railway] line, 15 miles from Maitland and 33 miles from Newcastle. Coal of

the finest quality is abundant and land is cheap. He said that he knew of 280 acres of land there, with a coal mine upon it, which he believed could . . . be bought for a mere song.[19]

In the event Federation in 1901 did not produce a concerted call for indigenous manufacture.

However, as a defensive measure, early in 1915 H.R. Lysaght purchased twenty-four acres of land (at £100 per acre) also beside the Hunter River at Newcastle, should it prove necessary to establish rolling mills and galvanising pots in competition with BHP.[20] The war had severely interrupted supplies of sheet to Australia and driven up the price of imported galvanised iron to £100 a ton.[21] Since the country possessed ample supplies of its own iron ore and coal, the view developed that the nation should never again allow itself to be dependent upon supplies from abroad. Accordingly in July 1915, the Federal Government approached H.R. Lysaght, then managing director of Lysaght's Galvanised Iron Pty, to suggest that they consider manufacturing in Australia. As a consequence, he travelled to Britain to discuss the matter with the full board in December 1916.[22] With the threat hanging over them that BHP would extend their rolling operations to include black sheets should Lysaghts insist on importing all their products, the directors concluded in principle that it 'was desirable that John Lysaght Ltd. should start manufacturing in Australia'.[23] W.R. Lysaght added that in a recent interview, G.D. Delprat, the general manager,[24] had indicated that BHP would be prepared to supply them with sheet bar and so long as Lysaghts obtained their supplies from them, the former also agreed not to roll sheet themselves. Even if the enterprise were initially undertaken at a loss, Lysaghts believed that its value from 'an advertisement and insurance point of view' was sufficient justification, adding that financial success was an 'improbability'.[25]

However, before committing the company to such a large capital expenditure, H.R. Lysaght had an interview with the Federal Minister for Customs to obtain an assurance that the embryonic industry would be protected by a tariff or bounty when an end to the war brought prices down.[26] In 1917, W.M. Hughes, the Prime Minister, made a public announcement that this assistance would be provided (and presumably the corresponding threat existed that should Lysaghts not proceed to invest in plant there, a protective wall would be erected to hinder the sales of British-made galvanised sheet).[27] Upon the news being cabled to Bristol, the board authorised the project. In the following year the head office was moved from Melbourne to Sydney to be closer to the planned manufacturing plant, and the name of the company changed to John Lysaght (Australia) Ltd. to reflect this broader strategy. Thomas Davey having resigned in his mid-eighties, H.R. Lysaght was appointed the first chairman.

In 1918 F. Lightfoot Walker, an engineer, who had been employed by

Lysaghts in the UK but transferred to Australia in 1913, proceeded to Newcastle to supervise the preparation of the site.[28] Most of the twenty-four, riparian acres were swampy, the only building being a two-roomed cottage, which was used as the works office for several years, just as farm buildings at Newport had become the office for the Orb rolling mills. To raise the level of the land, four feet of sand was pumped from the riverbed. To provide stability, over 1,000 piles of turpentine timber were driven to a depth of twenty feet into the ground. The first buildings, constructed from 2,000 tons of steel provided by BHP, and covered with galvanised sheet supplied by the Bristol works, housed four rolling mills, together with coal-fired re-heating furnaces, one pickling machine and two galvanising pots.[29] In 1919 Alfred Tysoe, chief constructional engineer at the Orb Works, arrived to supervise the completion of the buildings and installation of plant and machinery. Wherever possible, local materials were used: mill housings, coupling boxes and spindles, iron casings for mill furnaces, floor plates and other equipment were produced in Newcastle, mainly by BHP and Goninans, though the 1,300 h.p. electric mill motors had to be imported from England by Westinghouse.

While construction proceeded at Newcastle, skilled workmen from the British company were recruited in order to fill key positions and in due course pass on their experience. In January 1921 fifty-five sheet workers from Newport, most of them recently returned from the armed forces, sailed on the *Themistocles* with their wives and families.[30] Shortly afterwards, they were followed by twenty-seven galvanisers from Bristol and a further twenty men from Newport on the *Demosthenes*. About 70 brick cottages in the suburb of Mayfield, about a mile from the works, had been erected to house the married men and their families, with the option of rental or purchase. The furniture which had been provided could be bought, exchanged or rejected as the inhabitants pleased. When a major phase of extensions to the works was initiated in 1928–29, it proved necessary to gather a further group of trained employees from Britain, there being skilled labour shortages in Australia.[31]

On completion in April 1921, when the first sheets were rolled, the works had cost £300,000 to construct.[32] Outputs from the rolling mills for the month of December 1921 were 1,079 tons, all of which was galvanised, which together with some imported black sheet contributed to a total of 1,126 tons of galvanised sheet.[33] For 1923 the annual totals were 11,971 and 12,827 tons respectively (Table 10.2).[34] From about 1924 the market for black (or uncoated) sheet expanded and was reflected in a widening gap between total tonnages rolled and galvanised; the difference, very approximately, represented the quantity sold as black sheet.

Despite the ability of the Newcastle Works to come on stream swiftly and turn out a quality product, its early years were not greeted with commercial success. In January 1922 the mills were reported as running at a loss and a reduction in wages was ordered.[35] The workforce came out on strike and in March the works closed temporarily.[36] Manpower shortages had resulted in Australian rates of pay being comparatively high, and in August 1922 Lysaghts began to negotiate a new scale for Newcastle employees based upon, and fluctuating with, the minimum wage in Australia.[37] Eventually an agreement was reached in February 1923, but because of the industrial dispute only thirteen weeks had been worked during 1922.

Reflecting the fall which had taken place in prices and in an attempt to stimulate an economic revival, the Federal Government reduced the import tariff for sheet exported from Britain to £1 per ton from £3 12s. in September 1922, and for other nations to £1 10s from £5 10s.[38] In addition, a bounty of 52s per ton was introduced for locally made galvanised iron. By the end of 1923 a total of around 24,000 tons of

Table 10.2   Output from Newcastle works, 1923–43 (tons)

Year	Total output of rolling mills	Galvanised sheet	Zincanneal	Terne plate[a]	Black or uncoated sheet (approximate by difference)
1923	11,971	12,827	—	—	—
1924	15,956	15,587	—	—	400
1925	20,468	19,221	—	—	1,300
1926	25,138	24,065	—	—	1,100
1927	25,760	24,328	—	—	1,400
1928	26,077	24,238	—	—	1,800
1929	27,255	27,882	—	—	—
1930	35,984	32,429	—	—	3,500
1931	27,829	28,506	—	—	—
1932	58,479	55,815	—	—	2,800
1933	69,305	67,296	—	—	2,000
1934	66,865	69,914	—	—	—
1935	90,243	80,349	—	—	9,900
1936	103,613	86,664	—	—	16,950
1937	124,389	104,141	748	—	19,500
1938	99,438	78,543	1,739	—	20,150
1939	166,350	148,448	2,016	214	15,650
1940	138,025	102,739	4,358	2,011	28,900
1941	151,067[b]	85,251[c]	6,912[c]	2,840[c]	32,427
1942	193,845[b]	46,951[c]	8,736[c]	7,676[c]	93,440
1943	196,161[b]	36,043[c]	2,526[c]	4,488[c]	142,000

Notes: [a] Terne plate is sheet coated with an alloy which chiefly consists of lead and tin.
[b] Including bullet-proof plate, helmet steel and electrical steel sheets.
[c] For military projects only.

Source: BHP Central Products Division, Central Library, NSW, D1 (C), 'Works' Company History', 13 December 1945.

sheet had been produced by the Newcastle Works and although its annual capacity had risen to around 13,000 tons, this was still well below the Australian national demand, some 100,000 tons still being imported.[39] On 10 January 1924 the Prime Minister, Stanley Melbourne Bruce, met D.C. Lysaght[40] to assure him that the Federal Government would protect the sheet industry adequately should Lysaghts agree to proceed with extensions to the Newcastle plant.[41] Having obtained this promise, the UK board authorised the expenditure of £30,000 on the installation of two extra mills and a further galvanising pot.[42] This raised the works' capacity to around 20,000 tons a year, a mere 20 per cent of the country's consumption. During 1926 the seventh mill was laid down and the eighth was ready by the following year. The galvanising and packing shops were extended, which resulted in the mill motor, annealing furnace and pickling machine all operating at maximum capacity.[43] If output were to be increased any further then much of the plant needed to be duplicated.

The decision whether to supply the bulk of Australia's needs from the UK or to extend the Newcastle Works and increase domestic output was crucially determined by the level of subsidy offered by the Federal Government. In September 1924, for example, the Lysaght board calculated that the cost advantage obtained by the Newcastle Works over sheet imported from Britain was a mere 5s per ton which was insufficient without further protection to allow the mills to compete with exports beyond the boundaries of New South Wales owing to the costs of transporting orders within the continent.[44] In October 1926 while S.M. Bruce was on a visit to the UK, Lord Buckland, Sir John Field Beale, W.R., D.C. and H.R. Lysaght arranged to see him at the Savoy Hotel to ask for higher tariffs.[45] In the event, their request was refused, it being in the interests of the Australian economy to maintain the highly competitive market which then existed for galvanised sheet.[46]

Negotiations with the Australian government continued and on 1 January 1928 it was announced that rather than raise import duties, the bounty on domestically produced sheet would be increased from 52s to 72s per ton.[47] The grant of this incentive coincided with a decision by Lysaghts to undertake major extensions to the Newcastle Works. Discussions had also been held with BHP to obtain their assurance that they would supply the increased volume of steel bars which these developments would entail. To aid co-operation between the two companies, Essington Lewis, chairman of BHP, was elected to the board of Lysaghts' Newcastle Works Ltd,[48] and from 1928 to 1940 H.R. Lysaght served as a director of BHP, W.R. Lysaght being a member of BHP's London board. Alfred Tysoe travelled from Britain a second time to supervise the lengthening of the mill building and the extension of the galvanising shop. A further eight mills were laid down bringing the total to sixteen (capable of supplying 60 per cent of the nation's galvanised sheet)[49] and ten galvanising pots.[50] Yet the investment could not have been worse timed. Before the new plant could

Figure 14 Newcastle and Port Kembla Works, Annual Coated Sheet Production compared with Imports, 1920–45

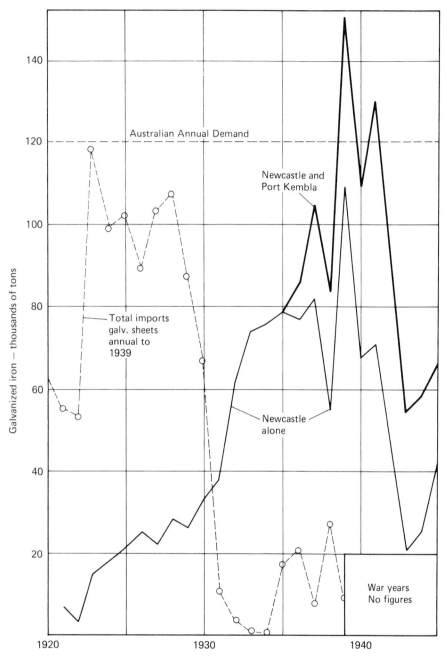

come into operation as planned in 1930, the depression hit the Australian economy hard. After ten years' struggle to meet continuously rising demand, in 1931 the Newcastle Works ran at 40 per cent capacity. Prices fell dramatically. In the spring of 1930, Newcastle Works reported a profit of only 5s per ton on their 'Orb' or their premium brand, while second quality sheet was sold at cost price.[51]

112   The manual mills at Newcastle Works in the early 1930s. The drive wheels (middle ground) were the largest in the southern hemisphere at the time (*BHP Steel*).

During the depression, in an attempt to protect Lysaghts against cheap imports, the Australian government raised the bounty from 72s to 90s a ton in January 1930.[52] The company had earlier been under the impression that the subsidy was to have been abandoned and the existing tariff of £1 per ton be increased to £5 10s.[53] Although this would have resulted in the company making a straight gain of 12s per ton if outputs remained constant, it might, in a period of falling demand, have encouraged Lysaghts simply to increase their prices (knowing that the new duty provided sound protection) or reduce output in an attempt to cut costs. The government, whose principal

Table 10.3   Galvanised sheet in Australia, 1923–31 (000 tons)

Years	Domestic production	Imports	Consumption	% Production to consumption
1923–24	16.2	99.5	115.7	14.1
1924–25	17.1	102.5	119.6	14.3
1925–26	18.9	89.4	108.3	17.5
1926–27	26.1	103.4	129.5	20.2
1927–28	22.9	107.4	130.3	17.5
1928–29	28.5	87.4	115.9	24.5
1929–30	24.1	67.1	91.2	26.5
1930–31	22.0	10.3	32.3	68.0

Source: Nancy Windett, *Australia as Producer and Trader, 1920–32*, Oxford (1933), p. 170.

concern was to raise the level of economic activity, preferred to provide incentives to raise manufacturing activity. However, because of the high-cost structure of the Australian industry and the fall in world prices, steel products could be imported more cheaply than the home product could be manufactured even when subsidised to the level of £4 10s. The Hon. F.M. Forde, the Acting Minister for Trade and Customs, speaking in the House of Representatives, recalled the pressure which the Hughes government had exerted on Lysaghts during the Great War to establish a galvanised sheet plant at Newcastle and concluded that the company 'has every reason to assume that a very definite obligation devolves upon the Commonwealth to ensure that its manufactures are adequately protected against competition'.[54] Accordingly, in June 1930 20s was taken off the bounty and placed on the duty, while in July the tariff rose by 2.5 per cent and the subsidy fell by 7s, followed by an increment of 4 per cent and reduction of 4s respectively in November.[55] These revisions weighed the balance substantially in favour of Australian-produced sheet and the UK board concluded 'that it would probably be necessary to manufacture at Newcastle the whole of the Australian requirements'.[56] Imports of galvanised iron by all companies totalled a mere 33,000 tons in 1930, the lowest figure (excluding the war years) since 1908.[57] By December 1930 exporters found themselves virtually excluded from the Australian market.[58]

The situation worsened during 1931 when Newcastle Works, operating at only 36 per cent of its capacity, turned out 27,829 tons of sheet.[59] The company's total sales in Australia reached a mere 37,500 tons, which suggested that only 9,700 tons had been exported from the Orb Works at Newport.[60] Although a small figure it compared creditably with the 886 tons that all other makers had succeeded in selling overseas. In part, this was explained by the differential duties which favoured British manufacturers, being £5 10s on UK imports and £6 10s rising to £7 10s on those from other nations. Early in 1932 the Federal Parliament, accepting the recommendations of the Tariff Board, agreed to leave these rates in force for the foreseeable future. Since the company had now achieved a virtual monopoly over the Australian market, its future seemed to be a profitable one. For in exchange for maintaining a high tariff wall, Lysaghts had reduced the price of their 'Orb' sheet by £1 to £26 10s 0d per ton, which in view of the anticipated rise in output, would, they believed, produce a profit of about £1 a ton, and £2 a ton on black sheet.[61] Their forecasts proved reasonably accurate as output for 1932 rose to 58,479 tons (about 82 per cent of capacity) and the average profit on 'Orb' sheet, allowing for depreciation and interest on capital, was approximately 15s.[62]

During 1933, Nos. 15 and 16 mills at Newcastle Works came into operation and from February the plant was at full capacity, having achieved the size that had been planned in 1921.[63] So long as protection remained in force, profitability was assured. Because the success of the enterprise was so crucially reliant upon government favour, decisions about pricing were effectively taken from the management's hands and passed to the Minister for Customs. In the spring of 1933, for example, the latter suggested that the company reduce their selling price by 10s a ton.[64] This they estimated would trim profits by only 3s 7d per ton as the basic wage had been cut by 1s 6d a week and the sum that they paid BHP for bars automatically followed a drop in the price of galvanised sheet. If the 'Orb' product sold at £24 10s per ton then on this new basis Lysaghts' profit was estimated at £2 8s a ton, subject to a deduction of £1 15s for depreciation, exchange rates and taxation.

Crucial to the commercial prosperity of Lysaghts was their relationship with BHP. In August 1921 they had signed a twenty-year agreement by which BHP undertook not to engage in the manufacture of galvanised iron in competition with Lysaghts so long as the latter purchased their entire supply of steel bar from the former. That BHP never sought to transgress or re-negotiate its terms owed much to the relationship forged between Essington Lewis and H.R. Lysaght. When the arrangement came to be renewed after the Second World War, E.C. Lysaght travelled to Australia as GKN's representative in what was believed to be the difficult task of obtaining an extension. Lysaght discovered to his surprise that Lewis was happy to renew the terms of the agreement without exerting undue pressure.

Following the example of the Orb Works where a mechanised hot rolling had been introduced in 1932–33 (p. 47), it was decided to initiate a programme of modernisation. In 1934, at a cost of £120,000, the works' first mechanical finishing mill (with the capacity of four hand mills) was laid down and came into production in the following year.[65] The unit proved to be so successful that a second was installed in 1936, costing only a further £30,000.[66] To supply both of them, a 3-high roughing mill, made by Macintosh Hemphill, was purchased from the United States.[67] At the same time, the galvanising plant was modernised, the baths being gas rather than coke-fired. Outputs (Table 10.2) increased dramatically, with over 100,000 tons being rolled in 1936 and 86,700 tons of galvanised sheet produced. By September of the following year, Lysaghts could report that no galvanised sheet was being imported and that the entire trade was in the hands of their Australian subsidiary.[68]

From the initial 102 workmen who travelled from Britain to set up the Newcastle Works, the numbers grew rapidly as operations extended. Recruitment was from the local population and newly arrived immigrants. By 1929, 550 men were employed[69] and as a result of the duplication of 1928–32, the numbers exceeded 1,000.[70] Industrial relations appear to have been relatively trouble free apart from the strikes in 1922 (p. 327), 1934 and that in January 1938 which lasted for six months.[71] The nature of the dispute was not recorded, though its protracted length suggested that it was about wage rates. Shortages of labour in Australia had strengthened the trade union's hand and

113 The 3-high Macintosh Hemphill mill installed at Newcastle in 1936 as part of a programme of progressive mechanisation (*BHP Steel*).

helped to earn employees comparatively high sums. During the dispute the Australian government authorised Lysaghts to import galvanised sheet from Britain, free of duty and primage, up to a total of 25,000 tons.[72] The sheet, supplied from the Orb Works, was to sell at £24 10s a ton which with the cost of shipping would result in a small loss. John Lysaght (Australia) Ltd felt that it was better to bear a short term financial penalty than to lose the goodwill of customers established over decades.

THE SPRINGHILL WORKS AND CRM WORKS, PORT KEMBLA

Reference has been made to the Lithgow Iron Works which in 1928 transferred to a site at Port Kembla where they laid down a steelworks. In 1933 the Australian Iron & Steel Co. Ltd (AI&S), the company's new name, decided to embark on the manufacture of sheet in an attempt to revitalise their fortunes after the depression. A manager travelled to America to purchase plant and engage a few key workers. Construction started in 1934 and a three-high rolling mill, two-high finishing mill, six annealing furnaces and two galvanising pots were installed.[73] Rolling began in May 1935 but AI&S experienced considerable trouble in the operation of their plant and outputs remained far below expectation.[74] After a major breakdown in the mill section in November 1935, Lysaghts generously offered to assist and Tom Hewitt, assistant mill manager at Newcastle, spent several weeks at Port Kembla in order to help AI&S resume production.[75] In the autumn of 1935 BHP acquired all the ordinary shares in the company[76] and offered to sell Lysaghts the sheet mill and galvanising plant if the latter then agreed to double its capacity so that the sheet bar producing facilities of the former AI&S Works could be worked at full output.[77] The transfer of ownership was concluded in March 1936.[78] It would have been difficult for BHP to have operated the works as they stood being party to an agreement with Lysaghts not to manufacture galvanised iron themselves.

Because no opportunity existed to extend the former AI&S site at Port Kembla, Lysaghts acquired land nearby on which to build a new works of double the capacity. In the meantime, they began operating the AI&S plant, achieving an output of 10,000 tons in 1936 and 22,000 tons in 1937.[79] Construction began at the Port Kembla site in 1937 (to be called the Springhill Works), and by the following year had progressed sufficiently for the transfer of plant and machinery from AI&S. In April 1938, for example, galvanising began at Springhill Works, to be followed by annealing in January 1939, and while hot rolling on the Lewis and No. 1 Finishing mills started at the same time, the seven stand Tandem mill did not come into full production until September 1939.[80] The depreciated mills and two galvanising pots formerly belonging to AI&S had been valued at £50,000,[81] and the cost, including land for the new works and a portion of the railway station (erected at Lysaghts's request), amounted to £171,000,[82] while the final cost of the Springhill Works amounted to £870,000.[83]

Because the Newcastle Works had grown in stages, responding to the vicissitudes of the market, it had the ability to specialise and deal with a considerable variety of widths, gauges, coatings and grades of steel. The modern mechanised Springhill Works could operate at maximum efficiency only when able to have long runs of set requirements. Accordingly, it became the mass producer, while Newcastle with its manual mills and flexibility concentrated on smaller and less common orders.[84]

The subsequent success of the Springhill Works owed much to the expertise in sheet rolling which had been acquired both at Orb Works in Newport and at Newcastle, NSW. This contributed to the design of the Port Kembla plant, which was supervised by Albert Bear, chief engineer of Newcastle Works, but also determined the staffing of the new enterprise. Key positions were filled from Newcastle Works including the manager (P.K. Parbury) and the three mill foreman, one for each shift (E. Stevens, H. Whittle and W. Matthews).[85] Thus, a fund of skill and experience which had been transferred on two occasions from

Newport (in 1930 a further 24 men emigrated from South Wales), found its way to the latest of the Lysaght mills.

In the spring of 1936 the American Rolling Mills Co. (Armco) applied to the Australian Minister of Customs for permission to import steel strip duty free to be rolled into automobile sheet. Whilst a decision was pending, H.R. Lysaght was requested by the UK board to announce the company's intention to erect the necessary plant for the production of high-grade sheet.[86] In the meantime, Lysaghts, together with Essington Lewis, a director of BHP, had met representatives of Armco to discuss whether a joint venture might be attempted. In October agreement was reached,[87] and the Commonwealth Rolling Mills Pty Ltd was formed, the share capital being subscribed on a fifty-fifty basis by Lysaghts and Armco.[88] Construction on a site at Port Kembla, close to the Springhill Works, started in 1938,[89] the original cost of the plant and buildings being £650,000.[90] The CRM Works, designed with an annual capacity of 30,000 tons, began operating in February 1939.[91]

MANAGERS AND MANAGEMENT

Much of the credit for the establishment of a highly successful manufacturing enterprise in Australia was owed to Herbert Royse Lysaght (1862–1940), the son of Thomas R. Lysaght (1828–90), an elder brother of John who founded the galvanising business. 'H.R.', having quarrelled with his uncle, originally emigrated to Australia to work for Lysaght Bros. & Co., wire-netting makers and galvanised sheet importers, but left them after a dispute to join the Sydney branch of the Commercial Banking Company of Australia.[92] S.R. Lysaght, his elder brother and a director of the Bristol holding company, recruited him in 1899 as the NSW manager for their distribution and sales outlet. A popular and liked man, he was responsible for persuading the UK board of the wisdom of rolling and galvanising in Australia. When Thomas Davey retired in 1917, he was appointed chairman and managing director of John Lysaght (Australia) Ltd and moved the head office from Melbourne to Sydney. Lysaght continued in these posts until June 1930 when ill-health forced him to take semi-retirement. A non-executive director of BHP (1928–40), he also joined the boards of the Australian Iron & Steel Co., Anthony Hodern & Sons, and Nettlefolds Pty. Lysaght died in June 1940, having seen an embryonic enterprise become one of the major industrial companies of Australia.

F. Lightfoot Walker took over a number of Lysaght's duties, having been appointed general manager of Newcastle Works and deputy managing director of John Lysaght (Australia) Ltd in July 1930. On his death in March 1936, a management committee was formed, and in January 1937 R.G.C. Parry-Okeden became general manager of Newcastle Works with responsibility for the new enterprise at Port Kembla.[93] Parry-Okeden had joined Lysaghts in January 1920 and, having worked both in Bristol and Newport, decided that prospects for promotion were greater in Australia, emigrating there in 1923.[94] On the death of H.R. Lysaght the chairmanship and post of managing director of John Lysaght (Australia) Pty. passed to C.E. Davey, while Parry-Okeden became chairman and managing director of Lysaght's Newcastle Works Pty.[95] D. Royse Lysaght, son of H.R., was elected to the Lysaght (Australia) board at the same time.[96] Although a sheep farmer with no experience of industry, D.R. Lysaght had been approached by Parry-Okeden and offered a temporary job with the company. When the former pointed out his lack of qualifications, Parry-Okeden conceded that it was his name that he wished to acquire for the board. Lysaght accepted and eventually became deputy chairman of the company.[97] V.A. Wardell had been made acting general manager at Newcastle in January 1937, but during the Second World War transferred to Spring-hill where he served as acting manager[98] in the absence of P.K. Parbury who was a Lt. Colonel in the infantry. Wardell, having read chemistry, worked as research superintendent at Newcastle during the thirties and was responsible for the introduction of 'Red Orb' for roofing, the use of inhibitors in pickling (an innovation which generated large economies by preventing iron loss) and the production of zincanneal.

In a sense, the managerial problems faced by John Lysaght (Australia) Pty. were complicated by having to consider the views of two major companies. On the one hand they remained a subsidiary of John Lysaght, and though the UK board did not interfere in the daily running of the works, questions of capital expenditure, the appointment of senior members of staff, and negotiations with the Australian government were all subject to its approval. Indeed, since John Lysaght Ltd was itself a subsidiary of GKN, sanction had ultimately to be sought from the latter's board. A glimpse at the potential complexity of this organisational arrangement can be seen in April 1924 when T.S. Peacock, then managing director of GKN, returned to England from a visit to Australia where he had been investigating the market for nuts, bolts and woodscrews. His presentation to the parent board included a reference to the excellence of the Lysaght sales and distribution network and 'to the desirability of closer combination and amalgamation between the two concerns'.[99] Nevertheless, GKN devolved a considerable amount of authority to John Lysaght (Australia) Pty., granting them considerable freedom to make operational decisions.

The nature of the relationship between John Lysaght (Australia) Pty. and their supplier BHP was a complex one. Since the latter were the only steelmakers in Australia capable of satisfying their requirements for sheet bar, they occupied a position of relative strength and hence the need, on Lysaght's part, for long-term trading agreements. The arrangement concluded in 1921, by which BHP undertook not to roll or galvanise sheet for a period of twenty years was honoured in 1935 when they sold the AI&S sheet-rolling and galvanising plant without hesitation to Lysaghts. The two companies worked closely together throughout the interwar period. In 1928, for example, when Lysaghts decided to lay down a further four mills at Newcastle that Essington Lewis, general manager of BHP's steelworks from 1921 and a director from 1926,[100] was appointed to the board of the works.[101] Detailed agreements were concluded between the two companies concerning price and delivery requirements. In 1921, for example, sheet bars supplied to Newcastle Works by BHP were to be purchased at one-third of the final sale price of the sheet.[102] BHP derived considerable advantages from the trading agreement from Lysaghts: the latter were their biggest customer and the low carbon steel that they consumed was easy to make providing them with regular and reliable orders; Lysaght incurred the supply and distribution costs of the product, leaving BHP to concentrate upon the early stages of manufacture. In 1930 Lysaghts calculated that they could have imported sheet bar from Britain more cheaply than BHP's price[103] and while this situation may not have always endured it gave the former a measure of bargaining power. Thus, throughout the 1920s and 1930s it remained in the interests of the two companies to operate in concert and the relationship worked well, but given the monopolistic position of BHP, the supplier, Lysaghts would always remain anxious when trading agreements required renewal.

THE SECOND WORLD WAR

As the prospect of war grew more certain early in 1939, the Australian works of John Lysaght were asked to assist in the production of galvanised sheet for air-raid shelters. With a weekly output of 500–1,000 tons, they eventually exported 41,000 tons of sheet during 1939, which was made into 125,000 shelters, the final shipments being despatched just after the hostilities were declared.[104]

Heavy restrictions imposed on the use of zinc, which was required in large quantities for war material, resulted in severe controls being placed on Lysaghts' ability to make galvanised sheet. By 1943 their output (36,043 tons) was less than one-third of the 1939 figure (148,448 tons). Nevertheless, a continuous and increasing demand for black sheets, needed in the war effort, helped to maintain output from the works' rolling mills. In 1940–41, for example, 10,000 tons of galvanised iron and 2,500 tons of black sheet and roofing ternes were sent to Egypt for use by the Australian Infantry Forces (2nd AIF) in the Middle East. The Lewis mill, which had originally been moved from the former AI&S Works to Springhill was transferred to Newcastle to replace two manual mills and raised the rolling capacity of the works, particularly for the heavier sheets and plates. It began operation in April 1941 and contributed to that year's record production of black sheets (133,000 tons), which was then used for the manufacture of various items such as ammunition boxes, jerricans, depth charges, aerial torpedoes, gun carriages, land mines, and small metal components needed in vehicles, ships and aircraft.

In addition, developmental work was undertaken on steels that had not hitherto been rolled into sheet in Australia: electrical steels for dynamos, motors and transformers, helmet steel, and special steels for aircraft.[105] As the war advanced it became clear that the country's ability to produce armour-plate was inadequate. BHP experimented with the manufacture of these new steels, which required less alloying elements as these were difficult to obtain in Australia. The manual mill at Newcastle Works was employed until the Lewis mill was installed and modified to roll large plates up to 11 mm thick. The laboratory staff of Newcastle, led by Mr Jack Hawkins, technical superintendent, re-fined the heat treatments which the metal required.[106] Once these new techniques had been mastered, rolling and annealing proved to be highly successful, and around 25,000 tons of ABP 3 (bullet-proof plate) were turned out by the Newcastle Works. Further, about 500 tons of non-magnetic armour was rolled for the Navy, using the same plant and steel made in electric furnaces by the Commonwealth Steel Co., a subsidiary of BHP, at Waratah, about two miles from Newcastle Works. The production and rolling of a novel type of weldable bullet-proof steel was a major achievement by Australian industry.

In the galvanising shop six of the pots were shut down owing to the shortages of zinc. The equipment was dismantled to provide space for other operations. Twenty-three portable Bellman hangars for aircraft were manufactured, while sheets for a hundred more assemblies of a similar type were cut, punched and slotted ready for construction.[107]

One important manufacturing enterprise at Port Kembla was entirely fortuitous in its origins. Vincent Wardell, then acting manager of the Springhill Works, stumbled upon a sugar-bag lying against a low wall near his garage in Wollongong, and was surprised to discover that it contained a submachine gun.[108] He returned it to the owner, Evelyn Owen, the son of a local solicitor, who had invented the .22-inch calibre model but had been unable to interest the ordnance department in its production.[109] Owen had enlisted in the Australian Infantry Forces and in September 1940 was on the point of leaving for military service in the Middle East. After a final burst from his prototype, aimed out to sea from the Wollongong beach, he left it in a sugar bag outside the flat of his neighbour. Wardell, realising that the sub-machine gun could be made more easily and cheaply than a standard rifle for military service, took the matter up with Essington Lewis, who promptly sent Owen to see Captain C.M. Dyer, secretary of the Army Central Inventions Board. Dyer then approached Wardell's brother, G.S. Wardell (chief engineer of the Springhill Works), to ask him unofficially to manufac-ture two further models of the gun. With Owen granted leave, .32-inch and .45-inch calibre versions were assembled and subjected to firing trials.[110] In the belief that American and British designs were greatly superior, it was reluctantly compared with other sub-machine guns, the Thompson and the Sten, and out-performed them under extreme conditions.[111] As a result, [Sir] Percy Spender, Minister for the Army, ordered 2,000 Owen guns from Lysaght in November 1941.[112] After unconscionable delays and the ill-advised decision to order 100 guns of 0.38in calibre, the Army finally decided upon a 9mm calibre weapon.

After considerable difficulties in obtaining the necessary machine tools, the production of the original order for 2,000 guns was completed at the beginning of July 1942.[113] An annexe was built at Port Kembla and the unused space in the Newcastle galvanised iron warehouse was turned into a machine shop and heat treatment plant. A peak production figure of 2,700 guns a month was reached and a total output of 45,447 weapons (at about £10 each) supplied with over half a million magazines.[114] The project employed about 105 workers at Port Kembla of whom 85 were females, together with a further 30 at Newcastle.

The spinner shop, erected in 1943 with expertise acquired from Sankeys at Hadley Castle, manufactured the streamlined cowlings for aircraft propeller hubs. Made from a spun aluminium sheet, and designed to rotate at the same speed as the propeller, spinners required to be balanced to fine limits of accuracy.[115] Altogether, around 900 were made for the Beaufort and Lincoln bomber and the Mosquito fighter. Almost all the work was carried out by locally recruited women. The superintendent of this project was E.B. Gosse, who had originally worked for BHP before joining the staff of Lysaghts' Newcastle Works in about 1938, and ultimately became chairman of John Lysaght (Australia) Pty. After the war the spinner shop was used as a sports and recreation centre until 1950 when it was commissioned as the press shop and tool room for Joseph Sankey (Australia) Pty., manufacturers of electrical laminations.

SUMMARY

By 1945, when the Second World War ended, John Lysaght (Australia) Pty. had established itself as a major manufacturing enterprise. In 1919, although work had commenced in laying down rolling mills and galvanising pots at Newcastle, the company remained in essence an importing and distribution business. With a network of offices and warehouses throughout Australia, it was able to supply the nation's needs by regular shipments from Britain. The threat of domestic production by BHP and the guarantee of protection through tariffs and bounties were sufficient to persuade the UK board that progressive investment in capital-intensive plant was a sound strategy. Under the executive authority of H.R. Lysaght, the company expanded and flourished such that by the mid-1930s Lysaghts were able to satisfy the entire Australian demand from their works at Newcastle and later Port Kembla. It probably remained the case, however, that had Lysaghts been permitted to continue supplying the Australian market from

Newport and Bristol throughout the interwar period, then their profits would have been greater as their UK plant was under-employed for much of the time and the investment required to raise exports from Britain would have been considerably less than that needed to erect new works on greenfield sites overseas. Yet the exigencies of the political and economic situation could not be ignored and if Lysaghts wished to retain these important Australian customers, then they had to bow to the wishes of the Federal Government.

References

1. The Australian Tariff Board's Report on Galvanised Iron (1932), quoted from *Lysaght's Newcastle Works Pty. Ltd.* (*c.* 1939), p. 9.
2. *The Lysaght Century 1857–1957*, Bristol (1957), p. 22.
3. John Lysaght Minute Book, Vol. 1 (1901–1909).
4. *The Lysaght Venture*, Sydney (1955), p. 2; *Lysaght's Silver Jubilee 1921–1946*, Sydney (1946), p. 18.
5. Neil Hood and Stephen Young, *The Economics of Multinational Enterprise*, London (1979), pp. 44–84; Peter J. Buckley and Mark Casson, *The Economic Theory of the Multinational Enterprise*, London (1985), pp. 60–98.
6. Alfred D. Chandler, *Economic History Review*, Vol. XXXIII (1980), 'The Growth of the Transnational Industrial Firm in the United States and the United Kingdom: A Comparative Analysis', p. 401.
7. C.B. Schedvin, *Australian Economic Review*, Vol. X (1970), 'Rabbits and Industrial Development: Lysaght Brothers & Co. Pty Ltd, 1884–1929', p. 28.
8. Lysaght Minute Book, Vol. 1, op. cit., 20 August 1907, pp. 256–7.
9. Ibid., 26 September 1907, pp. 259–60.
10. Ibid., 17 December 1907, pp. 271–2.
11. Lysaght Minute Book, Vol. 2, op. cit., 16 July 1912, p. 123.
12. Ibid., 21 June 1920, p. 21.
13. 'The Evolution of the Iron Industry in Australia' (typescript, June 1962), p. 1.
14. Ibid.
15. Lysaght Minute Book, Vol. 2, op. cit., 16 July 1912, p. 123.
16. *Seventy Five Years of BHP, Development in Industry*, Victoria, Australia [*c.* 1960], pp. 15–16.
17. Lysaght Minute Book, Vol. 2, op. cit., 21 November 1911, p. 81.
18. *BHP Seventy-Five Years*, op. cit., p. 18.
19. BHPL, Letter H.R. Lysaght to Thomas Davey, 4 September 1899.
20. Lysaght Minute Book, Vol. 2, op. cit., 16 February 1915, p. 239; Letter re purchase of land at Newcastle to A.A. Rankin, Solicitor, from Creer & Berkeley, 18 November 1914.
21. BHP, Coated Products Division, Central Library, Port Kembla (BHPL), D1(b) 'Some Facts in Connection with the Establishment of the Galvanized Iron Industry in Australia' (typescript, *c.* 1930).
22. Lysaght Minute Book, Vol. 2, op. cit., 21 December 1916, p. 333.
23. Ibid., 19 January 1917, p. 337.
24. *Seventy Five Years of BHP*, op. cit., p. 18.
25. Ibid.

26. Until then galvanised sheet carried a duty in only a few states; Neville R. Wills, *Economic Development of the Australian Iron and Steel Industry*, (1948), p. 30.

27. *Lysaght Venture*, op. cit., p. 3; Helen Hughes, *The Australian Iron and Steel Industry 1848–1962*, Melbourne (1964), p. 85.

28. BHPL, D1(d), 'Newcastle Works' (typescript, c. 1946), reprinted in *The Australasian Manufacturer*, 11 May 1946, p. 24.

29. Ibid; *Lysaght Venture*, op. cit., pp. 4–5; *Lysaght's Silver Jubilee 1921–1946*, Sydney (1946), pp. 23–26.

30. *The Orb*, Vol. 5, January 1988, Alan Stein, 'Our Pioneers'; *Lysaght Venture*, op. cit., p. 5.

31. Interview R.N.M. Ward with R.G.C. Parry-Okeden, July 1973.

32. *The Sydney Mail*, 18 May 1921, p. 16.

33. Lysaght Minute Book, Vol. 4, op. cit., 26 January 1922, p. 36.

34. BHPL, D1(c) 'Works Company History', 13 December 1945.

35. Lysaght Minute Book, Vol. 4, op. cit., 26 January 1922, p. 36.

36. Ibid., 23 March 1922, p. 48.

37. Ibid., 17 August 1922, p. 86.

38. Ibid., 20 September 1922, p. 97; JLAL, D1(c), 'Works Company History'.

39. *Lysaght Venture*, op. cit., pp. 5–6.

40. Lysaght Minute Book, Vol. 4, op. cit., 31 January 1924, p. 186.

41. BHPL, D1(c), 'Galvanised Industry', op. cit., p. 2; Geoffrey Jones, *British Multinationals*, op. cit., Edgar Jones, 'Steel and Engineering Overseas: GKN's Multinational Growth, 1918–1965'. p. 167.

42. Lysaght Minute Book, Vol. 4, op. cit., 19 September 1923, p. 163.

43. *Lysaght Venture*, op. cit., p. 6.

44. Lysaght Minute Book, Vol. 4, op. cit., 18 September 1924, p. 237.

45. Lysaght Minute Book, Vol. 5, April 1926–May 1931, 20 October 1926, p. 33.

46. Ibid., 22 July 1927, p. 88.

47. BHPL, D1(c), 'Works Company History', op. cit., p. 2.

48. Lysaght Minute Book, Vol. 5, op. cit., 20 April 1928, p. 138; 19 September 1928, p. 163.

49. Ibid., 17 December 1929, p. 250.

50. *Lysaght, Australian Sheet Steel* (1933), pp. 3–5.

51. Lysaght Minute Book, Vol. 5, op. cit., 18 March 1930, p. 270.

52. BHPL, D1(c), 'Works Company History'.

53. Lysaght Minute Book, Vol. 5, op. cit., 21 November 1929, p. 244.

54. Quoted from Hughes, *The Australian Iron and Steel Industry 1848–1962*, op. cit., p. 110; *Commonwealth of Australia, Parliamentary Debates*, 16 September 1931, pp. 13ff.

55. BHPL, D1(c), 'Works History', op. cit., p. 2.

56. Lysaght Minute Book, Vol. 5, op. cit., 1 October 1930, p. 305.

57. Ibid., 5 November 1930, p. 312.

58. Ibid., 3 December 1930, p. 319.

59. BHPL, D1(c), 'Works History', op. cit., p. 3.

60. Lysaght Minute Book, Vol. 6, June 1931–November 1935, 4 February 1932, pp. 67–8.

61. Ibid., 2 March 1932, p. 75.

62. Ibid., 1 December 1932, p. 133; *Lysaght Australian Sheet Steel* (1933), p. 17.

63. *Lysaght Venture*, op. cit., p. 7.

64. Lysaght Minute Book, Vol. 6, op. cit., 4 May 1937, pp. 173–4.

65. BHPL, D1(d), 'Newcastle Works', op. cit., p. 3.
66. Lysaght Minute Book, Vol. 6, op. cit., 6 June 1935, p. 336.
67. *Lysaght Venture*, op. cit., p. 8.
68. Lysaght Minute Book, Vol. 7, December 1935–July 1940, 4 November 1937, p. 151.
69. Advertisement, *Lysaght's Newcastle Works Ltd*, [*c*. 1929].
70. *Lysaght Venture*, op. cit., p. 7; *Lysaght, Australian Sheet Steel* (1933), p. 17.
71. Lysaght Minute Book, Vol. 7, 3 February 1938, pp. 170–1; 1 September 1938, pp. 208–9.
72. Ibid., 3 February 1938, pp. 170–1.
73. 'Port Kembla Works' (typescript, n.d.).
74. *Lysaght Venture*, op. cit., p. 18.
75. Alan Stein, 'Springhill Works, Golden Jubilee' (typescript), p. 4.
76. Lysaght Minute Book, Vol. 6, op. cit., 3 October 1935, p. 350.
77. Lysaght Minute Book, Vol. 7, December 1935–July 1940, 6 February 1936, p. 18.
78. Ibid., 2 April 1936, p. 30; *Lysaght, Springhill Works, C.R.M. Works, Port Kembla, NSW*, [*c*. 1956].
79. *Lysaght Venture*, op. cit., p. 19.
80. Alan Stein, 'Springhill Works, Golden Jubilee' (typescript, 1987), p. 2.
81. BHPL, 'Recollections' by Mr. P.K. Parbury.
82. BHPL, 'Port Kembla Works' (typescript, *c*. 1942).
83. BHPL, 'Brief History of Newcastle Works' (typescript *c*. 1948).
84. *Lysaght Venture*, op. cit., pp. 17–18.
85. Stein, 'Springhill Works', op. cit., p. 7.
86. Lysaght Minute Book, Vol. 7, op. cit., 4 June 1936, p. 54.
87. Ibid., 1 October 1936, p. 66.
88. *Lysaght Venture*, op. cit., p. 38.
89. Lysaght Minute Book, Vol. 7, op. cit., 1 September 1938, p. 209.
90. *Lysaght Venture*, op. cit., p. 38.
91. *Lysaght C.R.M. Works, Port Kembla, NSW* [*c*. 1956].
92. *The Farmer and Settler*, Sydney, NSW, Obituary 4 July 1940; Interview E. Jones with V.A. Wardell, May 1984.
93. BHPL, D1(c) 'Works Company History', op. cit., pp. 3–4.
94. Interview R.N.M. Ward with R.G.C. Parry-Okeden, July 1973.
95. Lysaght Minute Book, Vol. 7, op. cit., 4 July 1940, p. 354.
96. BHPL, D1(c) 'Works Company History', op. cit., p. 4.
97. Interview J. Cockroft with D.R. Lysaght, March 1973.
98. Interview J. Cockroft with J.C.F. Lysaght, March 1973.
99. Lysaght Minute Book, Vol. 4, op. cit., 24 April 1924, p. 208.
100. *Seventy Five Years of BHP*, op. cit., pp. 8, 18.
101. Lysaght Minute Book, Vol. 5, op. cit., 20 April 1928, p. 138.
102. Lysaght Minute Book, Vol. 4, op. cit., 19 August 1921, p. 7.
103. BHPL, 3B 1.1-FMI 'Parliamentary Debates on Galvanised Iron, 1931'.
104. *Lysaght Venture*, op. cit., p. 20.
105. *Lysaght Venture*, op. cit., p. 21.
106. Ibid., p. 23; D.P. Mellor, *The Role of Science and Industry*, Canberra (1958), pp. 79–81.
107. Ibid., p. 33.
108. Ibid., p. 33; Interview R.N.M. Ward with R.G.C. Parry-Okeden, July 1973, pp. 15–16.

109. D.P. Mellor, *Australia in the War 1939–45, The Role of Science and Industry*, Canberra (1958), p. 326; G.S. Wardell, 'The Development and Manufacture of the Owen Gun' (typescript, March 1982), p. 1.
110. Ibid., p. 327.
111. Ibid., p. 329; *War and Society* Vol. 5 (1987), R.G. Haycock and A.T. Ross, 'The Australian Owen Gun Scandal 1940–45', pp. 39–51.
112. Mellor, *Science and Industry*, op. cit., p. 331; G.S. Wardell, 'Owen Gun', op. cit., p. 10.
113. Wardell, 'Owen Gun', op. cit., p. 17.
114. *Lysaght Venture*, op. cit., p. 35; Interview E. Jones with V.A. Wardell, May 1984.
115. Ibid., p. 37; Interview of S.W.H. Fairbairn, 14 March 1973.

11 *Guest, Keen, Williams in India*

But I am not bound by this vast work of creation. I
am and I watch the drama of works.
I watch and in its work of creation nature brings forth
all that moves and moves not: and thus the revolutions
of the world go round.[1]

The *Bhagavad Gita*, 9

Although GKN had built up a considerable trade to India, particularly
in woodscrews and other fasteners, until 1934 they possessed no
manufacturing base in the subcontinent. However, in 1931, whilst on a
visit to assess market conditions and to improve sales, two of the
company's representatives (possibly T.S. Peacock and I.F.L. Elliot)
were approached by Owen Williams (1879–1958), chairman, of Henry
Williams India Ltd.[2] The latter as makers of bolts and nuts for the
railway and construction purposes had found himself in increasing
competition with GKN. Accordingly, Williams suggested that the latter
might wish to purchase a holding, given the similarity of the fasteners
and railway fittings produced in India and those exported by GKN from
its Darlaston bolt works, Bayliss, Jones & Bayliss at Wolverhampton
and Exors. of James Mills (EJM) at Bredbury. The matter appears to
have been held in abeyance whilst the Indian enterprise underwent a
reconstruction emerging as Henry Williams (1931) Ltd (HWI). In
September 1933, when Owen Williams was in England, a meeting was
arranged with J.H. Jolly and Allan Macbeth in Sheffield at which the
former presented his terms for selling a 57 per cent holding in HWI.
GKN agreed in principle to examine the plant and machinery at
Calcutta, but at a further meeting in Sheffield on 4 October obtained a
reduction in the price that Williams was asking for the majority
shareholding.[3] It was also decided that the tour of inspection would be
by I.F.L. Elliot and Allan Macbeth (managing director of EJM, which
made permanent way materials for railways, and whose cousin N.B.
Macbeth managed Macbeth Brothers & Co., the Indian agents, whose
Calcutta office acted for GKN).[4] Originally, T.S. Peacock was to have
gone, but he withdrew on medical advice, while Elliot was already
proceeding to India on matters connected with steel manufacture. In
considering the acquisition, the board had been influenced by GKN's
declining volume of trade with India, the domestic government's policy
of encouraging local manufacture by the institution of tariffs and by the
prediction that Indian railway companies were likely to place considerable orders over the next few years.[5]

Having received the report of Macbeth and Elliot, the GKN board approved a meeting between them, T.S. Peacock and Owen Williams, in April 1934 to discuss terms.[6] The latter offered to sell 51 per cent of the ordinary shares in the company at a premium of 60 per cent, a deal which they estimated would cost around £100,000. The reported results of HWI had shown only very small profits for the last two years but since these corresponded with a period of depression in India, the expectation was that when trade recovered and new, more stringent tariffs were introduced to protect the domestic market, the company's fortunes should improve. Accordingly, GKN approved the acquisition in May for £95,000 on the understanding that the vendors of the shares would re-invest 50 per cent of the proceeds in the company's preference share capital in order to provide funds for future development.[7]

In deciding to buy a majority shareholding in HWI, GKN were influenced by the group's declining exports to India. Given the Indian government's policy of erecting trade barriers to encourage domestic industry, it was felt that it would be considerably cheaper to invest in an established business rather than 'set up a competitive manufacturing organisation'.[8] The strategy of investing in an indigenous business might upset the merchant houses with whom they dealt though, GKN believed, their discontents could be placated if persuaded that the 'revised policy was not at the instigation of this company but was brought about by the fiscal policy of the Indian government'.[9]

In practice, the 51 per cent share capital of HWI was assigned as follows: 26 per cent to GKN, 20 per cent to EJM and five per cent to Joseph Sankey & Sons.[10] Owen Williams was confirmed in the offices of chairman and managing director for a further five years, subject to health, while Allan Macbeth, N.B. Macbeth (of Macbeth Bros & Co., Bombay) and T.S. Peacock were elected to the board representing the GKN shareholding.[11] Macbeth Bros. were to be liquidated over the next two years and its Bombay and Calcutta offices incorporated within HWI.[12] In October 1934, it was also agreed that the company should change its name, being registered as Guest, Keen, Williams in Calcutta on 19 December 1934.[13]

HENRY WILLIAMS INDIA

The company, Henry Williams Ltd. (HWI), had been registered with its office in Calcutta by Owen Williams in November 1921, and construction of the works at 97 Andul Road, Howrah, began shortly afterwards.[14] At the time, he was a director of Henry Williams Ltd of Darlington, manufacturers of permanent way materials and signal fittings for railways. The business, originally established at Polmodie near Glasgow in 1883, had built up a considerable reputation and, with expansion in mind, it was decided to enter the large Indian market. Accordingly, in 1910 Owen Williams, the third son of the founder,

114 Owen Williams
(1879–1958), chairman of
Henry Williams India Ltd
(*Sir Henry Williams*).

visited the subcontinent, earlier the destination of exports from Glasgow,
and appointed Turner Hoare & Co. of Bombay as agents for the import
and sale of HWI products from the Darlington Works.[15] The company's
trade was interrupted by the Great War but on its close and once the
supply of track fittings had resumed, Owen Williams returned to India
in 1921. His first visit had convinced him of the economic sense of
manufacturing indigenously (given the costs of transporting goods
from England) and he was now able to put his ideas into practice.

Owen Richard Williams had graduated from Glasgow University
with a BSc degree in engineering, being awarded the George Hawey
prize, and was admitted to an associate membership of the Institution
of Mechanical Engineers in 1922. Described as a 'man of scrupulous
honesty and integrity',[16] he could be a formidable opponent in any
financial transaction, as GKN discovered when they sought to purchase
the outstanding 44 per cent in the business that Williams had established (p. 357). An Indian employee, who worked at Andul Road from
its opening, recalled that he was 'a strict and conservative person; a tall,
reserved figure, he would occasionally appear in the factory aloof and

115 Owen Williams (right) seated in an inspection trolley touring Indian railways to win orders (*Sir Henry Williams*).

ghost-like, barely speaking to a soul but constantly observing and noting'.[17] Williams became chairman and managing director of the new enterprise. Although never taking up permanent residence in Calcutta, he usually spent four months of the year (November to February or March, the cooler, drier period) in the country so that he could take personal control of the business.

The Andul Road works came into production in March 1923, turning out permanent way and signal fittings, together with points and crossings.[18] It was designed to supplement orders despatched from Darlington, though some of these (switch levers in particular) were covered by patents, so that licences had to be granted for their manufacture in India.[19] As its production rose, so the level of exports from England declined. In 1937, for instance, output from this department had risen to 639 crossings, 468 switches and 277 turnouts.[20] A few years after the establishment of the Andul Road factory ('A' Works), a nearby site in Bharpara Road was rented from the Bengal–Nagpur Railway for 'B' Works.[21] There, plant capable of making steel sleepers, fish bolts, crossing bolts and dog spikes was installed. Steel sleepers (preferred in India to the timber variety because of their resistance to termites) were manufactured on two large Taylor & Challen presses in large numbers, an order for one million being placed by the Bengal-Nagpur Railway.[22] Always a particular problem was the supply of steel, as the only source within India, the Tata Iron & Steel Co., could not meet HWI's entire demand. Accordingly, the company had to purchase billets and sleeper bar abroad – mainly from Germany, Belgium, and later BHP in Australia. Low wages and the ability to buy

116 The laying of a siding from the Bengal–Nagpur Railway to the Andul Road Works (*Sir Henry Williams*).

117 At 'A' Works rails being sawn into shorter lengths for points and crossings (*Sir Henry Williams*).

cheap steel were crucial in the decision to continue transferring production to India and after the Second World War outweighed any considerations of protection by the Indian government.

In 1929, it was decided to lay down rolling mills ('D' Works) at Andul Road as a step towards self-sufficiency and in particular to obtain control over the rolling of special sections and close tolerance bars for the bolt works.[23] In England, Owen Williams travelled to Sheffield, then in the depths of the slump, where he purchased three Brightside double-duo mills which had been installed on their foundations but remained unused.[24] The financial difficulties into which their owners, Sheffield Steel Products,[25] had fallen forestalled the installation of their electric motors. Williams purchased the plant (comprising 14in, 10in and 8in mills) for £30,000, and bought the necessary motors from AEI. These mills were principally engaged in rolling billets down to bars for the bolt, nut, rivet and fstener department.[26] The highest monthly output recorded prior to January 1935 stood at 1,430 tons for the three mills, though Owen Williams consistently maintained that 2,000 tons was possible.[27]

Since the principal customers of HWI were the many different railway companies that spanned the subcontinent, it was essential to establish personal contact with the permanent way inspectors and engineers. To achieve this, Owen Williams maintained his own well-equipped carriage which could be coupled to a train heading to the place where business was to be conducted. Williams became an estab-

118 Loading coal for the gas producer, which heated billets for the rolling mills. Since labour was cheap the incentive to mechanise certain jobs was limited (*Sir Henry Williams*).

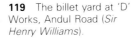
119 The billet yard at 'D' Works, Andul Road (*Sir Henry Williams*).

lished figure in the railway world and the arrival of his coach was often eagerly awaited.[28] The military and senior civil service officials in India sometimes tended to take a snobbish view of those involved in trade and commerce (called 'box-wallahs'),[29] an attitude said to have had its origins in the old East India Company's hostility to interlopers, but a figure of such influence as Owen Williams would have revealed the pretentiousness of these views. In part, they may have reflected the affluence of the successful businessman which stood in contrast to the tight financial position of many junior army officers.[30]

GUEST, KEEN, WILLIAMS

The demand by Indian railways for bolts and dog spikes having outstripped the capacity of the Bharpara Road works, and with financial support provided by GKN, it was decided to expand the bolt and nut capacity at Andul Road.[31] Known as 'C' Works, it was originally equipped with three Horsfall horizontal forging machines (purchased from the Bengal Bolt and Nut Co.) and four double-headed, vertical forging machines (which had been bought in 1931 from Etchell in England),[32] and was now supplied with steel rod from the adjacent rolling mills ('D' Works). 'C' works began producing the full range of products with the exception of ¾in and 1in fish nuts, which to qualify for the lower rate of import duty as unfinished were imported from Britain in an unthreaded state from Darlaston, the final operations being undertaken at Howrah.[33]

It is doubtful whether GKW would have recorded profits during the second half of the 1930s without the protection provided by import duties. Continental manufacturers, mainly in Belgium, and Germany, having all the advantages of economies of scale and a home market as a base, could cut margins to the narrowest in order to undersell an indigenous Indian business. In view of this continuing threat, in July 1935 A. H. Bishop was asked to review the question of tariffs and report to the government authorities.[34] Reference was made,

> in particular to the need for adequate protection to enable the Calcutta Works to compete successfully for the bazaar trade in bolts and nuts ... The following cable was agreed to be despatched: 'After reviewing the effect of [the] present duties [on] our dog spikes, taper keys, bolts and nuts [and] rivets [the] board consider it imperative you press for immediate fresh tariff enquiry.'[35]

The report presented by Bishop in October to impress on the government the importance of raising duties focused on the fact that raw material prices had advanced of late because of the protection afforded to Indian steelworks.[36] In addition, the argued that estimates used by the Tariff Board were based on factories working at full capacity, and, therefore, allowed no margin for seasonal or cyclic reductions in demand.

Table 11.1   Output and sales from 'C' works, the Bolt Mills, GKW, Howrah

Year	Sales (rupees)	Average monthly despatch (tons)
1935	604,589	197
1936	603,316	218
1937	1,221,273	352
1938	1,779,163	456
1939	2,340,858	657
1940	4,116,336	921
1941	4,800,000	1,159

Source: W.E. Murphy, 'Memories of GKW' (September 1964), p. 17.

120 Flats supplied by the Tata Iron & Steel Co. being carried into the cold press department (*Sir Henry Williams*).

Without detailed sales and profit data (which have been lost), the justice of this claim cannot be assessed accurately. Certainly, the profitability of GKW fell in the first six months of 1936, when a small surplus of around 40,000 rupees was estimated.[37] Stocks had increased considerably (valued at 1,202,095 rupees in December 1935 and 1,792,512 on 30 June 1936), suggesting a deepening sluggishness in demand. Profits recovered dramatically in the first half of 1937 to reach 421,000 rupees after allowances for depreciation and interest on loans.[38] Only 'A' Works showed a loss (11,000 rupees), while 'D' Works, the rolling mills, recorded a surplus of 350,000 rupees. The former continued to be problematical as in April 1939 figures for the previous two years revealed that sales from the original Andul Road factory had fallen without a corresponding reduction in wage costs.[39]

The takeover by GKN did not simply result in an injection of fresh capital and changes in management (p. 354), it also provided the company with an additional group of products. Exors. of James Mills (EJM), a subsidiary of GKN at Bredbury, near Stockport, had patented a

Table 11.2   Output from 'D' works, rolling mills, GKW, Howrah

Year	Output (tons)
1937	16,256
1938	16,954
1939	24,400
1940	33,966
1941	33,944
1942	30,654
1943	36,480

Source: W.E. Murphy, 'Memories of GKW' (September 1964), p. 18.

number of devices for attaching rails to sleepers (in particular the 'loose jaw' which, when used with the standard taper key, replaced the need for a clip bolt and nut for steel sleepers with flat-footed rails and Mills and Macbeth steel keys to replace the wooden key) and various agreements licensed GKW to manufacture these in Howrah on condition that EJM was to supply all orders which the Indian factory could not meet.[40] Some diversification from railway equipment followed; rice muller blades and horse shoes were manufactured, large quantities of the latter being sold to the army during 1937.[41]

MANAGERS AND MANAGEMENT

Because GKN had been allowed only to purchase a 51 per cent holding in HWI, the shares were divided into two groups, 'A' and 'B', reflecting the ownership of the two parties. GKN were granted three board members and the former HWI interest two. Allan Macbeth, N. Bruce Macbeth and Kenneth Swift Peacock were confirmed as the directors representing class 'A' shares in August 1934, while Owen Williams (chairman and managing director of GKW) and A. H. Bishop (a former director of HWI) were appointed on behalf of class 'B' shares.[42] Shortly afterwards a new accountant, Mr. E. H. Sims, took up his post on a six-month trial.[43] In June 1935, I. F. L. Elliot, who had been so closely involved in the negotiations leading to the acquisition of HWI, was also elected to the board of GKW[44] (retaining this post until July 1936 when he resigned from GKN),[45] though he would have remained, in practice, like the two Macbeths and Peacock, a non-executive director. Authority for the daily running of the business would have fallen to Owen Williams, who spent part of the year in Britain, travelling to India when necessary.

After a visit to the Howrah Works in the spring of 1936, Allan Macbeth reported to the GKN board that he discovered conditions

121 The durwans (watchmen) at Andul Road Works, 1937 (*Sir Henry Williams*).

there to be 'unsatisfactory'.[46] At a meeting between him, J. H. Jolly and Owen Williams, GKN suggested that the latter re-purchase the group's 51 per cent holding or that 'drastic alterations' be made to the management of the company.[47] The key issue appears to have been residence in Calcutta. Owen Williams reported that his health would not permit him to live there permanently and his contract allowed him to return to England for extended periods.[48] Given the insistence of GKN on this point, Williams agreed to relinquish his post as managing director forthwith and would resign as chairman on returning from his proposed visit to India in the autumn.[49] In the meantime, the board decided to appoint a general works manager.[50] W. E. Murphy was interviewed for this post in Birmingham by Peacock and Macbeth in September, and before setting sail for India on the S. S. *Strathmore* with Williams in the following month, undertook a detailed inspection of the works of Bayliss, Jones & Bayliss, F. W. Cotterill (Atlas Works), Henry Williams, and Exors. of James Mills.[51] The last was to brief Murphy on the manufacture of the 'Macbeth spring steel key', a device for holding rails to sleepers which it was hoped to fabricate in India. A further recommendation put forward by GKN was that 'a newly qualified accountant be sent to strengthen the secretarial and accountancy staff'.[52] This was H. H. Groves, who on arrival at Howrah set about re-organising the wages system and introducing methods for costing products.[53]

With the imminent retirement of Owen Williams, the appointment of his eldest son, [Sir] H. M. L. Williams (b.1913), took on a greater importance. Having read engineering at Corpus Christi College, Cambridge, the latter had for the past eighteen months been obtaining experience in the works of GKN, Henry Williams and the Great Western Railway. In July 1936, Owen Williams recommended that his son be placed in 'A' Works as assistant to the works manager,[54] where his first task was to improve the manufacture of rail anchors, loose jaws, keys and tie bars. This decision was confirmed in October, when it was also agreed that he should be employed elsewhere in the Howrah Works to deputise for officers on leave in order to broaden his understanding of the business.[55] He arrived at Calcutta in December 1936.

At the April 1937 board meeting Owen Williams tendered his resignation and was succeeded as chairman by Allan Macbeth,[56] while in June Jolly was appointed as the alternate director for Bruce Macbeth and would attend board meetings at 66 Cannon Street, London, when the former remained in India.[57] Because of pressure of work, K. S. Peacock resigned his directorship in July 1937 and his seat was taken by S. R. Beale.[58] At the same meeting, A. H. Bishop was appointed managing director; this promotion was accompanied by him resigning as representative of 'B' shareholders and immediate election representing the 'A' shareholders.[59] This, in part, enabled Owen Williams' brother, D. D. Williams (a director of the Darlington company) and H. M. L. Williams (at Calcutta), to be elected to the board on behalf of the 'B' shareholders.[60] A. H. Bishop had originally joined HWI from the Bengal-Nagpur Railway and succeeded C. M. Atkinson as general manager in Calcutta.[61] A dedicated and hard-working man respected by the Indian workforce, Bishop applied the same financial stringency to himself as to the business and even when travelling long distances by train, such as Calcutta to Lahore, never went more comfortably than second class.[62]

In summary, therefore, the GKW board in the summer of 1937 was composed of seven directors, four representing the GKN shareholding and three the former HWI company. The first (or 'A' group) comprised Allan Macbeth (chairman), A. H. Bishop (managing director), S. R. Beale and N. B. Macbeth, while the 'B' directors were Owen Williams, D. D. and H. M. L. Williams.[63] A further change was the resignation in November 1938 of N. B. Macbeth and his replacement by J. Leisk,[64] who had joined GKW upon its formation in 1934 as a result of a connection with Allan Macbeth whom he had known since 1925.[65] Throughout this period GKW remained a private limited liability company, its shareholding being retained by GKN and Owen Williams and his nominees.

Although Owen Williams had resigned the chairmanship of GKW in April 1937, as the founder of the enterprise and of an autocratic personality, he retained his directorship and continued to exercise a powerful hold over the running of the company which at times produced 'disruption and difficulties'.[66] When Henry Williams Ltd. of Darlington issued writs against GKW in respect of earlier consignment stocks which had been sent to the Indian company, Owen Williams met Allan Macbeth and reported that the former were prepared to settle these claims for £1,500 providing that the latter would agree 'to adopt a memorandum submitted by Mr. O. R. Williams for the re-organisation and future management of the company'.[67] This document proposed that

> the officers of the company should be controlled by a board in India; that Mr. Leisk and Mr. H. M. L. Williams should be appointed joint managing directors; that GKN, the majority shareholders, should confine their control to capital expenditure and dividend payments.[68]

S. R. Beale and J. H. Jolly, who had been empowered to negotiate with Owen Williams, refused to accept the scheme on the grounds that it was 'impracticable', and agreed, if the writs were found to be justified, to settle in full. Discussions continued and by October it was reported to the GKN board that 'agreement was imminent for the future organisation and management of the company ... the two actions against GKW by Mr. Owen Williams' Darlington company would be dropped on terms favourable to the Indian company'.[69]

However, the Second World War had begun and the matter of how the company was to be run could not be resolved. Jolly reported in December 1939 that the proposed settlement with Owen Williams had not been signed, and that he was 'again reviving old demands which could not be agreed'.[70] In addition, the flotation of GKW as a public company was proposed, and, subject to Williams' approval, 4,500 ordinary shares were to be offered for sale. It appears that he would not agree to the scheme and that GKN then sought to acquire his 49 per cent of the ordinary shares and entire holding of preference stock.[71] On the termination of hostilities negotiations were commenced in August 1945 but the price asked by Williams was considered 'excessive' by GKN.[72] In December, the latter raised their offer from six-and-a-half times par to seven-and-a-quarter times for the outstanding shares.[73] In the event, the purchase was agreed in February 1946, 2,560 'B' shares being obtained at nine times par value and a further 5,774 at ten times par.[74] The 6,500 preference shares of 100 rupees were to be exchanged for 32,500 ordinary shares of £1 each in GKN. Finally, the group became the outright owners. Owen Williams retired as a director of GKW in August 1946.[75]

There were several managerial changes during the war years. In October 1939, J. F. Heatly, who had joined HWI in 1926/27 after service with the North Western Railway in India, was appointed a director of GKW, and D. D. Williams retired to be replaced by Geoffrey Whitworth Taylor.[76] The outbreak of hostilities resulted in several ex-patriate managers volunteering for military service; H. M. L. Williams, for example, was commissioned as an Ordnance Mechanical Engineer (later REME). With younger men in the forces, older members of staff were asked to continue in office. However, in December 1943 A. H. Bishop, having almost completed twenty years service with the Indian company, announced his intention of retiring as managing director in 1944.[77] Accordingly, in June of that year, J. Leisk became a joint managing director[78] with Bishop, on the understanding that the latter would resign in December.[79] Other appointments to the GKW board included those of G. R. Thom (Bombay) and W. E. Murphy as general works manager in June 1944.[80] Recruited from a hollow-ware manufacturers in Wolverhampton in 1936, Murphy had travelled to Calcutta to take up the post of general works manager. With the return of H. M. L. Williams from the forces being imminent, it was initially proposed that he be appointed joint managing director with responsibility for technical matters, Leisk taking charge of commercial matters.[81] In the event, the latter appeared unhappy with this arrangement and Williams was appointed deputy managing director until Leisk retired.[82] Williams eventually became managing director in 1953, a post which he retained until retirement in 1962.

The auditors of HWI were Price, Waterhouse, Peat & Co.[83] and in view of their established expertise and in order to maintain continuity, they were re-elected after the takeover and change of name to GKW.[84] However, in July 1935, after A. H. Bishop had presented a report on the company's balance sheet, it was agreed that Price, Waterhouse & Co. should be asked to provide a supervising European auditor.[85]

Since the mid 1920s HWI had leased accommodation at 7 Church Lane, Calcutta, for its head office. However, with the setting up of GKW more space was required for the enlarged management and staff and they moved to larger premises at 7 Council House Street on the opposite side of Dalhousie Square in the city's business centre.[86] During the 1930s, board meetings were held there and at GKN's London headquarters, 66 Cannon Street, almost on an alternate basis.

The works, located on the outskirts of Howrah across the Hooghly river some seven miles distant, were reached by crossing the Howrah pontoon bridge constructed in 1874 and when this was closed to road traffic – a daily event dependent on the tides – the alternative route required a journey of not less than 90 minutes via the Wellington bridge at Kanchapara. In 1937 the Cleveland Bridge Company, in conjunction with three Calcutta engineering firms, Braithwaite, Burns and Jessops, began building a single span bridge in steel, for which GKW supplied all the rivets and other fasteners.

THE SECOND WORLD WAR

Many of the younger managerial staff of GKW enlisted in the armed forces, including H. M. L. Williams, K. J. Bhore, J. Baker, G. Lancaster (killed whilst piloting Leigh Mallory on a flight to India) and K. Sharpe.[87] GKW made up their military pay to the level they would have received if still working for the company, a practice common to most leading businesses in India.[88] Kenneth Bhore, the son of Sir Joseph Bhore, a senior official in the Indian Civil Service, had taken an engineering degree at Cambridge and was the first Indian graduate from a British university to obtain a managerial post in the company.[89]

By 1940, when it was clear that the conflict would prove protracted, GKW was called upon to manufacture munitions. The additional output that this demand created overstrained the electric power facilities at Andul Road and an expenditure of 30,000 rupees was authorised for the provision of a new transformer and cables.[90] In June 1942, the War Supply Department requested GKW to raise their capacity to manufacture nuts and bolts.[91] Initially, they proposed that they pay for a factory capable of producing 5,000 tons of nuts, bolts and rivets per annum and pass its management to GKW. However, 'it proved to be impossible to obtain suitable terms for this method of operation and it was therefore suggested that if adequate safeguards could be obtained GKW might provide the necessary additional capital and install and operate this plant'.[92] After negotiations with both the War Supply Department and the Revenue, the most important concession granted to GKW by the government was a depreciation allowance of 33.3 per cent with reference to income, super and excess profits taxes for a period of two years on the original cost of the buildings and plant. Further, the government promised not to develop any other sources of nuts, bolts or rivets unless the new enterprise were unable to satisfy the demand. 'It is anticipated', noted a board minute,

> that war and post-war demands should fully absorb the outturn of the existing and additional plant and that with the amount of depreciation allowed before taxation during the first two years the plant should be capable of being operated profitably on a commercial basis thereafter.[93]

In fact GKW had already considered the possibility of manufacturing fasteners in the western side of the subcontinent.[94] A rise in the cost of transport between Calcutta and Bombay further encouraged this plan, though a pre-war slump in the fastener market caused its postponement. The entry of the Japanese into the war exposed Howrah to attack, especially after their occupation of Burma, and provided the government with the fillip they needed to sponsor the scheme of transfer,[95] known at the time as the 'Bhandup Shadow Factory'.[96]

By August 1943, a plot of land (about 84,000 square yards) had been purchased for 87,625 rupees close to Bhandup Station, about 17 miles from Bombay Victoria. The site lay between the main Agra road and the railway, having access to both.[97] The plant and machinery had been ordered through the Machine Tool Control. In March 1944 it was estimated that the total cost of this scheme (including land, and 30,000 rupees to the Great Indian Peninsula Railway for the laying of a works' siding) would amount to 700,000 rupees.[98] The installation of plant at Bhandup bolt works was finally completed by November 1945,[99] but early in 1946 was moved back to Calcutta to increase production at 'C' Works and to allow plant for Sankey Electrical Stampings to occupy the new factory.

The need for increased billet and steel storage space prompted further development of the Andul Road site, and with a view to re-organising and improving the general layout of the works,[100] an area of adjacent land was acquired[101] at a cost of 73,000 rupees.[102] The scheme involved the purchase of a 3-ton overhead electric crane for 'A' Works, alterations to the 10ins mill and the transfer of the heat-treatment plant to the former spring-steel stocking bay; its cost was estimated at 350,000 rupees.[103]

Among the specific jobs performed during the war for the government was the rough machining of shells and trench mortar bombs. Several Great War shell lathes were purchased from Cossipore and installed in 'B' Works.[104] In addition, GKW manufactured shovels for the 14th Army in Burma, together with picket stakes and brass fuse bodies,[105] and undertook the rolling of copper driving bands for shells.

LABOUR AND CONDITIONS OF EMPLOYMENT

Whilst managers were for the most part recruited from the UK until after the Second World War, the labour force was almost exclusively Indian, with the exception of the few European foremen, and lived locally in Howrah or Calcutta.[106] It was estimated that by 1936 GKW was employing around 2,000 workers,[107] and in a country where labour was both cheap and plentiful, higher outputs could be satisfactorily achieved by increasing the size of the workforce rather than importing cost-saving but capital-intensive machinery.

Whilst the post-1934 forging machines employed in 'C' Works had mostly been purchased from GKN in Darlaston and therefore were designed to be operated by skilled or semi-skilled workers, the Indian labour force was largely untrained and inexperienced in the manufacture of fasteners.[108] Accordingly, Owen Williams adapted the vertical bolt headers to single shuffle double-blow machines so that they required considerably less manual effort with increased output. Tool life was slightly reduced as the single bottom die ran hotter, but tools were not costly to produce.[109]

In the interwar years a paternalistic attitude to labour persisted. If Owen Williams considered that the men were working well and that the business were flourishing, he would issue a bonus.[110] Demands for wage increases were not welcomed. When, for example, the office staff approached A. H. Bishop with a request for higher pay, he conducted a detailed inquiry into the cost of food and household expenditure and concluded that on their existing salaries they ought to be able to make small savings and consequently turned down their claim. Wages at the works were paid on a monthly basis and were calculated manually from clock cards.[111] By September 1940, when the number of employees at Andul Road had risen to around 3,000, considerable congestion arose in the time office, encouraging the construction of a larger building[112] and the purchase of a Hollerith machine to speed up accounting records. Rates of pay seem to have been determined as much by the cost of living as the profitability of the business – a situation that pertained in eighteenth-century England, when rises in the price of wheat could inspire industrial riots. In June 1944, for example, GKW agreed to increase the daily rate of those paid 8 annas by two annas, and of those receiving between 11 and 15 annas by one anna.[113] These increments were based on an assessment of recent inflation in the Indian economy and during the hostilities were accompanied by concessionary rates for foodstuffs supplied from the company's store. For example, the controlled price for rice was 6 annas and 6 pies per seer; GKW sold at 4 annas per seer. Atta, sugar, dal, mustard oil and salt were also provided at a discount.[114] J. Leisk, who as managing director was responsible for authorising these changes, observed,

> for the past two or three months, outputs in practically every department of the works have been disappointing and it is hoped that these increases and concessions will result in more co-operation being given by all workers as the total amount represents a very large sum to the company, and in order to continue to pay these rates, it is essential that higher outputs should be obtained.[115]

The concept of the works canteen was almost unheard of in India during the pre-war period and everybody had to bring or have food sent from home. The European managers employed a small boy who called at their Calcutta homes to collect lunch in a tiffin carrier and then served the meal after warming the ingredients.[116] In December 1941, however, proposals were presented for the provision of a further mess and changing facilities for junior and supervisory staff and for the construction of a small hospital and dispensary.[117] In the event, a portion of the quarters was allocated as a staff luncheon room.

SUMMARY

In a sense, it is difficult to judge the wisdom of GKN's acquisition of Henry Williams India (1931) Ltd in the period to 1945. The group gained outright control of the company only in 1946 when Owen Williams surrendered his holding of 49 per cent of the ordinary shares and the entire preference stock. As he had been responsible for founding and building up the business over some thirteen years, his desire to continue to exercise executive authority after the takeover in 1934 and his retirement as chairman in April 1937 was understandable. In the absence of annual profit figures for these and the war years, it has proved impossible to say whether GKN's investment yielded a valuable return.

It appears, however, that such surpluses as did accrue were ploughed back into the business. Indeed, the principal advantage to GKN during this period may have been an indirect and unquantifiable one. By taking over an indigenous manufacturing company, they were able to acquire the sales and marketing agents, Macbeth Bros. & Co., incorporating their Bombay and Calcutta offices. The GKN group exported woodscrews from Smethwick, nuts and bolts from Darlaston and railway fittings from Bredbury, and orders for these may have risen within India as a result of these improvements. Again, there are no figures to support this hypothesis.

Having constructed a factory at Bhandup, near Bombay eventually to be used by Sankey Electrical Stampings and GKW's screw works (and transferred its existing bolt and nut plant back to Howrah), acquired land to extend and improve the layout of the Andul Road Works, GKW was poised at the end of the Second World War to enter a period of expansion and commercial prosperity. The return of key managers from the armed forces, in particular H. M. L. Williams, strengthened its operations still further. Now a wholly-owned subsidiary of GKN, the parent board felt confident that they could invest further in the enterprise and appoint senior management from expatriates and Indian nationals trained in Britain.

References

1. The *Bhagavad Gita* (translated by Juan Mascaro) Harmondsworth (1962), pp. 80–1.
2. GKN Minute Book, Vol. 9, op. cit., 5 October 1933, it. 6377.
3. Ibid., 2 November 1933, it. 6398.
4. G. G. Jones, (Editor), *British Multinationals: Origins, Management and Performance*, Gower (1986); Edgar Jones, 'Steel and Engineering Overseas: GKN's Multinational Growth 1918–1965', p. 165.
5. Ibid., 5 October 1933, it. 6377.
6. GKN Minute Book, Vol. 9, op. cit., 12 April 1934, it. 6495.
7. Ibid., 3 May 1934, it. 6516.

8. Ibid., 12 April 1934, it. 6495.
9. Ibid.
10. Ibid., 7 June 1934, it. 6538.
11. Guest Keen Williams Ltd Minute Book, August 1934 to April 1948, 27 August 1934.
12. GKN Minute Book, Vol. 9, op. cit., 22 August 1934, it, 6559.
13. Ibid., 4 October 1934, it. 6576.
14. 'Guest, Keen, Williams, Fifty Years, An Historical Brief' (typescript, n.d.), pp. 3–4.
15. Interview J. Cockroft with Sir Henry Williams, 25 January 1972, revised by Sir Henry Williams, December 1983, p. 1.
16. 'GKW', op. cit., p. 4.
17. Ibid., p. 5.
18. *GKW News, Golden Jubilee Issue* (1972), p. 2.
19. Jones, 'Steel and Engineering Overseas', op. cit., p. 175.
20. E. E. Blyth, 'Memories of GKW' (February 1965), p. 15.
21. 'GKW', op. cit., p. 6.
22. J. Leisk, 'Memories of GKW' (September 1964), p. 2.
23. 'GKW', op. cit., p. 12.
24. 'GKW', op. cit., p. 13.
25. W. E. Murphy, 'Memories of GKW' (September 1964), p. 3; E. E. Blyth, ibid. (February 1965), p. 5.
26. J. Leisk, 'Memories of GKW' (September 1964), p. 5.
27. T. K. Walshaw, 'Memories of GKW' (August 1965), p. 36.
28. 'GKW', op. cit., p. 9.
29. Charles Allen (Editor), *Plain Tales from The Raj*, London (1977), pp. 97, 103.
30. Ibid., pp. 103–04.
31. 'GKW', op. cit., p. 7.
32. Ibid., p. 12.
33. Jones 'Steel and Engineering Overseas', op. cit., pp. 175–6.
34. GKW Minute Book, op. cit., 22 July 1935, it. 2.
35. Ibid.
36. Ibid., 8 October 1935, it. 4.
37. Ibid., 14 October 1936, it. 1.
38. Ibid., 28 September 1937, it. 2.
39. Ibid., 26 April 1939, it. 10.
40. Ibid., 29 August 1934, it. 4–5.
41. 'GKW', op. cit., p. 15.
42. GKW Minute Book, op. cit., AGM, 31 December 1934.
43. Ibid., 18 January 1935.
44. Ibid., 26 June 1935, it. 1.
45. Ibid., 30 June 1937, it. 17.
46. GKN Minute Book, Vol. 10, op. cit., May 1936, it. 6848.
47. Ibid.
48. GKW Minute Book, op. cit., 15 July 1936, it. 1.
49. GKN Minute Book, Vol. 10, op. cit., 2 July 1936, it. 6884.
50. Ibid., it. 2.
51. Ibid., 14 October 1936, it. 3.
52. GKN Minute Book, Vol. 10, 2 July 1936, it. 6884.
53. T. K. Walshaw, 'Memories of GKW', op. cit., p. 52.
54. GKW Minute Book, 15 July 1936, it. 13.

55. Ibid., 14 October 1936, it. 4.
56. GKW Minute Book, 14 April 1937, it. 4, 5.
57. Ibid., 30 June 1937, it. 1.
58. Ibid., it. 4.
59. Ibid., it. 5.
60. Ibid., it. 6.
61. J. Cockroft with Sir Henry Williams, op. cit., p. 4.
62. 'GKW', op. cit., p. 19.
63. Ibid., 31 August 1937, it. 8.
64. Ibid., 21 December 1938, it. 5; GKN Minute Book, Vol. 11, op. cit., 3 November 1938, it. 7194.
65. J. Leisk, 'Memories of GKW', op. cit., p. 1.
66. GKN Minute Book, Vol. 11, op. cit., October 1938, it. 7338.
67. GKW Minute Book, op. cit., 14 July 1939, it. 2.
68. Ibid.
69. GKN Minute Book, Vol. 11, op. cit., October 1938, it. 7338.
70. Ibid., 7 December 1939, it. 7364.
71. Ibid., 1 February 1945, it. 8028.
72. Ibid., 2 August 1945, it. 8301.
73. Ibid., 6 December 1945, it. 8358.
74. Ibid., 7 February 1946, it. 8391.
75. GKW Minute Book, op. cit., 26 August 1946, it. 4.
76. Ibid., 22 December 1939, it. 2–5.
77. GKN Minute Book, Vol. 12, op. cit., 2 December 1943, it. 8008.
78. Ibid., 1 June 1944, it. 8105.
79. GKW Minute Book, op. cit., 10 January 1945, it. 3.
80. Ibid., 27 July 1944, it. 4.
81. GKN Minute Book, Vol. 12, op. cit., 2 August 1945, it. 8301.
82. Ibid., 6 December 1945, it. 8358.
83. GKW Minute Book, op. cit., 31 December 1934.
84. Ibid., 20 February 1935.
85. Ibid., 22 July 1935, it. 11.
86. Ibid., 29 August 1934; *GKW News, Golden Jubilee Issue* (1972), p. 2.
87. GKW Minute Book, 4 September 1940, it. 3.
88. Ibid.
89. J. Cockroft with Sir Henry Williams, op. cit., p. 7.
90. GKW Minute Book, op. cit., 25 October 1940, it. 5.
91. Ibid., 22 June 1942, it. 2.
92. Ibid.
93. Ibid.
94. 'GKW', op. cit., p. 24.
95. Ibid.
96. J. Leisk, 'Memories of GKW', op. cit., p. 4.
97. Ibid., 19 August 1943, it. 4; 12 November 1943, it. 2.
98. Ibid., 25 March 1944, it. 16.
99. Ibid., 2 November 1945, it. 7.
100. Ibid., 6 December 1945, it. 5.
101. Ibid., 10 January 1945, it. 6.
102. Ibid., 2 November 1945, it. 9.
103. Ibid., 6 December 1945, it. 5.
104. E. E. Blyth, 'Memories of GKW' (February 1965), p. 11.

105. Ibid., p. 12.
106. J. Cockroft with Sir Henry Williams, op. cit., p. 14.
107. Ibid., p. 6.
108. W. E. Murphy, 'Memories of GKW', op. cit., p. 1.
109. Ibid., p. 12.
110. 'GKW', op. cit., p. 18.
111. Ibid., pp. 18–19.
112. GKW Minute Book, op. cit., 4 September 1940, it. 11.
113. GKW Minute Book, op. cit., 30 June 1944.
114. Ibid.
115. Ibid.
116. W. E. Murphy, 'Memories of GKW', op. cit., p. 2.
117. GKW Minute Book, op. cit., 23 December 1941, it. 4.

12 *Conclusions and Perspective*

> The externals of a past action, indeed, he cannot know with the
> precision of a contemporary; but his business is with its essen-
> tials ... The date of an action, then signifies nothing: the action
> itself, its selection and construction, that is what is all important.
> Matthew Arnold (1822–1888),   Preface to *Poems* (1853).[1]

GKN in 1925 was a much altered entity from the three companies which
had merged in 1900–2 to form the core of the group. By the early 1920s
it had collected a number of subsidiary companies; its activities were
extended by both horizontal and vertical integration; it was in the
process of building up several overseas subsidiaries, which by the 1930s
were to include Australia, India and Sweden within their territory.
Overall control of the company could no longer be mastered by one
man and a few deputies, advised by non-executive directors, as in the
days of Arthur Keen.[2] The complex and fluctuating circumstances of
the interwar period caused the group to take two major changes of
direction: first, into coal, and subsequently away from coal and heavy
steel towards its established base in light engineering. The 1920s and
1930s were difficult times for GKN and perhaps produced more
fundamental change, not all to the good, than had been seen over the
previous century.

   The most important consideration for any company is to preserve its
continuity through the earning of profits; they are the *sine qua non* of all
business activity. Accordingly, the historian in attempting to assess the
performance of GKN in the interwar years must first address himself to
the group's financial record (Table 12.1). In no year did a loss accrue,
though in 1933, when the published surplus was £133,665, it was a
close run thing. During the Edwardian period the group's profits had
levelled at around £400,000 per annum,[3] which roughly corresponded
with the figures reported for 1918 and 1919. This may not have been
entirely a coincidence, as the negotiations surrounding the payment of
Excess Profits Duty (based on standards achieved in the immediate pre-
war years) would have allowed a margin for adjustment. The jump to
£860,510 in 1920 may, in part, have reflected the post-war boom but

Table 12.1   Profits of GKN by constituent company, 1918–45

	£ GKN reported profits after tax	£ GKN adjusted	£ Nettlefolds	£ John Lysaght	£ Joseph Sankey
1918	446,645[c]	347,854	537,210	965,482[a]	39,103[a]
1919	417,141[c]	306,721	397,923	595,286[a]	37,055[a]
1920	860,510	545,317	660,551	499,090	26,952
1921	810,102	566,109	233,335	495,329	3,011
1922	567,220	488,983	173,747[b]	580,845	73,375
1923	844,919	757,096	415,166	616,332	84,844
1924	874,743	790,192	512,024	545,505	162,273
1925	937,613	840,155	508,804	—	103,391[b]
1926	948,298	870,798	533,329	—	129,550
1927	909,279	856,195	369,173	507,580	144,669
1928	966,244	921,110	356,694	—	79,273
1929	956,071	919,299	387,412	674,652	77,993
1930	968,698	968,698	364,975	483,404	83,260
1931	409,222	438,609	230,618	—	112,637
1932	201,569	221,261	189,393	—	73,497
1933	133,665	311,041	146,939	199,892	74,048
1934	274,960	307,906	225,935	409,230	138,380
1935	808,813	891,745	—	441,718	164,931
1936	820,445	883,149	—	397,746	166,493
1937	898,286	923,212	—	548,370	150,728
1938	1,075,467	1,089,632	—	315,270	156,980
1939	985,785	985,785	—	445,682	160,331
1940	1,003,170	861,830	—	401,136	154,147
1941	985,636	781,011	—	345,859	251,678
1942	858,624	680,368	—	351,205	202,999
1943	903,774	716,144	—	388,565	181,376
1944	965,028	759,465	—	364,511	—
1945	1,017,168	792,187	—	358,168	—

Notes: [a] not included within GKN profits,
  [b] nine months,
  [c] not including J. Lysaght.

Figures adjusted by the Bank of England's index of consumer prices, 1930 = 100.

was principally the result of the merger with John Lysaght. With the exception of 1922 (a depression year) GKN's reported profits remained well above £800,000 until the slump of 1931 when they tumbled to £409,000, falling to £202,000 in the following year and £134,000 in 1933.

If these results are indexed to remove changes in the value of money, the picture does not alter dramatically. The slump of 1931–33 remains the most prominent feature; cancelling out all the gains that had been made in the decade to 1930. The group recovered its position only by

1938 when the advent of another downturn and the outbreak of war altered economic circumstances.

In the absence of standardised accounting procedures, it is virtually impossible to say which were the profitable subsidiaries within the GKN group. Random figures and contemporary reports suggested that coal was a drain on the company's resources throughout the period until the formation of Welsh Associated Collieries in 1930. Dowlais and Dowlais–Cardiff struggled to earn a consistent surplus during the twenties and demanded heavy inputs of capital expenditure. It seems, therefore, from Table 12.1 that the Nettlefolds screw works, John Lysaght and its subsidiary, Joseph Sankey, comprised the consistent revenue earners for GKN. The Heath Street mills never fell into the red during this period; in 1933, possibly its worst year, for example, the screw works generated a surplus of £146,939, marginally more than the profit declared for the group as a whole. Unfortunately the Nettlefolds series survived only to the end of 1934 and it has not proved possible to discover their contribution for the late 1930s and war years.

John Lysaght was another profitable element within GKN, and appears to have avoided losses throughout the depression. Similarly, Joseph Sankey recorded growing surpluses throughout the interwar period, and because of its involvement with the expanding electrical and automotive industries escaped the full impact of the slump. As a subsidiary of Lysaght, it is assumed that the Sankey results were incorporated within the former's results. If this were the case, then Sankeys provided an increasing proportion of the Lysaght profits as the thirties passed. In 1920, for example, the Sankey share would have been a mere 5.4 per cent, but in 1938 it had risen to 49.8 per cent and in 1941 was 72.8 per cent.

Detailed profit series for the other leading GKN subsidiaries have not survived. F. W. Cotterill, the Darlaston nut and bolt company, incorporated within GKN in 1926, has not left its internal accounting records. However, given their size, the contributions of Bayliss, Jones & Bayliss, John Garrington and from 1930 of Exors. of James Mills would not have been of the same order as those of Lysaght, Nettlefolds or Sankeys.

With the high levels of investment necessary to fund the expansion of the group's Australian subsidiary, John Lysaght (Australia) Pty., it seems unlikely that there was a substantial net flow of income from GKN's overseas subsidiaries to the home company. Profits earned by Aug. Stenman, the Swedish manufacturer of fasteners, were never transferred to the UK, and it is improbable that Guest Keen Williams was a major source of finance to GKN as its Calcutta works did not earn great surpluses during the 1930s and required a measure of capital spending on plant and machinery; in 1943, for example, GKN agreed in principle to help fund the construction of a new nut and bolt plant near Bombay, though this was never built.

Was the GKN group which emerged from war in 1945 a stronger and better managed company than that of 1918? There had been weaknesses evident in the main board which had steered GKN through the Great War: few of its directors had broad industrial experience, and most were of advanced age, while the absence of a truly dynamic leader paved the way for an attempted take-over by Lysaghts. The board of 1945 was both larger, better balanced and possessed greater business acumen. Although Sir Samuel R. Beale served as chairman and managing director his role was, to a large extent, non-executive. The two most active and influential executives were J. H. Jolly and K. S. Peacock. Between them they devised strategy, monitored the performance of elements within the group, advanced the careers of talented managers and supervised the running of Nettlefolds, the principal revenue earner. Representing major subsidiaries were E. C. Lysaght (John Lysaght), Allan Macbeth (Exors. of James Mills), Lt.Col. H. B. Sankey (Joseph Sankey) and M. H. Tollit (Nettlefolds), while J. H. Bean (who also served as chairman of John Garrington), Sir Maurice E. Denny, Lord Hyndley and Edmund L. Hann could offer impartial business advice. The last two were leading figures in the coal industry and, in part, owed their appointment to GKN's minority shareholding in Powell Duffryn. T. S. Peacock and Lt.Col. C. H. C. Guest provided a measure of historical continuity, the former having once been joint managing director with responsibility for the group's fastener factories, and the latter represented the Guest family's interest.

In terms of activities the group was more broadly based and slightly less reliant on the traditional industries at the end of the Second World War. In 1918 GKN's fortunes rested on coal, steel and woodscrews, its two nut and bolt factories (the London and Stour Valley Works) having fallen into technical obsolescence, hence the acquisition of Cotterills in 1919. Its only overseas venture was a minority shareholding in the Orconera Iron Ore Co. With the exception of its woodscrew business, the group was particularly vulnerable to periods of depression since the traditional industries (coal, steel, shipbuilding and textiles) were those which fared worst during a downturn. GKN were practitioners in the first two and suppliers to the third. The merger with John Lysaght, the most important single event in this twenty-seven year period, brought a measure of diversification. First, it advanced GKN's steel operations into sheet for the automotive and electrical industries, secondly, it brought Joseph Sankey into the group (important not only as an earner of profits but as a further entrée into the motor car and electrical trades), and thirdly it dramatically extended manufacturing into Australia. Other acquisitions had led to factories in India (Guest Keen Williams) and Sweden (Aug. Stenman). Thus, by 1945, GKN had considerably broadened the scope of its enterprise and had successfully distanced itself from its two, least-profitable activities, coal and heavy steel.

The other major repercussion of the merger with John Lysaght was the introduction of H. Seymour Berry, later Lord Buckland, and Sir

David Llewellyn to the GKN board. Together they formed a powerful and dynamic team which soon dominated policy-making within the group. Using the Dowlais and Cyfarthfa collieries as a base, they set about acquiring pits and for the first time took GKN into anthracite mining. To consolidate their major position in the South Wales coalfield, they purchased marketing and sales companies such that the entire coal operation was within the group's hands. It was the company's misfortune that they happened to be associated with what was to prove a regional industry set in long-term decline. Falling prices in the face of tight international competition, ageing pits, inherent geological problems, limited opportunities for mechanisation and labour disputes conspired to ruin their grand plan. Had they implemented their strategy for coal in the pre-war period then GKN would have earned considerable riches, or had their experience been in growth industries such as car making, pharmaceuticals or electrical components, then their undoubled talent and expertise would have assured them of commercial success. With family roots in South Wales, both Berry and Llewellyn had been brought up in the coal trade; they remained committed to the activities they knew and would not have wanted to work elsewhere or in a different industry. As it was, GKN was kept alive during the slump by its woodscrew business together with contributions from Sankeys and the Orb rolling mills at Newport.

The death of Berry in 1928 and the less prominent role subsequently taken by Sir David Llewellyn opened the way for several younger executives. Prominent amongst these was K. S. Peacock, who at thirty-two was the youngest board member of GKN, and at thirty-four became a joint managing director. Of greater experience was J. H. Jolly, who had risen to deputy chairman and managing director from the office of company secretary and chief accountant. Although the two were temperamentally quite different – Peacock gregarious and expansive, Jolly taciturn and in favour of economy – they formed an executive team which managed the group under the overall supervision of Sir Samuel Beale.

With more specific responsibilities were E. C. Lysaght, an expert in the rolling of sheet steel, M. H. Tollit, who took charge of sales and marketing at Nettlefolds, Allan Macbeth, chief executive of Exors. of James Mills, and Lt.Col. H. B. Sankey, chairman of Joseph Sankey. J. H. Bean, a former automobile maker (Beans Cars) although chairman of Garringtons, was in essence a non-executive director,[4] as were Lord Hyndley (chairman of the coal factors and distributors, Stephenson Clarke, managing director of Powell Duffryn and from 1942 Controller General of the Mines Department),[5] Sir Maurice E. Denny (chairman of William Denny & Brothers, shipbuilders and engineers), Lt.Col. C. H. C. Guest, MP and Edmund L. Hann (chairman of Powell Duffryn).

In his analysis of large American companies from the latter part of the nineteenth century, Professor A. D. Chandler has suggested that the impact of market forces and changing technology can require the adoption of alternative strategies, which if they are to be properly implemented, require a new organisational structure – a managerial hierarchy in the form of a multi-divisional group, vertically-integrated, with a geographical spread and diversity of products.[6] 'The visible hand of management', he has observed,

> replaced the invisible hand of market forces where and when new technology and expanded markets permitted a historically un- precedented high volume and speed of materials through the processes of production and distribution. Modern business enter- prise was thus the institutional response to the rapid pace of technological innovation and increasing consumer demand in the United States during the second half of the nineteenth century.[7]

Within GKN, in common with most of the major industrial com- panies in Britain,[8] this process was by no means complete by 1945. For a variety of reasons (the market structure of the UK, size of manufac- turing units, the attitudes of managers, and the existence of cartels), the diversified, multi-divisional group was a feature of the post-war eco- nomy rather than the interwar period. GKN took an important step towards such a structure from 1960–61 when a system of 'sub-groups' was established. However, the harsh business climate of the twenties had produced some earlier organisational change within GKN. During the years preceding the Great War the principal manufacturing units which formed the group were all incorporated within GKN (having been placed into voluntary liquidation if, like Nettlefolds, they had previously existed as a limited liability company). There had to be a special reason to justify the creation of a subsidiary, as in the case of the British Screw Co. in Leeds, which preserved its identity after acquisition to suggest that it was a competitor. Crawshay Bros (Cyfarthfa), taken over in 1902, was never incorporated within GKN because it was purchased, not with a view to integrating its manufacturing capacity, but to control a neighbouring competitor, and was closed as a steel- works in 1910.[9]

After 1918 the situation changed. Acquired competitors were permit- ted to retain their names and boards of directors, being managed as subsidiaries with a high degree of devolved power. Control was exercised over major capital expenditure and information gathered by one or two GKN directors sitting on the subsidiary board. Bayliss, Jones & Bayliss, John Garrington and F. W. Cotterill were all run on this principle, though the latter was put into voluntary liquidation in 1926 and its assets incorporated within GKN. In order to co-ordinate the operations of similar or related companies various committees were established (Birmingham, Colliery, Steel) to operate between the sub- sidiaries and the holding company. Thus, when GKN merged with John Lysaght and its subsidiary Joseph Sankey, they were allowed to retain their legal identities, though their policies were monitored by an exchange of directors and informal rules regarding capital investment. The holding company with its growing number of subsidiaries became a fundamental characteristic of both GKN and large British companies during the interwar years.

The notion of strategic diversification was also introduced to GKN in the 1920s. Until then the group had grown either by moving into closely related areas in a policy of vertical integration or by acquiring competitors. Berry and Llewellyn introduced a new way of thinking. Having identified a market, in this case coal (albeit one with which both they and GKN had strong links), they decided to advance in a determined and aggressive manner. The practical failure of this strategy, rather than the philosophy which lay behind it, led to the abandonment of coal and a return to investment in tried and tested activities. It was not until after the Second World War and the decision to diversify into automotive components that a second major change of direction was effected.

In November 1779, having lived through the early phase of the Industrial Revolution, Dr Johnson was able to write to Mrs Thrale,

> Do not be frighted; trade could not be managed by
> those who manage it, if it had much difficulty.
> Their great books are soon understood, and their language
>> If speech it may be call'd, that speech is none
>> Distinguishable in number, mood or tense,
> is understood with no very labourious application.[10]

Whilst managerial theory was probably not of great importance during the early phases of industrialisation, by 1919 no senior director could hope to be successful without having some knowledge of company law, the structural organisations available to groups, accounting procedures, and the practical ramifications of manufacturing methods. Whilst management in Britain had yet to attain the status of a profession, retaining something of the ethos of the 'gentlemanly amateur',[11] it had become a very serious business. By 1945 GKN had established itself as an international and vertically integrated group; it employed 45,000 staff and workers, had annual profits, after tax, of over £1 million, and could count itself in the top ten British companies, ranked according to the market value of capital.[12] In 1919 GKN had been sixteenth (in reality this should have been twelfth as the listing occurred before the merger with Lysaghts). Although they had in effect moved up only two places, their assets had grown from £12.1 to £35.3 million. The group had consistently pursued a cautious policy towards borrowing and was virtually free of debt at the end of the Second World War. Given the unprofitability of coal and difficulties they had experienced with steel, GKN had done well to have held their own in such adverse economic circumstances; others, such as Armstrong Whitworth and United Steel, had fallen below them in the league table. The harsh years of the 1920s and 1930s had seen the group mature, often through vicissitude, into a semi-structured managerial hierarchy, and, as a result, was well equipped to reap the rewards of a world economy in which supply fell far short of demand.

POSTSCRIPT

It was originally envisaged that Volume Two of the GKN History would relate the fortunes of the group from 1918 to the mid 1970s and thereby bring this task to a close, at least for the forseeable future. In the event, the complexity of the subject matter and wealth of archival material available made it impossible to encapsulate this story within a single study. It was decided to end the second volume at 1945, a natural break in the development of GKN, and one which would eventually permit the completion of this plan in a work of roughly equal length. There remains much to discuss in the post-war period: the impact of successive phases of nationalisation, the introduction of structural change ('sub-grouping' followed by divisionalisation), a reshaping of overseas interests away from the former Empire towards the Continent and America, a strategic change of direction towards the automotive industry, together with a host of acquisitions and divestments. There is, therefore, an involved and exciting tale still to be told of the 30 years from the end of the Second World War.

References

1. Kenneth Allott (Editor), *Arnold, Poems*, Harmondsworth (1985), p. 245.
2. *DBB*, Vol. 3, London (1985), Edgar Jones, 'Arthur Keen', pp. 570–74.
3. Jones, *GKN, Vol. One*, op.cit., p. 369.
4. *DBB*, Vol. 1, London (1984), Edgar Jones, 'Lord Brookes', p. 463.
5. *DBB*, Vol. 3, London (1985), Jenny Davenport, 'John Scott Hindley', pp. 256–57.
6. A. D. Chandler, *The Visible Hand, The Managerial Revolution in American Business*, Harvard (1977), pp. 6–11.
7. Ibid., p. 12.
8. D. C. Coleman, *Courtaulds, An Economic and Social History Vol. 3, 1940–1965*, Oxford (1980), pp. 320–21.
9. Jones, *GKN, Vol. One*, op.cit., p. 354.
10. Quoted from A. S. Turbeville (Editor), *Johnson's England* Vol. 1, Oxford (1933), H. Heaton, 'Industry and Trade', Dr S. Johnson to Mrs Thrale, 16 November 1779, p. 225.
11. D. C. Coleman, *Economic History Review*, Vol. XXVI (1973), 'Gentlemen and Players', pp. 100–1, 109.
12. Hannah, *Rise of the Corporate Economy*, op.cit., 'Fifty Largest Companies in 1948', p. 190.

Sources

MANUSCRIPT SOURCES

The references to individual chapters should be consulted for a detailed record of the original sources. The following archives, libraries and institutions were of particular value: BHP Coated Products Division Library, Port Kembla, NSW; Birmingham Reference Library; Bristol Central Library; Bristol Record Office; British Library; Business Archives Council; Business History Unit, London School of Economics; Cyfarthfa Castle Museum; Glamorgan Archive Service, Cardiff; Gwent Record Office, Cwmbran; Institution of Mechanical Engineers; Merthyr Tydfil Central Library; Merthyr Tydfil Heritage Trust; Metal Society; National Library of Wales, Aberystwyth; National Museum of Wales, Cardiff; Public Record Office, Kew; and the Walsall Local History Centre.

JOURNALS

Business Archives
Business History
The Colliery Guardian
The Colliery Yearbook and Coal Trades Directory
The Economic History Review
The Engineer
Historical Metallurgy
The Iron and Coal Trades Review
The Ironmonger
Journal of the Iron and Steel Institute
Proceedings of the Institution of Mechanical Engineers
Transactions of the South Wales Institute of Engineers
Transactions of the Newcomen Society

SELECT BIBLIOGRAPHY

Alford, B. W. E., *Depression and Recovery? British Economic Growth, 1918–1938*, London (1972).

Allen G. C., *British Industries and their Organisation*, London (1951).

Ashworth, William and Mark Pegg, *The History of the British Coal Industry, Vol. 5, 1946–1982, The Nationalised Industry*, Oxford (1986).

Baber, Colin and L. J. Williams (Editors), *Modern South Wales, Essays in Economic History*, Cardiff (1986).

Barraclough, K. C., *Sheffield Steel*, Sheffield (1976).

Boswell, Jonathan S., *Business Policies in the Making, Three Steel Companies Compared*, London (1983).

Burn, D. L., *The Economic History of Steel Making, 1867–1939*, London (1940).

Carr, J. C. and W. Taplin, *History of the British Steel Industry*, Oxford (1962).

Chandler, A. D., *The Visible Hand, The Managerial Revolution in American Business*, Harvard (1977). *Economic History Review*, Vol. XXXIII (1980), 'The Growth of the Transnational Industrial Firm in the United States and United Kingdom: A Comparative Analysis'.

Chester, Sir Norman, *The Nationalisation of British Industry, 1945–1951*, London (1975).

Church, Roy and John Kanefsky, *The History of the British Coal Industry, Volume 3, 1830–1913, Victorian Pre-eminence*, Oxford (1986).

Coleman, D. C., *Courtaulds, An Economic and Social History, Vol. 3, 1940–1965*, Oxford (1980).

Crofton, C. Anthony, *The Nettlefolds*, Lewes (1962).

Davenport-Hines, R. P. T., *Dudley Docker, The Life and Times of a Trade Warrior*, Cambridge (1984).

Davenport-Hines, R. P. T. (ed.), *Markets and Business, Studies in the History of Marketing and British Industrial Performance, 1830–1939*, Aldershot (1986).

Edwards, J. R., *Company Legislation and Changing Patterns of Disclosure in British Company Accounts, 1900–1940*, London (1981).

Edwards, J. R., *A History of Financial Accounting*, London (1989).

Erickson, Charlotte, *British Industrialists, Steel and Hosiery, 1850–1950*, Cambridge (1959).

Fearon, P., *The Origins and Nature of the Great Slump, 1929–32*, London (1979).

Gale, W. K. V., *The British Iron and Steel Industry, A Technical History*, Newton Abbot (1967).

Goodall, Francis, *A Bibliography of British Business Histories*, Aldershot (1987).

Guest Keen & Nettlefolds Ltd., An Outline History of this Group of Companies, (c. 1925).

Gumbel, Walter and Kenneth Potter, *The Iron and Steel Act, 1949*, London (1951).

Hancock, W. K. and M. M. Gowing, *British War Economy*, London (1949).

Hannah, Leslie, *Rise of the Corporate Economy*, London (1983).

Herbert, Gilbert, *Pioneers of Pre-fabrication, The British Contribution in the Nineteenth Century*, Johns Hopkins (1978).

Holmes, A. R. and Edwin Green, *Midland, 150 Years of Banking Business*, London (1986).

Jeremy, David (Editor), *Dictionary of Business Biography*, 5 Vols, London (1984–86).

Jones, Edgar, *A History of GKN, Volume One: Innovation and Enterprise, 1759–1918*, London (1987).

Jones, Geoffrey (Editor), *British Multinationals: Origins, Management and Performance*, Aldershot (1986).

Kirby, M. W., *The British Coalmining Industry, 1870–1946*, London (1977).

Lewis, E. D., *The Rhondda Valleys, A Study in Industrial Development 1800 to the Present Day*, London (1959).

Liebenau, Jonathan (Editor), *The Challenge of New Technology, Innovation in British Business since 1850*, Aldershot (1988).

Llewellyn, Harry, *Passports to Life, Journies into many Worlds*, London (1980).

Lubin, I., and H. Everett, *The British Coal Dilemna*, New York (1927).

Anon., *The Lysaght Century, 1857–1957*, Bristol (1957).

Anon., *Lysaght Silver Jubilee, 1921–1946*, Sydney (1946).

Anon., *The Lysaght Venture*, Sydney (1955).

Mackworth, Margaret, The Viscountess Rhondda, *This was my World*, London (1933).

Marwick, Arthur, *The Home Front, The British and the Second World War*, London (1976).

Mellor, D. P., *Australia in the War of 1939–45, The Role of Science and Industry*, Canberra (1958).

Milward, Alan S., *War, Economy and Society 1939–1945*, London (1977).

Mitchell, B. R. and Phyllis Deane, *Abstract of British Historical Statistics*, Cambridge (1971).

Newport Encyclopaedia, Coronation Year and Royal Visit Souvenir, Bristol (1937).

Orwell, George, *The Road to Wigan Pier*, London (1937).

Owen, John A., *The History of the Dowlais Iron Works, 1759–1970*, Risca (1977).

Parker, R. H., *Understanding Company Financial Statements*, Harmondsworth (1972).

Ponsonby, Sir John, *The Ponsonby Family*, London (1929).

Richardson, H. W., *Economic Recovery in Britain, 1932–9*, London (1967).

Richardson, H. W. and D. H. Aldcroft, *The British Economy, 1870–1939*, London (1967).

Richmond, Lesley and Bridget Stockford, *Company Archives, The Survey of the Records of 1000 of the First Registered Companies in England and*

Wales, Aldershot (1986).

Schedvin, C. B., *Australian Economic History Review*, Vol. X (1970), 'Rabbits and Industrial Development: Lysaght Brothers & Co. Pty. Ltd, 1884–1929'.

Steer, Elsa, *Threads from the Family History*, Moulsford (1957).

Stenton, Michael and Stephen Lees, *Who's Who of Members of Parliament, Vol. 3, 1919–1945*, Brighton (1979).

Stevenson, John and C. Cook, *The Slump, Society and Politics during the Depression*, London (1977).

Stevenson, John, *The Pelican Social History of Britain, British Society, 1914–1945*, Harmondsworth (1984).

Supple, Barry, *The History of the British Coal Industry, Vol. 4, 1913–1945, The Political Economy of Decline*, Oxford (1987). *Economic History Review*, Vol. XLI (1988) 'The Political Economy of Demoralization: the state and the coalmining industry in America and Britain between the wars'.

Tolliday, Steven, *Business, Banking and Politics: the Case of British Steel, 1918–1939*, Cambridge Massachusets (1987).

Walshaw, G. R. and C. A. J. Behrendt, *The History of Appleby–Frodingham*, Scunthorpe (1950).

Walters, R., *The Economic British History of the South Wales Steam Coal Industry*, New York (1977).

Warren, Kenneth, *The British Iron and Steel Sheet Industry since 1840*, London (1970).

Williams, D. J., *Capitalist Combinations in the Coal Industry*, London (1924).

Index

379